T0397269

See the Studies in Legal History series website at
http://studiesinlegalhistory.org/

Studies in Legal History

EDITORS

Sarah Barringer Gordon, University of Pennsylvania
Holly Brewer, University of Maryland, College Park
Michael Lobban, London School of Economics and Political Science
Reuel Schiller, University of California, Hastings College of the Law

Other books in the series

Cynthia Nicoletti, *Secession on Trial: The Treason Prosecution of Jefferson Davis*

Edward James Kolla, *Sovereignty, International Law, and the French Revolution*

Assaf Likhovski, *Tax Law and Social Norms in Mandatory Palestine and Israel*

Robert W. Gordon, *Taming the Past: Essays on Law and History and History in Law*

Paul Garfinkel, *Criminal Law in Liberal and Fascist Italy*

Michelle A. McKinley, *Fractional Freedoms: Slavery, Intimacy, and Legal Mobilization in Colonial Lima, 1600–1700*

Mitra Sharafi, *Law and Identity in Colonial South Asia: Parsi Legal Culture, 1772–1947*

Karen M. Tani, *States of Dependency: Welfare, Rights, and American Governance, 1935–1972*

Stefan Jurasinski, *The Old English Penitentials and Anglo-Saxon Law*

Felice Batlan, *Women and Justice for the Poor: A History of Legal Aid, 1863–1945*

Sophia Z. Lee, *The Workplace Constitution from the New Deal to the New Right*

Michael A. Livingston, *The Fascists and the Jews of Italy: Mussolini's Race Laws, 1938–1943*

The First Modern Risk

Workplace Accidents and the Origins of European Social States

JULIA MOSES
University of Sheffield

CAMBRIDGE
UNIVERSITY PRESS

University Printing House, Cambridge CB2 8BS, United Kingdom

One Liberty Plaza, 20th Floor, New York, NY 10006, USA

477 Williamstown Road, Port Melbourne, VIC 3207, Australia

314–321, 3rd Floor, Plot 3, Splendor Forum, Jasola District Centre, New Delhi – 110025, India

79 Anson Road, #06-04/06, Singapore 079906

Cambridge University Press is part of the University of Cambridge.

It furthers the University's mission by disseminating knowledge in the pursuit of education, learning, and research at the highest international levels of excellence.

www.cambridge.org
Information on this title: www.cambridge.org/9781108426503
DOI: 10.1017/9781108657853

First published 2018

Printed in the United States of America by Sheridan Books, Inc.

A catalogue record for this publication is available from the British Library

ISBN 978-1-108-42650-3 Hardback

To my parents, and to H.

Contents

Figures

Tables

Acknowledgements

I would like to thank the individuals and institutions that made the research and writing of this book possible. For funding the initial research, I am grateful to the Gates Cambridge Trust; the Overseas Research Studentship Awards Scheme; the German Academic Exchange Service; the Prince Consort and Thirwall Prize Scholarship Scheme at the University of Cambridge; the Faculty of History at the University of Cambridge; and St John's College, Cambridge. I am especially grateful to my doctoral supervisors, Chris Clark and Martin Daunton, for their enthusiasm for the project and encouragement in seeing it through. My examiners, Peter Baldwin and Pat Thane, played an enormous role in helping me to sharpen the thesis and make it into a book. Not least, the University of Sheffield, and especially my various heads of department, have provided the essential environment in which to complete the manuscript. Michael Lobban has graciously and patiently enabled me to make my book project into a reality, reading multiple drafts and helping to shape the manuscript. I am also grateful to Tim Smith, Larry Frohman, Holger Nehring and the anonymous reviewers for Cambridge University Press for their comments on earlier drafts. Thanks, too, to my editor at the Press, Debbie Gershenowitz, and to Kris Deusch, as well as my excellent copyeditor, Christopher Feeney, for making the process of publishing this book a pleasure.

Many colleagues, friends and mentors along the way have proved formative for this book. I am deeply indebted to Jose Harris and Abigail Green at Oxford for encouraging me to pursue this research and pointing me in the right direction – even if it was to 'the other place'. Through their example of inspirational scholarship, I owe Deborah Valenze and Lars Trägårdh at Barnard College thanks for supporting my decision to abandon law and pursue the path of comparative history. Thanks, too, to colleagues around the world who have provided feedback on the project along the way, including Arnd Bauerkämper, Jürgen Kocka, Hartmut Kaelble, Bernhard Struck and other members of the

Collegium for Comparative European History at the Free University, Berlin, where I was a visiting scholar in 2005; my many excellent colleagues at Oxford, and especially at Pembroke and Brasenose Colleges; Paul-André Rosental and Laura Downs at the École des Hautes Études en Sciences Sociales (EHESS), where I had the immense privilege of visiting as a guest professor in 2010; Ingrid Gilcher-Holtey, Willibald Steinmetz and Bettina Brandt at the University of Bielefeld Graduate School of History and Sociology, where I enjoyed an inter-national guest lectureship in 2012; Michael Lobban, John Bell, David Ibbetson and the other members of the AHRC-funded European Legal Development Project; Paul-André Rosental, Martin Lengwiler, Bernard Thomann and mem-bers of the European Research Council's Silicosis project; Thomas Le Roux and members of the CNRS/EHESS Industrial Risks and Accidents project; Dan Rodgers, Susan Pedersen, Frank Trentmann and other participants in the Social Policy across Borders conference at Cambridge; participants in the Risk, Social Policy and the State conference at Sheffield, and especially my co-organiser Eve Rosenhaft; colleagues and collaborators in the Political Economy and Welfare Research Network at the Council for European Studies, and espe-cially my co-chairs Matthieu Leimgruber, Marius Busemeyer and Christine Trampusch, and in the Risk, Policy and Law Research Group and at the Centre for Medical Humanities at Sheffield, and especially my co-director Matthias Benzer; and interlocutors at Cambridge, including Simon Szreter, Deborah Thom, Richard Evans, Bonnie Evans, Sîan Pooley and Andrew Fearnley.

I am also enormously grateful to the hosts who have generously invited me to present on this research in seminars and conferences over the last many years, including at the University of Cambridge, the University of Oxford, the University of York, the University of Sheffield, King's College London, the University of Glasgow, Princeton University, the Graduate Institute at Geneva, the University of Groningen, the EHESS, Sciences Po and the University of Paris VII, the Free University in Berlin, the University of Cologne, the University of Bochum, the University of Gothenburg, the University of Stockholm, the New University of Lisbon, the Finnish Institute in Rome and the German Historical Institutes in Rome and in Washington, DC, as well as elsewhere.

Not least, I wish to acknowledge the many institutions and archives that have enabled me to pursue this research. In Britain, I would like to thank the staffs of the Working Class Movement Library in Salford, The National Archives in Kew, the Modern Records Centre at the University of Warwick, the West Yorkshire Archives Service at Wakefield and the Guildhall Archives, as well as Bill Noblett at Cambridge University Library. In Germany, the staffs of the Bundes-Archiv at Lichterfelde West and Hoppegarten and of the Geheimes Staats-Archiv Preußischer Kulturbesitz provided valuable aid and friendly rapport during a lonesome stay in Berlin. In Italy, the staffs of the Archivio centrale dello stato, the historical archives of the Foreign Office and the Archivio di stato in Rome provided helpful advice. The staffs of the historical archives at the Senate and the Chamber of Deputies, in particular, provided valuable assistance and information about the historical functions of each body. I am especially grateful to the staff of the historical archives and library at the Istituto nazionale della previdenza sociale for opening their doors to me and providing such a convivial atmosphere, along with numerous invaluable photocopies. Alberto Lucarelli, Gianpiero Ruspantini and Bernardo Sabetta at the Istituto nazionale per l'assicurazione infortuni sul lavoro went out of their way to allow me access to the closed and uncatalogued holdings there and shared their wealth of knowledge about accident insurance in Italy. Lutz Klinkhammer, Patrick Bernhard and Gerhard Kuck at the German Historical Institute in Rome provided helpful tips about pursuing research in Italy at the beginning of my stay there. I am also indebted to Bodo Nehring and Christopher Dowe for procuring valuable photocopies in Germany. Bodo and Waltraut Nehring provided a home away from home while working in the archives and on the manuscript in Germany, while Pia Schneider and Valerio Ialongo offered me an insider's view of Rome and much helpful advice about navigating my way through Italian archives.

I am especially grateful to several publishers for generously permitting me to draw on various aspects of my earlier publications, including: 'Accidents at work, security and compensation in industrialising Europe: the cases of Britain, Germany and Italy, 1870–1925', *Annual Review of Law and Ethics* 17 (Summer 2009): 237–58, for parts of Chapters 1 and 4; 'Foreign workers and the emergence of minimum international standards for the compensation of workplace accidents, 1880–1914', *Journal of Modern European History* 7/2 (2009): 219–39, for parts of Chapter 5; 'Risk, humanity and injuries to the body politic: governmental representations of "the industrial accident problem" in Britain, Germany and Italy, 1870–1900', in C. Smit et al., eds., *Imagination and commitment: representations of the social question* (Leuven: Peeters, 2010), pp. 209–32, for parts of Chapters 1 and 2; and 'Contesting risk: specialist knowledge and workplace accidents in Britain, Germany and Italy, 1870–1920', in K. Brückweh et al., eds., *Engineering society: the role of the human and social sciences in modern societies, 1880–1980* (Basingstoke: Palgrave, 2012), pp. 59–78, for parts of Chapters 1 and 4. Thanks, too, to the Geheimes Staats-Archiv Preußischer Kulturbesitz and to Bruno Müller, Hubert Steinke and Ulrich Woermann of the University of Bern for enabling me to reproduce Figures 4 and 5, respectively, here.

I dedicate this book to my parents, for their encouragement of intellectual curiosity and sacrifices made for my education, and to H. and F., who have provided me with a secure retreat from a world of risk.

Abbreviations

ACS	Archivio centrale dello stato
A. P. Cam.	*Atti parlamentari della Camera dei deputati del regno*
A. P. Sen.	*Atti parlamentari del Senato del regno*
BArch	Bundes-Archiv Berlin
BT	Board of Trade
Ccmi	Central Committee on Mobilisation (Italy)
CdAs	Camera dei deputati, Archivio storico
CNAIL	Cassa nazionale d'assicurazione per gl'infortuni degli operai sul lavoro
DDB	*Drucksachen des Deutschen Bundesrates*
DDNB	*Drucksachen des norddeutschen Bundes*
DDR	*Drucksachen des Deutschen Reichstags*
Div. Ind. & Comm.	Division of Industry and Commerce
FO	Foreign Office
GStAPK	Geheimes Staats-Archiv Preußischer Kulturbesitz
HC	House of Commons
HO	Home Office
ILO	International Labour Organization

INAIL	Istituto nazionale per l'assicurazione contro gli infortuni sul lavoro
INPS	Istituto nazionale della previdenza sociale
LAB	Ministry of Labour
Maem	Ministry of Arms and Munitions (Italy)
MAIC	Ministry of Agriculture, Industry and Commerce (Italy)
MdaeAs	Historical Archives of the Foreign Office (Italy)
MRC	Modern Records Centre
MT	Ministry of Transport
PCM	Presidenza del consiglio dei ministri
PIN	Ministry of Pensions
PP	*Parliamentary Papers* (British)
QS	*Quellensammlung zur Geschichte der deutschen Sozialpolitik 1867 bis 1914*
RECO	Ministry of Reconstruction
RGBl	*Reichsgesetzblatt*
SBDR	*Stenographische Berichte über die Verhandlungen des Deutschen Reichstags*
SdrAs	Senato del regno, Archivio storico
SPD	Sozialdemokratische Partei Deutschlands
TNA	The National Archives of the United Kingdom
TUC	Trades Union Congress
UGC	Ufficio del Genio Civile
WCML	Working Class Movement Library

Introduction

In August 2008, the British government released its first 'National Risk Register', which contained an 'assessment of the risks of civil emergencies facing people in the UK'. The Register has been updated every two years since 'to ensure that changes to the assessment of risks in terms of impact, plausibility and likelihood are correctly captured'. By 2015, the most significant risks facing Britons were identified as pandemic flu and issues associated with weather, from coastal flooding to heatwaves and gales, alongside 'catastrophic terrorist attacks' and 'widespread electricity failure'. 'Major industrial accidents' ranked just behind. Regardless of where each of these risks fell on the scale, it was clear that the state would be called upon to plan for and clean up after each of them.[1] Accordingly, a separate document on 'Central Government's Concept of Operations' outlined how, in theory, the state, with government as its agent, would act as risk manager.[2]

This development seems, perhaps, unsurprising. Over a hundred years earlier, at the 1889 meeting of the International Congress on Accidents at Work, delegates from across the globe had already identified what they called 'occupational risk', agreeing that it was a fact of everyday life and would require legislative action. Participants ranged from a General Consul of Brazil to representatives from Norway, Portugal and Romania, and they flocked to Paris for this inaugural meeting of the organisation. All came in search of, as the conference organiser put it, the 'true solution' to the problem of workplace

---

[1] 'National Risk Register', Reports, Cabinet Office, 27 March 2015, www.gov.uk/government/publications/national-risk-register-for-civil-emergencies-2015-edition, last accessed 5 December 2015.

[2] 'Central Government's Concept of Operations', Cabinet Office, 23 April 2013, www.gov.uk/government/publications/the-central-government-s-concept-of-operations, last accessed 10 November 2015.

accidents.[3] The conference coincided with the opening of the Eiffel Tower the same year, which stood as a reminder of the wonders – as well as the perils – of modern life in an industrial, and still industrialising, world. It seemed that modernity, with its various risks, from the workplace to, in 2015, terrorism and extreme weather, carved out a special role for the state. How has the state come to be seen as the manager of 'risks'? And how has social legislation contributed to this transformation?

It is tempting to describe this process as one of inevitable modernisation. One can point to changing socio-economic structures caused by industrialisation, urbanisation and democratisation and trace the parallel emergence of what have come to be known as 'welfare states'.[4] Others have highlighted the roles of policy learning and emulation that have been facilitated by the new technologies of modernity, such as the telegraph, daily newspaper and steamship.[5] To some, social policy has simply followed the 'logic of industrialisation': it grew in lockstep with industrialisation and related processes of modernisation, and it also served the function of keeping industrialisation going by appeasing those it most harmed: workers. To be sure, many have explained the changing role of the modern state by tracing the connection between political power and resources,[6] whether economic or cultural, and have pointed to 'welfare capitalism' as an outcome of this dynamic. As a consequence, we have come to learn a great deal about the role of interest groups in pushing for particular kinds of social programmes that aim to benefit middle-class voters or businesses,[7] stifle working-class unrest[8] or construct families based on male breadwinners and female housewives.[9] However, interpretations that look so persuasive with hindsight echo past debates about specific policy proposals, and linked to specific political aims.

---

[3] Édouard Gruner (ed.), *Exposition universelle internationale de 1889: Congrès international des accidents du travail*, vol. II: *Comptes rendus des séances et visite du congrès* (Paris, 1890), pp. 1, 7, 11ff., 19ff.

[4] Harold L. Wilensky and Charles N. Lebeaux, *Industrial society and social welfare* (New York, 1958); Gaston V. Rimlinger, *Welfare policy and industrialization in Europe, America and Russia* (1973; Aldershot, 1993).

[5] On these issues, see: Colin J. Bennett, 'What is policy convergence and what causes it?', *British Journal of Political Science* 21 (1991), pp. 215–33; David Dolowitz and David Marsh, 'Learning from abroad: the role of policy transfer in contemporary policy-making', *Governance: An International Journal of Policy and Administration* 13 (2000), pp. 5–24.

[6] Walter Korpi, *The democratic class struggle* (London, 1983).

[7] Isabela Mares, *The politics of social risk: business and welfare state development* (Cambridge, 2003); Peter Baldwin, *The politics of social solidarity: class bases of the European welfare state, 1875–1975* (Cambridge, 1990).

[8] Gøsta Esping-Andersen, *Politics against markets: the social democratic road to power* (Princeton, NJ, 1985).

[9] Susan Pedersen, *Family, dependence, and the origins of the welfare state: Britain and France, 1914–1945* (Cambridge, 1993); Jane Lewis, 'Gender and welfare in modern Europe', *Past and Present*, Supplement (2006), pp. 39–54.

My book offers an alternative perspective that emphasises the historical role of government in identifying and managing social risks. I focus on the case of workplace accidents as a lens into these processes and cast a spotlight on the essential role of law and administrative practices in shaping what I call 'social states'. In the early and mid nineteenth century, vastly different legal systems declared that accidents at work were a private matter with which workers and their families had to cope alone, even if the fortunate few could turn to contributory mutual funds or, for the less privileged, to the aid of local parish relief. As free agents in the labour market, workers could choose to take up dangerous jobs – and to live (or die) with the consequences. By the close of the century, however, the situation had altered considerably, as numerous countries and federal states across the world enacted social legislation that guaranteed workers compensation (Appendix, Table 2). These initiatives, although building on certain more specific laws and practices, addressed workplace accidents in a novel way. They assumed that accidents were an inherent occupational risk to which no one had consented. Since employers were seen as the main beneficiaries of the workplace, they were now required to compensate injured workers for occupational accidents regardless of the cause. Some countries, such as Germany in the 1880s, set up social insurance schemes to carry out the new policy, while others relied on market-based solutions such as commercial insurance. Despite these differences, and across national borders, these schemes were based upon a common assumption: accidents at work had become an issue for social legislation and were now to be governed, whether directly or indirectly, by law and through the state.[10]

In Europe, this thinking in terms of risk and the role of the state as an arbiter in social life seems to have continued from the late nineteenth century into the twenty-first, as the UK's 'Risk Register' (or almost any daily newscast) indicates. Policies for the compensation of workplace accidents helped to create this set of assumptions. Accident compensation laws were generally the first pieces of modern social legislation that set out, through national policy, to redistribute individual risks – which were consciously understood and articulated as 'risks' – systematically to a wider community (Appendix, Table 1). Of course, earlier social legislation had targeted the poor, sometimes on a national scale, as was the case in England since the seventeenth century, and soldiers' pensions were another early attempt to redistribute risk through the state.[11] However, to contemporaries in the late nineteenth century, accidents had seemed a

---

[10] For a related observation, see Alain Supiot, 'Grandeur and misery of the social state', *New Left Review* 82 (July–August 2013), pp. 99–113.

[11] See for example: Jonathan Healy, *The first century of welfare: poverty and poor relief in Lancashire, 1620–1730* (Woodbridge, 2014); Theda Skocpol, *Protecting soldiers and mothers: the political origins of social policy in the United States* (Cambridge, MA, 1992).

shadowside of industrial modernity[12] that would require a thoroughly modern solution: national social policy managed by a modern bureaucracy. Attempts to address the 'accident problem' marked the sudden intervention of the state in the market, transforming understandings about liberalism and, in particular, the freedom of contract.[13] In turn, they revolutionised thinking about both the obligations and the rights of individuals. Tort law, that 'bastard child of technology', provided an initial, and usually unsatisfactory, means to seek damages against employers for accidents at work in the wake of industrialisation.[14] As a consequence, commercial liability insurance for accidents became more prevalent as the nineteenth century wore on.[15] Nonetheless, tort law proved unable to address the core problem behind workplace accidents: no one could be held responsible for them. Accidents no longer seemed an interpersonal matter to be sorted out between workers and employers in court. Instead, they became a social problem and a target for social policy.[16]

Compensation for workplace accidents formed an essential, yet often neglected foundation for the subsequent history of European statehood, in which identifying and managing social problems has become a core mission.[17] In attempting to manage the first modern risk, governments played a central role not only in defining a task for themselves. They also made states in modern Europe into 'social states'. The '*État social*', '*stato sociale*', '*Sozialstaat*' and their equivalents are terms widely used in other languages, while the (frequently pejorative) 'welfare state' has taken hold in English. This linguistic distinction reveals what can be seen as an anglophone reluctance to acknowledge the positive social function of the state alongside a preference

---

[12] Anson Rabinbach, 'Social knowledge, social risk, and the politics of industrial accidents in Germany and France', in Dietrich Rueschemeyer and Theda Skocpol, eds., *States, social knowledge, and the origins of modern social policies* (Princeton, NJ, 1996), pp. 48–89.

[13] Peter Flora and Jens Alber, 'Modernization, democratization, and the development of welfare states in western Europe', in Peter Flora and Arnold J. Heidenheimer, eds., *The development of welfare states in Europe and America* (New Brunswick, NJ, 1981), pp. 37–80, at p. 38; Jose Harris, *Private lives, public spirit: Britain, 1870–1914* (London, 1993), p. 144. On the broader relationship between shifting concepts of liberalism and the origins of the welfare state in Britain, see Chris Renwick, *Bread for all: the origins of the welfare state* (London, 2017).

[14] Lawrence M. Friedman, 'Civil wrongs: personal injury law in the late 19th century', *American Bar Foundation Research Journal* 12 (1987), pp. 351–78, at p. 375.

[15] Peter Borscheid, 'Europe: an overview', in Peter Borscheid and Niels Viggo Haueter, eds., *World insurance: the evolution of a global risk network* (Oxford, 2012), pp. 37–66, at p. 38.

[16] For a related analysis of the relationship between modern states, the law and risk that builds on and overlaps with my earlier published and unpublished work and arguments, see Peter Itzen, 'Who is responsible in winter? Traffic accidents, the fight against hazardous weather and the role of law in a history of risks', *Historical Social Research* 41 (2016), pp. 154–75, and associated publications by the same author.

[17] Paradoxically, the *idea* of compensation, as a form of distributive justice, has been seen as the founding principle behind the welfare state. See, for example, John Finnis, *Natural law and natural rights* (1980; 2nd edn, Oxford, 2011), pp. 177ff.; Niklas Luhmann, *Political theory in the welfare state* (Berlin, 1990), pp. 22–3.

for market-based solutions to social problems.[18] Nonetheless, following the identification of occupational accidents as the consequence of known 'risks', a pan-European transformation unfolded in the governance of social problems. It included Great Britain as much as its continental counterparts, even if specific emphases and policy details differed. Social statehood was predicated on the sharing of risks – and the identification of analogous responsibilities, both for individuals and the state.[19] The 1870s marked a watershed for this kind of thinking, as earlier ideas about fate or the immorality of people who had fallen on 'hard times' began to wither away in favour of arguments based on probability. Social reformers across Europe and the emerging social sciences such as statistics, sociology and economics all seemed to prove that problems such as accidents, hunger and poverty were the consequences of specific risks that could be predicted,[20] whether those risks were related to one's job, natural fluctuations of the market or the lifecycle.[21] By 1911, the British sociologist Leonard Hobhouse could look back at the sea change within his own lifetime in coming to terms with hardship:

It was thought ...[that] by sternly withholding all external supports we should teach the working classes to stand alone, and if there were pain in the disciplinary process there was yet hope in the future. They would come by degrees to a position of economic independence in which they would be able to face the risks of life, not in reliance upon the State, but by the force of their own brains and the strength of their own right arms. These views no longer command the same measure of assent. On all sides we find the State making active provision for the poorer classes and not by any means for the destitute alone.[22]

Of course, the idea of risk was nothing new by the time Hobhouse was writing. Marine insurance across the northern Italian city states had been covering what it identified as 'risks', ranging from piracy to wrecked ships, already in the fourteenth century. The risks of winning and losing associated with gambling went

[18] A tension highlighted in Jose Harris' work. See, for example: 'Enterprise and welfare states: a comparative perspective', *Transactions of the Royal Historical Society* (5th series) 40 (1990), pp. 175–95.

[19] My reading of the 'social state' contrasts sharply in this regard with that put forward by Niklas Luhmann: *Political theory*, pp. 21–2.

[20] Thomas Osborne and Nikolas Rose, 'Do the social sciences create phenomena? The example of public opinion research', *British Journal of Sociology* 50 (1999), pp. 367–96. See, for example: Per Wisselgren, *The social scientific gaze: the social question and the rise of academic social science in Sweden* (London, 2015); Kerstin Brückweh et al., eds., *Engineering society: the role of the human and social sciences in modern societies* (Basingstoke, 2012); Michael J. Lacey and Mary O. Furner, eds., *The state and social investigation in Britain and the United States* (Cambridge, 1993).

[21] See, for example: James Vernon, *Hunger: a modern history* (Cambridge, MA, 2008); Jose Harris, *Unemployment and politics: a study in English social policy, 1886–1914* (Oxford, 1972); Pat Thane, *Old age in English history: past experiences, present issues* (New York, 2002).

[22] L. T. Hobhouse, *Liberalism* (1911; London, 1919), pp. 156–7.

back at least to ancient Egypt, and they would characterise attitudes towards buying shares in joint-stock companies in early modern Europe. By the mid eighteenth century, commercial insurance markets had taken off across much of Europe, covering risks to life and property.[23] Looking to the state as a guardian in times of risk was, however, a novelty of the late nineteenth century, as was the expectation that individuals owed something (beyond taxes or military service) in return. For Hobhouse, therefore, 'this view of social obligation [lay] increased stress on public but by no means ignores private responsibility'.[24] As I show in the following chapters, this thinking had become so deeply rooted by the 1920s that, through a major war, a global economic crisis and the birth pangs of Europe's early experiments in both democracy and social legislation, it seemed that social statehood was here to stay, and it was based on this web of mutual expectations about the sharing of risks and responsibilities.

By the late twentieth century, this consensus began to crack, leading to a chequered view of the social state's past and contemporary legacies. The economic downturn of the 1970s led several observers across the political spectrum to agree that the social state was a failure and to look for neoliberal alternatives – even if many elements of the social state would remain in place, and, not least, proliferate within this new political climate.[25] Under the Conservative British Prime Minister Margaret Thatcher, it seemed that benefit claimants merely took advantage of the system and avoided taking responsibility for their own lives. Similar thinking informed policy adjustments throughout the 1980s and into the early 2000s, evidenced by Thatcher's attempt to make tenants in public housing into home owners by selling off council estates; Conservative Prime Minister David Cameron's 'Big Society' vision of communitarian social care; the privatisation and 'Catholicisation' of welfare through the voluntary sector in northern Italy; and in recently reunified Germany, by the Social Democratic Chancellor Gerhard Schröder's aim to move long-term claimants off public assistance by requiring beneficiaries to take so-called 'mini-jobs', regardless of individuals' qualifications, ambitions or abilities.[26] Meanwhile, across the pond, the Democratic US President Bill Clinton dissolved Aid to Families with

[23] Peter L. Bernstein, *Against the gods: the remarkable story of risk* (New York, 1996), pp. 12–13, 89–95. On the eighteenth century as a turning point: Emily C. Nacol, *An age of risk: politics and economy in early modern Britain* (Princeton, NJ, 2016). For example: Geoffrey W. Clark, *Betting on lives: the culture of life insurance in England, 1695–1775* (Manchester, 1999).

[24] Hobhouse, *Liberalism*, p. 164.

[25] On the broader context, see Paul Pierson, *Dismantling the welfare state? Reagan, Thatcher and the politics of retrenchment* (Cambridge, 1995).

[26] Edward Ashbee, 'Neoliberalism, conservative politics and "social recapitalization"', *Global Discourse* 5/1 (2015), pp. 96–113; Georg Menz, '*Auf Wiedersehen*, Rhineland model: embedding neoliberalism in Germany', in Susanne Soederberg et al., eds., *Internalizing globalization: the rise of neoliberalism and the decline of national varieties of capitalism* (Basingstoke, 2005), pp. 33–49; Andrea Muehlebach, *The moral neoliberal: welfare and citizenship in Italy* (Chicago, 2012), pp. 60–5.

Dependent Children with a similar rationale, declaring 'today we are taking a historic chance to make welfare what it was meant to be: a second chance, not a way of life'.[27] Behind these disparate initiatives was the consensus that individuals should take responsibility for their own lives, and should be free to choose whether and how to make provisions for potential risks.[28]

Neoliberal critiques of the welfare state and calls for retrenchment permeated the centre and right as well as the left, leading not only to anxieties about the abuse of social assistance but also to analyses of the state as a social disciplinarian.[29] Some began arguing that new forms of knowledge about risk resulted in the growth of governmental power and legal regulation, with a resultant loss of individual liberties. For example, in his pathbreaking study of the origins and growth of the 'providential state' in nineteenth- and twentieth-century France, François Ewald claims that a 'decisive rupture' took place when workplace accidents came to be seen as the natural outcome of known risks (that could be predicted and therefore provided for), rather than as the consequences of individual responsibility. Subsequently, attempts to manage social risks through 'solidarity' gradually proliferated in the form of insurance and related measures. Ewald's argument was both a conscious critique of the French 'providential state', which had come under widespread attack during the 1980s, and a manifestation of his disappointment about the failure of radical social revolution in 1968.[30] For Ewald, the 'socialisation' of risk was a unidirectional – and gradually authoritarian – process that moved away from protecting individual 'liberty' towards promoting 'life', in the form of 'biopower'. From this perspective, the providential state was potentially totalitarian, akin to James C. Scott's high modernist states like the Soviet Union, whose grand 'schemes to improve the human condition' were bound to fail (and harm subjects in the process).[31] In parallel to these critiques, others proposed an alternative reading of the relationship between risk, modernity and the state. From the 1970s, scholarship on 'risk societies' led by the sociologists Ulrich Beck, Anthony Giddens and Niklas Luhmann posited that attempts to govern risk, especially through scientific and social knowledge, have become

---

[27] Quoted in Francis X. Clines, 'Clinton signs bill cutting welfare; States in new role', *New York Times* (23 August 1996), http://nyti.ms/194fPhs, last accessed 10 December 2015.

[28] An outline of this transition in the USA: Jacob S. Hacker, *The great risk shift: the new economic insecurity and the decline of the American dream* (Oxford, 2008). See also Yascha Mounk, *The age of responsibility: luck, choice, and the welfare state* (Cambridge, MA, 2017).

[29] For example: Larry Frohman, *Poor relief and welfare in Germany from the Reformation to World War I* (Cambridge, 2008).

[30] François Ewald, *L'État providence* (Paris, 1986), pp. 10–11. Michael C. Behrent, 'Accidents happen: François Ewald, the "antirevolutionary" Foucault, and the intellectual politics of the French welfare state', *Journal of Modern History* 82/3 (2010), pp. 585–624.

[31] Ewald, *L'État providence*, pp. 16, 25–7, 143, 275, 349–51, 374–5, 529–30, at pp. 10 and 401; James C. Scott, *Seeing like a state: how certain schemes to improve the human condition have failed* (New Haven, 1998).

the ubiquitous hallmarks of a new, postindustrial era. These exercises in risk management have been characterised by regulations on 'health and safety' at work, school and elsewhere, as well as by policies directed at new 'risks' such as ecological disasters, nuclear accidents and terrorist attacks. Postindustrial risk societies have been marked by their neutrality: on the surface, it seems that everyone suffers from global warming or the meltdown of a nuclear reactor in the same way.[32] Due to the ostensibly universal nature of postindustrial risks, the question of individual responsibility becomes irrelevant. Following this line of reasoning, modern states are not necessarily totalitarian, but they are predicated on risk management for society at large.

Contrary to received wisdom, I suggest that the state has not become unrelentingly interventionist over the last two centuries in attempting to manage 'risks'. Nor must questions of individual responsibility – to hold a job, return to work, maintain a home – stand either at the centre of our understanding of social legislation, as in critiques inspired by neoliberalism, or out of view entirely, as in the accounts of 'risk societies'. Instead, by studying how workplace accidents were made into the object of social policy, we can see how governments at the dawn of the twentieth century worked together with a wide range of actors to determine what counted as a 'risk' and what were deemed the obligations of both individuals *and* the state in dealing with that risk. In doing so, officials, from career bureaucrats to consulting attorneys, helped create the idea that modern states were the guardians of their citizens: whether acting as benevolent caretaker or stern warden, the state took on a mystical, almost spiritual quality.[33] In order to understand this process, we need to return our attention to government as the motor of social policy, and to adopt a comparative and historical analysis. Following Pierre Bourdieu, I emphasise the role of bureaucracy in taking up a range of practices, from collecting statistics to enacting laws or producing official memoranda, that created a sense of 'stateness' when attempting to deal with workplace accidents and their repercussions.[34] Officials contributed to this sense not only through their actions, but also through their beliefs about the specific nature of their own state *as*

---

[32] Ulrich Beck, *Risk society: towards a new modernity*, trans. Mark Ritter (Thousand Oaks, CA, 1992). An adumbrated version of this view distinguishes between earlier understandings of 'danger' and modern notions of 'risk': Niklas Luhmann, *Risk: a sociological theory* (New York, 1993), pp. 23–7; Anthony Giddens, 'Risk and responsibility', *Modern Law Review* 62 (1999), pp. 1–10, at p. 3.

[33] Following Max Weber, some have gone as far as suggesting that the state has replaced religion as the modern form of faith, a view to which I do not subscribe. See Pierre Legendre, *Leçons VI: Les enfants du texte. Étude sur la fonction parentale des états* (Paris, 1992).

[34] Pierre Bourdieu, *Sur l'État: cours au Collège de France, 1989–1992* (Paris, 2012), pp. 580–1. On 'stateness', see Peter Nettl, 'The state as a conceptual variable', *World Politics* 20 (1968), pp. 559–92. See also Philip Abrams, whose 'myth of the state' was a crucial analytical link between earlier theory and Bourdieu's work: 'Notes on the difficulty of studying the state (1977)', *Journal of Historical Sociology* 1 (1988), pp. 58–89.

a nation state.[35] The creation of Europe's social states paralleled the birth of many of its nation states, alongside a more widespread phenomenon: modern nationalism.[36] Official views about national specificity filtered into the details of policy proposals and the tone of government publications about social legislation. As Tim Mitchell has argued, the state 'occurs not merely as a subjective belief', but it is also 'represented and reproduced in visible, everyday forms, such as the language of legal practice, the architecture of public buildings, the wearing of military uniforms, or the marking out and policing of frontiers'.[37]

My concept of the 'social state' calls for this kind of cultural sensitivity to processes of policy making. This perspective enables us to tease out the meaning behind official wording and the symbolism inherent in official actions as well, of course, as inaction.[38] It also allows us to depart from viewing the state as an autonomous actor that is both rational and above the frays of civil society,[39] meaning that governments create and subscribe to closed rationalities with the result that policy is the self-propelling progeny of Max Weber's 'iron cage'.[40] At the same time, thinking in terms of 'social states' enables us to move beyond placing social policy into that murky quagmire of the 'social' which neo-Foucauldian scholars have located between civil society and the state.[41] The paradox of the 'social' as a category of analysis is that it assumes that the state continues to dole out social discipline, even if its (neo)liberal policies mean that individuals unknowingly choose to discipline themselves.[42]

[35] From a Marxist perspective, Philip Corrigan and Derek Sayer have made a similar argument about the creation of 'Englishness' that ran parallel to state formation in England: *The great arch: English state formation as cultural revolution* (Oxford, 1985).

[36] For a related argument that focuses on Germany, see Sandrine Kott, *Sozialstaat und Gesellschaft: das deutsche Kaiserreich in Europa* (Göttingen, 2014), especially ch. 6.

[37] Timothy Mitchell, 'The limits of the state: beyond statist approaches and their critics', *American Political Science Review* 85/1 (1991), pp. 77–96, at p. 81. These aspects of the 'state as effect', in Mitchell's words, have been highlighted for Britain in some recent important works. See, for example, Patrick Joyce, *The state of freedom: a social history of the British state since 1800* (Cambridge, 2013); Tom Crook, *Governing systems: modernity and the making of public health in England, c. 1830–1910* (Berkeley, 2016).

[38] And the emotions or lack thereof associated with those actions. See Michael Herzfeld, *The social production of indifference: exploring the symbolic roots of western bureaucracy* (Chicago, 1992).

[39] George Steinmetz, 'Introduction', in George Steinmetz, ed., *State/culture: state-formation after the cultural turn* (Ithaca, NY, 1999), pp. 1–50, at pp. 23–4.

[40] A possible reading of Oliver MacDonagh's landmark study of governmental problematising: *The pattern of government growth: the Passenger Acts 1800–1860* (London, 1961). This line of analysis can also be detected in some of the neo-institutionalist literature on the state, such as Peter Evans et al., eds., *Bringing the state back in* (Cambridge, 1985).

[41] *Pace* George Steinmetz for his otherwise brilliant *Regulating the social: the welfare state and local politics in imperial Germany* (Princeton, NJ, 1993), p. 1.

[42] Michel Foucault, 'Governmentality', in Graham Burchell et al., eds., *The Foucault effect: studies in governmentality, with two lectures by and an interview with Michel Foucault* (Chicago,

By contrast, an understanding of social states necessitates illuminating the interactive bureaucratic-societal dynamics that drove the evolution of social policy. It requires moving beyond seeing the state either as a kind of *deus ex machina* disciplinarian (or, from a Whiggish perspective, as a benefactor) or as the punching bag of interest groups hashing out their own visions of social justice.[43]

Britain, Germany and Italy offer ideal case studies to understand these dynamics. While Germany and Italy had recently unified as new nation states, in 1871 and 1859, respectively, Britain had existed, in various forms, as a sovereign country for centuries before the concept of social states began to take root at the end of the nineteenth century. These differences mattered for the nature of the social state in each country and make a comparison of their experiences with the evolving relationship between risk, responsibility and statehood especially meaningful. Of course, other countries could easily have been selected for such a comparison. France and Britain have often been compared in terms of their histories of industrialisation,[44] and the Nordic countries, due to their expansive late twentieth-century welfare states, are often the subject of comparisons of European social policy. Beyond Europe, a number of other countries, from the United States to Chile and Japan, might have convincingly been selected for such an analysis. However, in terms of the making of nation states in the nineteenth and early twentieth centuries, and its relationship to social provision, Germany and Italy offer perhaps the most analogous – and, by extension, telling – objects of study. Meanwhile, Germany and Britain, in many ways, offer a particularly important contrast in terms of historical development, due to the differing nature of their legal systems, bureaucracies and political structures. At the same time, contemporaries in Britain, Germany and Italy consistently looked to developments across each other's borders – and especially to the contrasting models of social legislation put forward in Britain and Germany – when reflecting on the nature of workplace risk and possible ways to manage it. For these reasons, France – which has also been the subject of considerable research in terms of accidents, risk and welfare, including important comparative work[45] – does not form a central part of the story presented here.

Of course, Britain, Germany and Italy shared the common problem of workplace accidents and similar solutions to that problem. Germany and Italy introduced accident insurance legislation in 1884 and 1898 respectively. By

---

1991), pp. 87–104. On the elision between neo-Foucauldian work and older studies of social control: Peter Mandler, 'After the welfare state', *Journal of British Studies* 39 (2000), pp. 382–8.

[43] A downside of Supiot's otherwise persuasive analysis: 'Grandeur and misery'.

[44] For example: Patrick O'Brien, 'Path dependency, or why Britain became an industrialized and urbanized economy long before France', *Economic History Review* 49 (1996), pp. 213–49.

[45] In particular, in Ewald, *État providence*, but also in a spate of subsequent work such as Rabinbach's *Human motor* and recent important research by Soraya Boudia, Nathalie Jas, Thomas LeRoux and Jean-Baptiste Fressenoz.

contrast, Britain enacted a workmen's compensation policy in 1897. Each of these laws targeted a finite group of workers employed in trades that were considered to be amongst the most dangerous, including miners, quarry workers and workers in factories with at least a certain number of employees.[46] Over the next several years, the scope of these laws was expanded considerably (Appendix, Table 3) while, at the same time, each country adopted a variety of separate legislation that targeted related issues of social security. Nonetheless, despite these commonalities, Britain, Germany and Italy also differed in several ways that are significant for an investigation of the relationship between individuals and the state that is forged through social policy. While Britain was governed centrally, Germany maintained a federal political system alongside a strong central government. Italy, like Britain, was administered centrally, but its government lacked authority throughout the peninsula after national unification. All three countries also differed in terms of their legal systems. Britain employed an unwritten common law that was based on precedent, while Italy relied on a civil code and Germany had several different legal systems that coexisted until the codification of its civil law in 1900. In addition to these differences, aspects of civil society in each of these countries, including levels of enfranchisement, the strength of trade unions and the development of social democracy, meant that responses to workplace accidents differed slightly in each case.[47]

Not least, Britain, Germany and Italy contrasted substantially in terms of their economies in the late nineteenth century, with significant implications for the nature of the accident problem in each country. While Britain had already begun to industrialise by the turn of the nineteenth century, Germany only initiated the process in the mid nineteenth century, and Italy underwent a rapid period of industrialisation starting in the 1890s. Consequently, each of these societies differed in terms of its economic composition,[48] and Italy remained largely agricultural into the first part of the twentieth century (Appendix, Table 4). Moreover, each of these countries maintained different forms of social provision for workplace accidents prior to the enactment of the social policies examined in this book. Workers in all three countries joined mutual

---

[46] Railway workers were included in the British and German legislation but excluded from the Italian law, as an earlier policy had already required the railway industry to establish its own insurance fund for industrial accidents.

[47] See Hartmut Kaelble, *A social history of Western Europe: 1880–1980* (Dublin, 1987), p. 85; Stefano Bartolini, *The political mobilization of the European Left, 1860–1980: the class cleavage* (Cambridge, 2000), p. 246; Joel Krieger, 'Britain', in Mark Kesselman et al., eds., *Introduction to comparative politics* (5th edn, Boston, 2010), pp. 47–98, at p. 56; Christopher S. Allen, 'Germany', in Kesselman et al., eds. *Introduction to comparative politics*, pp. 157–210, at p. 162; Martin Clark, *Modern Italy: 1871 to the present* (3rd edn, London, 2008), pp. 77–8, 156.

[48] Brian R. Mitchell, *European historical statistics, 1750–1970* (London, 1975), pp. 156, 158, 163, 355–7; A. Maddison, *Monitoring the world economy, 1820–1992* (Paris, 1995), pp. 23–4.

organisations that allowed benefits for accidents,[49] and, from the middle of the century, each country had a thriving private insurance sector with policies targeting accidental death and injury (Appendix, Table 5). For example, the first commercial personal accident insurance policies were introduced in Britain in 1848 and in Germany in 1853, and Italy's most important insurer began offering similar policies from the mid 1870s.[50]

My book seeks to establish the significance of these differences for thinking within government about accidents as a kind of 'risk' that should be addressed through the state. Yet, I also consider alternative influences, including the impact of transnational communication on policy learning and, not least, the timing of policy adoption.[51] From this perspective, we can attempt to trace how what contemporaries saw as national 'models' of accident compensation came to emerge *within* the context of transnational cultural encounters, for example, through exchanging periodicals or sending officials and experts affiliated with government on research visits. Hence, I investigate transnational and international contact through conferences and international organisations, and also examine the exchange of information and the transfer of practices related to compensation which resulted from international labour migration. As we shall see, it mattered for officials in Berlin *as well as* for those in Rome and London that Germany adopted accident insurance when it did, just as it mattered for civil servants in Rome that Italy had only begun to industrialise when other countries began enacting compensation policies. It was the combination of these various factors that contributed to the specific imprint of each country's social state.

In fact, in light of their contrasting social provisions, and in view of their vast political, social and economic differences, each of these countries has been subjected to various myths of national peculiarity, or 'special paths', in historical development. Britain has frequently been characterised in historical memory (as well as by historical actors) by its absence of a socialist labour movement,

[49] For example: Florian Tennstedt, *Sozialgeschichte der Sozialpolitik in Deutschland: vom 18. Jahrhundert bis zum Ersten Weltkrieg* (Göttingen, 1981), pp. 127–34; Alan J. Kidd, *State, society and the poor in nineteenth-century England* (Basingstoke, 1999), p. 112; Arnaldo Cherubini, *Beneficenza e solidarietà: assistenza pubblica e mutualismo operaio (1860–1900)* (Milan, 1991), p. 333.

[50] Note that it is impossible to compare authoritatively the insurance sectors within these countries because of the multitude of different kinds of policies that contained provisions for accidental injury or death at work. Moreover, comparing the total premiums collected in any given year can provide only limited insights into the size and scope of private accident insurance policies, given that the cost of living in each state differed substantially. Robin Pearson, 'Towards an historical model of services innovation: the case of the insurance industry, 1700–1914', *Economic History Review* (n.s.) 50 (1997), pp. 235–56, at pp. 238–40; *Le Assicurazioni Generali: cenni storici* (Trieste, 1966), p. 32.

[51] On these issues, see: Andrew Abbott and Stanley DeViney, 'The welfare state as transnational event: evidence from sequences of policy adoption', *Social Science History* 16/2 (1992), pp. 245–74.

political revolution and domestic violence.[52] According to this logic, Britain's history of a non-radical, 'peaceable kingdom', based on political consensus and an unwritten constitution, has both drawn upon and led to the continuous success of liberal, reformist forms of politics facilitated by a weak and non-interventionist central government. Britain has thus been seen as the apotheosis of liberal statehood.[53] By contrast, Germany has often been characterised by a negative path of development (a *Sonderweg*) following the failure of a liberal political revolution in the mid nineteenth century that resulted in the excessive power of agricultural and industrial interest groups, an exclusive and authoritarian government and the ultimate rise of National Socialism. The shadow of the Nazi state has tempered historical memory of German statehood, but already in the nineteenth century, many contemporaries saw that Germany was a kind of 'authoritarian' foil to 'liberal' Britain.[54] Scholars of Italy, like those of Germany, have been concerned to uncover the roots of political fascism in the twentieth century. They have, however, focused on the failure of governments in late nineteenth- and early twentieth-century Italy by looking to the nature of compromise (*trasformismo*) that characterised Italian politics. The politics of compromise in Liberal Italy has not only been linked to the rise of Benito Mussolini's Fascist government but also to a culture of clientelism that continues to characterise Italian politics in the twenty-first century.[55]

In many ways, these stories about 'special paths' not only echoed the views of contemporaries in the nineteenth century. They have also informed scholarship on the history of the welfare state, such as the 'conservative' continental European, 'social democratic' Scandinavian and 'liberal' Anglo-Saxon models outlined in Gøsta Esping-Andersen's influential typology. In highlighting the theme of 'liberal' Britain and its contrast to 'conservative' or even 'authoritarian' Germany, scholars have pointed to Britain's inclination towards progressive and gradual social reforms and contrasted these with Germany's ostensibly etatist programmes.[56] Others have pointed to a British 'tradition'

[52] A historical memory that may be revised after Britain's controversial 2016 referendum on exiting the European Union.

[53] David Blackbourn and Geoff Eley have elucidated the false pretext of this conception of British history and provide a helpful overview of this approach: *The peculiarities of German history: bourgeois society and politics in nineteenth-century Germany* (Oxford, 1984). See also E. P. Thompson, 'The peculiarities of the English', in E. P. Thompson, *The poverty of theory and other essays* (New York, 1978), pp. 35–91; Ross McKibbin, 'Why was there no Marxism in Great Britain?', *English Historical Review* 99 (1984), pp. 297–331.

[54] See the helpful overview of these issues in Helmut Walser Smith, 'When the Sonderweg debate left us', *German Studies Review* 31 (2008), pp. 225–40.

[55] See Lucy Riall, 'Progress and compromise in Liberal Italy', *Historical Journal* 38 (1995), pp. 205–13. On clientelism: Robert D. Putnam et al., *Making democracy work: civic traditions in modern Italy* (Princeton, NJ, 1993); Paul Ginsborg, *Italy and its discontents: family, civil society, state 1980–2001* (London, 2001).

[56] Gøsta Esping-Anderson, *The three worlds of welfare capitalism* (Oxford, 1990). Noteworthy historical comparisons: Gerhard A. Ritter, *Social welfare in Germany and Britain: origins and development* (Leamington Spa, 1986). An implicit comparison along these lines can be inferred

of voluntarism and minimal, but relatively universal state intervention in the nineteenth century that continued to inform social legislation after the adoption of the Beveridge Plan during the Second World War. This British 'model' has often been contrasted with a German system of 'Bismarckian' contributory social insurance based on male breadwinners that provided the foundation for all subsequent social policy, even if it drew on earlier forms of professional insurance schemes in Germany.[57] When Italian social provision has been compared to that in other European countries, it has often been scorned as a failed attempt to modernise the peninsula and a reason for the rise of the Fascist movement.[58] Alternatively, along with its neighbours around the Mediterranean, Italy has been consigned to a separate tier of European social legislation as a representative of the 'Southern model'.[59]

By subjecting these three countries to comparative analysis, I have sought to join up the dots, moving beyond single-nation studies and broad typologies of social policy in order to illuminate the contours of an experience with the identification and management of social risks that was genuinely European (and increasingly global) in scope – even if individual governments claimed that their social state was unique. Rather than viewing comparison as an (unpersuasive) exercise in isolating variables out of the complexity of the past, therefore, I have instead sought to throw new light on the ways in which different countries shared a common experience of grappling with modernity.[60] This experience had global repercussions, not least, through the transfer of thinking about 'social questions' and the function of the state across empires and in the transition to postcolonial states;[61] through Atlantic (and Pacific) crossings as contemporaries around the globe debated how to solve social problems at home;[62] and through the increasing impact of international organisations

in Hermann Beck, *The origins of the authoritarian welfare state in Prussia: conservatives, bureaucracy, and the social question, 1815–70* (Ann Arbor, MI, 1995).

[57] E. P. Hennock, *The origin of the welfare state in Britain and Germany: social policies compared* (Cambridge, 2007); Bruno Palier, ed., *A long goodbye to Bismarck? The politics of welfare reform in continental Europe* (Amsterdam, 2010).

[58] For example: Maria Sophia Quine, *Italy's social revolution: charity and welfare from liberalism to fascism* (Basingstoke, 2002).

[59] Maurizio Ferrera, 'The "southern model" of welfare in social Europe', *Journal of European Social Policy* 6 (1996), pp. 17–37; Martin Rhodes, ed., *Southern European welfare states: between crisis and reform* (London, 1997); Kees van Kersbergen and Philip Manow, eds., *Religion, class coalitions and welfare states* (Cambridge, 2009).

[60] Gurminder K. Bhambra, 'Comparative sociology and the state: problems of method', *Cultural Sociology* 10 (2016), pp. 1–17. See also Bernhard Rieger, *Technology and the culture of modernity in Britain and Germany, 1890–1945* (Cambridge, 2005).

[61] For example: John Murphy, *A decent provision: Australian welfare policy, 1870 to 1949* (Farnham, 2011); Amelia H. Lyons, *The civilizing mission in the metropole: Algerian families and the French welfare state during decolonization* (Stanford, CA, 2013).

[62] Daniel T. Rodgers, *Atlantic crossings: social politics in a progressive age* (Cambridge, MA, 1998); Gregory James Kasza, *One world of welfare: Japan in comparative perspective* (Ithaca, NY, 2006). Of course, the most frequent crossings were more localised: across the English

from the late nineteenth century.[63] Charting the rise of social states therefore requires a comparative history that is sensitive to broader connections at various scales of activity, from the local and regional to the imperial, international and global. I have chosen to focus on national case studies as a lens into these various and shifting scales, and as the most appropriate means to trace how contemporaries themselves understood social states: as nationally specific.[64]

Since my book is about the impact of ideas about risk on the origins of European social states, I have not therefore focused on various important aspects of occupational health and accidents, and I do not forefront the legislative evolution and details of the British, German and Italian policies on accident compensation. Both subjects have received due attention elsewhere.[65] Peter Bartrip and Sandra Burman have provided rich socio-legal studies on the history of workmen's compensation policy in Britain, building on earlier work focused primarily on legislative developments. Willibald Steinmetz has contributed to both approaches in his monumental social and cultural history of English labour law.[66] Greg Eghigian's illuminating work has focused on accident insurance and disability insurance policies in conjunction in order to analyse the politics of entitlement of German welfare recipients at the turn of the

---

Channel, for example, or the Rhine river. See Allan Mitchell, *The divided path: the German influence on social reform in France after 1871* (Chapel Hill, NC, 1991); E. P. Hennock, *British social reform and German precedents: the case of social insurance, 1880–1914* (Oxford, 1987).

[63] Key works include Sandrine Kott and Joëlle Droux, eds., *Globalizing social rights: the International Labor Organization and beyond* (Basingstoke, 2013); Daniel Maul, *Human rights, development and decolonization: the International Labour Organization, 1940–70* (Basingstoke, 2012); Madeleine Herren, *Internationale Sozialpolitik vor dem Ersten Weltkrieg: die Anfänge europäischer Kooperation aus der Sicht Frankreichs* (Berlin, 1993).

[64] Richard Snyder, 'Scaling down: the subnational comparative method', *Studies in Comparative International Development* 36/1 (2001), pp. 93–110; Sidney Tarrow and Doug McAdam, 'Scale shift in transnational contention', in Donatella della Porta and Sidney Tarrow, eds., *Transnational protest and global activism* (Oxford, 2005), pp. 121–50, at p. 123.

[65] See for example Francesco Carnevale and Alberto Baldasseroni, *Mal da lavoro: storia della salute dei lavoratori* (Rome, 1999); Dietrich Milles, *Gesundheitsrisiken, Industriegesellschaft und Soziale Sicherungen in der Geschichte* (Bremerhaven, 1993); P. W. J. Bartrip, *The Home Office and the dangerous trades: regulating occupational disease in Victorian and Edwardian Britain* (Amsterdam, 2002); Paul Weindling, ed., *The social history of occupational health* (London, 1985); Paul D. Blanc, *How everyday products make people sick: toxins at home and in the workplace* (Berkeley, CA, 2007); Christopher C. Sellers and Joseph Melling, eds., *Dangerous trade: histories of industrial hazard across a globalizing world* (Philadelphia, 2012).

[66] P. W. J. Bartrip and Sandra Burman, *The wounded soldiers of industry: industrial compensation policy 1833–1897* (Oxford, 1983); P. W. J. Bartrip, *Workmen's compensation in twentieth century Britain: law, history and social policy* (Aldershot, 1987); A. F. Young, *Industrial injuries insurance: an examination of British policy* (London, 1964); W. A. Dinsdale, *History of accident insurance in Great Britain* (London, 1954); David G. Hanes, *The first British Workmen's Compensation Act, 1897* (New Haven, 1968); Arnold Wilson and Hermann Levy, *Workmen's compensation* (2 vols., London, 1939–41); Willibald Steinmetz, *Begegnungen vor Gericht: eine Sozial- und Kulturgeschichte des englischen Arbeitsrechts (1850–1925)* (Munich, 2002).

twentieth century.[67] Wolfgang Ayass, Florian Tennstedt and Lothar Machtan
have all illuminated the role of Bismarck, the Prussian bureaucracy and business
interests in pushing for and shaping accident insurance legislation in Germany,
while Ernst Wickenhagen has detailed the development of accident insurance
from the perspective of the employers' liability associations that administered
insurance in Germany.[68] No full-length study of accident insurance exists for
Italy, although Arnaldo Cherubini and Italo Piva have focused on the political and legislative development of the policy in conjunction with other forms
of social legislation.[69] I have drawn upon these works, as well as literature on
workmen's compensation and accident insurance in other countries, such as
Martin Lengwiler's influential research on the relationship between actuarial
expertise and the development of the Swiss Accident Insurance Fund during
the interwar period.[70] Perhaps due to a national anxiety about litigation run
amok,[71] workmen's compensation has been the subject of much research for
the United States which has, in turn, been instructive for this book.[72] I have also
built on the rich social, cultural and intellectual history of accidents, workplace

[67] Greg Eghigian, *Making security social: disability, insurance, and the birth of the social entitlement state in Germany* (Ann Arbor, MI, 2000).

[68] Lothar Machtan, 'Risikoversicherung statt Gesundheitsschutz für Arbeiter: zur Entstehung der
Unfallversicherungsgesetzgebung im Bismarck-Reich', *Leviathan* 13 (1985), pp. 420–41; Florian
Tennstedt and Heidi Winter, '"Der Staat Hat wenig Liebe – Activ wie Passiv": die Anfänge des
Sozialstaats im Deutschen Reich Von 1871', *Zeitschrift für Soziale Reform* 39 (1993), pp. 362–
92; Florian Tennstedt and Heidi Winter, '"Jeder Tag hat seine eigenen Sorgen, und es ist nicht
weise, die Sorgen der Zukunft freiwillig auf die Gegenwart zu Übernehmen": die Anfänge des
Sozialstaats im Deutschen Reich von 1871', *Zeitschrift für Soziale Reform* 41 (1995), pp. 671–
706; Wolfgang Ayass, 'Regulierte Selbstregulierung in den Berufsgenossenschaften der gesetzlichen Unfallversicherung', in Peter Collin et al., eds., *Regulierte Selbstregulierung im frühen
Interventions- und Sozialstaat* (Frankfurt, 2012), pp. 123–43; Ernst Wickenhagen, *Geschichte der
gewerblichen Unfallversicherung: Wesen und Wirken der gewerblichen Berufsgenossenschaften*
(2 vols., Munich, 1980). See also Heinz Barta, *Kausalität im Sozialrecht: Entstehung und
Funktion der sog. Theorie der wesentlichen Bedingung: Analyse der grundlegenden Judikatur
des Reichsversicherungsamtes in Unfallversicherungssachen (1884–1914)* (Berlin, 1983).

[69] Arnaldo Cherubini and Italo Piva, *Dalla libertà all'obbligo: la previdenza sociale fra Giolitti
e Mussolini* (Milan, 1998). See also Giovanni Cazzetta, *Scienza giuridica e trasformazioni
sociali: diritto e lavoro in Italia tra Otto e Novecento* (Milan, 2007).

[70] Martin Lengwiler, *Risikopolitik im Sozialstaat: die Schweizerische Unfallversicherung, 1870–
1970* (Cologne, 2006).

[71] See Kenneth S. Abraham, *The liability century* (Cambridge, MA, 2009) and Lawrence M.
Friedman, *The republic of choice: law, authority and culture* (Cambridge, MA, 1990).

[72] In particular: Price V. Fishback and Shawn E. Kantor, *A prelude to the welfare state: the origins
of workers' compensation* (Chicago, 2000); John Fabian Witt, *The accidental republic: crippled workmen, destitute widows and the remaking of American law* (Cambridge, MA, 2004);
Jonathan Levy, *Freaks of fortune: the emerging world of capitalism and risk* (Cambridge, MA,
2012). In their pathbreaking work, David Rosner and Gerald Markowitz have touched on
related issues: David Rosner and Gerald E. Markowitz, *Deadly dust: silicosis and the politics of
occupational disease in twentieth-century America* (Princeton, NJ, 1991).

safety and risk that have been highlighted by other scholars.[73] For this reason, I do not explore in an authoritative manner the crucial impact of ideas that linked gender to work, accidents and compensation benefits which have been studied elsewhere.[74]

I instead examine the implications of thinking in terms of 'risk' in order to understand the relationship between states and individuals that is constituted through social policy. The articulation of workplace accidents as a problem of risk seemed to depoliticise class, although each country's policy on accident compensation was a form of 'class law' that specifically targeted manual labourers.[75] Moreover, the concept of risk embedded in the laws on accident compensation focused initially on those risks that were most *visible*, which were usually associated with heavy industry at home. This emphasis often served to minimise consequences of accidents that were invisible, such as repetitive strain injuries and industrial diseases encountered by women working in textiles and light manufacturing, as well as the work-related injuries and illnesses sustained by labourers employed overseas or in colonial outposts.[76] Through carefully reconstructing how social policy was made, we can trace how these assumptions about risk, agency and statehood were latent within it. We have heard aspects of this story before, in particular, through the pathbreaking work of François Ewald, but for a different context, and with a specific emphasis on

[73] See Anson Rabinbach, *The human motor: energy, fatigue, and the origins of modernity* (New York, 1990); Roger Cooter and Bill Luckin, eds., *Accidents in history: injuries, fatalities and social relations* (Amsterdam, 1997); Elaine Freedgood, *Victorian writing about risk: imagining a safe England in a dangerous world* (Cambridge, 2000); Andreas Killen, *Berlin electropolis: shock, nerves and German modernity* (Berkeley, CA, 2006); Ross Hamilton, *Accident: a philosophical and literary history* (Chicago, 2008); Jamie L. Bronstein, *Caught in the machinery: workplace accidents and injured workers in nineteenth-century Britain* (Stanford, CA, 2008); Jean-Baptiste Fressoz, *L'apocalypse joyeuse: une histoire du risque technologique* (Paris, 2012); Arwen Mohun, *Risk: negotiating safety in American society* (Baltimore, 2013); Dan Bouk, *How our days became numbered: risk and the rise of the statistical individual* (Chicago, 2015); Tom Crook and Mike Esbester, eds., *Governing risks in modern Britain: danger, safety and accidents, c. 1800–2000* (Basingstoke, 2016); Thomas LeRoux, ed., *Risques industriels: savoirs, régulations, politiques d'assistance, fin XVIIe–début XXe siècle* (Rennes, 2016); Mike Esbester, *The birth of modern safety: preventing accidents on Britain's railways, 1871–1948* (London, 2017).
[74] See Barbara Nelson, 'The origins of the two-channel welfare state: workmen's compensation and mothers' aid', in Linda Gordon, ed., *Women, the state and welfare* (Madison, WI, 1990), pp. 123–52; Barbara Harrison, *Not only the 'dangerous trades': women's work and health in Britain, 1880–1914* (London, 1996); Carolyn Malone, *Women's bodies and dangerous trades in England, 1880–1914* (Woodbridge, 2003); Arthur McIvor and Ronald Johnston, *Miners' lung: a history of dust disease in British coal mining* (Aldershot, 2007).
[75] Paul Johnson, 'Class law in Victorian England', *Past and Present* 141 (1993), pp. 147–69.
[76] Barbara Harrison, 'Are accidents gender neutral? The case of women's industrial work in Britain, 1880–1914', *Women's History Review* 2 (1993), pp. 253–75. On the 'invisibilisation' of occupational risk, see Judith Rainhorn, 'Les maux de la mine: Revisiter l'histoire minière au prisme des enjeux de santé au travail', in Judith Rainhorn, ed., *Santé et travail à la mine: XIXe–XXIe siècle* (Villeneuve d'Ascq, 2014), pp. 19–30, at p. 28. See also Gabrielle Hecht, *Being nuclear: Africans and the global uranium trade* (Cambridge, MA, 2012), p. 44.

the shadowside of this dynamic. My account is not, by contrast, triumphalist, nor does it seek to offer a monocausal explanation for the rise of 'welfare states' across Europe, which has been the emphasis of many comparative studies. Instead, I aim in this book to understand[77] how social states were created at the turn of the twentieth century and came to operate through the nexus of risk and responsibility. Only by comprehending this heritage can we overcome the social amnesia in contemporary Europe about modern states *as* social states: they are predicated on a reciprocal relationship with citizens that is constituted through everyday interactions with law, bureaucracy and those small symbols of stateness that have become ubiquitous, such as social security cards and forms of civil registration.

In telling this story, I have primarily employed rarely consulted governmental sources that have often been cast aside as dull remnants of the policy-making process and the so-called 'grey' literature that bureaucrats drew on as official and semi-official crib sheets for governing. This material has been neglected especially for Italy, and it has rarely been brought into a single cross-national analysis. I have drawn on the files of the ministries responsible for developing and administering policies on accident compensation in each country, including, for Britain, those of the Home Office, the Board of Trade, the Ministry of Reconstruction, the Labour Ministry and the Ministry of Pensions at the National Archives in London; for Germany, files held from the Imperial Office of the Interior, the Imperial Labour Office, the Imperial Chancellery, Imperial Chancellor's Office and the Imperial Insurance Office at the Bundes-Archiv Berlin at Lichterfelde and at Hoppegarten; the Ministry of Trade, the Ministry of Justice, the Ministry of Agriculture, the Ministry of Finance, the Ministry of the Interior and the Ministry of Welfare at the Geheimes Staats-Archiv Preußischer Kulturbesitz in Berlin; and, for Italy, files from the Ministry of Agriculture, Industry and Commerce, the Ministry of Munitions and the President of the Council of Ministers at the Archivio centrale dello stato in Rome, the Archives of the Chamber of Deputies, the Archives of the Senate and the Archives of the Foreign Office in Rome. In order to account for these discrepancies in official archives, the structures of each government and the national policies on workplace accidents, I have also relied on relevant sources from non-governmental bodies, including the commercial insurance records kept at the Guildhall Archives in London; the archives of the Trades Union Congress and various individual trade unions at the Modern Records Centre at the University of Warwick; and, the archives of the Amalgamated Society of Engineers and other trade organisations at the Working Class Movement Library in Salford. In addition, this study has selectively consulted several archives for information about the activities of local governments. These

---

[77] I. N. Bulhof, *Wilhelm Dilthey: a hermeneutic approach to history and culture* (The Hague, 1980), pp. 55–79.

include the Archivio di stato in Rome; the West Yorkshire Archive Service in Wakefield; and the Sheffield City Archives.

Due to the different administrative techniques at the time at which these files were created, as well as diverse archival practices in subsequent years, the source base for each country naturally varies. For example, the records of the British Cabinet Office in the nineteenth century and into the beginning of the twentieth have been stored at the National Archives in London, but they are of little use for this study due to the minimal information recorded in them. By contrast, the records of the Prime Minister's Office in Rome have been haphazardly archived but contain more valuable material. The German governmental records have been best archived and ordered. Many of the German sources on accident compensation policies have now also been published in the extensive *Quellensammlung zur Geschichte der deutschen Sozialpolitik 1867 bis 1914*. Although the collection is an invaluable resource, this book has instead relied primarily on the original documents, which demonstrate the wide scope of governmental activity, rather than a selection thereof, and reveal a clearer portrayal of how the administration worked. The sequence of correspondence and marginalia in governmental files provide information that is as important as the main contents in these files. Printed primary materials have also provided a valuable source base for this book, in two ways. Governmental publications and official delegations discussed in conference proceedings offer a source of information about developments related to each country's accident policies, *as well as* a means to understand how officials represented questions about risk and the related role of individuals and the state in addressing it. With this dual focus in view, I have relied extensively on official, legal and scientific periodicals; the proceedings of domestic, transnational and international congresses; newspapers; parliamentary minutes and documents; and periodicals from associations of workers, employers and the commercial insurance business.

My argument will unfold in the following six chapters. The first chapter shows how workplace accidents came onto the agenda of central government in Britain and recently unified Italy and Germany. I argue that, over the course of the nineteenth century, reformers, legal theorists, as well as workers' and employers' groups transformed understandings of the labour contract and, with it, the workplace as a public space that was open to scrutiny. Over time, it seemed clear that occupational accidents were not the result of individual misfortunes, incompetence or negligence: they resulted from foreseeable risks. Moreover, it seemed that workers were not in a position either to know about or consent to every risk related to their job, so they could not be held responsible for accidents at work. Instead, introducing liability law and, eventually, a no-fault compensation policy seemed the only option to redress the harms caused by work. The second chapter tells the story of how particular kinds of social policies such as workmen's compensation and social insurance for workplace accidents were viewed by contemporaries as appropriate for specific national contexts. It was through these early discussions that Germany came to be seen as the hallmark of 'state socialism', while contemporaries associated Britain with a *laissez-faire* approach to social policy and Italy with social legislation that sought to create a fragile kind of social peace across the peninsula.

As the following chapter shows, each country's policy on accident compensation was predicated on a more complex range of assumptions about risks, responsibilities and moral hazard. In Chapter 4, I trace how these views were tested at courtrooms across each country, as it became clear that workplace accidents and their consequences were anything but predictable. In various ways, worries about the equity of each country's compensation policy abounded, as did fears that workers were taking advantage of the system by malingering or making false claims. Chapter 5 shows how these concerns fed into considerations about entitlement to accident benefit, as a limited range of new workers were allowed access to compensation, while others were excluded from the policy. At the same time, central government was pushed to take on a greater role in overseeing (and being seen as overseeing) the quotidian management of the accident laws. In Chapter 6, I explore how ideas about the role of the state as a risk manager were transformed in the First World War, a total war that collapsed the clear divide between war and work and the risks associated with each.

I

Accidents, Freedom and Modernity in the Nineteenth Century

A cart fell over around midnight on 30 May 1835. It sparked one of the most significant verdicts on freedom and the role of the law in mediating inter-personal relations. The ruling implied that labour was a private matter that, only in exceptional circumstances, should be tampered with by the state. In the landmark case *Priestley* v. *Fowler*, a young butcher's assistant sued his employer when he was injured while trying to take a load of mutton to market in Lincolnshire. Fowler, the butcher, had ordered another worker to pack the cart full. The cart had been packed so full that an axle cracked, toppling the cart and dislocating Priestley's shoulder. Priestley lost in his claim for damages at court. The court ruled that the assistant had knowingly signed on for the job, including its associated risks. The fact that his colleague had overloaded the cart – at the behest of his employer – was simply a risk of the job that he would have to bear.[1] The verdict on Priestley's case resembled thinking about work across much of Europe, and indeed the globe, in the middle of the nineteenth century. It was not clear whether and to what extent work, and the social problems associated with it, was a concern for the state or the subject of legal regulation. To be sure, Britain had created a national factory inspectorate just two years earlier, in 1833, and various pieces of safety legislation, largely aimed at women and children, in subsequent years. Prussia, which would later form the core of unified Germany, followed suit with the introduction of a small fac-tory inspectorate in 1839 and a safety clause in its Commercial Code of 1845, while, on the Italian peninsula, Lombardy and Venice introduced child labour laws in 1843. Nonetheless, until the closing decades of the century, workers and employers generally addressed the consequences of workplace accidents on their own.

[1] *Priestley* v. *Fowler* (1837) 3 M & H 307–8.

The idea that individuals were free to sign on to the risks associated with their jobs reflected two broader contexts. First, until the late nineteenth century, central government was limited in Britain and in pre-unification Italy and Germany. Britain relied primarily on local governments and church parishes to administer the affairs of everyday life, which meant that 'the only agent of the central state whom the provincial citizen could regularly expect to encounter was the benign post office clerk'. Yet local government was hampered by limited finances. Local rate payers determined local policy and were reluctant to increase their financial contributions for this purpose.[2] As in Britain, in the German and Italian states, government was run primarily on a local level with a limited bureaucracy, and rate payers played an important role in determining policy.[3] Moreover, in the early and mid nineteenth century, Germany and Italy had not yet unified as nation states. Italy unified over the period between 1859 and 1870, while Germany unified between 1866 and 1871. Before unification, Germany and Italy consisted of numerous kingdoms, duchies and city states, each with their own bureaucracies and revenue streams.

Second, and against this backdrop, Britain, Germany and Italy relied primarily on civil law as the means to manage matters related to labour, including workplace accidents. In each country, the law made provisions for compensation which were based on an understanding of negative freedom. It implied that individuals, as free agents in the labour market, could choose to take up jobs that were known to be dangerous: work and its shadowside were matters for the individual, not the state. Further, individuals, alongside their families and, to a certain extent, their wider communities (whether confessional or occupational), should be held responsible for their actions and the consequences of those actions. In a sense, Britain as well as the German and Italian states, both before and shortly after national unification, operated as what Patrick Joyce has called 'liberal state[s]', in which 'political freedom', in this case, at work, formed a 'means of governance'.[4] In this light, it did not matter whether accidents stemmed from risks that were known to be inherent to work, nor was it relevant that those risks could perhaps be managed, even if not entirely prevented. Harms related to work were a matter for the private sphere and, more specifically, for individuals to handle on their own. In this light, the question of redistributing work-related risks through the state or on a national scale was unthinkable. By the 1870s and 1880s, however, officials in each country

---

[2] Pat Thane, 'Government and society in England and Wales, 1750–1914', in F. M. L. Thompson, ed., *The Cambridge social history of Britain, 1750–1950* (3 vols., Cambridge, 1990), vol. III, pp. 1–62, at p. 2.

[3] Dieter Langewiesche, 'Staat und Commune: zum Wandel der Staatsaufgaben in Deutschland im 19. Jahrhundert', *Historische Zeitschrift* 248 (1989), pp. 621–35; Raffaele Romanelli, 'Centro e periferia: l'Italia unita', in *Il rapporto centro periferia negli stati preunitari e nell'Italia unificata: atti del LIX congresso di storia del Risorgimento italiano* (Rome, 2000), pp. 215–48.

[4] Patrick Joyce, *The state of freedom: a social history of the British state since 1800* (Cambridge, 2013), p. 3.

began to embrace alternative arguments about responsibility, probability and the nature of workplace accidents that would have profound consequences for understandings of the relationship between individuals and the state.

GOVERNMENT AND THE GOVERNANCE OF WORKPLACE ACCIDENTS

Workplace accidents were certainly not a new development in nineteenth-century Europe. Workers had always suffered injuries and death due to accidents, and they had begun perceiving these as the consequences of 'accidents' since at least the Middle Ages. The modern concept of an 'accident' only crystallised, however, in the eighteenth century amidst the professionalisation of medicine, the evolution of commercial insurance and the related development of Enlightenment thinking about rationality and fate.[5] Eighteenth-century thinkers remained undecided about the role of fortune in causing accidents. Diderot's *Encyclopédie* of 1751 therefore cited 'accident' as a grammatical and philosophical concept: 'accident' was a synonym for 'chance'.[6] In subsequent years, the invention of steam-powered trains, the proliferation of railway networks and the gradual mechanisation of industry prompted new kinds of accidents, often on a grand scale. Not least, the boom in road transport in the early nineteenth century sparked an epidemic of fatal accidents. Between 1791 and 1795, there were 81 such accidents recorded in Britain; by 1836–40, the number peaked at 131.[7]

It is perhaps not surprising, therefore, that by the beginning of the nineteenth century, contemporaries began to reflect on workplace accidents not only as the results of new technologies, but also as the negative products of modernity. They argued that accidents had not only increased in number, but they had also become more brutal. In 1829, for example, the British politician Thomas Creevey claimed that a railway journey was, above all, 'frightful'. He explained that the train was 'really flying, and it is impossible to divest yourself of the notion of instant death to all upon the least accident happening'.[8] By 1844, two years after an axle snapped in a train on the Paris–Versailles line and caused the first major railway accident in Europe, a French 'Encyclopaedia

---

[5] Roy Porter, 'Accidents in the eighteenth century', in Roger Cooter and Bill Luckin, eds., *Accidents in history: injuries, fatalities and social relations* (Amsterdam, 1997), pp. 90–106; Geoffrey Clark, *Betting on lives: the culture of life insurance in England, 1695–1775* (Manchester, 1999), pp. 3, 8, 35–6, 193–4; Eve Rosenhaft, 'How to tame chance: evolving languages of risk, trust and expertise in eighteenth-century German proto-insurances', in Geoffrey Clark et al., eds., *The appeal of insurance* (Toronto, 2010), pp. 16–42.

[6] Quoted in Wolfgang Schivelbusch, *Geschichte der Eisenbahnreise: zur Industrialisierung von Raum und Zeit im 19. Jahrhundert* (1977; Frankfurt a. M., 2004), p. 118.

[7] Peter Halford, 'Lord Campbell and the Fatal Accidents Act', *Law Quarterly Review* 129 (2013), pp. 420–49, at p. 432.

[8] Sir Herbert Maxwell, ed., *The Creevey-papers* (2 vols., London, 1904), vol. II, p. 204.

of railways and steam-powered machines' included a nine-page article on the topic 'accident'. It declared that 'everything that man creates with his hand is subject to accidents ... [and] the more perfect machines are becoming, the more powerful accidents are becoming. For this reason, the most powerful and perfect industrial machines ... steam-powered machines and railways, can lead to the most serious and gruesome occurrences.'[9]

The British, German and Italian governments followed Thomas Creevey and other observers in the first half of the nineteenth century in linking accidents to modern technologies. Nonetheless, none sought to enact comprehensive legislation or regulatory systems to address the issue, as it appeared to fall beyond their remit. It seemed that the market and its problems stood outside the bounds of the state. In each country, financial and administrative constraints also played a role in decisions to keep intervention at a minimum.[10] Despite this broad point of commonality, there were nonetheless significant differences between Britain, Germany and Italy in terms of governmental structures, and these influenced how accidents were addressed. At the end of the eighteenth century, Prussia began a comprehensive programme of reform in order to modernise and standardise its bureaucracy.[11] Napoleonic France instituted similar reforms, which revolutionised the practice of administration in the lands that were conquered in the Napoleonic Wars. These included the Italian states, with the exceptions of Sicily and Sardinia, and the French–German border lands.[12] By contrast, Britain was run without a professional civil service and without any significant administrative reforms until at least 1854. It was then that Sir Stafford Northcote and Sir Charles Trevelyan reported to the prime minister that the British government needed to employ a professional civil service administered by trained professionals. Their emphasis on expertise reflects its first appearance in the English language several years later, in the 1860s.[13]

Despite the availability of a professional civil service in the German and Italian states, officials in each country focused mostly on regulating the economy as a whole, rather than labour in particular, and approached workplace accidents from this standpoint. In Germany, state governments were concerned about economic efficiency and the wealth of the state. From a paternalistic standpoint, they aimed at providing security for the general population

[9] Félix Tourneux, *Encyclopédie des chemins de fer et des machines à vapeur* (Paris, 1844), pp. 2–10, at p. 2.

[10] Thane, 'Government and society'; Langewiesche, 'Staat und Commune'; Romanelli, 'Centro e periferia'.

[11] Reinhart Koselleck, *Preußen zwischen Reform und Revolution: allgemeines Landrecht, Verwaltung und soziale Bewegung von 1791 bis 1848* (Stuttgart, 1967).

[12] Piero Aimo, *Il centro e la circonferenza: profili di storia dell'amministrazione locale* (Milan, 2005), part 2.

[13] Donald Read, *England, 1868–1914* (London, 1979), p. 133; Jennifer Hart, 'The genesis of the Northcote–Trevelyan report', in Gillian Sutherland, ed., *Studies in the growth of nineteenth-century government* (Cambridge, 1973), pp. 63–81.

in order to achieve this. The German states therefore governed by policing (*Polizei*) as a means to maintain public order. They intervened in the workplace primarily as a means to maintain social stability – and not to appease public outcry about accidents or other problems.[14] In Italy, state governments adopted a similar approach and relied on the administrative structure instituted during the Napoleonic Wars and, in the north, under Austrian influence.[15] As their primary concerns were economic efficiency and public order, the German and Italian state governments created minimal safety guidelines and regulations in response to public outcry about workplace accidents. Moreover, the limited safety stipulations that they enacted were not strictly enforced. Italy lacked factory inspectors until 1879, twenty years after unification. Even after the adoption of safety regulations in Prussia and several other German states, there were only four inspectors operating in Germany – all in Prussia. Moreover, the Prussian inspectorate reflected the ethos of policing that dominated contemporary governmental thinking on social problems. It focused primarily on the issue of child labour, for example, only expanding its remit to broader issues of workplace safety after 1878. While Prussia employed a small, yet professional, inspectorate, it, like other German states, relied on untrained local police to monitor workplace developments. In Italy, provincial commissioners served a similar function.[16]

In both Italy and Germany, regulating the workplace remained an issue for employers and workers to negotiate as an implicit aspect of the labour contract. Like Britain, neither country established a Ministry of Labour until decades later, leaving the regulation of the workplace to government departments that were preoccupied with various tasks.[17] Italian and German state governments therefore relied on self-regulation for the prevention of accidents. For example, the first Prussian commercial code, adopted in 1845, included a single vague

---

[14] Keith Tribe, *Governing economy: the reformation of German economic discourse, 1750–1840* (Cambridge, 1988), pp. 19–34, 51–4, 62–7; David F. Lindenfeld, *The practical imagination: the German sciences of state in the nineteenth century* (Chicago, 1997), pp. 17–22, 121–30.

[15] Emanuele Pagano, *Il comune di Milano nell'età napoleonica (1800–1814)* (1994; Milan, 2002), part 3, esp. pp. 178, 286–7; Lutz Raphael, *Recht und Ordnung: Herrschaft durch Verwaltung im. 19. Jahrhundert* (Frankfurt a.M., 2000), pp. 130–44.

[16] Michael Karl, *Fabrikinspektoren in Preußen: das Personal der Gewerbeaufsicht 1854–1945* (Opladen, 1993), pp. 57–74. On the function of the police in this capacity: Lorenz von Stein, *Handbuch der Verwaltungslehre*, vol. I: *Der Begriff der Verwaltung und das System der positiven Staatswissenschaften* (3rd edn, Stuttgart, 1888), pp. 184–5; Ministry of Agriculture, Industry and Commerce, Ufficio del lavoro, *L'ispezione del lavoro: studi sull'organizzazione di vigilanza per l'applicazione delle leggi operaie* (Rome, 1904), pp. 9–10.

[17] In each country, it was the First World War that ushered in the creation of targeted labour ministries: in 1916 in Britain and Italy and in 1919 in Germany. The Italian ministry was, however, a restructuring of the long-established Ministry of Agriculture, Industry and Commerce (MAIC) that had dealt with workplace accidents since the mid nineteenth century. Italy also set up an Office of Labour in 1902, which was based at MAIC, while Britain had established a Labour Department based at the Board of Trade, part of the Home Office, in 1893.

clause on the issue of accident prevention. It encouraged employers to 'take due care for the health and morality of employees, assistants and apprentices'. Yet, the clause contained no guidelines for how this should be achieved. The code instead relied on a presumed social consensus about due care and safety in the workplace.[18] This consensus emerged despite the spate of realist literature and reports of the era that exposed the misery of factory life and the hardships that befell families after workplace accidents. It also emerged despite the widespread panic following economic transition and eventual downturn in the 1830s and 1840s, which contributed to revolution across Germany in 1848. In fact, the issue of workplace accidents was almost sidelined altogether at a time when the role of the state in addressing recent social change was widely discussed in the writings of Marx and Engels, von Stein, Riehl, Rodbertus and others.[19] Although it featured in the objectives of several social reform groups, laws on the protection of workers did not take off.[20] The only exception to this rule was the case of miners in Prussia. This important state industry was also widely regarded as especially dangerous. As a means to secure it, Prussia enacted a law in 1854 that required miners to participate in mutual funds which offered accident compensation.[21]

Whether the state should intervene with any protective legislation at all remained fiercely contested in Italy before unification and continued afterwards. In part, this thinking reflected Italy's legal system, which was greatly influenced by the French *Code civil* of 1804 and predicated on a large degree of negative liberty when it came to employers.[22] The paternalist mindset of industrialists further bolstered this ethos.[23] The Italian states, and, later, unified

[18] Arne Andersen, 'Arbeiterschutz in Deutschland im 19. und frühen 20. Jahrhundert', *Archiv für Sozialgeschichte* 31 (1991), pp. 61–83, at p. 64.

[19] A key element of the panic was how to cope with the new industrial 'proletariat'. See Werner Conze, 'Vom "Pöbel" zum "Proletariat": sozialgeschichtliche Voraussetzungen für den Sozialismus in Deutschland', *Vierteljahrsschrift für Sozial- und Wirtschaftsgeschichte* 41 (1954), pp. 333–64; Joan Campbell, *Joy in work, German work: the national debate, 1800–1945* (Princeton, NJ, 1989), pp. 16–27; Eckart Pankoke, *Sociale Bewegung – sociale Frage – sociale Politik* (Stuttgart, 1970), pp. 49–100.

[20] Jürgen Reulecke, 'Die Anfänge der organisierten Sozialreform in Deutschland', in Rüdiger vom Bruch, ed., *Weder Kommunismus noch Kapitalismus: bürgerliche Sozialreform in Deutschland vom Vormärz bis zur Ära Adenauer* (Munich, 1985), pp. 21–59, especially pp. 32–6; Campbell, *Joy in work*, pp. 47–72.

[21] On the few regulations in place during this period: 'Schutz der gewerblichen Arbeiter gegen Unfall- und Erkrankungsgefahren in den letzten 100 Jahren', *Reichsarbeitsblatt* 29/30 (8 August 1925), pp. 483–7.

[22] Giovanni Cazzetta, *Scienza giuridica e trasformazioni sociali: diritto e lavoro in Italia tra otto e novecento* (Milan, 2007), pp. 3–12, 19–21; Stefano Rodotà, 'La libertà e i diritti', in Raffaele Romanelli, ed., *Storia dello stato italiano dall'Unità a oggi* (Rome, 1995), pp. 301–63. A typical expression of this: Alessandro Rossi, 'Le leggi sulle fabbriche in Inghilterra', *Nuova antologia* (4th series), 34 (1877), pp. 300–24. See also Raffaele Romanelli, *L'Italia liberale (1861–1900)* (Bologna, 1979).

[23] Roberto Romano, *Fabbriche, operai, ingegneri: studi di storia del lavoro in Italia tra '800 e '900* (Milan, 2000), p. 72.

Italy therefore generally adopted indirect measures that were aimed at encouraging industrial safety by propaganda and example. For example, in 1859, the Piedmontese Ministry of Agriculture and Industry established a consultative commission on industrial insurance that aimed at encouraging private ventures in regulating the workplace and preventing accidents.[24] Employing indirect measures to encourage workplace safety remained the *modus operandi* of unified Italy into the 1880s. New legislation, such as that creating a voluntary National Accident Insurance Fund in 1883, aimed at encouraging private solutions to work-related problems. Similarly, the central government in the newly unified country supported industrial exhibitions where not only new technology but also new safety devices could be displayed. State-sponsored competitions to create the best safety measures for machines were often a component of these. The administration in Rome also encouraged education in industrial safety, rather than edicts enforcing it, as was the case with the use of steam boilers. Throughout the 1880s, for example, the Ministry of the Interior and the Ministry of Agriculture, Industry and Commerce corresponded with prefects as well as local technology institutes, encouraging the education of workers and industrialists in the avoidance of boiler explosions. Through government periodicals, it also encouraged education in safety.[25] Rather than adopting comprehensive legislation on workplace accidents, Italy, like Germany, relied largely on voluntary action and voluntary associations to prevent them. In Italy, for example, the industrialist Ernesto De Angeli founded the Association of Italian Industrialists for the Prevention of Industrial Accidents in 1894. The group, which was based in Milan, was inspired by the positive information Italians heard about similar organisations founded in Mulhouse, in Alsace, in 1867, as well as in Paris, Brussels and elsewhere in subsequent years.[26] In time, De Angeli's association took on a semi-private status, as the Ministry of Agriculture and Industry enlisted it in the occasional inspection of factories and other workplaces.[27] In Germany, the regulation of steam power was largely left to numerous local and private or semi-private agencies, yet these worked in close conjunction with the government on overseeing safety legislation.[28]

[24] Dora Marucco, *Lavoro e previdenza dall'Unità al fascismo: il Consiglio della previdenza dal 1869 al 1923* (Milan, 1984), pp. 11–12.
[25] ACS: MAIC. Div. Ind. & Comm. Bta. 256A: unnumbered circular from the Ministry of the Interior, Directorate of Public Security, to the Prefects of the Kingdom of Italy, 21 August 1884; ACS: MAIC. Div. Ind. & Comm. Bta. 256A: unnumbered circular from the Ministry of Agriculture, Industry and Commerce, Second Division of Industry and Commerce, to the President of the Directive Advisories and the Directors of the Schools of Arts and Crafts, 10 November 1884.
[26] Raffaello Ricci, 'Per gl'infortuni del lavoro', *Nuova antologia* (4th series), 63 (16 June 1896), pp. 705–21, at p. 712.
[27] Romano, *Fabbriche, operai, ingegneri*, pp. 71–4.
[28] Ina vom Feld, *Staatsentlastung im Technikrecht: Dampfkesselgesetzgebung und -überwachung in Preußen, 1831–1914* (Frankfurt a.M., 2007), pp. 103–13. See, for example, the correspondence in: BArch: R1401: 430.

In contrast, the British government was more responsive to public concerns about workplace accidents in the early and mid nineteenth century, in part as a consequence of Britain's significantly earlier onset of industrialisation. Already in the late seventeenth century, Britain saw the emergence of what Jan de Vries has called an 'industrious revolution' characterised by an increase in work hours and workplace discipline, alongside an increase in consumption and demand for goods that could be bought on the market rather than manufactured at home. Gradually, mechanisation in both agriculture and industry, for example through James Watt's steam engine and Andrew Meikle's thresher at the close of the eighteenth century, began to meet that demand and, in the process, transformed the way in which individuals encountered work.[29] As a consequence, by the first half of the nineteenth century Britain intervened more directly and more frequently into questions related to labour than the Italian and German states – even though it lacked a professional civil service. To be sure, the efforts of several key political figures,[30] the influence of parliamentary politics on governmental action and growing working-class radicalism all played important roles in this transformation. And from the 1830s, Britain began a 'revolution in government' that reflected a broader shift in thinking about the role of the state as an arbiter in everyday life.[31] Numerous official investigations into issues such as workplace accidents were carried out, enabling later administrations to respond more directly to these matters.[32] Not only did these efforts provide an institutional platform for later action, they also legitimated the state as an actor when it came to questions about what contemporaries perceived as social ills. Nonetheless, and despite the expansion of governmental responsibilities and knowledge in this period, many political figures in Britain throughout the course of the nineteenth century sought to keep governmental involvement in the lives of its citizens to a minimum. Following the liberal ethos typified by John Stuart Mill, they instead aimed to 'provide a framework within which individuals could become self-supporting actors within the natural order'.[33] It was this tension that shaped how Britain addressed workplace accidents at the time and in years to come.

---

[29] Jan de Vries, *The industrious revolution: consumer behaviour and the household economy, 1650 to the present* (Cambridge, 2008).

[30] For example: Peter Mandler, 'Cain and Abel: two aristocrats and the early Victorian factory acts', *Historical Journal* 27 (1984), pp. 83–109.

[31] A meaningful starting point on this contentious topic: Oliver MacDonagh, 'The nineteenth-century revolution in government: a reappraisal', *Historical Journal* 1 (1958), pp. 52–67.

[32] Lawrence Goldman, *Science, reform and politics in Victorian Britain: the Social Science Association, 1857–1886* (Cambridge, 2002), especially ch. 2.

[33] Thane, 'Government and society', p. 18. See also Jose Harris, 'Society and the state in twentieth-century Britain', in Thompson, ed., *The Cambridge social history*, vol. III, pp. 63–119, at p. 67; Oskar Kurer, 'John Stuart Mill and the welfare state', *History of Political Economy* 23 (1991), pp. 713–30.

Following the efforts of social reformers such as James Kay-Shuttleworth who were involved in the broader movement to address questions of public health,[34] alongside the demands of workers, numerous parliamentary inquiries dealt with the question of safety in the workplace. Widespread discussion about the consequences of industrialisation marked the 1830s and 1840s, which was the moment when governmental investigation into labour took off. This was the era in which popular radicalism, such as the 'Captain Swing' riots of 1830, the Chartist movement of the 1830s and 1840s as well as unorganised social unrest emerged in response to a variety of factors. Upheaval grew out of the economic downturn following a series of poor harvests and the Napoleonic Wars and was exacerbated further by the enactment of the harsh New Poor Law of 1834 and the restrictive 1832 Reform Act, which sparked demands for enfranchisement and greater political rights. Popular radicalism also surfaced in response to the harassment of the factory bell, the hazardous work environment and unsympathetic employers. It was during this period, as E. P. Thompson has noted, that class consciousness crystallised, transforming class-based concerns into salient political issues.[35] The arguments of social commentators, such as Friedrich Engels, Thomas Carlyle and Charles Dickens, also drove contemporary discussions, revealing that the condition of British workers was abysmal.[36]

In 1833, the Factories Inquiries Commission noted that the danger of being killed or injured by a machine was 'one of the great evils to which people employed in factories are exposed'.[37] An 1832 committee had already supported these findings, while the 1835 Select Committee on Mines revealed the dangers associated with that industry. The questions of whether and how to regulate the workplace, however, remained unresolved at this time. Contemporaries debated whether the accident question was not exaggerated in these committees. Thus, for example, the Factory Act of 1833 prohibited the labour of children under eight years old and limited the hours of older children without making specific provisions for the prevention of accidents, such as fencing in machinery or providing adequate ventilation in enclosed workshops. Significantly, however, the 1833 Act recognised the need for a national

---

[34] For example, in his *The moral and physical condition of the working classes employed in the cotton manufacture in Manchester* (London, 1832).

[35] E. P. Thompson, *The making of the English working class* (New York, 1964), pp. 711ff. See also Patrick Joyce, *Visions of the people: industrial England and the question of class, 1848–1914* (Cambridge, 1994) and Gareth Stedman Jones, *Languages of class: studies in English working class history, 1832–1982* (Cambridge, 1983).

[36] Louis Cazamian, *The social novel in England, 1830–1850: Dickens, Disraeli, Mrs. Gaskell, Kingsley*, trans. Martin Fido (London, 1973); Michael Levin, *The condition of England question: Carlyle, Mill, Engels* (New York, 1998).

[37] PP 1833 (450) XX: 'Royal Commission on the Employment of Children in Factories: Report', p. 31.

factory inspectorate. Four inspectors and eight sub-inspectors were enlisted.[38] The creation of the factory inspectorate would fundamentally shape later discussions about industrial risk, and by the 1840s, Britain reached a turning point in thinking about workplace accidents. In 1840, the Parliamentary Select Committee to inquire into the operation of the Factory Act shifted the focus of labour legislation towards accident prevention. Financial incentives largely guided the ensuing Factory Act of 1844. Already in the 1830s, contributors to the accident debate such as Edwin Chadwick, the Chief Factory Inspector and hygiene reformer, had suggested that the best way to prevent accidents was to induce employers on monetary grounds.[39] The 1844 Act required employers to fence in dangerous machinery in an attempt to minimise accidents. It went further in linking the risk of accidents to the workplace, stipulating that employers could be fined for accidents due to machinery left unsecured. Whether employers were fined was another matter, as the enforcement of the policy varied greatly across the country. Nonetheless, the Act was significant, not least because it allowed injured workers to receive compensation from their employers if the Secretary of State for the Home Office sued employers on their behalf. No absolute right to compensation was established in the law, and there is no record of such a lawsuit being brought forward by the Home Office. However, the Act offered an alternative route to compensation for injured workers, through fines resulting from unsecured machinery involved in accidents. This clause was successfully invoked initially, but its use began to dwindle by the early 1860s. For example, in 1845, there were 42 prosecutions for safety breaches; by 1858–9, there were only five.[40]

Despite the relatively early establishment of a factory inspectorate as well as the enactment of a variety of ordinances related to accident prevention, as in Germany and Italy, voluntary regulation therefore remained a critical means for securing the work environment as well as its surroundings. This was especially the case with the inspection of steam boilers, whose explosions had long been known to cause extensive damage to factories and neighbouring properties. While various laws contained clauses relating to steam boiler use, boiler owners were left to determine their proper functioning. In 1855, the Association for the Prevention of Explosions was founded as a means for boiler owners to self-regulate. Similar organisations, such as the active Manchester Steam Users' Association, also flourished at this time. Remarkably, steam-powered railways, whose awesome speed and power had captivated and frightened the

---

[38] Jill Pellew, *The Home Office, 1848–1914: from clerks to bureaucrats* (London, 1982), pp. 122–49.

[39] *PP* 1833 (450) XX: 'Royal Commission on the Employment of Children in Factories: Report', pp. 72–4.

[40] P. W. J. Bartrip and Sandra Burman, *The wounded soldiers of industry: industrial compensation policy, 1833–1897* (Oxford, 1983), pp. 54–8; P. W. J. Bartrip and P. T. Fenn, 'The administration of safety: the enforcement policy of the early factory inspectorate, 1844–1864', *Public Administration* 58 (1980), pp. 87–102, at p. 95.

public since their introduction at the turn of the century,[41] remained relatively free from legislative intervention to protect workers. In the case of railways, in Britain as elsewhere, concerns about protecting *consumers* – rather than workers – came first. Following an 1839 parliamentary committee on the issue, a Railway Regulation Act was adopted in Britain in 1840. While the Act allowed for the inspection of railways and cited public safety as one of its aims, the implementation of safety regulations remained vague. Early railway regulation rather focused on commercial concerns, as indicated by the Board of Trade's, and not the Home Office's, role in overseeing that industry.[42] The safety of railway passengers and the general public, and not railway workers, was the main focus of early discussions because workers were seen as knowledgeable and free agents who had consented to the dangers of their job. By contrast, in theory, a passenger would probably be unaware of the intricacies of shunting tracks or the chaos of railway timetables. Moreover, having paid for the service of taking a train, passengers expected a guarantee of safe passage – and not the possibility of a derailment. Protecting passengers was a form of consumer legislation, not a concern for railway safety in general or labour in particular. Thus, a train passenger could successfully claim compensation if injured in a railway accident, while a worker could not.[43]

In the first half of the nineteenth century, therefore, it was not clear whether and to what extent work was a concern for the state. This was the case in both Britain and in pre-unification Italian and German city states, duchies and kingdoms. Until the mid nineteenth century in Britain and Germany, and until the late nineteenth century in Italy, workers and employers generally addressed the consequences of workplace accidents on their own, even though it seemed increasingly evident that accident numbers were on the rise. In Britain, for example, there were 51 work-related fatalities in factories in 1845 and 42 in railways. By 1881, the numbers had gone up to 409 and 521 respectively. Meanwhile, in Italy, 171 fatalities were recorded among miners in 1866, rising to 191 in 1880. And accidents involving employees at machine works in Germany rose from 39,040 in 1878 to 43,754 within just two years. It is important to bear in mind, however, that the accident statistics – especially for non-fatal accidents – that were collected until the end of the nineteenth century were often incomplete or varied widely from year to year in terms

---

[41] An overview: Schivelbusch, *Geschichte der Eisenbahnreise*; Simon Bradley, *The railways: nation, network and people* (London, 2015), ch. 6.

[42] Bartrip and Burman, *Wounded soldiers*, pp. 77–8.

[43] The result of these considerations was the Fatal Accidents Act 1846 (9 & 10 Vict., c.93), known as 'Lord Campbell's Act', which granted families of those who had died in accidents the right to sue for compensation. The Act was aimed at the general public, and not workers (and their families) because they were seen as knowledgeable about their jobs and therefore exempted from the policy. See William R. Cornish and Geoffrey de N. Clarke, *Law and society in England, 1750–1950* (London, 1989), pp. 503–4; R. W. Kostal, *Law and English railway capitalism, 1825–1875* (Oxford, 1994), pp. 290–6; Halford, 'Lord Campbell and the Fatal Accidents Act'.

of the categories that they described.[44] For example, until the introduction of
a liability law in 1880, British judicial returns for personal injuries included
cases involving workplace accidents alongside other incidents involving negligence.[45] Moreover, the meaning of 'factory', 'worker' and other terms observed
in statistical collections could vary greatly. Nonetheless, contemporaries noted
that accidents at work were growing in frequency and could have catastrophic
consequences.

In this context, numerous voluntary solutions to the widespread and severe
problem of injury or death from work-related accidents therefore thrived. In
each case, some form of compensation for workplace accidents dated back to
medieval guilds, and workers could later receive assistance through friendly
societies or mutual funds.[46] While coal miners in Britain and Germany had
relatively well-organised institutions for relieving the injured, certain railway
companies and factories offered financial provision for injury and death which
was financed through contributions from employers and workers. In the nineteenth century, there were also a variety of factory-based welfare organisations
which included accident provision and medical assistance for injured workers.
In factories such as the Krupp works in Germany, workers' welfare was often
seen as a matter for paternalistic care which would both secure social peace
and ensure economic productivity.[47] Not least, as in preceding centuries, local

---

[44] A point emphasised by Bartrip and Burman, *Wounded soldiers*, p. 42; see pp. 43–4 on accident
rates in Britain. For Italy and Germany, see 'Tavole delle morti accidentali ordinate secondo le
cause che le produssero e secondo il sesso, la professione o condizione dei defunti, estratte dalla
Statistica delle morti violente al 1866 al 1882 (escluso l'anno 1870) avvenute in tutti i comuni
del Regno e dalla statistica delle cause di morte negli anni 1881 e 1882 nei capoluoghi di provincia e di circondario del Regno', in *Atti per l'istituzione della cassa nazionale di assicurazione per
gli operai contro gli infortuni sul lavoro*, vol. I: *Relazione del Comm. Luigi Luzzatti, Deputato
al Parlamento* (Rome, 1884), appendix 1, pp. 94, 184; BArch: R1501: 100409: 7–14: 'Die
Unfall-Statistik des Deutschen Reichs nach der Aufnahme vom Jahre 1881', at p. 8.

[45] For example, in 1875, seven civil suits involving personal injuries due to negligence – excluding
those related to Lord Campbell's Act – were brought before the Queen's Bench. Twelve cases
related to Lord Campbell's Act were also heard. *PP* 1876 (C 1595) LXXIX: 'Judicial Statistics.
1875. England and Wales. Part I. Police – criminal proceedings – prisons. Part II. Common law –
equity – civil and canon law', p. 3.

[46] Cornelius Walford, *Cyclopaedia of insurance* (6 vols., London, 1871–80), vol. V, pp. 341–93;
Ernst Wickenhagen, *Geschichte der gewerblichen Unfallversicherung: Wesen und Wirken der
gewerblichen Berufsgenossenschaften* (2 vols., Munich, 1980), vol. I, pp. 18–20; John Kenneth
Hyde, *Society and politics in medieval Italy: the evolution of the civil life, 1000–1350* (London,
1973), pp. 94–123; Florian Tennstedt, *Sozialgeschichte der Sozialpolitik in Deutschland: vom
18. Jahrhundert bis zum Ersten Weltkrieg* (Göttingen, 1981), pp. 127–34; Alan J. Kidd, *State,
society and the poor in nineteenth-century England* (Basingstoke, 1999), p. 112; Arnaldo
Cherubini, *Beneficenza e solidarietà: assistenza pubblica e mutualismo operaio (1860–1900)*
(Milan, 1991), p. 333.

[47] John Benson, 'Coalminers, coalowners and collaboration: the miners' permanent relief fund
movement in England, 1860–1895', *Labour History Review* 68/2 (2003), pp. 181–94; Patrick
Joyce, *Work, society and politics: the culture of the factory in later Victorian England* (Brighton,
1980), chs. 4–6; Elisabetta Benenati, 'Cento anni di paternalismo aziendale', in Stefano Musso,

charities and poor relief provided forms of aid for injured workers and their dependants.[48]

FREEDOM OF CONTRACT AND EMPLOYERS' LIABILITY

For injured workers, recourse to civil law, rather than resorting to poor boards or making a claim against a friendly society, provided another option to seek out some form of relief against medical expenses and lost wages. And the relatively new area of accident law seemed to offer a promising avenue to this end. Over the course of the nineteenth century, liability law took off as an own field of jurisprudence due to both the professionalisation of legal education and the emergence of a variety of new social developments, including new consumer cultures, the expansion of property ownership and the boom in new and dangerous technologies such as the railways.[49] The implications were enormous: it meant, for instance, that injured railway passengers could expect a settlement for their injuries, just as property owners could expect to receive payment for damage to their property if it was caused by someone else.[50] However, legal discussions about liability for workplace accidents took a different line. They focused on a specific notion of occupational risk that was predicated on the freedom to close contracts. The assumption was that every worker understood the risks associated with a particular job when agreeing to that job. What was implicit in this logic was a free-market understanding of labour: workers were in a position to choose any job in the labour market. Due to the unlimited range of choice and their freedom to choose, they would take whichever job they preferred. According to this logic, workers might prefer to accept more dangerous areas of employment, such as in mining or railways, as they would

---

ed., *Tra fabbrica e società: mondi operai nell'Italia del novecento* (Milan, 1999), pp. 43–84, at pp. 51–64; Dennis Sweeney, *Work, race and the emergence of radical right corporatism in Imperial Germany* (Ann Arbor, MI, 2009), pp. 22–36.

[48] Tennstedt, *Sozialgeschichte der Sozialpolitik*, pp. 39–47, 92–103, 212–20; E. P. Hennock, *British social reform and German precedents: the case of social insurance, 1880–1914* (Oxford, 1987), pp. 23–6, 35–9, 50–6, 59–62; Giovanna Farrell-Vinay, 'The old charities and the new state: structures and problems of welfare in Italy (1860–1890)' (PhD, University of Edinburgh, 1989), p. 326.

[49] David J. Ibbetson, 'The tort of negligence in the common law in the nineteenth and twentieth centuries', in Eltjo J. H. Schrage, ed., *Negligence: the comparative legal history of the law of torts* (Berlin, 2001), pp. 229–71; Kenneth Reid and Reinhard Zimmermann, eds., *A history of private law in Scotland*, vol. II: *Obligations* (Oxford, 2000), chs. 16–19; Wolfgang Ernst, 'Negligence in 19th-century Germany', in Schrage, ed., *Negligence*, pp. 341–59; Michele Taruffo, *La giustizia civile in Italia dal '700 a oggi* (Bologna, 1980), pp. 107–50; Cazzetta, *Scienza giuridica e trasformazioni sociali*, pp. 27–114.

[50] To be sure, however, there were earlier legal precepts on compensation that were predicated on an understanding of interpersonal obligations. See Reinhard Zimmermann, *The law of obligations: Roman foundations of the civil law tradition* (Oxford, 1996).

be remunerated accordingly. The free market of labour would, therefore, dictate the values of salaries.

In Britain, common law determined how the negative consequences of workplace accidents were addressed. There were two forms of common law, one for England and Wales and the other for Scotland, and both contained personal injury provisions which allowed for claims against a negligent third party. However, making claims against an employer in the early and mid nineteenth century was more difficult than making claims against other third parties. As in British legislation on 'masters' and 'servants', the law generally turned a blind eye to the employment relationship. In Britain, as in other common law countries, the law assumed that this bond was 'private' and therefore closed to further regulation. The handling of employment as a private matter implied an essentially unequal treatment of employees.[51] This logic, in part, contributed to the court ruling that prevailed in Britain for most of the nineteenth century: in agreeing a contract to employment, workers had consented to all risks incidental to that work, or, *volenti non fit iniuria*.[52] Workers could request compensation only if they could prove that their employers were directly culpable for an accident.

Jurists began questioning this legal understanding of the employment contract by the early nineteenth century in England and Wales, and from the 1860s in Scotland. The government followed their discussions and became increasingly concerned about whether it should intervene with new legislation. Gradually, some courts began to conclude that employers had a 'duty of care' to ensure that workers did not become injured at work.[53] While judges began ruling in favour of workers in their claims against employers, whether workers could hold employers responsible for the actions of their workers was another matter. For instance, in his verdict on *Priestley* v. *Fowler*, Lord Abinger argued that holding an employer vicariously liable for the actions of his workers should be avoided because it could provoke a wave of mass litigation. The 'fellow-servant' rule established in *Priestley* would, therefore, stave off a crisis.[54] In any case, the 'implied terms' of a labour contract and the definition of a 'fellow-servant' remained open for judges to decide, often to the advantage

[51] Spiros Simitis, 'The case of the employment relationship: elements of a comparison', in Willibald Steinmetz, ed., *Private law and social inequality in the industrial age: comparing legal cultures in Britain, France, German, and the United States* (Oxford, 2000), pp. 181–202; Douglas Hay, 'England, 1562–1875: the law and its uses', in Douglas Hay and Paul Craven, eds., *Masters, servants and magistrates in Britain and the Empire, 1562–1955* (Chapel Hill, NC, 2004), pp. 59–116, especially pp. 109–16; Douglas Hay and Paul Craven, 'Introduction', in Hay and Craven, eds., *Masters, servants and magistrates*, pp. 1–58.

[52] For example: *Clarke* v. *Holmes* (1862) 7 H & N 937, 943.

[53] Ibbetson, 'The tort of negligence', p. 234; Elspeth Reid, 'The impact of institutions and professions in Scotland', in Paul Mitchell, ed., *Comparative studies in the development of the law of torts in Europe*, vol. VIII: *The impact of institutions and professions on legal development* (Cambridge, 2012), pp. 59–88.

[54] *Priestley* v. *Fowler* (1837) 3 M & H 307–8. See also *Hutchinson* v. *York, Newcastle & Berwick Railway Company* (1850) 5 Ex. 343 at 350 and *Wigmore* v. *Jay* (1850) 5 Ex. 354. An

of employers. Exclusive judicial interpretation of labour contracts meant that jurors, who often favoured workers in these cases, would not exert a pro-employee bias.[55]

As in Britain, in Germany, lawyers in the early and mid nineteenth century defined the problem of workplace accidents in terms of a traditional conception of workers' responsibilities. Despite the variety of legal practices throughout the federal state, which adopted a unified law code only in 1900, jurists generally invoked the principle of 'freedom of contract' when workers sought to claim compensation following accidents. The view in Germany was based on a liberal understanding of the *Rechtsstaat*, or constitutional state, which held that law should be neutral in order to safeguard individual freedoms.[56] This conception of the law echoed the British legal principle that workers had consented to on-the-job risks as part of their contracts. Moreover, as in British common law, German law held that employers could not be made liable for injuries to their workers if they were caused by fellow workers. Only in cases of deliberate negligence could an employer be held accountable for an accident. Proving culpability in these instances, however, was not easy, as the burden of proof lay on the injured, and the rules of evidence in court cases made this difficult to establish. In court, there-fore, workers generally fared poorly when attempting to hold employers liable for accidents under the standard liability rules of German law.

In Germany, jurists aimed to maintain an objective stance towards seemingly social issues, such as the increasing number of workplace accidents and their con-sequences. Members of the new 'Historical School' such as Friedrich Carl von Savigny sought to interpret private law scientifically, thereby allowing it to develop as an organic system naturally over time – without political intervention.[57] They therefore upheld a strict understanding of fault as the grounds for liability. In this light, legal theorists contended that, where fault could not be determined, the 'damage lay where it fell' (*casum sentit dominus*). As a result, the injured and his family were generally left with recourse only to charity or poor relief.[58]

---

overview: Michael Ashley Stein, 'Victorian tort liability for workplace injuries', *University of Illinois Law Review* 3 (2008), pp. 933–84.

[55] Kostal, *Law and English railway capitalism*, pp. 255–74. Occasionally, and increasingly from the late 1850s, judges became more benevolent in their interpretation of 'fellow-workers'. See Stein, 'Victorian tort liability', pp. 953–6 as well as Kostal, *Law and English railway capitalism*, p. 267.

[56] Ernst, 'Negligence in 19th-century Germany'; Franz Wieacker, *A history of private law in Europe: with particular reference to Germany* (Oxford, 1995), section II; Michael John, *Politics and the law in late nineteenth-century Germany: the origins of the civil code* (Oxford, 1989), pp. 5–6, 84, 86–9, 94–5.

[57] Hans-Peter Haferkamp, 'The science of private law and the state in nineteenth-century Germany', *American Journal of Comparative Law* 56 (2008), pp. 667–89, at pp. 669–71; Regina Ogorek, *Untersuchungen zur Gefährdungshaftung im 19. Jahrhundert* (Cologne, 1975), pp. 11–13.

[58] Zimmermann, *The law of obligations*, p. 1034. NB: Comprehensive federal statistics on success rates as a proportion of claims in these cases are unavailable until after the introduction of a national liability law in 1871.

The only exception to this legal practice in Germany was the case of railways. Already from the 1830s, civil servants and jurists in Prussia began connecting the concept of accidents to danger in certain industries. The owners of ostensibly dangerous industries therefore slowly became implicated in the accident problem. In 1838, three years after the installation of the first German railway line, connecting Nuremberg and Fürth, Prussia adopted a strict liability law for the railway industry. The policy was inspired in part by Savigny, who argued that railways merited special legislation because they affected the entire country, and everyone within it. The law was a revolutionary step towards viewing accidents as the result of occupational risk, rather than the consequences of workers' negligent actions. It stipulated that railway operators should be held accountable for all accidents during transport, whether they affected passengers, neighbouring land ignited by stray sparks from trains or individuals injured near tracks or workers.[59] Several other German states soon followed with similar legislation.[60]

In the Italian states, a civil code that stemmed from the peninsula's Napoleonic and Spanish inheritance governed disputes about workplace accidents. Soon after unification, the Italian government, in contrast to that in recently unified Germany, adopted a unified code. The Italian civil code was derived from a rereading of Roman Law, which made Italian legal interpretations of liability especially similar to those in Germany, where Roman Law also served as the main influence.[61] Three clauses within the civil code addressed the issue of liability, and these were reproductions of articles in the French *Code civil*. In Italian law, an employer could be held financially responsible for his own actions and those of his supervisors in the case of workplace accidents. Yet, employers could not be made liable for 'Acts of God' (*forza maggiore*) or accidents to which workers had contributed. The issue of occupational risk was especially important in the civil code's conception of liability: employers could not be held responsible for the risks that were seen to originate from the act of work. Therefore, as in Britain and Germany, in Italy, employers were held liable only if direct fault could be determined.[62] Moreover, in Italy, as elsewhere, the burden of proof lay on workers' shoulders.

[59] Theodor Baums, 'Die Einführung der Gefährdungshaftung durch F. C. von Savigny', *Zeitschrift der Savigny Stiftung für Rechtsgeschichte* 104 (1987), pp. 277–82.
[60] These included Saxony and Anhalt, which put the Prussian law into force for the Thuringian and Anhaltian lines, Holstein, with a law from 1840 and Mecklenburg with an Act from 1855. See Jens Scherpe, 'Technological change and the development of liability for fault in Germany', in Martín Miguel-Casals, ed., *The development of liability in relation to technological change* (Cambridge, 2010), pp. 134–84.
[61] Taruffo, *La giustizia civile*, p. 113; Italo Piva, 'Problemi giuridici e politici della "responsabilità" alle origini dell'assicurazione infortuni sul lavoro in Italia', *Rivista degli infortuni e delle malattie professionali* (1980), pp. 649–66, at pp. 654–61.
[62] Piva, 'Problemi giuridici e politici della "responsabilità"', p. 655.

By the 1860s in Germany, and by the 1870s in Britain and Italy, consensus around these legal practices began to falter rapidly. And, significantly, the governments in each country closely monitored and participated in legal debates about introducing a law that would increase the liability of employers in the case of accidents at work. These discussions resulted in the adoption in 1871 of a liability law in unified Germany and in 1880 of a liability law in Britain. In Italy, by contrast, these debates served to redefine judicial understandings of the civil code, but attempts to enact a separate liability law proved unsuccessful. In each case, these discussions challenged understandings of free choice and individual responsibility that had informed prior legal and administrative thinking about workplace accidents. For example, in Britain, the question of personal responsibility dictated the course of official discussions and set the tone of the Parliamentary Select Committee of 1876–7 that was established to consider legislating on employers' liability. This committee resulted from long-running discussions in the Home Office, which had drawn up several draft bills on employers' liability between 1871 and 1874, following a failed 1862 proposal that had been jointly penned by a Liberal and a Conservative MP. The arguments that ran against this early bill, and helped to ward off any further proposals for the next decade, had come under attack by the 1870s, in part due to the lobbying efforts of the recently organised Trades Union Congress.[63]

Nonetheless, different opinions about employers' responsibilities persisted within the Select Committee. For example, George Fereday Smith, a key witness and chairman of the Mining Association of Great Britain, was not alone in arguing that the common law dealt appropriately with workplace accidents. He claimed that it was based on the assumption of both personal freedom and authority that had been exemplified in the 1835 report of the Select Committee on Accidents in Mines. The report was right to argue, contended Smith, for workers 'to be acquainted with their individual responsibilities'. He concluded that it was 'in the public interest that the workmen should be self-reliant, intelligent, and industrious'.[64] Smith's view reflected common conceptions at the time of the labour process: that workers were skilled and worked in unmechanised industry; they were therefore in complete control of what happened in the workplace. Moreover, by citing the self-reliance and industriousness of workers as being in the 'public interest', he rejected a concept of work that included any role for government. For Smith, governmental intervention in the labour market would not be necessary, as workers alone should be responsible for the labour process and its impact on the public. This opinion echoed the common law conception of employers' liability: an employer could not be held liable for the actions of a worker resulting in injury, as the employer had taken

---

[63] Bartrip and Burman, *Wounded soldiers*, ch. 3, pp. 111–15, 124–44.
[64] *PP* 1877 (C 285) X.551: 'Report from the Select Committee on Employers' Liability for Injuries to their Servants; together with the Proceedings of the Committee, Minutes of Evidence, Appendix', pp. 35–7.

reasonable care in selecting his employees, who were supposed to be suited to their particular jobs and take due care in carrying them out. This maxim was especially significant in the case of skilled trades, such as coal mining, to which Smith had been alluding. Like other members on the committee, he assumed that workers were specialised in their tasks and should therefore be in a position to work safely.

The general view of members of the committee, which included officials from the Home Office as well as several barristers and judges, instead reflected the growing perception that work had changed considerably in recent years. The majority argued that modern industry was characterised neither by self-reliance nor by the direct management of employers over workers. Instead, they saw that 'the development of modern industry has created large numbers of employing bodies, such as corporations and public companies, to whom it is not possible to bring home such personal default'. Therefore, the committee concluded that employers could be held liable for the actions and orders of supervisors.[65] It also decided that employers should not be made liable for the actions of co-workers, even if they resulted in the death or injury of other employees. Instead, the committee claimed that an adjustment in the rate of wages might address this lingering risk.[66] A Home Office report later reflected on the issue, suggesting that the costs of these risks might fall to the consumer, rather than the employer or the employed.[67] These debates resulted in the enactment of an Employers' Liability Act in 1880, which was based on a Home Office bill put forward by the Liberal government under William Ewart Gladstone. The Act was the first significant strike against the contested maxims upheld under the common law. It removed the doctrine of 'common employment' in cases in which workers were injured while obeying the orders of their employers or superintendents.[68] However, the Act proved troublesome for workers. In claims cases, the burden of proof lay on the injured, and contributory negligence of the injured party was often interpreted by the courts as a reason not to grant compensation. While the new law made employers liable for their own actions and orders as well as those of supervisors, it did not hold employers responsible for the actions and orders of all of their employees. The fellow-servant rule thus remained largely untouched. Moreover, the Act included a clause that enabled employers to 'contract out' of it by arranging alternative provisions for workers in cases of injury or death related to workplace accidents. By 'contracting out' of the Liability Act, workers might instead receive compensation through a mutual fund or insurance policy, thereby bypassing costly court cases predicated on the question of responsibility.[69]

[65] *PP* 1877 (C 285) X.551: 'Report from the Select Committee on Employers' Liability', p. v.

[66] *PP* 1877 (C 285) X.551: 'Report from the Select Committee on Employers' Liability', pp. iv, 27–8.

[67] TNA: HO 45/9458/72731A: unnumbered: 30 July 1881.

[68] Patrick S. Atiyah, *The rise and fall of freedom of contract* (Oxford, 1979), pp. 587–9, 703–7.

[69] Employers' Liability Act, 1880 (43 & 44 Vict. c. 42).

In Germany, official discussions about liability for workplace accidents were much less contentious than in Britain. Debates about creating a liability law for the most dangerous industries emerged in the 1860s following the partial unification of Germany in a series of wars with Denmark and Austria. The enactment of a national liability law would, therefore, enable the government of the newly unified North German Confederation, the precursor to the German Empire, to begin a degree of administrative and legal state building. Moreover, the enactment of a liability law for the most dangerous industries would mark a less radical transition in Germany than was the case in Britain, as several German states had already enacted laws on the liability of railway operators. The German discussions about enacting a comprehensive policy on employers' liability began in 1868, when the National Liberal Karl Biedermann, a law professor from Leipzig, petitioned the parliament of the North German Confederation to create a liability law for railways and other industries. The policy was intended to rectify the problems with the current railway liability law and the liability provisions in the law codes of the various member states in the new confederation. As in Britain, in Germany, debates about liability for workplace accidents hinged on the issue of individual responsibility. Biedermann's petition sought compensation from employers for workplace accident claims, as long as the injured was not responsible for the injury.[70] The law proposal did not differ greatly from those in Britain, but it was received in German political discussions with relatively little debate. A parliamentary commission approved the proposal, even pointing out that the situation with workplace accidents was worse than stated in the petition. After consulting with local governments about the issue, the Prussian Ministry of Trade drafted the liability law that would soon follow. Broad political consensus about the petition as well as experience with similar legislation were important factors in its smooth reception. However, so was an element of legal state building: a national liability law would eradicate the many coexisting liability traditions that were still in effect throughout the German Empire. Not only the Ministry of Trade realised this; so, too, did the petition's advocates.[71]

The Ministry of Trade's bill maintained strict liability for railway companies, meaning that they were held liable for all accidents regardless of fault. However, the proposal only allowed for general liability in other industries. As a consequence, for a worker to claim compensation, his employer would need to be found personally responsible for causing the accident. Although the policy was restrictive, it nonetheless proved revolutionary in its re-evaluation of the relationship between probability, accidents and fault. As the Minister of Trade, Count Heinrich von Itzenplitz, put it, the only way to 'justify' special regulations for the compensation of workers for accidents involving railways would be to view the damage caused there as 'the consequence of the special

[70] *DDNB* 1868, Nr. 56 and Nr. 130.
[71] Ogorek, *Untersuchungen zur Gefährdungshaftung*, pp. 100–3.

dangerousness of railway businesses'. If a unique 'danger' existed, implementing a policy to address this could be justified.[72] His argument was pathbreaking: it linked danger to the workplace, thereby exonerating workers from total
responsibility for accidents in particularly risky industries. Yet, Itzenplitz's view
also reflected a trend that had slowly been brewing in German legal circles since
the 1830s and that had been typified by the 1838 law on railways. In light of
the radical changes to social life related to new technologies, economic downturn and commercial relations, jurists such as Savigny, and, later, Hermann
Roesler and Otto von Gierke, began calling for special legislative provisions
that would correct some of the injustices associated with the contract-driven
nature of private law. Roesler and Gierke even argued for a new kind of 'social
law'.[73]

The 1871 Liability Law that resulted from these discussions acknowledged
certain industries, including mechanised factory work, railways, and mining,
as particularly dangerous and therefore worthy of special legislation. The
connection between responsibility and danger encapsulated in the policy is
particularly telling: workers in railways were addressed with a special clause
that endowed them with compensation while altogether removing the burden of proof for culpability. This swift transition to a national liability law
reflected the fact that intervention in the face of dangerous industries had long
been accepted in the case of the railways in several *Länder*. As in Britain, in
Germany, workers injured in the other trades included within the law would
still need to prove that their employer or supervisor was somehow responsible,
which was no easy matter. Another difficulty associated with the policy was
that it expressly excluded accidents along railways that occurred 'through a
Higher Power', meaning 'Acts of God' in English legal and actuarial parlance.
German law did, however, grant compensation for accidents caused by the
negligence of supervisors, and, as in the Prussian policy on railway liability,
contracting out was forbidden.[74]

In Italy, as in Germany and Britain, determining responsibility for workplace
accidents was at the core of legal thinking about liability. The Italian word for
liability, *responsabilità*, reflects this conception. By the 1870s, the Italian government became especially concerned to protect workers in what it viewed as
a particularly dangerous process of modernisation. It therefore supported the

[72] GStAPK: I. HA. Rep. 120BB. Abt. VII. Fach. 1. No. 16. Vol. 1: 2: on behalf of the Chancellor
of the North German Confederation to Count Itzenplitz, the Prussian Minister of Trade and
Commerce, 5 May 1868; 14: Itzenplitz to the Chancellor of the North German Confederation;
27–32: Itzenplitz to the Chancellor of the North German Confederation, 24 July 1868.

[73] Felix Schmid, *Sozialrecht und Recht der sozialen Sicherheit: die Begriffsbildung in Deutschland,
Frankreich und der Schweiz* (Berlin, 1981), pp. 67–74; Michael Stolleis, *Geschichte des
Sozialrechts in Deutschland: ein Grundriß* (Stuttgart, 2003), p. 41.

[74] At first, contracting out was allowed and widely practised by the Prussian railways, but the law
was revised in 1869 following growing disgruntlement about the lack of provision for workers
who had contracted out of it.

legislative endeavours of Liberal parliamentarians to introduce a liability law and also wrote several proposals for a liability law. None of these succeeded in parliament.[75] Historians have often derided the 'failure' of Liberal Italy due to the 'transformist' nature of politics in which politicians aimed at compromise rather than legislative change.[76] Administrative and broader political discussions about workplace accidents demonstrate, however, that the government in newly unified Italy, like those elsewhere in the mid nineteenth century, was engaged in conceptualising questions of risk and individual responsibility. Its participation in these early debates shaped Italy's later legislation on workplace accidents.[77] Introducing a policy for the compensation of workplace accidents was first discussed in 1879, when Pietro Pericoli, a progressive liberal member of parliament, proposed a law to remove the burden of proof on injured workers when seeking compensation from employers. He called for the policy to apply only to the more dangerous industries, which he outlined in a report. Pericoli justified his proposal by arguing that the articles in the civil code which addressed liability proved cumbersome when put into effect. This was especially evident with developments in court. However, he also contended that industrial risk had transformed in recent years. Echoing the British discussions of two years earlier, Pericoli observed that the conditions of modern industry had changed relations between employers and workers. Yet, he also claimed that employers had been negligent in how they approached industrialisation. Trying to keep production costs down, employers had not put sufficient safety measures in place.[78]

Pericoli's bill failed in parliament, and the government, like legislators at this time, was undecided about how to approach the issue. Under the liberal Prime Minister Agostino Depretis, the Ministry of Agriculture, Industry and Commerce investigated for years, putting forward a number of diverse legislative proposals. When outlining a bill on employers' liability in 1884, the Minister of Agriculture at the time, Bernardino Grimaldi, claimed that the causes of accidents could not be traced sufficiently to determine who was responsible. In this estimation, he was rebutting the allegation of his immediate predecessor, Domenico Berti, who had claimed that one third of accidents stemmed instead from employer negligence.[79] By the mid 1880s, the Ministry

---

[75] On these debates, see Giulio Monteleone, 'La legislazione sociale al parlamento italiano: la legge del 1886 sul lavoro dei fanciulli', *Movimento Operaio e Socialista* 20 (1974), pp. 229–84.

[76] For example: Quine, *Italy's social revolution*.

[77] Susan A. Ashley, *Making liberalism work: the Italian experience* (Westport, CT, 2003), pp. 35–6. See also Lucy Riall, 'Progress and compromise in Liberal Italy', *Historical Journal* 38 (1995), pp. 205–13.

[78] A. P. Cam., Disc., Sess. 1878–9, 17 March 1879, pp. 4958–61; Doc., Nr. 191, p. 2.

[79] A. P. Cam., Doc., Nr. 73A, 8 April 1884, p. 4; A. P. Cam., Doc., Nr. 73, 19 February 1883, pp. 6–8. See also: A. P. Cam., Disc., XV/1, 18 May 1885, p. 13786. A source of inspiration for these debates was Adolf Held, 'Bericht über verschiedene Ansichten, betr. die Haftpflichtfrage', *Schriften des Verein für Social-Politik* 19 (1880), pp. 139ff. For the general debate, see: Volker Sellin, *Die Anfänge staatlicher Sozialreform im liberalen Italien* (Stuttgart, 1971), pp. 154–70.

of Agriculture, Industry and Commerce settled on the view that Italy was in a process of industrial modernisation in which workers would increasingly fall victim to accidents.[80] Echoing broader legal discussions which had also resonated in Germany, legislators came to see that law had a social function. As Berti would claim shortly after leaving office, 'the law is the idea that prevails, and it is that with which the workers' revolution is being carried out'.[81] Nonetheless, the question remained whether workers should be held liable for the consequences of this growth in industrial risk. In the several bills following Pericoli's, a concept of 'occupational risk', as it was called in legal and political discussions at the time, was advanced as a way to alter the legal conception of employers' responsibilities. The theory built upon contemporary discussions about the social functions of the law that had been elaborated at length in the work of Gian Pietro Chironi on accidents and employers' liability. The idea of 'occupational risk' suggested that a causal relation between work and accidents justified a right to compensation. According to this logic, employers, in creating and nominally managing the workplace, must be held responsible for all accidents associated with it. As the legal theorist Guido Fusinato argued, it was difficult to ascribe fault in cases of workplace accidents, so accidents should be dealt with outside the realm of liability. A consensus began to emerge across the political spectrum, encompassing opponents on both the Historical Left and the Historical Right of Italian politics: the circumstances of modern, industrial life required a shift from private law to public law. Whether accidents should be handled with special legislation was, however, another matter.[82]

Advocates of a liability law, including the several Liberal ministers of agriculture in office between 1879 and 1886, therefore called for greater accountability on behalf of employers. In the various governmental and parliamentary proposals from this period, it was argued that at least the burden of proof should be reversed. The policy would imply that employers were, in principle, responsible for the activities in their businesses. This aspect of these proposals appealed to workers, in particular, who urged the government to adopt a liability law.[83] Despite a growing consensus about the unavoidable rise of industrial risk and the inadequacy of current solutions, no liability law was adopted at

---

[80] For example: 'Circular No. 9, 11 July 1883', from MAIC to the mutual aid societies, printed in *Bolletino di notizie sul credito e la previdenza* 1 (6 August 1883).

[81] Domenico Berti, *Le classi lavoratrici e il parlamento* (Rome, 1885), p. 55, quoted in Cazzetta, *Scienza giuridica*, p. 81; on the social function of the law: pp. 73–90.

[82] Ada Lonni, 'Fatalità o responsabilità? "Le jatture" degli infortuni sul lavoro: la legge del 1898', in Maria Luisa Betri and Ada Gigli Marchetti, eds., *Salute e classi lavoratrici in Italia dall'Unità al fascismo* (Milan, 1982), pp. 737–62, at pp. 752–3; Cazzetta, *Scienza giuridica*, pp. 96–7, 103–8; Gustavo Gozzi, *Modelli politici e questione sociale in Italia e in Germania fra otto e novecento* (Bologna, 1988), p. 115.

[83] For example: the Third Congress of the Confederation of Lombardian Workers, Varese, 1883; the Workers' Congress of March 1884 at Forlí; the Second Congress of the Italian Workers' Party, Mantua, 1885. See Lonni, 'Fatalità o responsabilità?', p. 751.

the time. After a series of bills, the issue was ultimately put aside in 1886. A proposal had successfully passed through both the Chamber of Deputies and the Senate in 1885 but fell by the wayside when government ended the legislative session.[84] A major concern in parliament and in legal circles about Pericoli's and subsequent proposals was that these law proposals did not sufficiently justify bypassing the civil code with a statute. Instead, opponents of a liability law argued that judges could broaden their interpretation of the relevant articles in the civil code, and it was this tack that prevailed for the next several years. Developments in France, where a liability law was also being considered at this time, played an important role in these considerations.[85] Ultimately, this is how liability developed in Italy: judges became increasingly generous towards workers when interpreting the code.[86] Nonetheless, and in parallel, workers and employers were expected to make provisions for themselves against the consequences of workplace accidents. For instance, one of the proponents of a liability law was Luigi Luzzatti, the under-secretary at the Ministry of Agriculture, Industry and Commerce and a long-time advocate of cooperatives and savings funds.[87] In the face of legislative failure on liability law, he turned to voluntary compensation as a possible solution to the accident problem. Inspired by the creation of the Italian Post Office Savings Bank as well as information about mutual funds he saw at the International Exhibition in Paris in 1867 and the International Exhibition held in Milan in 1881, Luzzatti proposed the development of a semi-private National Accident Insurance Fund, which was ultimately established in 1883.[88] The fund enabled employers and workers to contribute on a voluntary basis to the payment of insurance premiums that would provide for injured workers. Instead of adopting a strict liability law, as the German and British governments had done, Italy managed the accident problem by relying on the combination of individual self-help through insurance and the growing lenience of judicial interpretation of the civil code. Until the enactment of the 1898 accident insurance law, it was left to the courts to modify legal understandings of responsibility in the workplace and to workers and employers to sort out insurance payments.

---

[84] Ashley, *Making liberalism work*, pp. 80–4.

[85] For example: Marco Besso, 'Il nuovo progetto di legge sugli infortuni del lavoro', *Nuova antologia* (2nd series), 30 (1 December 1881), pp. 498–520.

[86] Cesare Biondi, 'La Legge sugli infortuni del lavoro nel diritto e nella medicina', *Rivista di diritto e giurisprudenza. Patologia speciale e medicina forense sugli infortuni del lavoro e sulle disgrazie accidentali* 4 (1903), pp. 4–6; Piva, 'Problemi giuridici e politici della "responsabilità"', pp. 649–66.

[87] Maurizio Degl'Innocenti, *La società volontaria e solidale: il cantiere del welfare pubblico e privato* (Rome, 2012), pp. 227–57.

[88] Luigi Luzzatti, *Memorie autobiographiche e carteggi*, ed. Elena Carli (3 vols., Bologna, 1931–66), vol. II, p. 190; Luigi Luzzatti, 'Le rivelazioni della previdenza all'Esposizione nazionale di Milano', *Nuova antologia* (2nd series) 30 (1881), pp. 3–31, 203–24, 681–700.

PROBABILITY, RISK AND RESPONSIBILITY

Novel scientific conceptions of workplace accidents underpinned this movement towards new policies on employers' liability. Moreover, the development
of new management structures bolstered the argument that workers were
only partly responsible for their actions at work. By contrast, earlier in
the century, thinking about workplace accidents frequently echoed popular and early scientific representations of accidents as humanitarian problems whose solutions were interpersonal and moral rather than societal and
objective. Although officials continued to echo these humanitarian ideas
about workplace accidents, the emphasis of discussions in each government began to shift by the 1860s and 1870s. It was also at this time that
each country began collecting comprehensive statistics on workplace accidents, which only confirmed officials' suspicions: there was a causal connection between work, accidents and risk. From the 1830s, for example,
Britain began intensively investigating problems related to work. At first,
the task was left to parliamentary and royal commissions, but Home Office
Departmental Committees later took charge of the matter. The objective
of these inquiries was, in part, humanitarian: to gather evidence on the
issue at hand as a means to expose the 'evils' of factory life that liberal
reformers such as James Kay-Shuttleworth cited. In the case of the 1835
Parliamentary Select Committee on Accidents in Mines, this meant inter-
viewing miners, mine owners and mine inspectors to ascertain how and
why accidents occurred and what their consequences were.[89] In this respect,
the investigation of workplace risk echoed the broader movement in public
health in Britain in which Kay-Shuttleworth, Edwin Chadwick and others
were involved.[90] And, as in public health, the findings of these kinds of commissions brought Britain to introduce new regulatory measures. However,
they did not create a clear image of work-related risk. Instead, their reports,
which were published for public consumption as voluminous 'Blue Books',
'subverted demand for transparency by complying with it excessively'.
What these reports supplied was 'masses of detail'. This detail did, however,
reveal evidence that workplace accidents were widespread and devastating
to the individuals they struck.[91] By vividly elaborating on the injuries and
penury befalling individuals and families, these accounts seemed to create a

[89] *PP* 1835 (603) V.1: 'Report from the Select Committee on Accidents in Mines, together with the
      Minutes of Evidence and Index'.
[90] See Christopher Hamlin, *Public health and social justice in the age of Chadwick: Britain 1800–
      1854* (Cambridge, 1998).
[91] Oz Frankel, *States of inquiry: social investigations and print culture in nineteenth-century
      Britain and the United States* (Baltimore, 2006), p. 69; Thomas W. Laqueur, 'Bodies, details, and
      the humanitarian narrative', in Lynn Hunt, ed., *The new cultural history* (Berkeley, CA, 1989),
      pp. 176–204, at p. 177.

'pornography of pain' that could both heighten awareness of the problem and create public demand for more information.[92]

Commission reports, not unlike the writings of social reformers, incited a humanitarian response from readers. The humanitarian depiction of accidents focused on the devastation related to ambiguous dangers rather than known risks which could be foreseen and which, at least implicitly, individuals had chosen to take on.[93] The dangers associated with industry were somehow linked to it, but how they were linked to industry, whether they were definite and whether anyone could be held accountable remained unclear. On the one hand, commission reports extensively examined machinery involved in accidents in order to understand their cause and the connection between workers' actions and accidents, and they investigated safety equipment used to prevent accidents (Figure 1).[94] On the other hand, they portrayed the causes of workplace accidents as originating outside those 'struck' by misfortune, indicating that danger was unmanageable and perhaps even supernatural. These early accounts did not, therefore, create a clear impression of occupational risk, which was governed by the laws of probability and predictable causal connections. For example, the 1835 parliamentary committee on accidents in mines found that many accidents were never investigated because local authorities assumed that certain accidents, such as the collapse of a mine shaft, were due to misfortune rather than individuals' actions or improper safety procedures.[95] Moreover, humanitarian accounts frequently focused on the effects of accidents, rather than the causes, which further emphasised the theme of misfortune. By focusing especially on women and children, who not only appeared innocent but were also limited in their ability to legal consent, these investigations seemed to demonstrate that the sufferers of workplace accidents were not responsible for their occurrence. Instead, humanitarian portrayals of accidents, like those of other issues at the time, seemed to call on readers to feel a personal connection to the injured and some degree of agency in their injury.[96]

While the British government was unique in the form and number of investigations it carried out on workplace accidents during this period, its interest in these details was not. In each country, governmental discussion and commissions were often spurred by what they represented as 'disasters' or 'catastrophes' involving the deaths of numerous workers in mining, railways and

---

[92] Karen Halttunen, 'Humanitarianism and the pornography of pain in Anglo-American culture', *American Historical Review* 100/2 (1995), pp. 303–34; Laqueur, 'Bodies, details', pp. 190–3.

[93] On the distinction between danger and risk: Niklas Luhmann, *Soziologische Aufklärung* (6 vols., 2nd edn, Opladen, 1993), vol. v: *Konstruktivistische Perspektiven*, pp. 131–69.

[94] For example: *PP* 1835 (603) V.1: 'Report from the Select Committee on Accidents in Mines'; *PP* 1852–5 (691) XX.1: 'First Report from the Select Committee on Accidents in Coal Mines, with the Minutes of Evidence and Appendix'.

[95] *PP* 1835 (603) V.1: 'Report from the Select Committee on Accidents in Mines', p. 23.

[96] Thomas L. Haskell, 'Capitalism and the origins of the humanitarian sensibility, part 1', *American Historical Review* 90/2 (1985), pp. 339–61, at p. 358.

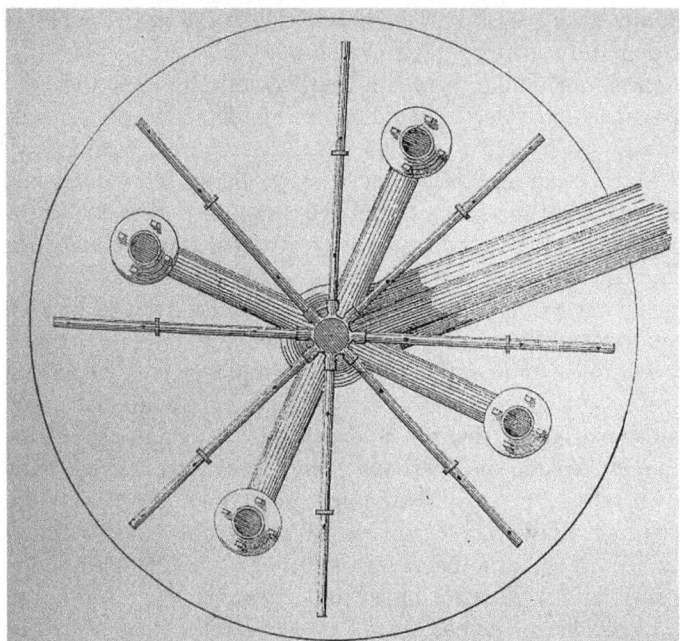

FIGURE I. 'Diagram of Goldsworthy Gurney's apparatus for ventilating mines'.
Source: *PP* 1849 (613) VII.1: 'Prevention of Accidents in Coal Mines Committee',
appendix 1, plan I, figure 3.

industries involving the use of steam boilers, which were prone to explosion.
In part, widespread media reportage of large-scale accidents impelled each
government to act.[97] By the 1860s, governments in each country increasingly
portrayed accidents as the result of workplace risk, and statistics proved a
meaningful tool for drawing a connection between the two. Over the course
of the nineteenth century, statistics became an increasingly important method
for governments to recognise and communicate about 'social questions'.[98] For
Britain, Germany and Italy, as elsewhere, the rise of statistical thinking within
governmental networks occurred largely in response to widespread concerns
about poverty and civil disorder during the mid nineteenth century. Each of

---

[97] For example: *PP* 1870 (C 370) X.459: 'Report from the Select Committee on Steam Boiler
Explosions, together with the Proceedings of the Committee, Minutes of Evidence, and
Appendix'; MAIC, Direzione generale dell'agricoltura, *Pubblicazioni del Corpo reale delle
miniere. Studio sulle condizioni di sicurezza delle miniere e delle cave in italia* (Rome, 1894);
GStAPK: I. HA. Rep. 120BB. VII. Fach. 1. No. 16. Vol. 1: 33–5: Prussian Minister of Trade,
Commerce and Public Works Itzenplitz to the Royal Railway Directorate of Hanover, 19
June 1868.

[98] Stuart Woolf, 'Statistics and the modern state', *Comparative Studies in Society and History* 31
(1989), pp. 588–604.

these countries developed central statistical bureaus between the 1830s and 1870s that increasingly collected material on social concerns ranging from public health to accident rates.[99] These new agencies emerged in 'an avalanche of numbers', when curious individuals and governments alike began calculating everything from annual national exports to suicide rates. Some scholars have gone so far as to claim that the sudden and intense development of statistics in the early and mid nineteenth century formed a 'probabilistic revolution' in thinking, even a 'paradigm shift' about agency, fate and the laws of nature.[100] From the late 1860s, the British, German and Italian governments began collecting comprehensive statistics that included accidents at work. Since these statistics could prove particular trades to be especially dangerous, each government could call on them to indicate which industries might require special regulation. Moreover, by creating a nexus of causation between industry and accidents, statistics helped to shift the onus of an accident away from individual workers and instead onto the workplace. The link between the probability of accidents and industry as their cause provided the three governments with grounds to call for compensation within the more dangerous industries.

An examination of the accident statistics collected during this period reveals how each government made the conceptual connection between accidents, work and risk, and how, in the process, each defined the concept of an accident that was taken up in legislative discussions. The early British statistics, first collected in 1845, were compiled by factory inspectors under the Factory Act of 1844. These early calculations did not draw a direct link between injury or death and specific risks; they instead correlated the generic categories 'by machinery' or 'not by machinery' with a limited range of consequences, including 'amputations', 'death', 'fractures', 'injuries to head and face' and 'other injuries'. These early statistics were compiled using the returns of local certifying surgeons, who were required to investigate the causes and consequences of accidents at factories if an injured worker did not resume work by the morning following an accident. The returns from this period excluded any specific reference to kinds of industry, thereby creating an abstract impression of work. It is remarkable that these early returns embedded the category of 'accidents'

[99] Michael J. Cullen, *The statistical movement in early Victorian Britain: the foundations of empirical social research* (Hassocks, 1975); Jürgen Reulecke, 'Pauperismus, "social learning" und die Anfänge der Sozialstatistik in Deutschland', in Wolfgang J. Mommsen and Winfried Schulz, eds., *Vom Elend der Handarbeit* (Stuttgart, 1981), pp. 358–72; Silvana Patriarca, *Numbers and nationhood: writing statistics in nineteenth-century Italy* (Cambridge, 1996), pp. 85–121, 178–80.

[100] Ian Hacking, 'Making up people', in Thomas C. Heller et al., eds., *Reconstructing individualism: autonomy, individuality, and the self in western thought* (Stanford, CA, 1986), pp. 222–36, at p. 222; Ian Hacking, 'Was there a probabilistic revolution, 1800–1930?', in Lorenz Krüger et al., eds., *The probabilistic revolution*, vol. I: *Ideas in history* (Cambridge, MA, 1987), pp. 45–55; Ian Hacking, *The taming of chance* (Cambridge, 1990); Theodore M. Porter, *The rise of statistical thinking, 1820–1900* (Princeton, NJ, 1986).

FACTORIES (ACCIDENTS).

RETURN to an Address of the Honourable The House of Commons,
dated 26 June 1873;—*for*,

"RETURN of all Fatal and other ACCIDENTS reported in the REPORTS of the INSPEC-
TORS of FACTORIES for the Year ending the 31st day October 1870, in the following
form :—

Pursuit or Occupation where Accident occurred.	Killed.		Requiring Amputation.		Other Injuries.		TOTAL.
	Males.	Females.	Males.	Females.	Males.	Females.	
Blast Furnaces and Iron Works							
Engineering Works							
Shipbuilding Yards							
Cotton Factories							
Woollen „							
Worsted „							
Flax „							
Silk „							
Calico Printing							
Bleach Dye Works							
Breweries							
Sugar Refineries							
Potteries							
All other Works included in the "Factory Acts"							
TOTAL							

FIGURE 2. Statistical representation of accidents at work in Britain in 1869–70.
Source: PP 1873 (C 355) LXI.39: 'Return of Fatal and other Accidents reported in
Reports of Inspectors of Factories, October 1869–70: Total of Accidents and Deaths in
Works under Factory Acts'.

within the form, rather than categorising the return as a whole as a collection
of accident statistics. By contrast, the statistics collected for the 1869–70 period
under the same Act explicitly labelled the return as relating to 'accidents' and
focused on industries, places of work and machinery that were already widely
perceived to be dangerous: shipping, mining, factories, roadways, steam boilers
and explosives (Figure 2).[101] Statistics from railways, which officials, following
popular perceptions, saw as an especially dangerous industry, were represented
in their own form from 1870, as these had not been included under the 1844
Factory Act and revisions to it. Railway companies sent their statistical returns
directly to the Board of Trade.

[101] PP 1871 (C 488) LVI.591: 'Accidental Deaths: Return of the Number of Lives Lost through
Accident during the Last Two Years for which Information is Available; &c.'.

What is remarkable about the evolution of the forms used in Britain to collect these statistics is how they represented different impressions of industrial risk. The earliest returns relating to accidents were more specific in outlining different kinds of injuries, but they were less detailed about the types of industries involved. Instead, they focused on a variety of categories of individuals in workplace accidents, including male and female 'adults', 'young persons' and 'children'. These categories reflected widespread concerns at the time about the labour of women and children. By contrast, the later forms collected under the Factory Acts no longer included 'children' or 'young people', focusing only on 'males' and 'females'. This shift in focus seems to reveal a change from thinking primarily in terms of humanitarianism. Over time, accidents were seen increasingly as events that could be determined probabilistically. Moreover, the concept of an 'accident' uncovered in these statistics reflected governmental perceptions that industry had become 'modern', chaotic and dangerous. In the British forms from the 1860s and 1870s, therefore, the consequences of accidents were broken down into three broad categories: those causing death, 'requiring amputation' or 'other'. Instead of prioritising individuals and the harms to them, these forms enumerated a wide variety of industries in order to create a causal connection between industry and its negative consequences.

In Italy, governmental statistics also portrayed accidents as the consequences of risks related to work. However, the conception of an accident in Italy was much broader than it was in Britain, which likely points to the fact that the peninsula was not nearly as industrialised at this time. Officials in Rome first began tabulating accident statistics between 1866 and 1882 by relying on reports forwarded from regional prefects. Unlike the British government, its Italian counterpart did not begin the collection of statistics as the continuation of earlier policies on workplace regulation. Instead, the administration in Rome sought to collect information on accidents as a means to gain greater authority throughout the recently unified kingdom but also to make the kingdom appear unified, at least on paper. As a first move in this direction, the central government compiled a census of the population in 1861.[102] The collection of statistics five years later focused on the broad category 'violent deaths' rather than exclusively on workplace accidents, which revealed the government's limited concern about the issue at this time. Instead, the administration focused primarily on growing worries across the peninsula about violence and the breakdown of social order.[103] It therefore sought statistics that linked all 'violent deaths' to each other, compiling in a single compendium 'accidental deaths' and deaths from other causes, including suicide, homicide, duels and capital execution. The focus on 'violent death' in general rather than deaths

[102] Raffaele Romanelli, 'La nuova Italia e la misurazione dei fatti sociali: una premessa', *Quaderni storici* 15 (1980), pp. 765–78; Patriarca, *Numbers and nationhood*, pp. 189–209.
[103] See John A. Davis, *Conflict and control: law and order in nineteenth-century Italy* (Basingstoke, 1988), part II.

MORTI ACCIDENTALI secondo le cause che le produssero e la professione o la condizione dei defunti.

AVVENUTE NELL'ANNO 1866.

CONDIZIONI E PROFESSIONI	TOTALE	Ingombro di veicoli	Estenuazione	Assideramento	Annegamento	Soffocamento	ESPLOSIONE di polverire	di armi da fuoco	SCOPPIO incendi o vapori	di fulmine	di caldaie	di mine	Lesioni nell'esercizio professionale	Cadute	Rovine di fabbricati	FRANE di cava o miniere	di terreno o pietre	SCHIACCIAMENTO per cadute d'alberi	sotto veicoli	Violenze d'animali	Disastri di strade ferrate	Combattimento	Cause ignote e diverse
1. Agricoltori	1302	11	2	3	533	46	....	75	113	36	2	2	4	419	10	15	28	17	82	42	1	2	54
2. Calzolai, sellai e conciatori	35	..	..	1	6	5	....	1	1	..	..	..	..	14	..	..	1	....	1	1	..	..	3
3. Clero regolare e secolare	21	..	..	..	6	..	....	..	3	1	..	..	..	1	..	..	1	....	..	..	..	..	4
4. Commercianti	126	2	1	..	46	2	1	7	12	..	..	2	3	32	3	1	..	....	8	2	1	..	3
5. Conduttori di vetture e animali	114	..	..	..	18	..	....	1	1	2	..	..	33	25	..	2	1	....	18	10	..	..	3
6. Domestici	129	..	..	..	40	5	....	9	12	1	1	..	2	41	1	..	1	....	5	2	..	..	9
7. Fornai e pastai	44	..	..	..	19	..	....	..	3	..	1	..	7	2	..	..	1	2	5	..	..	..	3
8. Lavoranti in legnami	25	..	..	..	6	1	2	..	3	..	..	..	..	7	..	..	1	1	1	..	..	..	2
9. Lavoranti in metalli	58	1	..	1	14	1	....	5	1	..	..	1	2	15	..	1	1	3	2	1	..	..	2
10. Macchinisti e guardie ferrov.	11	..	..	..	..	..	....	..	..	..	..	..	8	3	..	..	..	....	..	..	..	..	..
11. Marinai e barcaiuoli	66	..	..	..	35	..	1	..	9	2	1	..	6	9	..	..	..	....	2	..	..	..	1
12. Militari (1)	101	..	..	1	50	..	....	10	..	..	..	..	3	16	..	..	..	1	3	2	1	4	1
13. Muratori e minatori	171	..	..	..	10	3	....	3	3	..	1	13	57	37	5	12	10	....	6	1	1	..	3
14. Pirotecnici	7	..	..	..	..	1	....	..	3	..	..	..	2	..	1	..	..	....	....	..	..	..	..
15. Professioni liberali	52	..	1	1	16	..	....	2	3	..	..	..	3	17	..	..	..	....	..	4	..	..	..
16. Sarti e cucitori	24	..	..	2	7	1	....	..	2	1	..	..	..	9	..	..	..	....	..	..	..	..	2
17. Tessitori e filatori	37	1	..	..	4	4	....	..	7	3	..	..	..	13	1	..	..	....	2	1	..	..	1
18. Zolfatai	48	..	..	..	..	..	....	..	..	..	..	..	..	..	..	1	48	1	....	..	..	..	..
19. Diverse e ignote	800	7	1	6	267	32	13	40	102	9	12	3	25	203	6	13	12	2	48	17	..	1	41
COMPLESSO...	3431	22	6	15	1097	105	17	169	268	54	17	23	162	866	27	57	58	26	183	82	4	7	131

1 Non sono compresi in questi numeri i militari, sia dell'esercito regolare che dei volontari, i quali lasciarono la vita nelle battaglie combattute in quell'anno contro l'Austria per il riscatto della Venezia. Il numero di questi è di 1512 e cioè 1161 appartenenti all'esercito regolare e 351 al corpo dei volontari.

FIGURE 3. Statistical representation of accidents, risk and death in Italy.
Source: 'Tavole delle morti accidentali', p. 94.

related to work perhaps also reflected officials' anxieties about intervening in industry and agriculture alike.[104]

In order to collect its statistics on 'accidental deaths', the General Division of Statistics based in the Ministry of Agriculture devised a form that tallied the deaths of individuals in particular trades, as diverse as agriculture, mining and tailoring, and calculated death tolls according to causes as varied as suffocation, explosions and 'violence by animals' (Figure 3). The broad categories in the form took into account the particularities of the Italian economic landscape during this period, as they revealed its predominantly agricultural nature. Unlike the British forms, which were directed specifically at uncovering information about workplace accidents, their Italian counterparts elaborated at length on the kinds of individuals affected by accidents. Not only sex and age were represented as linked to accidents, but marital status was included as well. Despite the fact that the General Division of Statistics had sought to collect this information as part of a larger project on violent deaths, the specificity of the Italian forms allowed for a much more elaborate depiction of workplace risk than in Britain. Nonetheless, the Italian government's focus on death rather than injury meant that the majority of workplace accidents remained unrecorded, which greatly skewed officials' perceptions of the problem.

[104] 'Tavole delle morti accidentali'; Patriarca, *Numbers and nationhood*, pp. 182–3.

Unlike in Italy and Britain, in Germany, comprehensive statistics on workplace accidents were only collected *after* the enactment of a national liability law. During discussions about adopting the policy, civil servants in Prussia, which played a leading role in spearheading the law, instead relied on inchoate understandings of dangerous industries in order to argue against workers' agency in accidents. It was only during the 1870s, following the enactment of a national commercial code in 1869 and the liability law of 1871, and amidst intragovernmental debates about whether Germany should create legislation on factory safety, that the administration began collecting accident statistics.[105] In 1873, the Prussian Ministry of Trade drew up forms and asked local governments to complete them with information about workplace accidents that had caused fatalities or serious injuries. The Ministry of Trade was specific in its instruction, asking for information about only those injuries causing the 'inability to work' for at least eight days as a 'consequence' of an 'accident'. It outlined detailed categories of injuries which could be listed, such as bone breaks or fractures, crushing, fire damage, hernia, concussion, general wounds and, ultimately, death. Local governments throughout Prussia began completing the returns annually.[106] Germany's early accident statistics were remarkable in their lack of specificity about the individuals involved. Unlike the Italian or British forms, the early forms adopted by the Prussian Ministry of Trade included no references to sex or age. They instead elaborated on the timing of reported accidents, representing a seemingly precise conception of the risks and consequences involved in particular types of misfortunes (Figure 4).

It was only several years later, after the government's first accident insurance bill was rejected in parliament in 1881, that officials attempted to forge a more complete picture of workplace risk. The Imperial Office of the Interior sent a directive to the state governments across Germany, asking them to enlist the services of local authorities, including chambers of trade and trade associations, in collecting information on workplace accidents over several months in 1880. Prussia devised a new form for compiling this data, which also took into account sex and age. As in the earlier Prussian statistics, the new series outlined the timing of accidents and their consequences, connecting the risk of incidents with particular times of day, days of the week and seasons of the year.[107] The elaborate detail in the returns reflected Germany's growing interest at the time in devising an insurance-based solution to workplace accidents. Specific accident statistics could later serve as the basis for the formulation of 'risk classes'

---

[105] On these debates: Renate Zitt, *Zwischen innerer Mission und staatlicher Sozialpolitik: der protestantische Sozialreformer Theodor Lohmann (1831–1905)* (Heidelberg, 1997), pp. 434–48.

[106] GStAPK: I. HA. 120BB. Abt. VII. Fach. 1. No. 4. Vol. 4: 111–13: Minister of Trade and Commerce to the Collective Royal Governments, Police Presidia and *Landdrostereie*, 30 June 1873.

[107] GStAPK: I. HA. Rep. 77. Tit. 923. Nr. 1. Vol. 2: 63–5: Imperial Office of the Interior to the collective state governments, 11 July 1881.

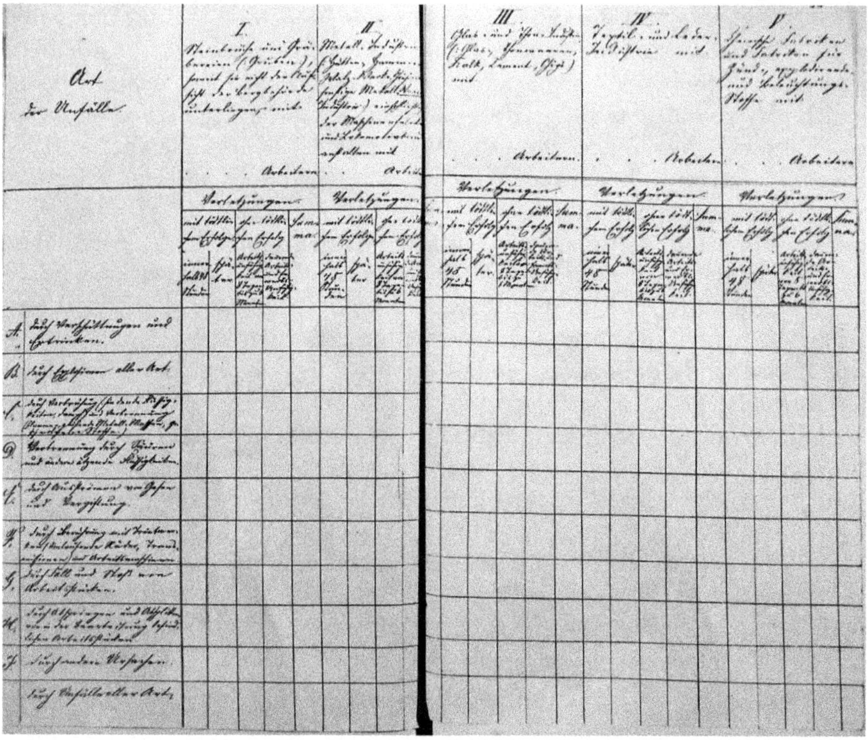

FIGURE 4. Statistical representation of workplace accidents in Prussia.
Source: GStAPK: I. HA. Rep. 120 Ministerium für Handel und Gewerbe, BB VII 1 Nr. 4a: 93–4. Courtesy GStAPK.

used to devise premiums.[108] In fact, the Prussian Ministry of Trade consulted closely with commercial insurance firms and insurance experts when devising these numbers.[109] This later compilation of statistics on workplace accidents proved crucial for the government's proposal to adopt a national policy on accident insurance.

[108] This was especially the case from the early 1880s. See Chapter 2 about the creation of premiums.
[109] GStAPK: I. HA. 120BB. Abt. VIII. Fach. 4. No. 1. Vol. 1: 309–10: Royal Statistical Office to the State Secretary of the Interior, 11 November 1880; 311: the Deputy Secretary of the Ministry of Trade and Commerce (Lohmann) to Professor Dr Heym, 21 November 1880; 88: Deputy Secretary of the Ministry of Prussian Trade and Commerce (Jacobi) to Professor Dr Heym and to the Governmental Adviser Stämmler, 27 September 1880; 106–37: Report from Jacobi to 'Seiner Durchlauth' (the Chancellor), 8 October 1880; 277–8: response from Heym to Dr Jacobi, Deputy Secretary, 24 October1880; 279–80: report from Stämmler; GStAPK: I. HA. 120BB. Abt. VIII. Fach. 4. No. 1. Vol. 2: 16–17: Royal Prussian Statistical Bureau to the Minister of Trade and Commerce, 29 November 1880.

Britain, Germany and Italy collected accident statistics against the backdrop of three related developments: a transnational community of statisticians who met regularly at congresses from the 1850s, a network of scientists of work that slowly extended across Europe from the 1840s onwards, and new management practices that began to take hold in certain economic sectors from the latter part of the eighteenth century and became increasingly prevalent from the middle of the nineteenth century. The contemporaneity of the early statistical collections of the British, German and Italian governments perhaps resulted from a degree of mutual observation facilitated by the transnational networks of statisticians and scientists of work. Widespread international discussion about the development of statistics as a social science emerged with the first International Statistical Congress in 1853. The following congresses, which met every two to three years, were a particularly important source of information for social scientists at the time, many of whom had links to government.[110] For example, the Statistical Society of London, later the Royal Statistical Society, counted several MPs and even a few prime ministers amongst its members. An active participant in these international conferences, the Statistical Society transmitted information from international networks of experts back to government. Similarly, Ernst Engel, head of the Prussian Statistical Office, and Luigi Bodio, head of the General Division of Statistics at the Italian Ministry of Agriculture, attended the meetings. The goal of the congresses was foremost practical; they aimed both to advance statistics as a science and to utilise them in solving political problems. By its seventh meeting in 1869, the Congress resolved that 'governments should be invited in the preparation of forms or statistical tables, to take into serious consideration the interests and needs of science as well as of administration'. It was hoped that members would soon be able to use this information to create a 'Statistique internationale de l'Europe', which would provide the basis for comparison of social and economic circumstances across Europe.[111]

In later discussions, mutual observation amongst the three governments, as well as further afield, played an increasingly important role in confirming the risk of accidents at work. When Germany introduced statutory accident insurance in 1884, officials in Italy and Britain monitored the wording of the legislation as well as subsequent developments. German decisions about which industries should be included in the policy and how particular consequences of accidents should be compensated proved important for shaping discussions abroad about the probability and meaning of accidents. This was particularly the case for Italy. For the next several years, the Ministry of Agriculture obtained

---

[110] Nico Randeraad, 'The international statistical congress (1853–76): knowledge transfers and their limits', *European History Quarterly* 41 (2011), pp. 50–65.

[111] Samuel Brown, 'Report of the seventh International Statistical Congress, held at the Hague, 6th–11th Sept. 1869', *Journal of the Statistical Society of London* 4 (1869), pp. 391–410.

copies of German accident statistics and compensation rates.[112] Similarly, from the 1880s, when New Zealand, several Canadian provinces and Australian colonies began contemplating and introducing accident compensation legislation, the British Home Office carefully monitored new developments and the wording of bills.[113] The Liberal Unionist Joseph Chamberlain, Secretary of State for the Colonies from 1895 until 1903 and a long-time advocate of workmen's compensation, played an important role here as an informant on the accident problem in the empire.[114]

A significant conduit of information on industrial risk at this time was the International Congress on Industrial Accidents and Social Insurance. The body met every two to three years and had a standing committee based in Paris as well as a regular *Bulletin* that discussed the international development of social policy.[115] Germany began sending official representation at the second of these congresses, which was held in Berne in 1891, and it aimed to spread information about its approach to accident insurance for other countries to emulate.[116] Both the Italian and British governments also sent representatives, including Luigi Luzzatti, who served as the honorary president of the standing committee of the congress organisation, and Alfred Edward Bateman, chief of the Commercial Department of the Board of Trade and an honorary secretary

[112] For example, the Italian government commissioned a full-length study of the German system, published as a special issue in a series of the MAIC: Ugo Mazzola, *L'assicurazione degli operai nella scienza e nella legislazione germanica: relazione a S. E. il Ministro di agricoltura, industria e commercio* (Rome, 1885). See also: 'Le associazioni professionali nell'anno 1886', *Bollettino di notizie sul credito e la previdenza* 6 (31 July 1888), pp. 829–40. The British government commissioned several reports from the Foreign Office, while it also observed developments in Germany and elsewhere in the media. For example: *PP* 1886 (C 4784) LXVII.571: 'Reports by Her Majesty's Representatives Abroad on the Laws Regulating the Liability of Employers in Foreign Countries' and Foreign Office, *Report on the question of employers' liability in Germany* (London, 1894). See also: TNA: HO 45/9841/B11058: unnumbered: memorandum of the Secretary of State of the Home Department, 2 February 1892.

[113] On the transnational contours of developments in Britain, and the shifting concept of risk within British discussions about workplace accidents, see also my article 'La (re)découverte du risque professionnel: l'indemnisation des ouvriers britanniques dans la perspective d'une histoire croisée', *Mouvement Social* 249 (2014), pp. 187–204.

[114] TNA: HO 45/9867/B13816H: unnumbered letter from Edward Treager, Secretary of the Department of Labour in New Zealand, to Joseph Chamberlain, Secretary of State for the Colonies, 27 March 1897; TNA: HO 157/3/234: Sir Kenelm Digby, Under-Secretary of State in the Home Office to William Onslow, Under-Secretary of State for the Colonies, 15 October 1900; TNA: HO 45/9866/B13816D: unnumbered letter from R. H. Meade, of the Colonial Office to the Home Office, 27 June 1893; TNA: HO 45/9867/B13816H: unnumbered letter from Edward Wingfield of the Colonial Office to the Under-Secretary of State of the Home Office, 13 August 1896.

[115] On these conferences: Julia Moses, 'Policy communities and exchanges across borders: the case of workplace accidents at the turn of the twentieth century', in Davide Rodogno et al., eds., *Shaping the transnational sphere, 1830–1950* (New York, 2014), pp. 60–81.

[116] BArch: R 1501: 101093: 7–10: President of the Imperial Insurance Office to the Secretary of the Interior, 30 March 1899.

of the Royal Society for Statistics in London, who also served on the standing committee of the congress organisation. This particular organisation was crucial for crystallising a common international standard of occupational risk – based on the concept underpinning the German accident insurance law of 1884. Already at its first meeting, members of the congress called for the collection of accident statistics using 'uniform principles'. They argued that the 'nature and duration' of injuries should be taken into consideration and suggested sending a form to national governments for this purpose.[117] By the 1894 International Congress on Industrial Accidents and Social Insurance, participants resolved that governments should compile annual and comprehensive statistics on the circumstances of industrial accidents, including both the nature of injuries and the length of disability, and that the different countries participating in the congress should use the form of the Imperial Insurance Office in order to compile their statistics.[118] It is unclear to what extent the congress' efforts in standardising accident statistics had an impact on the activities of member governments, which had generally been collecting relatively similar statistics by this point. Nonetheless, there is some evidence that the congress' efforts did have an impact. For example, the Italian National Fund had adopted the statistical categories proposed at the congress in 1891, and the British Home Office began re-evaluating its method for collecting accident statistics as a result of these conferences.[119] In any case, by the following meeting in Brussels in 1897, participants were unanimous in recognising the principle of 'occupational risk': certain trades were probabilistically bound to specific rates of accidents that varied according to time of day, day of the week and the sex and age of the worker.[120]

The International Congress on Industrial Accidents and Social Insurance was one of many national and international congresses focused on industrial hygiene and accident prevention at this time. In these various venues, participants did not only seek to trace 'occupational risk' through the study of accident statistics. They also engaged with what Anson Rabinbach has called the 'science of work' that began emerging gradually out of physiology and physics from the 1840s. By

[117] Édouard Gruner, ed., *Exposition universelle internationale de 1889: Congrès international des accidents du travail*, vol. II: *Comptes rendus des séances et visite du congrès* (Paris, 1890), p. 21.
[118] BArch: R 1501: 100645: 100–1: copy of the resolutions from the 1894 International Workers' Accident and Social Insurance Congress in Milan.
[119] *Congrès international des accidents du travail et des assurances sociales. Sixième session tenue à Düsseldorf du 17 au 24 Juin 1902, publié par les soins du comité allemande d'organisation* (Breslau and Berlin, 1902), pp. 921–3; TNA: HO 45/9841/B11058/7: departmental memorandum of 2 February 1892, asking for information on all existing sources of official statistical information on industrial accidents. The resonance of the congress's later resolution related to the Home Office's increasing emphasis on statistical collection at the time. See Pellew, *The Home Office*, pp. 52–7.
[120] Ernesto de Angeli, 'Il congresso degli infortuni nel lavoro a Bruxelles', *Nuova antologia* (4th series) 70 (16 August 1897), pp. 666–84, at p. 668.

the late 1880s and 1890s, when the first congresses on workplace accidents met, researchers in France, Germany, Belgium, Italy and Austria had begun developing comprehensive studies of the relationship between work and fatigue which linked industrial accidents to the activities of work rather than the choices of workers.[121] Studies of industrial fatigue were predicated on the findings of the German physicist Hermann von Helmholtz's discovery of the first law of thermodynamics in 1847. The concept of 'labour power' (*Arbeitskraft*) emerged as a rereading of Helmholtz's research in the 1850s, when Karl Marx and Friedrich Engels saw it as the power of individual workers to trade in their only commodity: their labour.[122] The concept of labour power to which Marx and Engels referred reflected contemporary understandings of the labour contract and workers' free choice to find employment. By the 1880s, the concept of 'labour power' transformed, as a new field of science around work, including industrial hygiene, engineering and medicine emerged across much of Europe and investigated 'labour power' as a finite resource that could be drained.

This 'energetic' conception of work had enormous significance for understandings of workplace risk and accidents. The idea of 'labour power' applied Helmholtz's law on the conservation of energy to the activity of work. Understood in this light, the meaning of work could be extricated from moral understandings of indolence and diligence. Instead, researchers of work argued that the activity of labour was a structure in which the human body operated as a component – as a 'human motor'. In this formulation, human will was removed from the equation, indemnifying workers for accidents in which they were involved. The idea found widespread support, as physicists such as James Clerk Maxwell attempted to place free will against the laws of nature. Helmholtz's second law of thermodynamics helped to support this notion. It outlined the process of entropy, the inevitable and gradual decline of energy, which could be transferred to the sphere of labour in order to account for worker fatigue. If a worker did not perform optimally, fatigue, rather than irresponsibility, could be to blame. The application of the law of entropy to the workplace found such widespread support that, by the early 1900s, physicians began calling for regular work breaks in order to make the workplace both safer and more efficient.[123] According to this physical understanding of work, accidents were the result of risks related to the process of work; they were not

[121] Anson Rabinbach, *The human motor: energy, fatigue, and the origins of modernity* (Berkeley, CA, 1990).

[122] The concept merited an entry in the Grimm brothers' dictionary as early as 1854. 'Arbeitskraft', in Jacob and Wilhelm Grimm, *Deutsches Wörterbuch* (16 vols., 1854–1960; repr. Munich, 1984), vol. i; Friedrich Engels, 'Review for the *Fortnightly Review*', in Friedrich Engels, *Engels on capital* (New York, 1937), p. 19; Rabinbach, *Human motor*, pp. 72–3.

[123] For example: Thomas Oliver, 'Occupation diseases due to excessively repeated muscular actions', in Thomas Oliver, ed., *Dangerous trades* (London, 1902), pp. 815–26. Rabinbach, *Human motor*, chs. 1 and 7; Matthew Stanley, 'The pointsman: Maxwell's demon, Victorian free will and the boundaries of science', *Journal of the History of Ideas* 69 (2008), pp. 467–91.

the result of human agency, nor did they stem from the ambiguous dangers emanating from technology or misfortune.

Researchers of work at these congresses also noted that expanded managerial control and new industrial structures during this period had fundamentally altered the responsibilities left to individual workers, which was a point that the British government discussed when considering the question of liability for workplace accidents.[124] In Britain, in particular, new management structures were becoming widespread by the time government began investigating the accident problem, and they played a role in shaping officials' views.[125] Industrialisation was marked by the centralisation and mechanisation of labour in order to improve efficiency. In many industries, the built environment underwent significant transformation. Employers, inspired by Jeremy Bentham's 'panopticon' designs of 1785, sought to construct new workplaces where the focus of architecture was efficiency. The Round Mill in Belper, England, for example, adopted this model in 1811. By the 1830s, technical manuals began calling for the spatial rationalisation of the workplace.[126] British woollen mills from the mid nineteenth century were generally arranged 'like closed, defensive fortresses', with 'various rooms for spinning, for assembling the warps, and for weaving [that] formed a ring enclosing a central courtyard'. These altered structural conditions at work, characterised not only by the machine but also the factory clock, may have affected worker behaviour and influenced their role in accidents.[127] To observers, it seemed that workers were no longer free agents to do as they chose; they were cogs in a larger industrial machine.

As we have seen in this chapter, the second half of the nineteenth century witnessed a dramatic shift in thinking about workers' agency, the causes of accidents and the role of the state in addressing social problems. This transformation took form in Britain, Germany and Italy, regardless of their vastly different political structures, legal systems and economies.

This shift in thinking marked a transition from conceptualising accidents primarily in humanitarian terms, in the case of women and children, or as a negative by-product of the labour market, in the case of adult men. Workers

---

[124] For example: Gruner, ed., *Exposition universelle internationale de 1889*, vol. II, pp. 19–21.

[125] For example: *PP* 1877 (C 285) X.551: 'Report from the Select Committee on Employers' Liability', p. v. This contemporaneity also influenced the American experience with workplace accidents: John Fabian Witt, 'The transformation of work and the law of workplace accidents, 1842–1910', *Yale Law Journal* 107 (1998), pp. 1467–502.

[126] For example: Andrew Ure, *Philosophy of manufactures* (London, 1835); Evan Leigh, *The science of modern cotton spinning* (2 vols., 2nd edn, London, 1873). See Germano Maifreda, *La disciplina del lavoro* (1787; Milan, 2007), pp. 88–126.

[127] Richard Biernacki, *The fabrication of labor: Germany and Britain, 1650–1914* (Berkeley, CA, 1995), pp. 93–111, at p. 128; E. P. Thompson, 'Time, work-discipline and industrial capitalism', in E. P. Thompson, *Customs in common: studies in traditional popular culture* (New York, 1993), pp. 352–403.

had previously been seen as consenting to potential dangers associated with their jobs. In theory, as free agents in the labour market, they could agree to whichever job they preferred. That is, workers could choose to take up dangerous employment knowingly, perhaps with the hope of earning more income in return. Of course, this understanding of consent to risk was predicated on the assumption that workers were always adult men; women and children were not in a legal position to consent to employment. By the end of the century, however, workers were no longer viewed as agreeing to dangers associated with employment. Social reformers, government officials, engineers and physicists, let alone workers and lawyers, doubted whether workers were capable of consenting to risks associated with modern industry. Modern industry came to be seen as especially hazardous, with predictably unpredictable risks for which no one could be held accountable.

The existence at the end of the century of greater institutional capacities and governmental knowledge about society was crucial for this paradigm shift. This was especially the case in Germany and Italy, which dealt with the problem of workplace accidents while simultaneously attempting to build new states following national unification. Workers, too, played a pivotal role in questioning whether they should bear the brunt of the costs arising from modern industry. They had long relied on various arrangements to address the consequences of occupational accidents – from friendly societies to family help or assistance for the poor. However, they increasingly took to the courts, in part, with legal aid from trade unions, to demand that employers pay instead. For example, in 1880, its first year in effect, Britain's Employers' Liability Act elicited 118 actions at court in England and Wales, with 8 in the City of London alone. By 1890, the numbers rose to 371 and 17. Meanwhile, in Germany, the Supreme Commercial Court heard 91 cases between 1871 and 1880 related to the 1871 Employers' Liability Law.[128] That the industrial workforce in each country had grown considerably throughout this period, and would continue to rise in subsequent years, might also have fuelled the rise in litigation. In Britain, the number of workers employed in manufacturing alone increased by 191 per cent between 1841 and 1891. Meanwhile, in Germany, the industry grew by 23 per cent between 1882 and 1895, and it increased in Italy by 31 per cent between 1871 and 1901.[129]

However, the fact that Britain's and Germany's liability laws and Italy's civil code had only partially addressed workplace accidents meant that the issue

---

[128] *PP* 1881 (C 3333) LXXV.1: 'Judicial Statistics of England and Wales, 1881', pp. xli–xlii; *PP* 1890–1 (C 6443) XCIII.1: 'Judicial Statistics of England and Wales, 1890', pp. xxxviii–xxxix; John M. Kleeberg, 'From strict liability to workers' compensation: the Prussian Railroad Law, the German Liability Act, and the introduction of Bismarck's accident insurance in Germany, 1838–1884', NYU *Journal of International Law and Politics* 36 (2003), pp. 53–132, at pp. 106–7.

[129] Brian R. Mitchell, *European historical statistics, 1750–1970* (London, 1975), pp. 156, 158, 163.

would soon emerge again at the forefront of national debate. By 1877, for example, a local official in Düsseldorf wrote to the Minister of Trade in Berlin to declare that 'the current situation is intolerable'. His view reflected the growing consensus in Germany at the time and in Britain and Italy over the next 20 years: their laws on workplace accidents had failed because they were based on a false assumption. The policies in each country looked for the *causes* of accidents in the actions of employers and supervisors. However, as the official in Düsseldorf, along with numerous others, saw it, accidents stemmed from the risks of modern industry, and no individual – neither workers nor employers – could be blamed.[130]

By the 1880s and 1890s, this constellation of governmental activity, new forms of legal and scientific expertise and contestation at court marked a turning point. It seemed that compulsory, no-fault compensation, guaranteed through the state, was the only solution to the accident problem. Neither workers nor employers could be held responsible for accidents: accidents stemmed from work, and work was not simply a matter of the market. Nor was the market entirely free, as workers were hardly in a position to agree to all aspects of their jobs. Work, with accidents as its shadowside, was a matter for the state. Amidst these debates, new questions therefore emerged about the role of the state in redistributing occupational risk, which is the subject of the next chapter. What kind of social legislation seemed acceptable in each country? Could the state go as far as mandating that its citizens buy social insurance?

---

[130] GStAPK: I. HA. Rep. 120BB. Abt. VII. Fach. 1. No. 16. Vol. 1: 176–82: Royal Government in Düsseldorf, Department of the Interior, to the Prussian Minister for Trade and Commerce, 2 August. 1877. See also, for example: BArch: R43: 507: 99–105: H. Woltersdorf, Head of the Committee of the League of German Millers, 20 December 1880; BArch: R1501: 100402: 4: Annual Report on Factory Inspection, 1878; 4 *Hansard* HC vol. 8 (20 February 1893), c. 1961; *Smith* v. *Baker* [1891] AC 325; *Proceedings*, TUC Congress (1891), p. 64; *PP* 1886 (C 192) VIII.1, 'Report from the Select Committee on the Employers' Liability Act (1880) Amendment Bill', pp. 66–7, 110; *A. P. Cam.*, Doc., Leg. XVI, Sess. 4 (1889–90), Nr. 116, 'Disegno di legge presentato alla camera dei deputati dal ministro di agricoltura, industria e commercio (Miceli), nella seduta dell'8 febbraio 1890: Provvedimenti per gl'infortuni sul lavoro', p. 4; Relazione al Consiglio della previdenza, 'Allegato B: Relazione del professore Carlo Francesco Ferraris sul tema: "Gli infortuni del lavoro e la legge"' (1897), 207–9.

2

Occupational Risk, Work and the Nation State

'If the law thus takes to protecting men, whether tenant farmers or pitmen or railway servants, who ought to be able to protect themselves, it tends to weaken their self-reliance, and thus, in unwisely seeking to do them good, it lowers them in the scale of moral beings.' By 1881, argued the moral philosopher T. H. Green, such a view could no longer hold sway in Britain. It seemed an outdated relic of the evangelical Christian faith in duty, commitment to individual character and belief in divine justice that had blended seamlessly with liberal economics in the early nineteenth century. Instead, Green maintained that law could be used as a tool to enable individuals, while freedom could result in subjugation, especially of workers, women and children.[1] He was not alone in this view. By the end of the nineteenth century, freedom of contract had come to be seen as a fiction across much of Europe. Workers no longer seemed in a position to consent to the risks associated with their jobs. The era of liberal risk, based on a belief in the agency of individuals, to negotiate fair contracts, to take up dangerous professions and to provide for their own future, had withered away. In its place, a new regime of risk regulation took form. The concept of occupational risk – that certain trades were especially dangerous, provoking injuries for which no one could take personal responsibility – seemed to require a novel role for 'the state', with the law as its agent, as an intermediary in social relations.

It was in this context that Britain, Germany and Italy, like many countries across the globe during this period, spearheaded new legislation that required employers to compensate workers for accidents regardless of their cause.

---

[1] T. H. Green, 'Lecture on liberal legislation and freedom of contract (1881)', in R. L. Nettleship, ed., *Works of Thomas Hill Green* (London, 1906), vol. III, pp. 365–86, at pp. 365, 370–1. On the conflation between 'morals and markets', see: Boyd Hilton, *The age of atonement: the influence of Evangelicalism on social and economic thought, 1785–1865* (Oxford, 1991); G. R. Searle, *Morality and the market in Victorian Britain* (Oxford, 1998).

Germany and Italy enacted accident insurance policies in 1884 and in 1898, while Britain adopted a workmen's compensation law in 1897 that allowed, but did not require, employers to insure themselves against claims for compensation. Implicit in the details of the new policies were views about what role the state should play in regulating the social problems surrounding workplace accidents.[2] How the management of occupational risk came to be seen as a task for the state is the subject of this chapter. It argues that each country attempted to address workplace accidents in a similar way: by holding employers, as the owners and presumed managers of the workplace, financially liable. This understanding of *work* as a source of risk lay at the core of each country's policy on accident compensation. Work not only sparked accidents, potentially pushing families over the edge of poverty. It was also a source of strength for what were increasingly seen as *national* economies. Accidents, as both a disruption to work and as a potential source of social upheaval – whether through strikes, court cases or strains on poor boards – came to be seen as a pressing concern that should be addressed through the state.

The new compensation laws declared that only those accidents which occurred in 'the course of employment' or 'at work' were eligible for remuneration. British legislation cited 'compensation to workmen for accidental injuries suffered in the course of their employment', while its Italian counterpart addressed 'gli infortuni degli operai sul lavoro': 'the accidents of workers at work'. The German laws addressed 'die Folgen der bei dem Betriebe sich ereigenden Unfälle', or 'the consequences of accidents happening in the operation [of work]'. It is significant that the German policy targeted the mechanistic actions associated with labour rather than the more abstract understanding of work embodied in the word *Arbeit*. Its language revealed the assumption that had begun to take hold amongst scientists of work from the middle of the nineteenth century: that workers served as part of the machinery of production, toiling as human motors without individual attributes or agency. However, the legislation in Germany, as in Britain and Italy, was careful to differentiate between types of labour, initially focusing on 'dangerous' industries, where accidents were seen as a consequence of *workplace* risk rather than the actions of either employers or workers. It seemed that certain forms of labour created an altogether new kind of worker, and a new type of political and moral subject. As Green argued, workers were not 'lower[ed] ... in the scale of moral beings' due to the availability of social policies like compensation laws. Instead, it was the nature of modern industry that had stripped workers of agency. The concept of occupational risk denoted this view of workers' and,

[2] A point also emphasised by Ulrike Haerendel in her examination of the German disability and old-age insurance policy adopted several years later: *Quellensammlung zur Geschichte der deutschen Sozialpolitik, 1867–1914*, sect. 2, vol. vi: *Die gesetzliche Invaliditäts- und Altersversicherung und die Alternative auf gewerkschaftlicher und betrieblicher Grundlage* (Darmstadt, 2004).

indeed, employers' subjectivity. And it implied a new role for the state to mitigate the harms caused by accidents.

How the state would become involved in the 'accident problem' was a question that spoke to concerns about its legitimacy as an arbiter in everyday life.
Could the state take on accident compensation within its sphere of activity? And
would a national policy that guaranteed injured workers benefits ruin individual
character, despite Green's claims? In this context, contemporary beliefs about specific and appropriate *national* paths in social legislation assuaged anxieties about
the sharing of risks on a social basis. The idea that there were different national
models for dealing with workplace accidents drove early legislative debates. In
Germany and Italy, the development of new nation states following political unification in 1859 and 1871 overlapped with the creation of their own and other
European social states, based on national welfare legislation. The enactment of
social legislation seemed to indicate the legitimacy of the newly unified nation
states. In Britain, fears about 'lagging behind' cast a shadow on discussions about
how to address the 'accident problem', as the development of European and colonial social legislation pointed towards yet another area of decline at home.

In each country, policy ideas were conceived in national, cultural and often
competitive terms. Comparisons abounded as contemporaries grappled with
the changes wrought by modernity and how different societies had dealt with
them.[3] Germany was the first country to enact a national policy that required
compensation for workplace accidents, a point on which the German government capitalised. It argued that Germany was spearheading a new form of
social legislation, guided by a novel kind of state that symbolised the country's modernity and progressiveness. In Germany, 'state socialism' would ease
the woes of industrialisation, whether in the form of workplace accidents or
political unrest. Civil servants in Rome deliberated about the German system
of accident insurance, reflecting widespread insecurity about state intervention
but also deeper fears about Italian 'backwardness' that pervaded domestic politics throughout this period.[4] Britain continued to struggle with an inefficient
liability law long after Germany had introduced a policy on accident insurance,
and the German example often served as a tool to demand new social legislation in Britain. However, it also offered a foil against which to argue for what
contemporaries saw as a more neutral, less involved state that seemed better
suited to life in Britain.[5] Despite rhetorical sparring against what they saw as

---

[3] See David Strang and John W. Meyer, 'Institutional conditions for diffusion', *Theory and Society*
22 (1993), pp. 487–511; Katharina Holzinger and Christoph Knill, 'Causes and conditions of
cross-national policy convergence', *Journal of European Public Policy* 12 (2005), pp. 775–96.

[4] Romilda Scaldaferre, 'L'origine dello "stato sociale" in Italia (1876–1900)', *Pensiero Politico*
19 (1986), pp. 223–40. See also Silvana Patriarca, *Italian vices: nation and character from the
Risorgimento to the Republic* (Cambridge, 2010).

[5] E. P. Hennock, *British social reform and German precedents: the case of social insurance, 1880–
1914* (Oxford, 1987). A parallel debate focused on education: David Phillips, *The German
example: English interest in educational provision in Germany since 1800* (New York, 2011).

'foreign' models of compensation, in the case of Britain and Italy, and boasting about its novelty, in the case of Germany, civil servants shared across national borders at the end of the nineteenth century a core belief: workplace accidents were caused by occupational risk that should be managed by the state. The ideology of liberal risk, in which workers and employers operated freely in a fair market of labour relations, had lost credibility.

STATE SOCIALISM

Civil servants in Germany, like others across Europe, battled over various policy proposals when deciding how to address workplace accidents. In the end, compulsory insurance emerged as the only viable option because it acknowledged that neither individual employers nor workers were in a position to take full responsibility for accidents. The risk of something going wrong at work had to be shared by a larger community – not least, because work was important for what was increasingly seen as the *national* economy. As a consequence, the state could and should oversee this process of redistributing workplace risk. The German government worked hard to defend this decision in public, crystallising the idea that social insurance was not only a German novelty but also the hallmark of a particular kind of state. Only through 'state socialism', as officials and other contemporaries called it, could social ills be rectified. Social insurance came to be associated both in Germany and abroad with the German welfare state. Paternalistic and inclusive (or, in the eyes of many at the time, authoritarian and integrationist), it offered a wide range of social provision, with the tripartite system of insurance for sickness (1883), accidents (1884) and disability and old age (1889) as an anchor. The programme has often been associated with the German Chancellor Otto von Bismarck, who pushed for a policy on accident insurance as a means to integrate workers who might otherwise succumb to the siren calls of social democracy.[6] However, mandatory insurance was not a foregone conclusion in Germany when determining how to deal with occupational risk. Over the course of the 1870s, several members of central government, like their counterparts across the German federal states and throughout the country's cities, participated in heated debates about addressing the 'accident problem'.[7]

The Prussian Commerce Department worked up the legislative proposals on accident insurance that were eventually carried out across Germany. The section was relatively small and allowed for ample personal input into legislative initiatives from the civil servants staffing it. The head of the department, Rudolf Jacobi, and other members of government, such as the conservative

[6] For example: Hans-Ulrich Wehler, *The German empire, 1871–1918* (Leamington Spa, 1985), ch. 3, especially pp. 131–7.

[7] See, for example, on the poverty question: Larry Frohman, *Poor relief and welfare in Germany from the Reformation to World War I* (Cambridge, 2008).

Robert Bosse, the Deputy Directory of the Imperial Office of the Interior, saw that something needed to be done not only to address the grievances of workers, which were becoming known through the reports of factory inspectors, but also to avert revolution, which had broken out just a few years earlier in neighbouring France, most notably under the banner of the Paris Commune in 1871. For Jacobi and Bosse, as for other senior civil servants in the German government, confession may also have played a role in espousing new legislation. Both were devout Protestants and saw social reform, whether through philanthropic initiatives or public policy, as an essential aspect of Christianity.[8] By 1878, Theodor Lohmann, a senior member of the Commerce Department and one of Jacobi's allies, called for a fundamental revision of Germany's liability law.

Lohmann advocated what he saw as the British approach to social problems: a combination of voluntary solutions such as membership in friendly societies or commercial insurance funds, along with regulation such as factory inspection.[9] For Lohmann, occupational risk was a problem that needed to be addressed through some form of public policy. However, he saw that workers and employers should organise themselves in addressing the aftermath of accidents. It was up to the state, by contrast, to encourage the prevention of accidents from occurring in the first place. Lohmann's interest in this kind of approach was not unique. Like Bosse and Jacobi, Lohmann was a committed Protestant, with strong ties to both the Inner Mission social reform organisation and the progressive Social Policy Association (Verein für Socialpolitik). His links to these groups may have informed his views on the predictable nature of occupational risk and suitable strategies to address it. In fact, numerous social and economic theorists in Germany, such as Lujo Brentano and Hermann Schulze-Delitzsch, proposed similar plans to combine safety legislation with voluntary enrolment in friendly societies or cooperative organisations. Several of these reformers, like Lohmann, looked to Britain in order to advocate what they saw as a double-pronged attack on workplace accidents.

This focus on prevention rather than compensation resonated with German workers. Although less prominent in early trade union campaigns than higher wages and shorter working hours, safety at work eventually became the target of a failed legislative proposal by the Social Democratic Party in 1877.

---

[8] Florian Tennstedt and Heidi Winter, '"Der Staat hat wenig Liebe – active wie passiv": die Anfänge des Sozialstaats im Deutschen Reich von 1871', *Zeitschrift für Sozialreform* 39 (1993), pp. 362–92, at p. 368; 'Einleitung', in Volker Mihr et al., eds., *Sozialreform als Bürger- und Christenpflicht. Aufzeichnungen, Briefe und Erinnerungen des leitenden Ministerialbeamten Robert Bosse aus der Entstehungszeit der Arbeiterversicherung und des BGB (1878–1892)* (Stuttgart, 2005), pp. 9–42, at p. 10.

[9] Theodor Lohmann, *Die Fabrik-Gesetzgebungen der Staaten des europäischen Kontinents* (Berlin, 1878); Florian Tennstedt, 'Sozialreform als Mission: Anmerkungen zum politischen Handeln Theodor Lohmanns', in Jürgen Kocka et al., eds., *Von der Arbeiterbewegung zum modernen Sozialstaat: Festschrift für Gerhard A. Ritter zum 65. Geburtstag* (Munich, 1994), pp. 528–59.

Calling for a ten-hour work day for adult men and eight hours for women and children, it also outlined the creation of a national factory inspectorate and the surveillance of occupational hazards through the Imperial Health Office.[10] The proposal saw limited success, inspiring a new national commercial code the following year. Some labour organisations, like the Association of Tobacco Workers, argued for a more dramatic intervention into workplace safety by overhauling Germany's feeble liability law. As the Association of German Engineers suggested, the policy had only provoked collusion amongst employers and newfound strategies amongst commercial insurance firms to swindle workers out of compensation.[11] Encouraging neither safety at work nor offering a guarantee of compensation for the consequences of accidents, liability law was seen by workers as having failed to deal with occupational risk. Rather than relying on liability law to solve the 'accident problem', these groups called for improved safety regulation that would be governed by a benevolent, interventionist state.

Some workers, however, like members of the left-liberal trade unions associated with the labour economist Max Hirsch, were reluctant about amending liability law, especially if it meant introducing state-mandated insurance. As Hirsch claimed, state-organised insurance, unlike cooperatives or a free market of commercial insurance, would strip workers of their free will and lead to a new form of 'feudalisation'. 'Even more', he argued, it would lead to the 'corporative organisation of commercial society and the state'.[12] Hirsch was unusual in his *laissez-faire* outlook on workplace accidents in the early 1880s. Not least, he was unusually outspoken. Workers and their advocates rarely took a clear stand on occupational risk. They may have been reticent to speak up for fear of dismissal, which was especially pronounced amongst those employed by larger, rural and semi-rural firms and living on factory grounds. For example, several years later, a factory inspector in Baden noted that five workers had been let go after consulting with him during a routine visit.[13]

In the end, the demands of groups like the Association for Tobacco Workers went unheeded, as did Hirsch's warnings about 'feudalisation'. Theodor Lohmann's efforts to improve industrial safety were railroaded by his employer, the German Chancellor and the head of the Prussian government,

[10] *SBDR* 3/1 (1877), Drucksache Nr. 92: 'Antrag der Reichsgasabgeordneten August Bebel, et al. mit Gesetzentwurf' (1 April 1877).

[11] 'Wahlaufruf … mit Entwurf eines Arbeiterschutzgesetzes', *Der Botschafter: Organ für die Mitglieder des Deutschen Tabakarbeiter-Vereins* 8/50 (13 December 1873), quoted in *QS* I/3: *Arbeiterschutz* (Mainz, 1996), pp. 190–4; and 'Sitzungsprotokoll der 15. Hauptversammlung des Vereins Deutscher Ingenieure', *Zeitschrift des Vereins Deutscher Ingenieure* 18 (10 September 1874), pp. 692–8, quoted in *QS* I/3: *Arbeiterschutz* (Mainz, 1996), pp. 228–34, at p. 230.

[12] 'Berufsgenossenschaft und Umlageverfahren in der deutschen Unfallversicherung', *Gewerkverein* 23 (6 June 1884), quoted in *QS* II/2, part 1 (Stuttgart, 1995), pp. 625–8, at p. 626.

[13] Gerhard A. Ritter and Klaus Tenfelde, *Arbeiter im Deutschen Kaiserreich, 1871–1914* (Bonn, 1992), p. 328.

Otto von Bismarck, feeding directly into the fears outlined by many workers. In agreement with a consortium of industrialists and left-leaning liberals, Bismarck opposed new safety measures because he sought to intervene minimally in the relations between employers and workers.[14] Instead of addressing factory safety directly, and rather than encouraging safety measures through a revised liability law, Bismarck sought an entirely different approach to occupational risk. He advocated a new kind of policy that would require employers to take out state-organised insurance for workplace accidents. In Bismarck's eyes, neither employers nor workers could be held directly accountable for the consequences of workplace accidents since these stemmed from predictable yet unavoidable occupational risks. Mandating safety measures could, therefore, only go so far. In any case, he saw that introducing regulations to prevent accidents, like fencing in machinery, could interfere too greatly in the autonomy of workers and employers. It was the role of the state to manage occupational risk, but the state could only go so far in governing daily interactions in the workplace.

To be sure, financial and social considerations also informed Bismarck's views on the matter. The Chancellor was well aware of the financial burden that a new liability law could bring employers, as court settlements could prove costly and unpredictable. He also feared that resolving accident claims at court could further ignite social unrest. A policy on compulsory insurance meant that employers could be left to sort out the repercussions of workplace accidents directly with their workers; neither the legal system nor the state would need to play a substantial role in industrial relations.[15] Viewing insurance as the only appropriate option, the Chancellor purged the civil service of political opponents. He dismissed Lohmann's supervisor, replacing him with an ally in Karl von Boetticher, who would head the Imperial Ministry of the Interior for the next two decades. Bismarck avoided further conflict over social insurance by making himself the Prussian Minister of Trade and Commerce.[16]

Bismarck took up the idea of compulsory insurance from prominent industrialists in one of the most dangerous economic sectors: mining.[17] Mining offered the ideal case for considering occupational risk: working underground, removed from the view of pit masters, miners could – and frequently did – suffer accidents. Determining who was responsible often proved impossible,

[14] Only after Bismarck's retirement in 1890 did Germany see any new safety legislation as part of a 'new course' in domestic policy. Gerhard A. Ritter, *Soziale Frage und Sozialpolitik in Deutschland seit Beginn des 19. Jahrhunderts* (Opladen, 1998), pp. 52–61.

[15] A point emphasised by Lothar Machtan: 'Risikoversicherung statt Gesundheitsschutz für Arbeiter: zur Entstehung der Unfallversicherungsgesetzgebung im Bismarck-Reich', *Leviathan* 13 (1985), pp. 420–41.

[16] Otto Pflanze, *Bismarck: der Reichskanzler* (1998; Munich, 2008), p. 406.

[17] See E. P. Hennock, *The origin of the welfare state in England and Germany, 1850–1914: social policies compared* (Cambridge, 2007), p. 96; Dennis Sweeney, *Work, race and the emergence of radical right corporatism in Imperial Germany* (Ann Arbor, MI, 2009), pp. 42–7.

especially in the large-scale catastrophes that regularly hit mines, killing hundreds of workers in an instant. For example, an 1869 explosion at a coal mine in Freital killed 276. A decade later, 89 workers perished in a similar incident in Zwickau. The difficulty of tracing responsibility for these accidents certainly made the proposals on insurance compelling. For mine owners, paying for insurance – rather than dealing directly with individual accident claims at court – may also have appealed as a means to freeload. Insurance could enable dangerous businesses to exploit the premiums paid by less hazardous workplaces and industries and even take advantage of the contributions of workers, if they were to be included in an insurance scheme.

Despite the immediate appeal of freeloading, the proposals on insurance were driven by more complex reasoning. The steel magnate and mine owner Carl Ferdinand von Stumm was a conservative member of parliament who had proposed insurance for old age and disability, but not workplace accidents, in 1878. An Evangelical Protestant, Stumm had established welfare programmes in his steelworks and encouraged social reform throughout the Empire.[18] As the head of one of the country's most powerful families of industrialists, he was closely connected to the Emperor and an ally of Bismarck's. While his project never reached parliament, it provoked Bismarck in 1880 to ask another mine owner, Louis Baare, to put together a proposal for accident insurance.[19] In part, Stumm and Baare looked to the mutual insurance funds for sickness and disability (*Hilfskassen*) that industrial workers had been required to join since the implementation of a national law in 1876. They also drew on the successes of the mining funds (*Knappschaftskassen*) that various German states already required employers to run. The funds were meant to address two issues: the risks associated with mining and the smooth operation of that industry, especially in light of its importance to both regional and national economies in Germany. The mining funds made a suitable model for dealing with the accident problem because they could ensure similar economic growth and stability across the country. State intervention to ensure economic growth seemed entirely appropriate for recently unified Germany.

Although these funds provided Bismarck with a model for accident insurance, he argued in public that Germany was undertaking a novel enterprise with the policy. He called for the enactment not only of compulsory accident insurance but also of other forms of 'social insurance' that would target old age, disability and sickness as part of a unified reform of the social sphere. And, echoing the views of Bosse and Jacobi, he claimed that these policies symbolised the kind of state that Germany was, where a conservative, paternalistic form of

---

[18] Sandrine Kott, 'Éléments pour une histoire sociale et culturelle de la religion en Allemagne au XIX siècle', *Revue d'Histoire Moderne et Contemporaine* 5 (2001), pp. 92–111, at pp. 94–7.
[19] *DDR* 4/2 1879, vol. 4, Anlage Nr. 16; BArch: R43: 507: 2–7: Memorandum from Louis Baare, general-director of the Bochum Verein für Bergbau und Gußstahl Fabrikation and Royal Commercial Adviser in Bochum, 30 April 1880.

'state socialism', based on 'practical Christianity', meant that the state would care for workers, who were the 'victims of industry'.[20] Modern industry had brought about modern risks, and workers were victims rather than agents of the accidents that befell them. Bismarck's emphasis on 'practical Christianity' rather than 'state socialism' alone is noteworthy. The rhetoric may, in part, have evolved from his anti-Catholic politics during the *Kulturkampf*, or cultural struggle, of the 1870s, when local, regional and central governments in Germany sought to limit the role of Catholic institutions. It highlighted the role of a caring state that could positively integrate all its members, including Catholics (and perhaps Germany's Jewish minority) as well as Social Democrats, whose activities were severely curtailed during this period.[21]

By emphasising the 'imperial duty' to legislate on workplace accidents, Bismarck's and other governmental representations of accident insurance linked the policy to the 'moral foundation of ... Christian folk life'.[22] In this light, social insurance stemmed from an ethical consensus within Germany about redistributing individual risks to a broader community. As an 'imperial duty', redistribution was not only a task for civil society. Civil society had been proven unable to address the 'accident problem', as evidenced by the unsatisfying wake of court cases that trailed behind German liability law. Instead, it was the obligation of the German state to rectify the problems caused by occupational risk. Drawing comparisons with foreign countries helped Bismarck and other members of government to distinguish this uniquely German ethos about social regulation. For Bismarck, France provided an ideal foil to the German approach to social questions. Manipulating French socialist rhetoric from the revolution of 1848, for example, he claimed that the citizens in other (that is, politically liberal) states might have the 'right to starve'; by contrast, those in Germany would be cared for because the state would require them to have insurance.[23]

Of course, the idea of 'state socialism' that shaped administrators' views about social insurance was neither an invention of Bismarck's nor of the Ministry of Trade's. It was an ingrained component of a broader public debate in Germany about social welfare. Ideas about 'state socialism' had their roots in the writings of the economist Johann Gottlieb Fichte, as well as those of

[20] Otto v. Bismarck, 'Introductory statement' for the proposal of a law for the insurance of workers occupied in mines, factories and other firms against accidents occurring at the firm, January 13, 1881, *DDB* 1881/2, No. 6, pp. 14–50, at p. 19. *SBDR* 2 May 1884, p. 481; *SBDR* 2 May 1884, p. 481.
[21] See Hans-Ulrich Wehler, *Deutsche Gesellschaftsgeschichte*, vol. III: *Von der deutschen Doppelrevolution bis zum Beginn des Ersten Weltkrieges, 1849–1914* (Munich, 1995), p. 803.
[22] *SBDR* 9 January 1882, pp. 485ff.
[23] *SBDR* 2 April 1881, vol. 62, 712; 15 March 1884, vol. 75, 87–8. See also: 4 April 1881, vol. 62, 743, 739; *DDB* 1881/2, no. 6: 'Begründung' of the 'Proposal of a law for the insurance of workers occupied in mines, factories and other firms against accidents occurring in the firm', pp. 14–50, at p. 14. A full examination of his turn to 'state socialism': Pflanze, *Bismarck*, pp. 399–434.

Johann Karl Rodbertus-Jagetzow, a Pomeranian land baron who sought to integrate conservative and radical thinking in order to address what he saw as the travesty of his era: the treatment of the working classes. Rodbertus was not alone in his writings on state socialism. He was in contact with Ferdinand Lassalle, a radical socialist whose ideas about the role of the state also influenced Bismarck.[24] The central question for German political and legal theorists of the mid nineteenth century was the role of the state in society: would the German states continue with aristocratic rule, governed by patronage and paternalism, or develop into constitutional states (*Rechtsstaaten*) where the rule of law determined all relations? If traditional, aristocratic forms of rule were to subside, how would the modern constitutional state address social problems that had been dealt with previously by paternalistic rulers? And would Germany's citizens – who gained universal manhood suffrage in 1871 – now be responsible for handling their own lives, and their own risks? Discussions about 'state socialism' sat squarely within these more generalised concerns about the role of the modern state in Germany. By the 1870s and 1880s, the concept was relatively widespread, and it drove debates within parliament and the wider public political sphere. It was so contentious that it even split members of the Association for Social Policy, such as Lujo Brentano and Adolph Wagner, who were divided over whether and how the state should intervene in addressing social problems such as accidents at work.[25]

When the government set forth its four legislative proposals on accident insurance between 1881 and 1884, questions about the role of the state in addressing social problems became politically explosive. In parliament, left-liberals tendentiously linked the concept of 'state socialism' with the doctrines of the French socialist left. Its association with Lassalle, the Silesian Jewish radical with a French surname, made the idea appear all the more inappropriate. By contrast, National Liberals and conservatives adopted Bismarck's stance on compulsory insurance, underscoring the difference between their 'state socialist' strategy and foreign models of minimalist government.[26] Even many Social Democrats agreed, condemning the 'night watchman state' associated with left-liberals and the so-called '*Manchesterthum*' in Germany's parliament.[27] The divide over the issue roughly mirrored the fault lines of national politics at the time: liberals had been largely sidelined since the late 1870s, when

[24] Jonathan Steinberg, *Bismarck: a life* (Oxford, 2011), pp. 199–206.
[25] Walter Euchner et al., *Geschichte der sozialen Ideen in Deutschland: Sozialismus, Katholische Soziallehre, Protestantische Sozialethik: ein Handbuch* (2nd edn, Wiesbaden, 2005), pp. 55–64, 211–13; Erik Grimmer-Solem, *The rise of historical economics and social reform in Germany, 1864–1894* (Oxford, 2003), pp. 189–203.
[26] *SBDR* 15 March 1884, vol. 75, 73; 2 April 1881, vol. 62, 712; 31 May 1881, vol. 63, 1446. For similar arguments, see 1 April 1881, vol. 62, 681, 685; 2 April 1881, vol. 62, 712, 716; 4 April 1881, vol. 62, 743; 31 May 1881, vol. 63, 1446; 15 March 1884, vol. 75, 74–5; 2 May 1884, vol. 75, 481.
[27] *SBDR* 31 May 1881, vol. 63, 1453, 1455.

Germany, following Bismarck's lead, took a decided shift towards the centre-right in terms of domestic politics and international trade.[28] In this context, proponents of both free trade and free association were pejoratively termed the *Manchesterthum*, or the Manchester School. The epithet evoked the grim textile mills of the northern English city, which seemed not only a hallmark of capitalism gone wrong but also thoroughly un-German. Conservative advocates of social insurance went further, claiming that members of the *Manchesterthum* were akin to the 'Nihilists in Russia', 'the Social Democrats in Germany' and the 'Communists in France'.[29] They stood as the 'arch-enemies of Christianity' because 'Jewish Manchester efforts' would always 'translate into gold' any 'social goods' which the proponents of state intervention sought.[30]

Outside the political realm, the government's proposals were equally divisive. To be sure, commentators cited concerns about the philosophy of 'state socialism'. The Chamber of Commerce of Bielefeld, for example, tore apart the government's plan for compulsory insurance, declaring it a token of 'socialism'. The association between social insurance and socialism provided a particularly potent device to reject the government's proposals – especially in light of widespread contemporary anxieties about the rise of socialism as a political force in Germany.[31] From the 1860s, German socialists had been split in two camps: Lassallians, who sought reform under the auspices of the state, and followers of Karl Marx, who sought radical social transformation. In 1875, the competing strands merged into a united front, and the newly formed Social Democratic Party managed to win 12 seats in parliament just two years later. Socialism increasingly appeared a credible threat. A series of bungled assassination attempts on the Emperor towards the end of the decade provided the ideal opportunity to side-line the party for inciting political radicalism. As a consequence, the SPD was effectively outlawed between 1878 until 1890.

In this context, 'state socialism' offered the ideal counterpart to political socialism, mapping out a means to address occupational risk without casting off capitalism or overturning the political system. The government in Berlin sought allies in its quest to mandate insurance for workplace accidents and consulted on the matter with an advisory committee of land owners, industrialists and workers, as well as regional governments. It was these groups, as well as a variety of social-reform organisations, who supported the government's proposed plan of 'state socialism' based on compulsory insurance. They all recognised what a factory-owner on the advisory committee claimed: 'self-help',

---

[28] A brief overview of this shift: Edgar Feuchtwanger, *Bismarck* (London, 2002), pp. 200–11.

[29] *SBDR* 31 May 1881, vol. 63, 1453.

[30] *SBDR* 28 April 1883, vol. 70, 2190; 15 January 1885, vol. 79, 627; see also: *SBDR* 31 May 1881, vol. 63, 1453.

[31] BArch: R1501: 100394: 5–10: Petition from the Chamber of Commerce of Bielefeld to the Bundesrat and Reichstag, 1 March 1881.

in practice, did not really work.[32] The concept seemed a relic of the economic liberalism that had triumphed in Germany in the first half of the nineteenth century, when workers gained new freedoms: to migrate, to consent to contracts, even to marry. The shadowside of this sea change had by now become apparent: workers were not always free to help themselves. Many workers could not afford the financial burden of buying accident insurance or contributing to mutual aid funds. Nor were they in a position to consent to all aspects of their jobs. In the eyes of many contemporaries, it was this decisive rejection of 'self-help' that would need to define Germany's response to occupational risk. By rejecting 'self-help', German commentators also distanced themselves from the economic liberalism associated with Britain. The concept itself was a British import that had gained currency following the translation of Samuel Smiles' eponymous volume.[33]

The government latched onto the idea that 'state socialism', in the form of compulsory accident insurance, was a uniquely German method for addressing occupational risk. Nonetheless, by 1884, the year that Germany enacted its first law on accident insurance, Tonio Bödiker, the head of the new Imperial Insurance Office, argued that the global rise of accident insurance laws was 'inexorable'. In a government publication aimed at a domestic audience, he outlined stages of progress towards solving the problem of workplace accidents. Different countries were placed at each stage. While Germany and Austria were the most advanced because they had chosen what he identified as 'models' of compulsory insurance, Italy trailed slightly behind and Britain and Switzerland followed next. He implied that each country was in the midst of a race for social policy, and it was only the 'cultured states' that would come out on top. Eleven years later, Bödiker again emphasised this view in another official pamphlet on social insurance. He now argued that 'workers' insurance will take its successful course around the world, just like steam power and electricity'. The development of social insurance (as opposed to liability law or commercial insurance) was intimately linked to understandings of progress in technology, statecraft and social values. For Bödiker, as for other German administrators, social insurance 'form[ed] an integrative part of the cultural progress (*Kulturfortschritt*) of mankind'.[34] Its rise was seen to be as natural

---

[32] BArch: R1501: 100379: 58: Minutes of the *Volkswirthschaftsrath*, 29 January 1881: statement of Mr Kalle-Biebrich; BArch: R1501: 100394: 99: 100–3: *Concordia* (*Verein zur Förderung des Wohles der Arbeiter*) to Bismarck, 15 April 1881; BArch: R1501: 100401: 132–3: State Ministry of Bavaria to the Ministry of the Interior, 16 February 1884; 134–9: State Ministry of Württemberg to Ministry of the Interior, 30 January 1884; BArch: R1501: 400: 88: Royal Legation in Dresden to Bismarck, 22 March 1881.

[33] The first German translation appeared more than a decade before these debates: Samuel Smiles, *Die Selbsthülfe in Lebensbildern und Charakterzügen*, trans. Josef M. Boyes (Hamburg, 1866).

[34] Tonio Bödiker, *Die Unfallgesetzgebung der europäischen Staaten* (Leipzig, 1884), pp. 1–4; Tonio Bödiker, *Die Arbeiterversicherung in den europäischen Staaten* (Leipzig, 1895), pp. iii–iv. See also 'Office report of the Imperial Commissioner', repr. in Georg Zacher, ed., *Die*

and inevitable as the increase in workplace accidents following industrialisation. 'State socialism', characterised by social insurance, was simply part of this process of modernisation, and its origins mirrored the gradual reformulation of risk as an unavoidable aspect of working life.

PRACTICABLE POLICY

Many observers of Germany's legislative experiment also touted the view that social insurance signified modernity, and they frequently pointed to the German system as an example of how to address the 'accident problem'.[35] In Britain, Germany's compulsory, state-organised and completely non-commercial accident insurance proved an ideal point of comparison in the years leading up to the Workmen's Compensation Act in 1897. The policy appeared entirely novel and unlike anything in Britain.[36] Ultimately, however, it seemed too radical, too difficult to implement and potentially too illiberal. Civil servants in Whitehall agreed that workplace accidents must be addressed with more effective legislation, and they saw that the state should provide a basic framework for redistributing occupational risk from workers to employers. However, 'state socialism' had no place in Britain. Instead, workplace accidents were seen as an essentially commercial issue; they were a trade-off that stemmed from commerce – from labour that undergirded the market – and should be absorbed by commerce. The only suitable response to the problem would be one that allowed for a great degree of continuity with previous practices, and a minimal role for the state. In Britain, the concept of occupational risk had given rise to a new type of political and moral subject. It not only relieved workers from the burden of proving that they were not to blame for injuries from work. It also granted employers a new responsibility, impelling them as wardens of their workplaces to *choose* how to deal with the consequences of accidents.

Years of observing German accident insurance – and the responses of the British public to it – had led to this conclusion. The Home Office had first commissioned a report from the ambassador in Berlin in 1880 on German liability law, which was followed in subsequent years with accounts on accident insurance and general labour questions in Germany.[37] By 1894, the Foreign Office

---

Arbeiter-Versicherung im Auslande, vol. XIX: *Gesammelte Aufsätze über die Arbeiterversicherung im In- und Auslande* (Berlin, 1908), p. 144.

[35] Daniel T. Rodgers, *Atlantic crossings: social politics in a progressive age* (Cambridge, MA, 1998); Gustavo Gozzi, *Modelli politici e questione sociale in Italia e in Germania fra Otto e Novecento* (Bologna, 1988), pp. 105–8, 111–23; Hennock, *British social reform*.

[36] For example: William Harbutt Dawson, *Social insurance in Germany 1883–1911: its history, operation, results and a comparison with the National Insurance Act, 1911* (London, 1912); William Harbutt Dawson, *Bismarck and state socialism: an exposition of the social and economic legislation of Germany since 1870* (London, 1890).

[37] *PP* 1880 (C 2607) LIX.233: 'Reports on Laws in France and Germany with regard to Insurance of Persons Employed in Mines, and Legal Liability of Employers'; *PP* 1886 (C

commissioned another update, and Percy Wyndham at the embassy in Berlin wrote persuasively about the merits of the German system. He argued that it had brought 'but little increase' to the 'price of the manufactured article' and was an overall success.[38] Civil servants from various branches of government came to similar conclusions: mandating employers to provide accident insurance would not harm the economy. Germany's seemingly meteoric economic success in the latter part of the nineteenth century only served as testament to this point. By 1913, Germany had risen from an industrial backwater to the second greatest economic power in the world, responsible for 13 per cent of world trade alone (just behind Britain's 15 per cent).[39]

However, Wyndham was not just convinced of the merits of requiring employers to provide accident insurance to offset the costs of workplace accidents. Instead, he saw the virtues in a state-run system of social insurance, and he was not alone in this thinking. The International Congress on Accidents and Social Insurance passed a resolution in 1891 in support of the policy.[40] Both the Superintending Inspector of Factories at the Home Office and the Head of the Commercial Department of the Board of Trade had attended the conference and agreed with the resolution. Meanwhile, in parliament, the Liberal Unionist MP Joseph Chamberlain latched onto Germany's state-run system of accident insurance as a model for Britain. Having owned screw- and wire-making factories and having served as mayor of the rapidly industrialising Birmingham, Chamberlain was aware of the pitfalls of industry and saw that attempting to pin liability for workplace accidents on employers would be illogical. Accidents stemmed from occupational risk, and employers could be held no more accountable than workers. Insurance would be the only way out of this quagmire of blame.[41]

In part, it was public anxiety about Britain's status as a late-comer to social insurance – rather than concerns about workplace risk – that provoked so much debate about adopting a policy on accident insurance. This outcry emerged as part of a more widespread fear that Britain was falling behind Germany economically, which was most clearly typified by E. E. Williams' 1896 publication *Made in Germany*. It also foreshadowed the eugenicist tone of the

4784) LXVII.571: 'Reports by Her Majesty's Representatives Abroad'; Foreign Office, *Report on the present state of the labour question in Germany* (London, 1891).

[38] Foreign Office, *Report on the question of employers' liability in Germany* (London, 1894), pp. 13–14.

[39] See Toni Pierenkemper and Richard Tilly, *The German economy in the nineteenth century* (Oxford and New York, 2004), p. 149.

[40] 'International congress on accidents to workmen', *The Times* (29 September 1891); see also: 'Politics for the people: an interview with John Gorst', *Help* 1/2 (1891).

[41] 4 *Hansard* HC vol. 8 (20 February 1893), cols. 1961–4. See Travis L. Crosby, *Joseph Chamberlain: a most radical imperialist* (London, 2011), pp. 8–10, 104; W. C. Mallalieu, 'Joseph Chamberlain and workmen's compensation', *Journal of Economic History* 10 (1950), pp. 45–57.

debates about 'national efficiency' that erupted in the wake of the Boer War of 1899–1902.[42] For example, the same year that Williams' tract was published, the British Medical Association decried that the 'Anglo-Saxon' race was miles behind its 'Teutonic' counterpart in terms of social legislation. The following year, the *Daily Chronicle* noted that 'even the most backward legislatures in Europe' were addressing the accident problem.[43] It seemed that Britain was losing out, and the implications might imperil the 'race', perhaps leading to swathes of injured workers and a consequent decline in production. Germany's economic success, despite the financial burden of social insurance, seemed to indicate that the policy could contribute to a healthier and wealthier population. In any case, it seemed that social insurance was simply something that states did. If even the 'most backward legislatures in Europe' had introduced the policy, why had Britain, the 'workshop of the world', failed to follow suit? What Britain was considering, a workmen's compensation bill, was a sign of Albion's degeneration. As the *Morning Post* put it, the policy was merely the 'crippled offspring of the continental legislation'.[44]

There was just as much public anxiety about following Germany down the path of social insurance. Many workers opposed the policy for the same reason they objected to the use of insurance in opt-out clauses under British liability law: insurance for all accidents, whatever their cause, could destroy any incentive for employers to institute costly safety provisions. Moreover, insurance encouraged recklessness amongst employers and workers alike. As the Women's Trade Union League noted, the German system proved that accident rates only *rose* after the law was introduced. Not least, employers could use the system as a means to swindle workers by reducing wages to pay premiums. In effect, it was workers in Germany who were paying for their own compensation – while suffering more accidents in the bargain. The prospect of losing wages to insurance payments was a particular concern for women workers, noted the League, because they were often low earners and nonunionised, making them particularly vulnerable. The group nonetheless recognised that some form of social provision for accidents must be introduced in Britain, even if the German 'scheme' was unattractive. The risk of workplace accidents was inevitable, and finding fault on the part of workers, supervisors or employers was often impossible: 'it is obvious that a state of things in which the great

---

[42] E. E. Williams, *Made in Germany* (London, 1896). See also Paul M. Kennedy, *The rise of the Anglo-German antagonism 1860–1914* (London, 1982); Geoffrey R. Searle, *The quest for national efficiency: a study in British politics and political thought, 1899–1914* (Oxford, 1971), ch. 3.

[43] 'The welfare of the worker', *British Medical Journal* 2 (26 December 1896), pp. 1839–40; TNA: HO 45/9867/B1381H: unnumbered booklet: *The workers' tragedy: an account of the law of employers' liability in England and of the working of the universal insurance system in Germany*, by the Special Commissioner of the the the *Daily Chronicle*, reprinted in the *Daily Chronicle* in 1897, at p. 15.

[44] 'Compensation to workmen', *Morning Post* (26 May 1897), p. 4.

proportion of accidents go uncompensated because no one is responsible is doomed'. Even if social insurance was unappealing, it was clear that 'the death or disablement of the worker at his work is a matter the responsibility for which must be placed on his employer's shoulders'.[45]

The fact that social insurance was associated with Germany made it all the more contentious to workers in Britain. Many, such as Henry Broadhurst, a former stone mason and Nottingham Lib-Lab MP, feared that the 'German model' might be introduced as an attempt to tame the British working classes. The allegation echoed claims of German socialists about Bismarck's programme.[46] These fears came at a time when the British labour movement was strengthening in numbers and political consciousness. The late 1880s witnessed a wave of strikes under the militant New Unionism that had opened trade unions to workers beyond those employed in the traditional crafts or elite trades such as mining and engineering. For example, 1888 saw the match girls at Bryant and May go on a highly publicised strike for safer working conditions, while 100,000 dock workers went on strike the following year for higher wages.[47] Britain saw the rise of the Independent Labour Party shortly afterwards, in 1893. In this context, arguments about the potentially repressive nature of German social insurance were particularly resonant. Other working-class groups rejected the idea of compulsion because they prioritised voluntary solutions in principle. Foreshadowing the backlash against National Insurance in the early years of the twentieth century, advocates of friendly societies invoked a trope of respectability, based on 'self-reliance' and 'manfulness' as particularly 'English' characteristics that a German-style compulsory insurance scheme would tarnish.[48] The *Daily News* helped synthesise these views when it sent out a questionnaire on compulsory insurance to the heads of trade unions. The majority argued that safety should be prioritised, yet it could not be ensured by requiring employers to buy insurance. Moreover, compulsory insurance for workplace accidents would 'injure' the trade unions by removing them from a key aspect of industrial relations. The survey concluded that most unionists were against a 'German-style compulsory insurance scheme'.[49] Nonetheless, many workers saw the value of amending the existing system of

[45] 'Employers' liability or workmen's insurance?', *Women's Trade Union Review* (1 January 1897), p. 5.

[46] 3 *Hansard* HC vol. 331 (7 December 1888), col. 1430.

[47] Louise Raw, *Striking a light: the Bryant and May match women and their place in history* (London, 2009), pp. 159–67.

[48] 'Compensation for accidents', *Oddfellows Magazine* 29/277 (January 1898), pp. 11–12, at p. 11. See Pat Thane, 'The working class and state "welfare" in Britain, 1880–1914', *Historical Journal* 27/4 (1984), pp. 877–900; Timothy Alborn, 'Senses of belonging: the politics of working-class insurance in Britain, 1880–1914', *Journal of Modern History* 73/3 (2001), pp. 561–602.

[49] 'Labour's death roll: employers' liability versus insurance: a trades union plebiscite: what the leaders of a million workmen say', *Daily News* (8 February 1897).

liability law, and some, such as the Labour MP and engineer John Burns, even admitted that mutual insurance could lower accident rates.[50]

These debates about the German policy, along with more pragmatic worries such as requiring small-scale employers to pay for insurance, shaped British legislative proposals on workplace accidents. As Home Secretary under the Liberal government, H. H. Asquith proposed a 'strict' liability law in 1893. The proposal reflected ambivalence under Gladstonian liberalism towards the role of the state in everyday life. A new law on compensation should be enacted, Asquith argued, but only 'if it were possible and *practicable* to do so'. He called for amending liability law by getting rid of the doctrine of 'common employment' which prevented workers from claiming compensation when accidents had involved co-workers rather than employers or supervisors. According to Richard Haldane, Asquith's colleague in the Liberal Party, the maxim had created a 'fictitious … distinction' that only served to harm workers. The artificial nature of the doctrine justified legislative action as a means to undo it. For Liberals like Haldane and Asquith, governmental intervention was warranted in cases such as this, when harms emerged from human tampering with the natural order of economic and social life. On the same ground, Asquith argued against allowing employers to 'contract out' of a new liability law by purchasing insurance or signing up for a mutual scheme. Echoing his Oxford mentor T. H. Green, he claimed that the doctrine of freedom of contract had created a pretence about the equal position of employers and workers in making agreements.[51]

For Asquith, a barrister by training, workplace accidents were a matter of tort law, not social policy. In his view, therefore, a policy on compensation should seek to provide workers with some form of 'solatium' for accidents. It is significant that he referred to the legal concept that guided common-law reasoning about compensation. This thinking highlighted his main concern: compensation as a means to mollify injured workers, but also as an incentive for employers to make their workplaces safer. In this sense, a strict liability law could encourage smooth industrial relations without significantly involving the state. He was not concerned to redistribute occupational risk to employers. Instead, he sought to let the court system continue to balance arguments about fault and responsibility. His proposal for a strict liability law would have shifted the burden of proof for accidents to employers, denoting the broad consensus by the 1890s that accidents usually derived from the process of work *and not* the negligence of workers. The bill acknowledged that workers did not consent to the risk of accidents related to their jobs. It did not, however, cast off

[50] Robert Asher, 'Experience counts: British workers, accident prevention and compensation, and the origins of the welfare state', *Journal of Policy History* 15 (2003), pp. 359–88, at p. 364.
[51] 4 *Hansard* HC vol. 48 (3 May 1897), cols. 1434ff.; Green, 'Lecture on liberal legislation', p. 373.

the cycle of blame at the root of the earlier era of liberal risk.[52] The Workmen's Compensation Act of 1897 contrasted with the principles of Asquith's failed proposal because it assumed that accidents were not preventable. Working through the court system and attributing blame to employers would not, therefore, make sense. In this respect, workmen's compensation echoed the ideas about agency, causation and the nature of modern industry that underpinned Germany's accident insurance policy.

The British and German laws differed, however, on the question of how the state would govern occupational risk. Since the 1870s, an 'idealist' philosophy about the organic relationship between state and society had flourished in various circles throughout Britain, from Balliol College in Oxford, where Green had embraced neo-Kantian thinking, to the meetings of the Fabian Society and the Charity Organisation Society. Idealist thought about social problems varied greatly, with some of its advocates calling for public policy, while others appealed to members of civil society to work together, for example, through philanthropic measures such as the growing settlement movement that sought to combat urban poverty. From an idealist perspective, social problems were to be solved by bringing *communities* together, whether through civic associations or legislation, in a form of romantic organicism.[53]

Although various civil servants like Asquith had been influenced by idealist thinking, they were driven by utilitarian and legal concerns when it came to legislating on workplace accidents. Benthamite utilitarianism had infused the British bureaucracy since the 1830s, and its influence continued into the late nineteenth century.[54] From this perspective, introducing a state-run insurance scheme like that in Germany was out of the question because it would be too radical a break with existing structures and practices. Even Chamberlain, who had initially come out as a supporter of Germany's social insurance, came to reject the idea. Now a member of Salisbury's Conservative government, which had taken up a policy of 'practical social reform', he argued that a German-style system of social insurance would be 'objectionable to English people'.[55] It went too far in addressing what was essentially a legal and technical issue

---

[52] V. Markham Lester, 'The employers' liability/workmen's compensation debate of the 1890s revisited', *Historical Journal* 44 (2001), pp. 471–95.

[53] Stefan Collini, 'Hobhouse, Bosanquet and the state: philosophical idealism and political argument in England, 1880–1918', *Past and Present* (1976), pp. 86–111; Jose Harris, 'Political thought and the welfare state, 1870–1930: an intellectual framework for British social policy', *Past and Present* (1992), pp. 116–41; Sandra den Otter, 'Thinking in communities: late nineteenth-century liberals, idealists and the retrieval of community', *Parliamentary History* 16/1 (1997), pp. 67–84; Mark Bevir, *The making of British socialism* (Princeton, NJ, 2011), pp. 336, 225–7.

[54] Thomas Osborne, 'Bureaucracy as a vocation: governmentality and administration in nineteenth-century Britain', *Journal of Historical Sociology* 7 (2006), pp. 289–313.

[55] 4 Hansard HC vol. 48 (3 May 1897), col. 1467; E. H. H. Green, *The crisis of conservatism: the politics, economics and ideology of the British Conservative Party, 1880–1914* (London, 1995), pp. 128ff.

within the common law. As Colonial Secretary, he helped provide the Home Office with alternative policy models, collecting reports on liability systems throughout the empire, from Australia to Canada, in 1896. Chamberlain, like many observers in Britain at the time, recognised that colonial practices might be more meaningful for Britain. British colonies shared the same common law legal heritage, meaning that the problem with workplace accidents could be solved in similar ways throughout the empire.[56] The white-settler colonies, Australia, New Zealand, Canada and South Africa, also seemed to resemble Britain culturally and administratively, which led civil servants to examine colonial social policy time and time again from the 1880s.[57]

The Workmen's Compensation Act of 1897 reflected these concerns about British particularity: its common law, heritage of classical liberalism and tradition of friendly societies and other voluntarist arrangements that could provide care for the injured and their families. The policy was predicated on the maxim of occupational risk: neither workers nor employers could be held accountable for accidents because they stemmed from the process of work. The cycle of blame and accountability inherent in the common law and in Britain's later liability law had been broken. In its place, a new understanding of responsibility had emerged: employers, as both the beneficiaries and nominal overseers of a workplace, were now compelled to manage occupational risk by buying commercial insurance coverage or paying compensation out of pocket. The only role for the state in this arrangement was dictating that employers must compensate their workers. In this respect, the policy allowed for a great deal of continuity with the 1880 Employers' Liability Act, which had permitted employers to 'contract out' of it by purchasing insurance.

In fact, the old employers' liability law continued to operate side by side with the 1897 Workmen's Compensation Act. Just as the new system had endowed employers with a choice about how to pay compensation, it granted workers a decision. They could now choose which policy to invoke when making a compensation claim. By contrast, in Germany, the introduction of social insurance meant that workers were no longer allowed to claim compensation under liability law. While the Workmen's Compensation Act guaranteed a limited amount of remuneration, a successful case made under the liability law could be much more lucrative. To be sure, the continued operation of the Employers' Liability Act in Britain, which granted workers compensation if employers were found at fault for accidents, was seen as an incentive for employers to improve safety measures. However, its continued operation pointed to the view that accidents were a legal matter with roots in common law. In the opinion of civil servants, workmen's compensation was a 'practicable' solution to the

---

[56] TNA: HO 45/9867/B13816H: unnumbered: R. D. to Kenelm Digby, 13 August 1896; TNA: HO 45/9867/B13816H: unnumbered: Edward Wingfield to Kenelm Digby, 13 August 1896.

[57] Edmund Rogers, '"A most imperial contribution": New Zealand and the old age pensions debate in Britain, 1882–1912', *Journal of Global History* 9/2 (2014), pp. 189–207.

defects of common law and its offspring tort. In contrast to Germany, the radicalism of 'state socialism' had no place in Britain when it came to workplace accidents.[58]

SOCIAL PEACE

In Italy, civil servants vacillated for years about introducing a compensation law for workplace accidents because they were divided over what the policy would mean for relations between the state and citizens. Upon national unification in 1859, the peninsula's varied landscape of vast agricultural expanses and ancient city states was centralised through a new administration based in Turin and, later, Rome. Under the conservative and royalist governments of the Historical Right under Camillo Benso di Cavour, Italy rapidly embarked on a process of state building by laying down railway networks and establishing a national postal service, knitting together its polity while aiming to foster economic growth.[59] Despite these early efforts, the country remained predominantly rural. By the late 1870s, civil servants in the new government of the Historical Left were keen to develop the national economy further, and they looked to Britain as a model that Italy could emulate. Anglophilia gripped many liberal politicians and economists throughout the peninsula and served as a background to social reform efforts, which aimed to balance anxieties about maintaining 'social peace', in the words of contemporaries, with the desire to modernise the country. In this context, even those who aspired to a greater degree of governmental intervention conceded that the state could best supply a framework for independent action.[60] It was with this version of liberalism in mind that Luigi Luzzatti, a member of the Chamber of Deputies and a former Under-Secretary of State at the Ministry of Agriculture, suggested establishing a voluntary National Accident Insurance Fund, which was founded in 1883. A lawyer and political economist by training, he had long been involved in efforts that encouraged workers to save, having founded the People's Bank of Milan several years earlier. For Luzzatti, a voluntary fund for accident insurance would encourage individuals to sort out compensation on their own – without further governmental involvement. In his view, requiring employers or workers to take out insurance was unnecessary.[61]

[58] Although the concept found many advocates in Britain during this period, most notably amongst the Webbs. See Bevir, *The making of British socialism*, pp. 173–94.

[59] Albert Schram, *Railways and the formation of the Italian state* (Cambridge, 1997), pp. 22–62; Gabriella Romani, ed., *Postal culture: reading and writing letters in post-unification Italy* (Toronto, 2013), pp. 4–5.

[60] Volker Sellin, *Die Anfänge staatlicher Sozialreform im liberalen Italien* (Stuttgart, 1971), ch. 1; Susan A. Ashley, *Making liberalism work: the Italian experience, 1860–1914* (Westport, CT, 2003), pp. 22–7.

[61] Luigi Luzzatti, *Memorie autobiographiche e carteggi*, ed. Elena Carli (3 vols., Bologna, 1931–66), vol. II, p. 190.

Luzzatti's proposal came at a time when Germany was well underway with the legislative process towards an accident insurance law, and he attempted to tap more widespread worries about moving towards a seemingly authoritarian, German style of state. By creating a National Accident Insurance Fund and encouraging citizens to take up insurance voluntarily, he argued that Italy could 'be spared the cyclopean proposals for compulsory insurance for sickness, accidents and the disability of old age, which, in Germany, have tried to solve social problems with the same method of blind military discipline with which a powerful standing army would be organised'.[62] Luzzatti's dismissal of the German approach to accident compensation was part of an entrenched debate about the purpose of the state that had raged in Italian legal, political and economic communities since the 1870s.[63] The moderate conservative lawyer Antonio Salandra was amongst Luzzatti's sparring partners in these debates. Nonetheless, echoing critics in Britain and across the border in France,[64] he agreed that German accident insurance was a product of 'state socialism' of the worst kind. For Salandra, compulsory accident insurance served as an example that 'the best of foreign scientific production is not always diffused'; rather, 'imports [are like] a vogue that favours certain doctrines, certain writers, certain countries'.[65] According to this thinking, it would be best for Italy to avoid modish forms of governance and continue its liberal course.

Salandra's critique was particularly poignant in the context of newly unified Italy. The government was at pains to establish legitimacy throughout the peninsula from its centre in Rome amidst demands for greater local and regional autonomy, which often resulted in the complete neglect of edicts from the centre.[66] At the same time, it was attempting to wrest control of charitable spending, bringing the state into direct conflict with the Catholic Church.[67] In this context, accident insurance became another means through which the state could gain authority, despite – or perhaps because of – its status as a relative latecomer to industrialisation. Under Domenico Berti, a leading figure on the left in Piedmont, the Ministry of Agriculture began considering an insurance law already in the early 1880s. It would have placed responsibility for the consequences of workplace accidents squarely on the shoulders of employers.

---

[62] Luigi Luzzatti, 'La Cassa nazionale di assicurazione per gli infortuni degli operai sul lavoro', *Nuova antologia* (3rd series) 21 (May 1889), pp. 312ff, at p. 328.

[63] Sellin, *Die Anfänge staatlicher Sozialreform*, ch. 1.

[64] Allan Mitchell, *The divided path: the German influence on social reform in France after 1870* (Chapel Hill, NC, 1991), pp. 14–15, 310.

[65] Antonio Salandra, 'Un caso del socialismo di stato: lo stato assicuratore', *Nuova antologia* (2nd series) 27 (1 June 1881), pp. 444–79, at p. 445.

[66] Raffaele Romanelli, *Il comando impossibile: stato e società nell'Italia liberale* (1988; Bologna, 1995), pp. 33–78; Lucy Riall, 'Elites in search of authority: political power and social order in nineteenth-century Sicily', *History Workshop Journal* 55 (2003), pp. 25–46.

[67] Maria Sophia Quine, *Italy's social revolution: charity and welfare from liberalism to fascism* (Basingstoke, 2002), pp. 43–63.

As custodians of workplaces, they seemed liable, at least financially and perhaps also morally, for bearing the cost of unavoidable occupational risks. By contrast, Luzzatti's voluntary scheme, which allowed employers and workers to pay jointly for insurance, failed to take a stand on questions of risk and blame, and it kept the state on the sidelines by leaving workplace accidents a matter for the courts rather than social policy. Although he was responsible for inaugurating the National Accident Insurance Fund, Berti saw it as a stopgap measure before introducing some form of social insurance.[68] His successor Bernardino Grimaldi went a step further. In his failed proposal for a liability law, he included a clause indemnifying employers if they purchased accident cover.[69] Like Berti, Grimaldi was a progressive who endorsed the expansion of state competences. In fact, he oversaw the extensive growth of the Italian rail network in the latter part of the century.

In this way, accident insurance became yet another battleground in *trasformismo* politics, in which a delicate political compromise was forged in parliament and government alike by folding conservatives into the progressive camp headed by Prime Minister Agostino Depretis in order to form a centrist coalition. The strategy eventually became synonymous with Giovanni Giolitti's social legislation at the turn of the century. In this context, the German and Austrian models of compulsory insurance provided powerful political arguments. Germany's accident insurance was reprehensible in the eyes of those like Luzzatti who advocated left-liberalism and its ostensible hallmarks of a small state and thriving civil society.[70] However, his colleagues at the Ministry of Agriculture took a different view. In 1884, the Ministry commissioned Ugo Mazzola, an insurance expert, to write a report about German social insurance.[71] Mazzola focused on the compulsory aspect of the policy, reflecting on the philosophy that underpinned the German system. In Mazzola's eyes, the German legislation drew on Emanuel Hermann's 'theory of insurance from an economic point of view'. From this perspective, insurance was a sort of 'game of chance' meant to 'eliminate the unfavourable case by means of the redistribution of risk'. It was a desirable solution to the accident problem because it would cost less than focusing on prevention: accident rates could be calculated, and appropriate premiums could be raised on a regular basis, making insurance

[68] A. P. Cam., Doc., Leg. XV, Sess. 1, Nr. 74 (19 February 1883): 'Cassa nazionale di assicurazione per gli operai contro gli infortuni sul lavoro (Berti, ministro di Agricoltura)', p. 3.

[69] A. P. Cam., Disc., Leg. XV, Sess. 1., p. 13819 (15 June 1885); A. P. Sen., Doc., Leg. XV, Sess. 1, Nr. 209 (17 June 1885).

[70] Luigi Luzzatti, 'Le rivelazione della previdenza all'Esposizione nazionale di Milano, II', *Nuova antologia* (2nd series) 30 (November 1881), pp. 203ff., at pp. 208ff.; Ulisse Gobbi, 'I provvedimenti per gli infortuni sul lavoro', *Giornale degli economisti* 5/1–2 (1890), pp. 3–28, at p. 27.

[71] Germany's influence on Italian social policy would later extend to debates about old-age and disability pensions: Enrico Gustapane, 'L'influenza tedesca sull'istituzione in Italia della Cassa di previdenza per l'invalidità e per la vecchiaia degli operai', *Jahrbuch für europäische Verwaltungsgeschichte* 5 (1993), pp. 179–214.

a cautious policy that could take advantage of known probabilities.[72] For Italy, its allure was obvious: insurance could allow factories and other workplaces to take off with ease, without installing preventive devices that were not only expensive but could hinder productivity.

Before drawing a conclusion, Mazzola also considered the political philosophy of Lujo Brentano and Rudolf Gneist, who advocated non-state solutions to social problems. Brentano was one of the leading sceptics of compulsory insurance, as he favoured an English style of guild socialism whose features could also be found in the various cooperatives and mutual associations (*Genossenschaften*) across Germany. The cooperative movement appealed to those like Luzzatti who sought a voluntary arrangement for addressing occupational risk. On closer inspection, however, German *Genossenschaften* emphasised solidarism, thereby retaining an element of compulsion that placed the interests of individuals beneath those of the community. Similarly, in his important work on English administrative law, Gneist advocated self-government, which would, for example, enable citizens to choose whether to have insurance at all. The implication was a liberal form of responsibilisation, whereby individuals shared in the burdens of their chosen community.[73] Methods drawn from the cooperative movement would therefore allow for the redistribution of occupational risk, yet favoured a non-state framework for social action.

In the end, Mazzola echoed Grimaldi, and indeed Tonio Bödiker, the head of the German Imperial Insurance Office, in declaring that social insurance should be embraced as part of the 'natural development of the state'.[74] Like workplace accidents, social insurance seemed an inevitable part of the process of economic and political modernisation. In reaching this conclusion, he drew on the writings of Adolph Wagner, one of the main advocates of 'state socialism' in Germany, an ally of Bismarck and a proponent of compulsory insurance as a public good. To appease sceptics like Luzzatti, however, Mazzola concluded that there was no need to fear the development of 'state socialism' or even genuine 'socialism' in adopting a system of compulsory insurance in Italy. Despite his positive review of social insurance, the policy was not taken forward for several years. The Ministry of Agriculture had repeatedly attempted and failed to introduce a liability law between 1879 and 1886, and the debate about social insurance subsided briefly with the last of these attempts.

By the late 1880s, the logic of encouraging individuals to buy insurance voluntarily through the National Accident Insurance Fund had eroded. The

---

[72] Ugo Mazzola, *L'assicurazione degli operai nella scienza e nella legislazione germanica: relazione a S. E. il Ministro di agricoltura, industria e commercio*, special issue of *Annali del credito e della previdenza* (1885), pp. 2–3.

[73] Mazzola, *L'assicurazione degli operai*, pp. 3–24. See also: Adolph Wagner, *Der Staat und das Versicherungswesen: socialökonomische und socialrechtliche Studien* (Tübingen, 1881); Lujo Brentano, *Die Arbeiterversicherung gemäss der heutigen Wirthschaftsordnung* (Leipzig, 1879); Rudolf von Gneist, *Das englische Verwaltungsrecht* (Berlin, 1883).

[74] Mazzola, *L'assicurazione degli operai*, pp. 24–5.

returns on membership in the Fund revealed that neither workers nor employers had taken to it in great numbers. In 1884, a year after it was founded, the Fund insured only 443 workers. While this amount increased dramatically in subsequent years – it insured 172,869 workers by 1897 – the number of workers guaranteed compensation through insurance remained noticeably scanty. The small number of workers insured outside the National Fund supported the finding that, without compulsory insurance, Italians were unlikely to insure against or receive compensation for workplace accidents.[75] It seemed to administrators that the liability clauses in the civil code had hardly succeeded in leading employers to buy insurance. In his 1897 governmental report on the matter, the progressive economist Carlo Francesco Ferraris argued that, in order to be 'effective', accident insurance would have to be mandatory.[76] In an earlier report, he also argued that compulsory insurance would have an additional benefit: it would be the best method of compelling employers to use better safety regulations. In his view, the only way to co-opt employers into taking responsibility for occupational risk was through requiring them to purchase insurance. Yet, for Ferraris, as for Mazzola, the main advantage of compulsory insurance was that it provided for foreseeable expenses. The probabilistic aspect of workplace accidents led Ferraris to claim that insurance contained an aspect of 'morality' because it made provisions for a known 'problem'. *Not* adopting an insurance law would be an admission not only of immorality, but also of inept government.[77]

Ferraris wrote his reports in a period when worries about national backwardness shaped considerations about the meaning of social insurance for the nation state. The idea of Italian underdevelopment had troubled intellectuals throughout the peninsula since at least the 1840s during the *Risorgimento*, and it permeated various strains of political and social-scientific thought, sometimes emerging in a racialised notion of degeneration.[78] By the 1880s and 1890s, when government was debating the accident question, the discourse had become so widespread that it helped to trump previous arguments about voluntary solutions to address the consequences of workplace accidents. In the eyes of those like Mazzola and Ferraris, anxieties about national backwardness pointed to the lack of a strong central state in recently unified Italy. In this view, social insurance would not only solve the accident question. It would also establish Italy as a modern country.[79] To members of government, anxieties about backwardness were especially significant because they pointed directly

---

[75] INPS, *La Cassa nazionale di assicurazione per gli infortuni sul lavoro nel suo quarantennio* (Rome, 1923), p. 60.

[76] 'Allegato B' (1897), pp. 205–322, at pp. 215–16.

[77] 'Allegato B: Relazione del professore Carlo Francesco Ferraris intorno all'assicurazione obbligatoria e alla responsabilità dei padroni ed imprenditori per gli infortuni sul lavoro', *Annali del credito e della previdenza* (1889), pp. 238–79, at pp. 248–9, 241–2.

[78] Patriarca, *Italian vices*, pp. 133–61.

[79] For example: A. P. Cam., Doc., Leg. XVI., Sess. 4 (1889–90), Nr. 116, pp. 571–86, at p. 103.

to the failings of the new state, and government within it, in regulating the social sphere. Thus, every legislative proposal that the Ministry of Agriculture put forward on accident insurance pointed to the numerous countries that had already adopted a version of the policy, underscoring the fact that Italy was behind its neighbours, not only in terms of social legislation, but as a state in general.[80] These concerns also led the government to host an international congress on workplace accidents even before adopting a policy on the issue. At the congress, a representative from the Ministry of Agriculture emphasised the general need for state intercession on workplace accidents. Italy therefore appeared particularly advanced in its handling of the problem at a time when government had made no legislative progress with its several bills on the matter.[81]

To be sure, a law on compulsory insurance for workplace accidents was widely opposed in parliament. In the senate, Grimaldi's proposal had encountered intense opposition in 1885, and intellectuals as well as business groups like the Association of Sardinian Mineowners continued to lobby against the policy in subsequent years, either in principle or because it seemed too large an expense to bear.[82] By contrast, socialists, anarchists and republicans saw that the government's proposals from the 1880s, alongside its plans for the reform of the penal code and the protection of women and child workers, did not go far enough. Amidst growing industrial unrest, including uprisings in 1882, 1884 and 1885 across the northern agricultural belt of Emilia Romagna and Lombardy, pushing forward with a policy on accident insurance seemed especially necessary. The cause seemed urgent from 1890, when the leading parties on the extreme left joined together in the *Patto di Roma* and demanded that employers be held accountable for workplace accidents.[83] Two years later, the Socialist Party of Italy was established and continued the lobby for labour rights. Meanwhile, the Pope joined the debate with his encyclical *Rerum novarum*, demanding that 'some opportune remedy must be found quickly for the misery and wretchedness pressing so unjustly on the majority of the working class'. To that end, Leo XIII suggested creating a fund that would care for

---

[80] For example: *A. P. Cam.*, Doc., Sess. 1882–3, Nr. 73; *A. P. Cam.*, Prima Sessione 1885, 'Discurso pronunziato dal ministro di agricoltura, industria e commercio (Grimaldi) nella discussione generale del disegno di legge sulla responsabilità civile dei padroni ed imprenditori per i casi di infortunio degli operai sul lavoro', 18 May 1885, pp. 13781–95.

[81] For example: *Congrès international des accidents du travail et des assurances sociales. Troisième session, Milan, 1–6 octobre 1894*, vol. I: *Rapports présentés par M. M. Asnago … et publiés par les soins du comité italien d'organisation* (Milan, 1894), pp. 8–10.

[82] For example: CdAs: Leg. XX, Sess. 1897–8, Proposte di legge: Bta. 664: Petition from the *Associazione mineraria sarda* to the Chamber of Deputies, 24 February 1898.

[83] Giorgio Candeloro, *Storia dell'Italia moderna*, vol. VI: *Lo sviluppo del capitalismo e del movimento operaio* (8th edn, Turin, 1981), pp. 293–4, 362–3.

workers 'not only in the cases of accident, but also in sickness, old age, and distress'.[84]

By 1898, when parliament finally approved the last of the Ministry of Agriculture's proposals for compulsory accident insurance, anxieties about rising labour unrest were shared widely in government. The recent wave of industrial action, together with the growing success of political socialism, seemed to connect with long-standing concerns about the failings of the Italian state. Following the bloody repression of numerous strikes that year under the conservative Prime Minister Antonio di Rudinì, the liberal ministers in his government rallied around the idea that the state should be socially conscious and reformist. The government's mishandling of the strikes only served to underscore Ferraris' point about administrative ineptitude and the need for a new form of state action. It was this strand of thought that characterised di Rudinì's Minister of Agriculture, Francesco Cocco-Ortu, and other members of the circle around the reformist former and future prime minister Giovanni Giolitti.[85] Under the *trasformismo* politics of the 1890s, their ideas about the role of the state in solving the accident problem were able to guide policy in what remained, at least nominally, a conservative administration.

When Italy introduced a law on accident insurance in 1898, the country had only just begun to industrialise. On the surface, the policy seemed irrelevant in the predominantly rural peninsula. However, members of government were so anxious about administering competently that they proposed the law in any case – even though they had estimated only a limited number of Italians to be at risk. In fact, the law on accident insurance pertained to merely 1,347,501 workers in the 1898–1902 period, while the population numbered just over 32 million.[86] For the Italian government, the ideology of backwardness, together with the linked goals of creating a strong central state and fostering economic growth, were the primary factors in adopting the policy. Ultimately, administrators' anxieties about these issues not only contributed to the adoption of the new law. They also paved the way for the fall of the old, Anglophile version of Italian liberalism connected with Luzzatti and his political allies.[87]

It was this intertwined heritage of an Anglophilic left-liberalism mixed with progressive, Germanophilic reformism that shaped Italy's accident insurance policy. A year following its enactment, the legal philosopher Gioele Solari observed:

---

[84] Pope Leo XIII, *Rerum novarum* (On capital and labour), 15 May 1891, quoted from http://w2.vatican.va/content/leo-xiii/en/encyclicals/documents/hf_l-xiii_enc_15051891_rerum-novarum.html, accessed 23 October 2014.

[85] Aldo A. Mola, *Giovanni Giolitti: lo statista della nuova Italia* (Milan, 2006), pp. 224, 235.

[86] INPS, *La Cassa nazionale*, table 3. See also Vera Zamagni, *The economic history of Italy, 1860–1990* (Oxford, 1993), chs. 1–2.

[87] Laura Cerasi, 'Anglophilia in crisis: Italian liberals, the English model and democracy in the Giolittian era', *Modern Italy* 7 (2002), pp. 5–22.

[W]hile Germany tends to prefer to model its social laws on a new ideal of the state and new *collectivistic* inspirations, [and] while England aims to resolve its social problems through the opportune and gradual extension of its *individualistic* ideal ... the Latin nations, and above all, Italy ... converge in their attempts ... to rebalance that equilibrium of the elements that are a condition of *social peace*.[88]

In Italy, the accident insurance law pointed to a new consensus in government that maintaining social peace required sharing risks. In the case of occupational risk, employers would be held accountable financially and, to a certain extent, morally, as Ferraris had claimed, because they were the chief beneficiaries of industry. However, litigating through the civil code's liability clauses had hardly contributed to social peace. The drill of casting blame not only seemed to cause hardship, as well as the resentment of workers and their socialist and Catholic advocates. It was also inefficient. By contrast, as Mazzola had pointed out, the logic of insurance appeared seamless: accidents could be predicted, and it would be possible to account for their potential harms. Moreover, through *social* insurance under the aegis of the state, Italy could create a harmonious national community characterised by economic growth and limited, yet responsive, government.

The governments in Britain, Germany and Italy pursued policies on accident compensation because they recognised that existing law had failed to rectify the problems associated with workplace accidents: their debilitating and sometimes fatal consequences, related poverty and potential for social strife between business and labour. Since workers and employers were naturally unequal, the agreement of labour contracts would fail to account adequately for the possibility of accidents. Moreover, liability law in Germany and Britain, and the use of liability clauses under the civil code in Italy, had begun a cycle of blame that only fostered social unrest and achieved few real gains for workers. New legislation would therefore be necessary to address the root issue behind accidents at work: occupational risk. Neither employers nor workers could be held personally responsible for everyday accidents because they were statistical occurrences in which free will played no role. Despite their agreement about the nature of the problem, however, officials sought very different policies on compensation. In large part, the distinctive national laws reflected the reality that economic, social and political circumstances differed greatly between the three countries. The German government was open to a corporatist policy which was entirely different from those in Britain and Italy partly because of its close relationship with mining magnates. Similarly, the existence of a national fund for accident insurance played an important role in the decision-making process of Italian administrators. Likewise, the availability of strong commercial and mutual insurance sectors, in conjunction with

---

[88] Author's italics. Gioele Solari, *La legge degli infortuni sul lavoro: introduzione al commento della legge italiana 17 marzo 1898 sugli infortuni* (Civitanova-Marche, 1899), p. 79, quoted in Gozzi, *Modelli politici*, p. 123.

widespread disapproval of social insurance, meant that officials in Britain felt that they would have difficulty justifying building a system anything like that in place in Germany.

However, these factors were merely one aspect of governmental decision making. Beyond deliberations about pragmatic constraints and established institutions, officials relied on their own views about the purpose and nature of the state. And these views reflected a broader understanding about the relationship between social policy and national identity. As Daniel Béland and André Lecours have noted, 'social policy preferences are fundamental aspects of the characterization of the nation'. The language behind social policies like accident insurance and workmen's compensation, let alone how the laws are implemented, reflects specific beliefs about social solidarism, including the 'contours of the community where this solidarity should occur'.[89] In recently unified Germany and Italy, creating social insurance was seen as a means to garner legitimacy for the new nation state as well as its new government. In Germany, the quest for authority often took form in official rhetoric about 'practical Christianity' or social pacification, while in Italy, it was manifested in laments about national 'backwardness'. However, the search for legitimacy did not merely imply creating an authoritative image in a precarious period. Instead, it pointed to concerns about the role of government as the safeguard of social stability and the overseer of the national economy. By spreading risk through social insurance, new national communities could take form in recently unified Germany and Italy. The policy cast aside questions about blame and responsibility, at least nominally, ensuring social stability that would be overseen by an ostensibly benevolent state. To be sure, the mechanics of each policy differed, which is the subject of the following chapter. Nonetheless, the motivations were remarkably similar.

By contrast, in Britain, gaining authority through social insurance was never a serious concern for government. Instead, officials were anxious to adopt a just and effective policy that, at the same time, accorded with both their own *and* popular ideas about freedom of choice and a limited role for the state. Despite the onslaught of organised labour in the 1880s and the rise of the Independent Labour Party in the 1890s, concerns about maintaining social peace failed to reach a climax, as they had in Italy and Germany. Instead, one of the chief worries in Britain was upholding the country's tradition of voluntary mutual funds and commercial insurance, and the concern cut across class lines. While Britons agreed about the precept of occupational risk, they were reluctant to accept a social insurance policy that would distribute it widely. Instead, the Workmen's Compensation Act of 1897 proved a compromise. It allowed *both* the sharing of risk and the casting of blame. On the one hand, it enabled workers to seek recompense through the courts in liability claims

[89] Daniel Béland and André Lecours, *Nationalism and social policy: the politics of territorial solidarity* (Oxford, 2008), pp. 5–6.

rather than under workmen's compensation. On the other, employers were allowed to purchase insurance as a means to pay for compensation under the new law. As Gioele Solari remarked, the system seemed the ultimate solution for guaranteeing individualism. In practice, however, Britain's policy shared many common features with social insurance on the continent.

3

Spreading Risk, Forging Solidarity

'Workers should render a significant contribution to the costs of accident insurance', argued the Bochum Chamber of Commerce in Germany's industrial heartland just a few months before the policy was signed into law. 'This won't only result in giving workers a right to take part in the administration [of the system]', argued the petition, which was likely penned by the steel magnate Louis Baare. Incorporating workers into the governance of accident insurance '[would] also enable them to identify their own material interest – alongside that of employers – in preventing accidents and fighting the annual increase in malingering'.[1] The petition pointed to a broader concern that pervaded debates about how accident compensation would work in practice, which is the subject of this chapter. To Baare and many others, the policy seemed rife for exploitation. Employers closely followed proposals to redistribute the costs of accidental injuries amongst different kinds of businesses, evincing a divide between smaller firms and larger ones and between benign and dangerous industries. For example, landowners repeatedly claimed that they might be exploited if their insurance contributions helped pay for accidents in industrial work.[2] As the petition from the Bochum Chamber of Commerce indicated, however, there was perhaps even greater fear about workers unfairly taking advantage of the system. Not least, many workers saw that accident insurance and workmen's

---

[1] 'Simulation', another term for malingering, is cited in the text. See Chapter 4 below for an elaboration on the concept and the backlash against it. GStAPK: I. HA. 120BB. Abt. VII. Fach. 4. No. 1. Vol. 5: 47–77: Petition of the Chamber of Commerce in Bochum to the Prussian Minister of Trade Otto von Bismarck.

[2] See, for example: GStAPK: I. HA. 120BB. Abt. VIII. Fach. 4. No. 1. Vol. 2: 153–62: 'Zusammenstellung der von den bayerischen Handels- und Gewerbekammern über den Entwurf eines Reichsgesetzes betreffend die Versicherung der in Bergwerken beschäftigten Arbeiter gegen die Folgen der beim Betriebe sich ereigenden Unfälle', n.d. [c. 8 February 1881]. See also: Isabela Mares, *The politics of social risk: business and welfare state development* (Cambridge, 2003), pp. 71–6.

compensation policies would result in employers cutting costs with shoddy safety provisions or miserly salaries. The only way forward, argued some, would be a corporatist arrangement in which workers and employers joined forces to oversee compensation and accident prevention. The state, in turn, would oversee this arrangement, ensuring that it was carried out in a just and uniform manner. Solving the problem of occupational risk would require a new form of social solidarity that would cut across regional, economic and social divides.

A guiding motivation behind the accident policies of the late nineteenth century was the creation of peaceful and productive national communities in the face of risks that affected some and left others untouched. Nonetheless, as this chapter shows, various rationales shaped *how* risk was redistributed and responsibility was allocated in practice. At the heart of the accident insurance and workmen's compensation laws lay concerns about moral hazard like those outlined in the Bochum petition, sparking a long-running debate across Europe about the relative benefits of social security for different social classes, generations and branches of industry that would continue from the nineteenth century to the present.[3] Would dangerous businesses take advantage of the system? Could workers be held accountable for their negligence or for fraudulent claims if they were insured in a no-fault compensation policy? And should the state not only set the rules but also referee this game? The language of moral hazard had, by this time, percolated into English-language discussions, drawing on earlier debates about the value of gambling, including through the game hazard.[4] While the term was absent in Germany and Italy, the idea was certainly implicit in contemporary discussions about the potential dangers of social insurance.

Assumptions about social class coursed through these considerations and were evident in the new 'risk classes' created in the German and Italian social insurance systems, which paradoxically stratified class hierarchies by trade while fostering new forms of social solidarity. Through insurance, employers and workers were co-opted into a system that required sharing the financial burdens of accidents. The policy was predicated on cooperation that cut across class divides while leaving those divides intact. In Britain, workmen's compensation was also guided by assumptions about class divisions, even though the policy gave employers the choice to insure against accidents or pay compensation out of pocket and did not identify specific 'risk classes'. Workmen's

---

[3] In addition to Mares, see also, for example: Peter Baldwin, *The politics of social solidarity: class bases of the European welfare state, 1875–1975* (Cambridge, 1992); Peter Swenson, *Capitalists against markets: the making of labor markets and welfare states in the United States and Sweden* (Oxford, 2002); Thomas Paster, *The role of business in the development of the welfare state and labor markets in Germany: containing social reforms* (London, 2011); Cornelius Torp, *Gerechtigkeit im Wohlfahrtsstaat: Alter und Alterssicherung in Deutschland und Grossbritannien von 1945 bis heute* (Göttingen, 2015).

[4] Tom Baker, 'On the genealogy of moral hazard', *Texas Law Review* 75/2 (1996–7), pp. 237–92.

compensation was based on the view that Britain was *already* a class society, characterised by 'masters' and 'servants', in the waning nomenclature of the mid nineteenth century, alongside the 'residuum' below and the 'aristocracy' and 'gentry' above.

As Ulrich Beck has argued, this emphasis on class characterised industrial modernity in the nineteenth and early twentieth centuries: the risks of modernity were determined by social status, meaning that industrial workers around the globe were affected in much the same way, regardless of geography.[5] At the close of the nineteenth century, however, it was far from obvious who, precisely, was at risk, let alone how that risk could be absorbed elsewhere. It seemed a foregone conclusion that workers in certain sectors, and especially in mechanised industries or those involving explosives, were at a greater risk of encountering workplace accidents. Widespread discourse about the perils of machinery and modernity, alongside the growing unionisation of industrial workers, may have contributed to this focus. Nonetheless, the perils of agricultural work were also widely discussed and, in Britain and Germany, legislated upon early on. However, it remained unclear whether all workers, or only those in the industries deemed most accident-prone, should be covered by the new social legislation. Moreover, commercial insurance for employers' liability thrived in Britain, Germany and Italy, which complicated questions about spreading risk through new instruments like social insurance. Not least, it was uncertain whether workers even *wanted* any kind of social provision that was organised through the state, let alone by employers. Joining friendly societies and other kinds of mutual funds often seemed preferable, allowing workers a degree of self-governance and control of their own affairs.[6]

This chapter shows how each country's policy on accident compensation was predicated on a complex range of assumptions about risks, responsibilities and moral hazard which were manifested in the fine print of the laws, from the criteria for membership to the rules on benefit payments. For Britain, workmen's compensation was seen as an important means to foster social peace and industrial productivity. However, the policy was founded on the consensus that Britons already shared a national community and knew to look to Whitehall in times of need, even if they did so rarely. Communal ties were civic and

---

[5] Ulrich Beck, *Risk society: towards a new modernity*, trans. Mark Ritter (Thousand Oaks, CA, 1992).

[6] For example: 'Berufsgenossenschaften und Umlageverfahren in der deutschen Unfallversicherung', *Gewerkverein* 23 (6 June 1884), quoted in Florian Tennstedt and Heidi Winter, eds., *QS*, sect. 2: *Von der kaiserlichen Sozialbotschaft bis zu den Februarerlassen Wilhelms II (1881–1890)*, vol. ii.i: *Von der zweiten Unfallversicherungsvorlage bis zum Unfallversicherungsgesetz vom 6. Juli 1884* (Stuttgart, 1995), pp. 625–6. On the broader contours of this debate for the British context, see Jose Harris, 'Did British workers want the welfare state? G. D. H. Cole's survey of 1942', in J. Winter, ed., *The working class in modern British history* (Cambridge, 1983), pp. 200–14; Pat Thane, 'The working class and state "welfare" in Britain, 1880–1914', *Historical Journal* 27/4 (1984), pp. 877–900.

established through the everyday bonds of civil society: through membership in mutual funds, trade unions and insurance. Employers could thus turn to established insurance agencies like Lloyd's, which had begun selling marine insurance in London in the seventeenth century and had extended its market to cover workplace accidents in the 1880s. They could also turn to newer firms like the Sickness and Accident Assurance, Ltd., which began in 1885 in response to increased demand following the introduction of the Employers' Liability Act in 1880. And workers could be relied upon to continue to join friendly societies and trade unions that would care for their members, in part through setting strict rules on behaviour.[7] In this light, commercialisation seemed the most appropriate means to spread occupational risk. Workplace accidents were a problem of the market and could be solved within the market. In Germany and Italy, by contrast, civil servants saw social insurance as an important tool to create new forms of solidarity in the face of industrial hardships. The 'state', as a symbol of national community, would play a central role in facilitating this goal. Regardless of these differences, the accident insurance and workmen's compensation policies provided government with a means to inscribe itself in society, garnering authority through everyday tasks such as determining 'risk classes', adjudicating accident claims and dictating procedures. Through these everyday bureaucratic practices, moral hazard could be combated directly, by weeding out unscrupulous employers and workers, and indirectly, by contributing to the idea that workers and employers were bound in a national community under the auspices of the state.

DANGEROUS TRADES

Officials in Britain, Germany and Italy were united in identifying which groups to include in their initial accident schemes, because it seemed clear that certain workers were most vulnerable to occupational risk. At the same time, these workers were often placed on the frontlines of heavy industry, employed in mining, steelworks and related trades which seemed to provide the basis for modern national economies. In Germany, policy makers argued that the Accident Insurance Law of 1884 should first apply only to workers who had already been included in the Employers' Liability Law of 1871 because they were employed in the most dangerous industries. The new law included miners, quarry workers and factory workers who earned less than 2,000 marks per year, as higher wage earners would be more expensive to insure and also better able to afford commercial insurance. Workers involved with railways were left outside the scope of the policy on accident insurance, as the 1871 law had already introduced strict liability for the industry. The accident insurance

---

[7] W. A. Dinsdale, *History of accident insurance in Great Britain* (London, 1954), pp. 8–9, 60–1; Jose Harris, 'Victorian values and the founders of the welfare state', *Proceedings of the British Academy* 78 (1992), pp. 165–82.

policy was also limited to factories with more than ten employees; smaller businesses seemed unable to bear the financial burden of the new law, even with the redistribution of risk across accident funds.[8] Limiting the policy to these groups was a controversial measure, and even defining a 'worker' proved difficult. The Minister of Agriculture in Prussia, Baron Robert Lucius von Ballhausen, along with industrialists in trades with a high proportion of female workers, enquired whether the policy would apply to women. Surprisingly, even the Minister of War raised the issue. Nonetheless, official statistics on accidents seemed to indicate that including women in the accident scheme might be superfluous: between 1872 and 1878, for example, only 0.01 woman per 1,000 was killed in a mining accident, compared to 1.51 men.[9] Although the Ministry of Trade had never doubted that the policy should also apply to female workers, it questioned whether the sex of workers should be noted at all.[10] The law proposals always phrased the noun 'worker' in the masculine case in German, and the discussion of dependants further complicated this impression of a male world of work. Dependants were always characterised in these discussions as widows – not widowers – and their children. Early discussions about women thus tended to focus on how long widows would outlive their husbands and receive accident benefit payments.[11] Nonetheless, the policy ultimately followed the convention of German labour laws by including women in the rubric of 'workers' and men in that of 'dependants'. As Heinrich von Friedberg, the Minister of Justice, had pointed out, most family members in the working classes contributed to the economic survival of their households.

While the risks that female workers encountered seemed uncertain, members of government had no doubt about the perils of agricultural work, such as run-ins with animals and accidents with threshing machines. This was made especially clear in the lobbying efforts by representatives of trade organisations, landowners and Ballhausen alike.[12] However, both Friedberg and Bismarck, who took over as the Minister of Trade in 1880 while still serving as the

---

[8] Ludwig Lass and Friedrich Zahn, *Einrichtung und Wirkung der deutschen Arbeiterversicherung: Denkschrift für die Weltausstellung zu Paris, 1900* (Berlin, 1900), p. 163.

[9] BArch: R1501: 100405a: 39–71: Statistics prepared by Herr Schulze for the Ministry of the Interior, 21 January 1881.

[10] BArch: R43: 507: 147–50: Minister of War to the Chancellor, 5 January 1881; GStAPK: I. HA. Rep. 84a:11030: 77–82: Vote of the Ministry of Agriculture, Domains and Forests on the first accident insurance law proposal, 23 December 1880; BArch: R1501: 100379: 65–9: Minutes of the Permanent Committee of the *Volkswirthschaftsrath*, 1 February 1881.

[11] BArch: R1501: 100405a: 125–49: Dr Heym, Memorandum on premiums, n.d. [1881].

[12] For example: GStAPK: I. HA. 120BB. Abt. VIII. Fach. 4. No. 1. Vol. 5: 11 March –1 July 1884: 48–62: Petition of the Chamber of Trade of Bielefeld to the *Reichstag*, 23 March 1884; GStAPK: I. HA. Rep. 84a:11030: 77–82: Vote of the Ministry of Agriculture, Domains and Forests on the first accident insurance law proposal, 23 December 1880; *DDR* 1 April 1883, Nr. 14: 'Denkschrift des Deutschen Landwirtschaftsraths zur Frage der Ausdehnung der obligatorischen Versicherung auf die landwirthschaftlichen Arbeiter in den Gesetzentwürfen betreffend die Unfall- und Krankenversicherung'.

Imperial Chancellor, were more concerned about the administrative difficulties of including agricultural workers, who were often transient due to the seasonal nature of their employment. A similarly pragmatic issue was how to organise this seemingly amorphous sector of industry into accident funds.[13] In the end, workers in agriculture were excluded from the policy, as were those in several trades that had previously been identified as dangerous, such as the construction industry. Officials decided first to enact the law and build the new system of insurance from the ground up. They would monitor how it developed before granting insurance to further groups of workers. Shortly after the policy was implemented, though, accident insurance was extended to rural labourers and a host of other workers.[14] The risk involved in agriculture proved only one reason for extending accident insurance to this important sector of the economy. As a master weaver on the People's Economic Advisory Board pointed out, including these workers in the scheme was necessary for their integration in German society. His concern spoke directly to Bismarck's motivations for adopting social insurance. If agricultural workers were included in the scheme, he argued, they would know that 'the Fatherland watch[ed] over [them]' and develop a sense of 'patriotism'.[15] Through the sharing of risk amongst workers across the country, whether in urban factories or vast landed estates, social insurance held the potential to foster a feeling of national belonging.

In Italy, who counted as a 'worker' provoked a similar debate, but officials' main concern was the practicality of extending social insurance throughout the country. In light of the peninsula's infrastructure, would this even be possible? Would including all workers within the scheme drain the economy? The government distinguished between three classes of workers: those employed outside of their homes, supervisors and apprentices. These categories defined the terms of the new policy on accident insurance. In contrast to Germany, where officials deliberated about whether 'workers' eligible for accident insurance could be female, in Italy, there was no significant discussion of gender. The main consideration was not who counted as a worker. Instead, it was which industries should be covered. The Italian law, like that in Germany, targeted workers

[13] GStAPK: I. HA. Rep. 84a:11030: 52–64: Vote of the Ministry of Justice on the first accident insurance law proposal, 31 December 1880; GStAPK: I. HA. Rep. 84a:11031: 160–7: Minutes of the Permanent Committee of the *Volkswirthschaftsrath*, 17 March 1882; GStAPK: I. HA. Rep. 84a:11030: 191–6: Vote of the Ministry of Trade and Commerce, 15 February 1881.
[14] BArch: R1501: 100651: 2–3: Minister of the Interior to the Imperial Insurance Office, 12 July 1884. The accident insurance law was extended to workers for the post, telegraph and railway industries as well as those in the navy and army, with the exception of soldiers and sailors, who were granted compensation through earlier legislation. It also extended the law to domestic shipping and related transport industries. In 1886, agricultural workers were included in the law, and in 1887 two different laws extended compulsory accident insurance to workers in construction and those involved in shipping. For information about further extensions, see Chapter 4.
[15] Quoted in BArch: R1501: 10037: 65–9: Master Weaver Hessel from Berlin, quoted in the minutes of the Permanent Board of the *Volkswirthschaftsrath*, 1 February 1881.

that the government perceived to be in 'dangerous' trades. The Minister of Agriculture, Industry and Commerce Augusto Barazzuoli explained this aim in his proposal on accident insurance, which was ratified in 1898. He claimed that the law 'divides all forms of industrial or quasi-industrial work into two large categories: one comprises those industries that, with respect to accidents, are held to be dangerous; the other encompasses the rest'.[16] All workers in the most dangerous industries would be included in the new policy, regardless of the size of the firm where they worked. As in Germany, in Italy, society was suddenly divided into two classes: those at risk from industry, and everyone else.

This rationale was evident as early as 1889, when the Advisory Commission on Insurance Institutions and Labour at the Ministry of Agriculture began positing an accident insurance law.[17] Barazzuoli cited dangerous industries as mining, quarries, construction, servicing steam boilers, the production of electricity, gas or telephone lines, and anything involving the use of explosives. As in Germany, the only industry that was conspicuously absent from the new law was railways: these had been subject to a law on pension funds, including pensions for accidents, since 1885. The policy targeted government employees as well as those in the private sector, as long as they met these criteria. Members of the 1889 committee had already pointed out the need to apply the law to servants of the state. Unlike other workers, though, government employees were required to enrol in the National Fund, perhaps as a means to augment the flailing body while also fostering loyalty towards the central state.

Anxieties about harming the national economy played a large role in outlining the rest of the policy, and these echoed the long-standing trope in Liberal Italy about overcoming economic backwardness. Workers in industries where machines 'powered by an inanimate agent', meaning machines driven by mechanised rather than animal power, would therefore be insured in the new law, but only if the firms where they worked had more than five employees. Overburdening smaller companies was a major concern. Moreover, as in Germany, in Italy, civil servants identified the practical problem of requiring insurance in industries where work took on an irregular nature. As Barazzuoli noted, it would be difficult to monitor the new law in agriculture and smaller firms, especially those linked to individual households. For this reason, the government sought to exclude agriculture in its first law on accident insurance. It

---

[16] *A. P. Cam.*, Doc., Leg. XIX, Sess. 1 (1895), Nr. 60: 'Infortuni sul lavoro: Disegno di legge presentato dal ministro di agricoltura, industria e commercio (Barazzuoli) nella seduta del 13 giugno 1895'.

[17] 'Allegato B: Relazione del professore Carlo Francesco Ferraris intorno all'assicurazione obbligatoria e alla responsabilità dei padroni ed imprenditori per gli infortuni sul lavoro', *Annali del credito e della previdenza* (1889), pp. 238–79. The *Commissione consultiva per le istituzione di previdenza e sul lavoro* was founded in 1869 and renamed the *Consiglio della previdenza* in 1894. On this institution, see Dora Marucco, *Lavoro e previdenza dall'Unità al fascismo: il Consiglio della previdenza dal 1869 al 1923* (Milan, 1984).

would follow Germany's model by proceeding with the new law 'in degrees'.[18] Providers of agricultural accident insurance responded by lobbying against the decision. For example, an accident fund based in Milan petitioned parliament to include rural workers because 'accidents [in agriculture] are rather more frequent and serious than one believes'. Indeed, the government's own accident statistics from the 1880s corroborated this point by highlighting the frequency of 'violent deaths' caused by animals.[19] Yet, the first accident law adopted the Ministry of Agriculture's streamlined approach. By 1903, the government followed through with extending the law to workers in agriculture – as long as they were working directly with machines. The question of rural risk would, therefore, continue to haunt policy makers in Italy for the next decade, until the issue was finally resolved in 1917 as a response to social unrest during the First World War. The long delay may have reflected the concern that Italy could not bear the expense of extending accident insurance to the majority of its workforce. Italy could, however, signal its status as a modern state to citizens and foreign observers alike by introducing social insurance, regardless of its meagre scope.

In Britain, in contrast to Italy, a substantial proportion of the workforce was included in the initial compensation law. Within ten years, 76 per cent of the British workforce was included, compared to just 10 per cent in Italy (see Appendix, Table 3). It was clear which industries to single out for the new policy in Britain: mining, quarries, railways, factories, engineering works and the construction of tall buildings. It seemed that workers could not be held responsible for accidents in these trades due to their inherent riskiness, associated mechanisation or loose management structures. Of course, various trade unions, including the Government Workers' Federation, also demanded access to workmen's compensation when it was initially introduced. Some called for the new law to be applied to all workers or at least all workers in particular industries, such as construction.[20] However, these requests found little response. As the Conservative Home Secretary, Matthew White Ridley, claimed, he sought to avoid creating the kind of accident policy in place in

---

[18] *A. P. Cam.*, Doc., Leg. XIX, Sess. 1 (1895), Nr. 60. On the gradual extension of the law, see also: 'Allegato B' (1897), pp. 205–322, at pp. 221–2; *A. P. Cam.*, Doc., Leg. XVI, Sess. 4 (1889–90), Nr. 116; *A. P. Sen.*, Doc., Leg. XVII, Sess. 1 (1890–1), Nr. 33.

[19] CdAs: Leg. XX, Sess. 1895–7, Proposte di legge: Bta. 613: A. C. 60: 'Petizione alla camera dei deputati del patronato per gli infortuni del lavoro, amministratore della fondazione G. B. Ponti in Milano, chiedente alcune modificazione al progetto di legge sugli infortuni del lavoro, presentato dal ministro d'agricoltura, industria e commercio, 4 dic. 1895'.

[20] *PP* 1893–4 (C 284) XI.907: 'Report from the Standing Committee on Law and Courts of Justice and Legal Procedure on the Employers' Liability Bill', pp. 194–5; WCML: L25/64: Associate Shipwrights' Society: unnumbered: 'Sixty-Second Quarterly Report of the Associate Shipwrights' Society', July–September 1897; TNA: HO 45/9867/B13816L/69: United Government Workers Federation to Sir Matthew White Ridley, 17 June 1897; TNA: HO 45/9867/B13816L/111: Francis Mowath of the Treasury Chambers to the Under-Secretary of State, 10 July 1897.

Germany. Its 'extremely elaborate system', he argued, was 'utterly foreign to this country'.²¹ Despite Ridley's plea to avoid complexity, the Home Office found that it had to step in to resolve the question: who was a 'workman'? The issue came to the fore in debates about distinguishing between 'workmen' and those involved in less strenuous labour. Already in earlier discussions about revising the Employers' Liability Act, a Parliamentary Select Committee noted that many workers were not granted compensation because of the strict definition of 'workman' used in the law. Due to the risks inherent in their jobs, however, Committee members argued that these groups should have been entitled to compensation.²² In later discussions about revising the Employers' Liability Act, the Standing Committee on Law noted that the word 'servant' might be a more appropriate term for demarcating who should be covered. Members of the Committee argued that 'servants' could stem from a larger group of people, including those working in service industries who also encountered dangers related to their jobs. Moreover, as one member of the Committee observed, the term 'workman' was simply a neologism, a mere '[creation] of the Employers' Liability Act', while the word 'servant' was an 'old English word' and better suited to describing those employed in the British economy.²³ This linguistic distinction proved particularly poignant, as it reflected broader a debate about whether the relationship between workers and employers should be characterised by 'status', as in earlier legislation on 'masters' and 'servants', or by 'contract'.²⁴ The Workmen's Compensation Act that emerged from these discussions reflected acceptance of the more recent term 'workman' and the assumptions upon which it was based. The term 'servant' seemed an antiquated remnant from an earlier stage of British economic, political and legal development. By contrast, the modern British economy was not only characterised by industry and its associated risks. It was governed, through law, by the state. Through legislation and everyday bureaucracy, government had become the new 'master' of industry, and both workers and employers were its 'servants'.

²¹ *Proceedings*, TUC Congress (1895), p. 43; WCML: L26/64: Associate Shipwrights' Society: unnumbered: 'Report of Proceedings of the Seventh Annual Meeting of the Federation of Engineering and Shipbuilding Trades of the United Kingdom', 26 May 1897; TNA: HO 45/9868/B13816M/2: Hull Building Trades Federation to the Secretary of State of the Home Department, 19 May 1897; TNA: HO 45/9868/B13816M/3: Preston Building Trades' Council to the Secretary of State of the Home Department, 8 May 1897. For the government's explanation: 4 *Hansard* HC vol. 48 (3 May 1897), cols. 1430, 1433.
²² PP 1886 (C 192) VIII.1: 'Report from the Select Committee on the Employers' Liability Act (1880) Amendment Bill', p. 110.
²³ PP 1893–4 (C 284) XI.907: 'Report from the Standing Committee on Law and Courts of Justice', pp. 2–3.
²⁴ Douglas Hay, 'England, 1562–1975: the law and its uses', in Douglas Hay and Paul Craven, eds., *Masters, servants and magistrates in Britain and the Empire, 1562–1955* (Chapel Hill, NC, 2004), pp. 59–116.

ORGANISING RISK

Across national borders, it was relatively clear which workers were most vulnerable to occupational accidents. Determining how to pay for accident benefit proved much more difficult, as it meant making a decision about whether and how to use public institutions. In Germany, government, employers and several insurers were united against commercial insurance as a means to pay compensation for occupational accidents. Insurance companies like the Magdeburg General worried about whether they could afford the onslaught of claims stemming from the policy.[25] The only other solution seemed obvious: creating some sort of state-organised insurance system that would relieve commercial funds of any possible costs. The Prussian Ministry of Trade contacted insurers and the chambers of trade in response to the Magdeburger's claim that the accident policy would wreck the commercial insurance industry. In response, most insurers rejected the argument, and several went on to claim that insurance was inherently a moral good because it made provisions for known risks. Creating an accident policy that did not draw on insurance would be unethical.[26] However, it was still uncertain whether accident insurance should be purchased on the market or organised instead by some other means. It was clear to civil servants such as the Royal Railway Commissioner and the head of the Royal Upper Mining Office in Dortmund that commercial insurance was not always generous or efficient, making it unsuitable for the paternalistic policy that the Ministry of Trade had espoused.[27] The proposal in 1880 from the industrialist Louis Baare reinforced these views. Baare argued for the creation of a single national accident insurance fund to manage the problem of occupational risk, and the idea of a national fund resonated with officials: Adolph Wagner, an economist and one of the key writers on 'state socialism', had argued that insurance was a *public* good that should be provided by the state.[28] The Ministry of Trade in Prussia put forward the suggestion at a meeting of the Prussian Economic Advisory Board, which consisted of employers, workers

---

[25] GStAPK: I. HA. Rep. 120BB. Abt. VII. Fach. 1. No. 16. Vol. 1: 231–7: *Magdeburger Allgemeine Versicherungs-Gesellschaft* to the *Reichskanzleramt*, 12 September 1878.

[26] For example: GStAPK: I. HA. Rep. 120BB. Abt. VII. Fach. 1. No. 16. Adh. 2:81: Chamber of Trade of Braunsberg to the Minister of Trade and Commerce, 10 January 1879; GStAPK: I. HA. Rep. 120BB. Akt. VII. Fach. 1. No. 16. Vol. 1: 313: Ministry of Public Works and Ministry of Trade and Commerce to the Chancellor, 4 June 1879.

[27] GStAPK: I. HA. Rep. 120BB: Abt. VII: Fach. 1: No. 16. Adh. 2: 382–7: Royal Upper Mining Office of Dortmund to the Minister of Trade, 15 January 1879; 460–73: Royal Railway Commissioner in Berlin to the Minister of Trade, 14 January 1879.

[28] BArch: R43: 507: 2–7: Memorandum from Louis Baare, General-Director of the Bochum *Verein für Bergbau und Gußstahl Fabrikation* and Royal Commercial Adviser in Bochum, 30 April 1880; Adolph Wagner, 'Der Staat und das Versicherungswesen. Principielle Erörterungen über die Frage der Gemeinwirthschaftlichen oder Privatwirthschaftlichen Organisation dieses wirthschaftlichen Gebiets im Allgemeinen', *Zeitschrift für die Gesamte Staatswissenschaft* 37 (1881), pp. 102–72.

and landowners, as well as governmental representatives. They agreed that commercial insurance was an 'immoral' method for managing workplace risk because it attempted to profit from a public concern. Moreover, in striving for profits, commercial insurance would inevitably cost more money to administer than public insurance. In a meeting on the issue, the collective of Prussian ministers agreed, arguing that a state-run insurance fund would need to operate on the principle of efficiency, not profit.[29]

The Prussian government found widespread support for the idea from workers' and manufacturing groups.[30] Yet, the idea of a public fund was greeted, unsurprisingly, with apprehension from the private insurance sector, business groups and employers who had established firm-based mutual funds. It was also met with resistance from the regional governments throughout Germany. For private insurance firms, the issue with public insurance was clearly the loss of potential profits from future clients as well as the loss of current policies. How existing policies would be transferred was one of their major concerns. The question was ultimately resolved by allowing for a brief transfer period from private insurance policies to state-sponsored accident insurance after the enactment of the law. This procedure ensured that no one would be burdened with paying insurance premiums twice.[31] The Imperial Ministry of the Interior also responded to the other major concern of the insurance industry: the mass unemployment that would follow if the accident insurance law did not allow employers to use commercial policies. When Germany enacted its law on accident insurance, which did not allow employers to take out commercial policies, the Ministry invited redundant employees from private insurance firms to work within the government's new public insurance system.[32]

---

[29] GStAPK: I. HA. Rep. 84a:11030: 138–42: 1st session of the Permanent Committee of the *Volkswirthschaftsrath*, 1 February 1881; GStAPK: I. HA. Rep. 84a:11031: 150–9: Minutes of the 7th session of the *Volkswirthschaftsrath*, 7 March 1882. This was the argument presented in the government's law proposal: *DDB* 1881/2, no. 6 (13 January 1881): 'Begründung', pp. 14–50, at pp. 29–30. See also: GStAPK: I. HA. Rep. 84a:11030: 4–6: Minutes of the Prussian State Ministers, 28 August 1880.

[30] BArch: R1501: 100394: 161–6: Copy of the lecture by Philipp Dessauer, *Verein deutscher Papierfabrikanten*, 20 June 1881; 211–14: *Verein deutscher Eisengiesserein* to the Imperial Chancellery, 25 November 1881.

[31] 'Zur Frage der älteren Versicherungsverträge', *Amtliche Nachrichten des Reichs-Versicherungsamt* 1 (6 December 1884). See also: GStAPK: I. HA. Rep. 84a:11030: 269–77: Proposal from the *Gegenseitige Lebens-Invaliditäts-und Unfall-Versicherungs-Gesellschaft* 'Prometheus' in Berlin and several other insurance companies from throughout Germany to the Reichstag, 21 March 1881; F. von Cotteritz, *Das Reichs-Unfall-Versicherungs-Projekt: eine sachliche Kritik mit neuen Vorschlägen, dem Reichstag gewidmet* (Berlin, 1881).

[32] For example: BArch: R101: 331: 1–2: Petition of the employees of the *Allgemeiner Deutscher Versicherungs-Verein* in Stuttgart (*Reichstag* petition Nr. 44); BArch: R1501: 100403: 2–5: Department for Accident Insurance of the *Magdeburger Allgemeine Versicherungs-Actien-Gesellschaft*, 14 May 1881, to the *Bundesrath*.

For the regional governments, the possibility of a public insurance system was only a cause for concern if the system were to be centralised, with a base in the German capital Berlin and little input from the periphery. Anxieties about centralisation, characterised by a form of German state building that gave Prussia a dominant role, had dominated German politics throughout the second half of the nineteenth century. The individual member states of the North German Confederation had sought policies of internal state building through modernisation before national unification succeeded between 1864 and 1871.[33] After unification, they were granted a voice in national politics through the upper chamber of parliament, the *Bundesrat*, and they were allowed to determine their own state budgets and the shape of state-based political issues and administrative competences such as education. Of the regional governments, only Bavaria maintained a significant degree of autonomy within the federal system, as it was allowed to maintain its own standing army, was granted a disproportionately large amount of votes in the *Bundesrat* and refused to ratify the constitution for unified Germany.[34] It is not surprising, therefore, that the Bavarian government suggested establishing regional insurance systems rather than a national one – especially in light of the fact that the Prussian Ministry of Trade was behind the creation of a national insurance fund. The government in large and highly industrialised Saxony offered a similar solution.[35] Even the Prussian envoy in Württemberg argued that Prussia's wide-reaching plan for a national insurance fund would 'interfere in the administrative measures of the individual federal states'. Instead, he suggested, a national fund might operate in conjunction with other funds.[36]

These arguments against a single national insurance fund proved influential, but they did not result in the creation of the regional system that several state governments suggested. Instead, accident insurance in Germany would be run through a corporatist scheme based on employers' liability funds. The funds

---

[33] Abigail Green, *Fatherlands: state-building and nationhood in nineteenth-century Germany* (Cambridge, 2001).

[34] Rudolf Morsey, 'Die öffentlichen Aufgaben und die Gliederung der Kompetenzen zwischen Norddeutschen Bund, Reich und Bundesstaaten, 1867–1914', in Kurt G. A. Jeserich et al., eds., *Deutsche Verwaltungsgeschichte*, vol. III: *Das Deutsche Reich bis zum Ende der Monarchie* (Stuttgart, 1985), pp. 128–37.

[35] BArch: R1501: 100399: 92–3: G. Werthern of the Royal State Ministry of the Interior, Department for Agriculture, Commerce and Trade in Munich to the Foreign Secretary of Germany (Bismarck), 31 December 1880; BArch: R1501: 100400: 100–63: n.d. [c. mid April 1881]: Royal State Ministry of the Interior, Department for Agriculture, Commerce and Trade in Munich to the Foreign Secretary of Germany (Bismarck); 88: Royal Legation in Dresden to the Foreign Secretary, Bismarck, 22 March 1881; BArch: R1501: 100399: 144–5: Royal Legation in Saxony to Bismarck, 31 December 1880. See also: BArch: R1501: 100399: 183–7: Great Archduke of Mecklenburg-Schwerin, Minister-President Count Bathewitz, to Bismarck, 10 December 1880.

[36] BArch: R1501: 100399: 150: G. Donhoff, Prussian Legation in Württemberg, to Bismarck, 2 January 1881.

would, in turn, be coordinated through a central supervisory board based in the federal capital. The solution stemmed from the politics of federalism in Germany, alongside considerations about the nature of German industry and the different occupations within it. Germany's corporatist system of accident insurance was not, therefore, merely a means to 'status differentials; rights ... attached to class and status', as scholars on welfare capitalism have posited,[37] even if the policy ultimately resulted in that end. To be sure, however, the solution emulated the suggestion put forward by the mining and steel magnates Louis Baare and Carl Ferdinand von Stumm, who drew on their experience with mutual funds that brought together workers in the same industry.[38] After the widespread rejection of a national fund for accident insurance, this corporatist system emerged as the compromise. To civil servants in Berlin, it seemed more efficient and moral than commercial insurance, and its public nature meant that it could operate as a means towards national social integration. The fact that the model stemmed from mining made it particularly appealing; Prussia, which spearheaded the policy on accident insurance, had long organised and run its mining sector, only liberalising the field in the 1860s.[39] In this respect, a solution from mining seemed particularly relevant for the German government but not for Britain and Italy, where the sector was entirely private.

The government used Baare's model to create a network of employers' liability funds (*Berufsgenossenschaften*) that consisted of similar industries within a particular region or across Germany. These were broken down into sections that related to location and 'risk classes', as they were called at the time and in subsequent years, which determined the premiums that needed to be paid. The idea of risk classes was a natural progression from the government's initial classification of 'dangerous industries' in its earlier liability legislation. Defining these was a straightforward exercise: Prussia had already begun to calculate statistics on risk with an eye towards adopting an accident law, and the Ministry of Trade called on insurance experts and looked to the regulations and statistics of commercial insurance firms when considering how to draw up a plan of risk classes for the new accident insurance law. It also observed how premiums were calculated at the Krupp and Bochum steel firms.[40] A particular industry

---

[37] For example: Gøsta Esping-Anderson, *The three worlds of welfare capitalism* (Oxford, 1990), p. 27.

[38] *DDR* 4/II 1879, vol. 4, Anlage Nr. 16.

[39] Although Prussia continued to run mines in Silesia and parts of the Saarland. William O. Henderson, *The rise of German industrial power, 1834–1914* (Berkeley, CA, 1975), pp. 72, 132, 151.

[40] GStAPK: I. HA. Rep. 84a:11030: 65–72: Presidium of the State Ministry to Chancellor Bismarck, 21 December 1880; GStAPK: I. HA. Rep. 84a:11030: 162–9: Fifth Session of the Permanent Committee, 7 February 1881; GStAPK: I. HA. 120BB. Abt. VIII. Fach. 4. No. 1. Vol. 1: 1–5: 23 September 1880. The first comprehensive compilation of statistics that included danger classes and provided a reliable basis for structuring the new law: *Unfall-Statistik des Deutschen Reichs*, special issue of the *Monatshefte zur Statistik des Deutschen Reichs für das Jahr 1882* 53 (Berlin, 1882). Later comprehensive statistics were collected by the insurance expert Thilo

was placed in a risk class not only based on its accident rate. Risk classes also took into account the amount of compensation that injured workers and their dependants could receive following an accident and how the result of an accident, whether death or temporary or permanent disability, burdened a worker. Workers were therefore divided not only based on their exposure to risk, but also on their earnings: the risk classes in German social insurance echoed broader social divisions amongst Germany's working classes.[41]

Moreover, the system of liability funds distributed the cost of occupational risk only between similar kinds of firms, which were placed within the same fund. Social insurance was organised in this way because premiums were collected only from employers, with no state subsidy provided by tax payers, no contribution from local poor boards and no contribution from workers. Financial redistribution was also relatively limited within the employers' liability funds: the first 50 per cent of compensation payments came from the section of the fund in which an injured worker's firm was a member. The remaining amount came from the other sections. Bismarck had suggested levying part of the burden for accident insurance on local poor boards, as the new accident insurance law would relieve these funds of paying for injured workers or their families. This proposal was, however, rejected adamantly on the grounds that redistributing the risks willingly taken on by negligent employers would not be fair to other members of society who paid poor rates. Landowners within the Prussian People's Economic Advisory Board were especially keen to point this out, as they conceded that agriculture, unlike industry, was unlikely to produce serious workplace accidents.[42] These groups were particularly concerned about the potential moral hazard of dangerous industries. However, others decried the possibility of a state contribution to social insurance on the grounds that it would be 'a dangerous, socialistic movement of the law'.[43] Bismarck was soon isolated in pushing for the public funding of accident insurance, as other members of government argued that the policy had nothing to do with provision for the poor and should be kept an entirely separate institution. As one official put it, 'workers' insurance [was] a matter of the inner household of industry'.[44]

von Seebach and sent to the Ministry of the Interior: BArch: R1501: 100408: 4–92: n.d. [*c.* 21 February 1884].

[41] *DDB* 1881/2, no. 43: 'Gefahrenklassen und das Gefahrenverhältniß zwischen den verschiedenen Gefahrenklassen'.

[42] GStAPK: I. HA. 120BB. Abt. VIII. Fach. 4. No. 1. Vol. 2: 153–62: 'Zusammenstellung der von den bayerischen Handels- und Gewerbekammern über den Entwurf eines Reichsgesetzes betreffend die Versicherung der in Bergwerken beschäftigten Arbeiter gegen die Folgen der beim Betriebe sich ereignenden Unfälle', n.d. [*c.* 8 February 1881].

[43] BArch: R1501: 100394: 102–5: Petition of the Chamber of Commerce for the *Kreis* Essen to the *Reichstag*, forwarded to the Chancellor, 19 April 1881.

[44] GStAPK: I. HA. Rep. 84a:11030: 65–72: Presidium of the State Ministry to Chancellor Bismarck, 21 December 1880; BArch: R1501: 100379: 75–82: Secret Commercial Adviser Heimendahl-Crefeld in the minutes of the Permanent Committee of the *Volkswirthschaftsrath*, 3 February 1881.

However, the idea of including workers' contributions gained greater traction. For example, the Minister of the Interior, following the suggestions of several industrialists, noted that having workers participate in this way would help to integrate them into society more generally.[45] Whether workers could afford to do this was another matter. The government initially put forward a proposal for a tax-based subsidy of workers with lower salaries. Ultimately, however, the arguments against tax-based subsidies, along with the powerful claim that employers were ultimately responsible for whichever risks emerged in their workplaces, won out. Employers, alone, would be responsible for paying for this system of accident insurance. In order to avoid overburdening employers, however, workers could receive compensation only after thirteen weeks of disability. During these thirteen weeks, they would have to turn to their health insurance fund, to which both they and their employers contributed. This thirteen-week waiting time was also added as a means to deter spurious claims, because only two-thirds of a worker's lost salary could be earned during this period.[46] While the policy pacified employers by offsetting some of the costs of accidents, workers' organisations, alongside both conservatives and liberals in parliament, opposed it.[47] The only aspect of this system that would require funding from tax payers was the bureaucracy involved in supervising it. This included paying for the Imperial Insurance Office, which operated as a branch of the Imperial Ministry of the Interior, as well as funding officials involved in supervising on local and regional levels. Since the accident insurance law required the liability funds to take charge of workplace inspections of their members, government and tax payers were relieved of paying for them. Through this corporatist arrangement, Germany created a public institution with national reach, governed through a new central office in Berlin. The policy bound workers and employers together across the country to share the financial burden of workplace accidents. It also balkanised them in separate risk classes and employers' liability funds.

The Italian government bypassed many of the issues that Germany had confronted because it resolved without much debate to retain an insurance-based system similar to that which was already in place across the country. It chose

[45] BArch: R43: 510: 159: Directorate of the *Centralverband Deutscher Industrieller* to Chancellor Bismarck, 31 May 1881; BArch: R1501: 100413: 74–85: Petition of the *Verein zur Wahrung der gemeinsamen wirthschaftlichen Interessen der Saar Industrie* to the *Reichstag*, 25 November 1882; GStAPK: I. HA. Rep. 84a:11030: Vote of the Ministry of the Interior, 21 December 1880.

[46] The imperial subsidy was advocated by the Chancellor, the People's Economic Advisory Board and the industrialist Louis Baare: GStAPK: I. HA. Rep. 84a:11031: 160: Minutes of the ninth session of the *Volkswirthschaftsrath*, 17 March 1882; GStAPK: I. HA. Rep. 77. Tit. 923. No.1. Vol. 1: 76–81L: Vote of the Presidium of the State Ministry to Chancellor Bismarck, 21 December 1880; GStAPK: I. HA. Rep. 84a:11030: 170–6: Sixth session of the Permanent Committee of the *Volkswirthschaftsrath*, 8 February 1881.

[47] For example: 'Die neueste Unfallvorlage und die Arbeiter', *Der Gewerkverein* 4 (25 January 1884), p. 480.

to base the system on the National Accident Insurance Fund that had been operating on a semi-private basis since 1883. The National Fund was endowed from a variety of mutual societies and banks throughout the country, and its headquarters was based in Milan. Unlike commercial accident insurance funds, the National Fund was treated as a quasi-public body. It had a non-profit status, and it used local post office branches throughout the country as points of administration. The Fund was in constant contact with central government, with a member of the Ministry of Agriculture sitting on its board, and it was required to seek royal approval for premiums and any changes to its statutes.[48] In these ways, the National Accident Insurance Fund offered a symbolic centre for Italy's new system of social insurance, even if not all employers chose to insure their workers through it.

The Italian government had already decided in the late 1880s that the best way to organise a system of compulsory accident insurance was to allow employers to insure workers through the National Accident Insurance Fund or through one of several approved commercial insurance companies. The advisory commission on insurance based at the Ministry of Agriculture unanimously voted against creating a monopoly for the National Fund or erecting 'that ponderous system of professional insurance corporations that characterises the German system' because it would be too much of a breach with the Italian tradition of liberalism.[49] The minimum compensation that workers received would be based on the premiums used at the National Fund and approved by government. Government devised this system out of concern that employers might otherwise arbitrarily choose premium amounts that would not adequately pay for compensation.[50] As in Germany, in Italy, the National Fund drew up what it called 'risk classes', and it was these risk classes that were used when calculating premiums. The Italian policy had distinguished between those 'at risk' of accidents and everyone else, but it further stratified workers into categories that were more or less affected by the dangers of work and, by implication, into different occupational groups.

In Italy, there was little debate about where the risk of workplace accidents should be redistributed: to employers. All government proposals for an accident insurance law, from the first in 1890 to the last in 1898, outlined that employers pay the entirety of premiums. Neither state subsidies, derived from taxes, nor co-payments by workers were seriously considered in government. From the start, officials argued that employers should pay for accident insurance because the policy was being adopted as a means to circumvent a strict liability law.[51] The Italian administration decided, however, to distribute part

---

[48] Legge 8 luglio 1883, n. 1473, serie 3a.
[49] A. P. *Cam.*, Doc., Leg. XVI, Sess. 4 (1889–90), Nr. 116.
[50] 'Allegato B' (1889), pp. 238–79.
[51] A. P. *Sen.*, Doc., Leg. XVII, Sess. 1 (1890–1), Nr. 33: 'Provvedimenti per gli infortuni sul lavoro: Progetto di legge presentato dal ministro di agricoltura, industria e commercio

of the cost of occupational risk to workers. Unlike Germany, Italy had not adopted a comprehensive insurance system in which health insurance and accident insurance worked in conjunction, which meant that the indirect contribution of workers to accident insurance was not a possibility. As a compromise, Italian workers would need to pay for the first two weeks of living costs and recuperation fees after an accident. Already in early discussions, both Ferraris and Luigi Miceli, the first Minister of Agriculture to put forward a bill on the matter, argued that workers could cover these costs through joining mutual funds, which they saw as an ideal solution because it meant that workers would pay for the consequences of less severe accidents. This meant, they hoped, that the new law would deter minor claims and fraud by making workers, in part, responsible for addressing the consequences of accidents.[52]

As in Italy, in Britain, government never seriously considered spreading the cost of occupational risk to tax payers, nor the possibility of requiring workers to pay. One of the main reasons behind choosing workmen's compensation, rather than compulsory insurance, was that the policy avoided redistributing the cost of accidents from individual employers to other members of society.[53] Many businesses felt that they had been short-changed in having to bear the full financial burden for accidents and argued that the cost of workmen's compensation should be distributed throughout the national community. As a group of manufacturers claimed, 'it did not seem fair that while the benefit of the consumption of coal was enjoyed by all, from the wealthiest to the poorest, that all the risk should be thrown upon the actual company mining the mineral'.[54] The Federation of Master Cotton Spinners' Associations even argued that the state, rather than the employer, should pay for compensation because it was Britain as a whole that benefited from labour.[55] However, unlike the voices of Carl Ferdinand von Stumm and other representatives of heavy industry in Germany, those of the Cotton Spinners did not echo loudly in the halls of Whitehall. There was never any significant discussion about their proposal or any other suggestions to offset the cost of accidents onto taxpayers.

In fact, workmen's compensation required employers to pay entirely for compensation, whether out of pocket or through a policy based at a commercial

(Chimirri) al senato del regno nella tornata del 13 aprile 1891'; 'Allegato B' (1889), pp. 238–79, at pp. 244–5.

[52] 'Commissione consultiva per le istituzione di previdenza e sul lavoro, 29 novembre 1889', *Annali del credito e della previdenza* (1889), pp. 146–9; 157–8; A. P. Sen., Doc., Leg. XVII, Sess. 1 (1890–1), Nr. 33.

[53] *PP* 1893–4 (C 284) XI.907: 'Report from the Standing Committee on Law and Courts of Justice', pp. 21, 23–4.

[54] TNA: HO 45/9867/B13816L/30: unnumbered: excerpt from the *Birmingham Daily Gazette*, 21 May 1897, forwarded to the Home Secretary by Mr Robert P. Yates, 22 May 1897.

[55] TNA: HO 45/9867/B13816L/29: 'Report on the Workmen (compensation for accidents) Bill, prepared and adopted by the Parliamentary Committee of the Federation of Master Cotton Spinners' Associations', 14 May 1897.

insurance company, mutual fund or friendly society that was approved by the Chief Registrar of Friendly Societies. In the case of employers without insurance, the possibility of bankruptcy was a problem.[56] The law therefore included a special provision that granted injured workers preferential status as creditors if their employers went bankrupt. Employers were required to adhere to the provisions of the new law, making the payment of compensation a ubiquitous concern. They were not allowed to mandate that their workers 'contract out' of the scheme, but they were allowed to offer compensation through an approved fund. The condition for government approval of a fund was not only its solvency, but, most importantly, that it would be able to pay the amount of compensation outlined in the new law. Workmen's Compensation required government to oversee its successful operation, but it was predicated on the notion that civil society should be made responsible for solving its own problems. In this light, commercial – rather than social – insurance seemed the most appropriate tool for disseminating the financial burden of occupational risk. As elsewhere, employers were responsible for paying the entirety of premiums if they chose to take out insurance. On the surface, this aspect of the British law seemed similar to the systems established in Germany and Italy. However, the underlying rationale differed substantially. Since Britain opted for a compensation policy, but *not* social insurance, the idea of having workers pay compensation to themselves did not make sense. This aspect of the policy most clearly reflected its roots in Britain's earlier Employers' Liability Act. Paying part of an insurance premium, as had been considered in Germany and Italy, might have been an option had compulsory insurance been adopted in Britain. The only instance in the British system when workers could provide a co-payment would be if they received additional compensation as a result.[57]

COMPENSATION AND THE STATE

Workmen's compensation reflected lingering attachment to the ideas of personal responsibility that had guided the common-law treatment of workplace accidents. With the enactment of the policy, Britain clearly shifted responsibility in its entirety to employers. By contrast, neither the German nor the Italian government was particularly concerned to maintain any traces of this thinking in their new social insurance systems. Both decided to hold employers financially liable for accidents, but moral and legal ideas about responsibility or culpability were not behind this decision. Instead, social insurance assumed that society, under the aegis of the state, shared the burden for *social* problems. By contrast, workmen's compensation seemed to denote a market-based solution to an unfortunate consequence of the market: occupational accidents. As

---

[56] *PP* 1893–4 (C 284) XI.907: 'Report from the Standing Committee on Law and Courts of Justice', p. 7.

[57] See Edward W. Brabook, *Provident societies and industrial welfare* (London, 1898), pp. 128–9.

primary beneficiaries of that market, employers should be held liable, even if that spelled their financial ruin. These differences revealed a more significant discrepancy between the British and continental policies: the *function* of compensation. In Germany, for instance, once the 'insurance principle' was settled upon, the question of how to compensate injured workers simply followed the guidelines that were used in the practice of commercial insurance. In this respect, compensation under the accident insurance law deviated markedly from that granted under the liability law of 1871.[58] Premiums reflected the risk of a particular trade and the pay of a worker, as compensation would be paid as a proportion of one's salary. In order to deter malingering, though, the Ministry of Trade decided to cap the maximum salary at two-thirds of one's final salary at the time of injury. This cap was also introduced because the families of deceased workers might have some other means of income anyway.[59] The implication behind the policy was that social insurance provided more than a basic minimum for workers and their families in times of need. Instead, by linking the regular payment of premiums with the attendant return of accident benefit, social insurance served as a kind of social contract through which workers, employers and the state were united. Setting an upper limit meant holding all parties to that contract: like employers, who were obliged to pay premiums, workers were made responsible for living frugally while on accident benefit and therefore deterred from making claims in the first place.

From this contractual perspective, the system was necessarily fine-tuned to the needs of individual workers, based on their individual circumstances. The percentage of one's final salary was correlated directly to the degree of a worker's injury. An injured worker's liability fund was responsible for determining how far the injury would prevent the worker from being able to earn: disability was registered in the language of the time as an 'inability to earn', and compensation was granted on that basis.[60] The concepts 'total', 'partial', 'temporary' and 'permanent' disability determined how much compensation a worker might receive. Workers could claim their compensation payments through the local post office. The families of deceased workers, including spouses, children and other dependants, were also entitled to compensation. They were, however, granted only a fraction of what the wage-earner was entitled to: 20 per cent of the salary for a spouse, 15 per cent for children and up to 20 per cent for other dependants, depending on individual circumstances. The law granted the status of 'children' to biological and adopted minor dependants up to the age of 15;

---

[58] GStAPK: I. HA. Rep. 84a:11030: 65–72: Presidium of the State Ministry to Chancellor Bismarck, 21 December 1880; GStAPK: I. HA. 120BB. Abt. VIII. Fach. 4. No. 1. Vol. 1: 1–5: Report of the Prussian Ministry of Trade on the 'Insurance of Commercial Workers against Accidents', 23 September 1880.

[59] GStAPK: I. HA. 120BB. Abt. VIII. Fach. 4. No. 1. Vol. 1: 1–5: Report of the Ministry of Trade on the 'Insurance of commercial workers against accidents', 23 September 1880.

[60] An elaboration on how this worked: Lass and Zahn, *Einrichtung*, p. 175.

afterwards, these individuals were no longer eligible for benefit unless, for some specific reason, they were still deemed dependent. The definition of dependency was wide-reaching in the case of children, as it allowed for the compensation of illegitimate children and acknowledged the fact that child labourers were low-paid and generally relied on income from their parents. Moreover, this level of compensation for dependants was generous compared to earlier suggestions in government that sought to limit compensation only to those cases when the deceased served as the 'sole nourisher', that is, the breadwinner for a family. As the Minister of Justice pointed out, the model of family based on a male breadwinner did not, in reality, exist.[61] His concern highlighted the fact that the accident insurance policy targeted working-class families, in which both spouses – as well as children – were likely to be involved in some form of employment. Social insurance would therefore not only apply to working-class men engaged in heavy industry. It was intended to integrate all members of the working classes within the German national community by rectifying individual injuries through national solidarity.

As in Germany, in Italy, the purpose of compensation was protecting workers against known hardships that they or their families could encounter following an accident. For members of the Italian and German governments, choosing insurance to deal with workplace accidents pointed directly to their roles as social planners: it enabled them to garner authority by overseeing the fine details of the policy. Moreover, it reflected the bureaucratic tradition of understanding government as a form of policing, whose goal was the maintenance of public order. Since both the Italian and German laws required insurance, they therefore granted compensation according to the standards used in commercial accident insurance rather than the standards used in liability cases. Under liability law, which both the Italian and German accident insurance policies were replacing, lump sums were granted as a form of compensation which aimed to assuage suffering, financial loss and lost opportunity. Compensation under liability law did not, however, attempt to pay the real cost of injuries: potentially, no longer being able to carry out the same line of work and, almost certainly, lost wages and medical treatment.[62] By contrast, the compensation practices of commercial insurance ensured the routine payment of benefit during a worker's recovery or following his death. Social insurance accorded with the same principles. By taking up the policy, the Italian and German governments placed themselves in situations where they would be responsible in some measure for overseeing the recovery and well-being of injured workers and their families.

---

[61] GStAPK: I. HA. Rep. 84a:11030: 52–64: Vote of the Ministry of Justice on the first accident insurance law proposal, 31 December 1880.

[62] Francesco Parisi, 'The genesis of liability in ancient law', *American Law and Economics Review* 3 (2001), pp. 82–124.

In Italy, it was clear to the Ministry of Agriculture that accident compensation should operate according to actuarial principles correlated with known occupational risks and their potential effect on the earnings of individual workers. As in Germany, the system was based on salary rather than need. The department therefore consulted with the renowned Milan-based Medical Institute for Industrial Accidents when determining how to measure disability.[63] Workers who were partially disabled received compensation amounts that corresponded directly with the level of their injuries, which were calculated as a percentage of total ability. The government met resistance in deciding to adopt this system of compensation based on salary rather than need. For example, the Sardinian Mining Association lobbied against the policy because of its potential financial burden. The Association, like the Union of Italian Railways, had been reluctant from the start about universally requiring insurance when it seemed that only those businesses at risk of bankruptcy from accident claims would need it. If compelled to pay for insurance, then employers would at least need a safeguard against malingerers who no longer required assistance, lest the policy turn into 'a fount of earning for the heirs of the person struck by an accident'.[64]

For accident insurance to remain equitable to employers and workers alike, it would need to stipulate against abuse. As in Germany, maximum compensation amounts were limited: workers could receive up to half the amount of their lost earnings due. This maxim applied to both permanent and temporary cases of partial disability. For cases of permanent total disability, however, the Italian law deviated from the norms of commercial insurance. It instead granted a lump-sum payment of six times one's annual salary. An annuity based on this payment would be distributed monthly through the National Fund for Disability and Old Age Pensions, which was erected as a semi-private voluntary fund several months after the accident insurance law was ratified in 1898. Similarly, for cases of temporary total disability, a worker would receive half of his full salary on a daily basis until recovery. Like German workers, those in Italy would be able to receive accident pensions through their local post office. The new system would continue the practice that had been in place

---

[63] In Italian, this was called the Istituto medico contro gl'infortuni degli operai sul lavoro: 'Allegato A: Relazione della commissione, composta dei signori Conte Aldo Annoni, senatore del regno, Comm. Enea, cavalieri, e commendatore Vincenzo Magaldi, sullo schema di regolamento per la esecuzione della legge 17 marzo 1898, n. 80, per gli infortuni sul lavoro', *Annali del credito e della previdenza* (1898), pp. 185–8, at p. 187.

[64] CdAs: Leg. XX, Sess. 1897–8, Proposte di legge: Bta. 664: A. C. 146: 'Disegno di legge già approvato dal senato del regno presentato dal ministro di agricoltura, industria e commercio – Guicciardini – infortuni sul lavoro, seduta 7 luglio 1897'; unnumbered: Petition from the Sardinian Mining Association to the Chamber of Deputies, 24 February 1898; unnumbered: Petition from the Union of Italian Railways with Local Subsidiaries to the Chamber of Deputies, 23 February 1898.

since 1884, when the National Fund began distributing compensation through post office branches.[65]

Caps on compensation amounts and the distinction between different levels of disability were attempts to mitigate against the potential harms of redistributing occupational risk on a mass basis. As the Sardinian Mining Association had made clear, social insurance could result in the double burden of depleting resources from industry while spurring a new moral economy of claims making. It therefore demanded that only family members who were truly dependent on an injured worker receive accident benefit.[66] The administration in Italy recognised that households relied on multiple wage earners, and civil servants saw it as their duty to ensure that the complex networks of familial dependence were acknowledged in compensation claims. Thus, the Ministry of Agriculture proposed that dependent children of deceased workers receive compensation payments until they turned 18, unless they were unable to work, in which case they would receive benefit for the rest of their lives. Family members would receive regular payments based on an annuity from a lump-sum amount of five times the worker's annual salary. The same benefit level applied to ascendants, which included dependent parents and grandparents, and dependent siblings. For spouses in Italy, compensation was less generous than it was in Germany because the Italian government assumed that a greater range of dependants would rely on a wage-earner's salary. Spouses were entitled to two-fifths of the total compensation amount if children were also eligible, and three-fifths if they were vying against ascendants or the deceased's siblings for their share of compensation. Spouses did, however, receive the entirety of compensation if no other family members could stake a claim. This varied system of compensation reflected officials' concerns that multiple generations of Italian families, as well as the members of a worker's wider kinship network, were likely to rely on each other for financial support. Through social insurance, Italian families could also come to look towards the state as a protector, whose authority was symbolised by the local post office branches where compensation payments would be collected regularly. However, they would be deterred from taking advantage of employers by the relatively stingy compensation amounts that were guaranteed under the new scheme.

In Britain, workmen's compensation was awarded on a case-by-case basis at court, creating what appeared to be a chasm between the state and civil society as well as between individuals within civil society, who fought out

---

[65] 'Regio decreto che approva il regolamento dei rapporti cogli uffici postali e le autorità comunali, 1 settembre 1884, no. 2684, serie 3a', *Bollettino di notizie sul credito e la previdenza* 2/16 (1 November 1884), pp. 448–52.

[66] CdAs: Leg. XX, Sess. 1897–8, Proposte di legge: Bta. 664: A. C. 146: 'Disegno di legge già approvato dal senato del regno presentato dal ministro di agricoltura, industria e commercio – Guicciardini – infortuni sul lavoro, seduta 7 luglio 1897'; unnumbered: Petition from the Sardinian Mining Association to the Chamber of Deputies, 24 February 1898.

their cases on their own terms. The policy did not create a new social insurance fund, nor did it require employers to take out insurance against accident claims. Moreover, the law did not set out compensation amounts following actuarial principles, and officials saw no need to calculate the costs associated with particular disability levels. In contrast to Germany and Italy, where the governments drew up disability guidelines that would assist judges and arbitrators in determining compensation amounts, no such schedule existed in Britain. It was left to medical referees, arbitrators and judges to decide disability levels and compensation amounts on an individual basis. The practice pointed to civil servants' concerns to maintain a position of distant neutrality in compensation claims. Nonetheless, as in Germany and Italy, in Britain, the Home Office drew up a general classification of disability. 'Partial', 'total', 'temporary' and 'permanent' disability were the main categories. Moreover, compensation amounts were not based on need. Instead, as elsewhere, they reflected the extent to which an injury interfered in a worker's ability to earn his usual salary or wages. Compensation and disability were, therefore, directly linked. Workmen's compensation, like social insurance, aimed to go beyond setting out a basic minimum for living costs. The policy was not intended as a mere replacement for the Poor Law. Instead, it was predicated on a notion of contractual obligation between workers and employers.

Due to the lack of a fixed schedule of compensation in Britain, officials saw the need to create a basic yardstick which could ensure that this obligation would be upheld in practice. Employers were especially anxious about the possible economic burden of paying for compensation, and their concerns shaped the Workmen's Compensation Act. Following the lobbying efforts of employers, the Home Office decided that it could prevent malingering by capping the maximum amount of compensation at one half of an injured worker's total average salary in the case of total or partial disability.[67] It also decided to limit the potential economic burden to employers by allowing workers to make claims only after two weeks' disability, meaning that lesser injuries were not subject to compensation. The government therefore established maximum and minimum amounts as part of the law: workers were allowed to receive a weekly payment of up to half of their former salary if totally disabled and a proportion of that if partially disabled. After six months, employers or workers could apply for compensation to be paid off as a lump sum, which workers could invest as an annuity. Similarly, dependants of deceased workers would receive lump-sum payments of three times a worker's former salary, which the arbitrator could invest in a post-office savings fund. Significantly, the law did not allocate proportions of compensation to different categories of dependants. The task was left to judges and arbitrators to determine.

---

[67] TNA: HO 45/9867/B13816L/14: Home Office notes, 15 May 1897, in response to a letter from B. Huntsman, 19 May 1897.

Through these basic guidelines and the rulings of judges and arbitrators, workmen's compensation sought to create a delicate balance of mutual obligation between employers and workers in the face of occupational risk. However, unlike social insurance in Germany and Italy, the policy stopped short when it came to questions of fault. Neither the German nor the Italian accident insurance laws enabled employers to claim that workers had contributed to an accidental injury – unless they had done so criminally, for example, by self-maiming. The Workmen's Compensation Act, by contrast, included a clause that forbade compensation for injuries resulting from 'serious and wilful misconduct'. The clause harked back to the thinking behind liability law and, before that, common law. For example, between 1869 and 1873, the majority of injuries involving railway workers were attributed to negligence. Under common law, any degree of contributory negligence precluded a claimant from receiving damages.[68] 'Serious and wilful misconduct' was not seen as a criminal act. It was instead a form of *fault* which could be determined at the discretion of a judge. In turn, the workmen's compensation law also allowed workers to hold their employers accountable for accidents. British workers could choose to try their luck at court by suing employers under liability law rather than claiming through the new compensation scheme. A successful liability suit held the potential to be much more lucrative, but it required workers to prove that their employers had in some way caused an accident to happen.

GOVERNING RISK

Various factors shaped how occupational risk would be administered on a day-to-day basis. In Germany, the corporatist system based on the practices of Prussian mining funds seemed the ideal way in which to tackle occupational risk because it compelled workers and employers to address accidents together, while also working with local and regional authorities and, as a last resort, central government. The policy conceded a fair amount of local and regional input in granting local authorities a role in administration and allowing for the establishment of regional insurance boards which would serve as appeals courts for disputes about compensation. The system therefore allowed for a degree of continuity in local and regional relations with political authorities. For example, in the province of East Prussia, the upper administrative authority in the new insurance system was the governmental president at Königsberg, while the lower administrative authorities were community-based officials. For urban areas, these were magistrates from the municipal police, while, in rural areas, they would be the *Landräte*, or district administrators, who had long

---

[68] Audrey C. Giles, 'Railway accidents and nineteenth-century legislation: "misconduct, want of caution or causes beyond their control"', *Labour History Review* 76/2 (2011), pp. 121–42.

been responsible for a variety of local concerns.[69] In fact, the involvement of local support that this system provided was an argument put forward by the Ministry of Agriculture, which recognised the need for local knowledge, especially in handling Germany's vast rural estates.[70]

This programme also allowed for a great degree of private involvement on the local and regional levels by establishing the employers' liability funds, the regionally based mutual insurance societies that consisted of employers in similar trades. Yet, the Imperial Insurance Office, which was set up in Berlin in 1885, would administer the whole system. It acted as the final court of appeals for disputes about compensation and oversaw premium rates and the efficient running of the funds, which included monitoring their statutes, finances, accident rates and safety provisions. At conferences and social museums as well as through a variety of official and semi-official journals, the Imperial Insurance Office also communicated with local and regional governments, staff members of the funds and the general public about changes to accident insurance policy and related developments. The government saw this combination of national, regional and local administration in conjunction with the funds as the ideal means to address the consequences of workplace accidents. It conceded that employers in like industries would know best how to regulate each other. The government would oversee this process, thereby endowing social insurance with special legitimacy while contributing to the sense that Germany indeed had a paternalistic state that would care for its citizens. Officials also sought to involve workers in the administration of the new system because they saw social insurance as a means to integrate members of society with the aid of that paternalistic state.[71] The wording of the law even included a section on the 'representation of workers', a theme that was taken up again and again in later official representations of the German social insurance system that were used at domestic and international congresses.[72] Equal numbers of workers and employers sat alongside a local official on the boards of arbitration for accident claims that served as a first court of appeal for disputes regarding compensation amounts. Similarly, both employers and workers sat in equal numbers as representatives at the regional and national courts of appeal for accident claims, which acted outside of the main court system.

However, workers' involvement in the administration of the employers' liability funds remained limited, as they did not pay insurance premiums. Workers were granted representation within the funds, in equal numbers to employers

[69] 'Bekanntmachung betreffend die von den Zentralbehörden der Bundesstaaten gemäß bestimmten höheren und unteren Verwaltungsbehörden', *Amtliche Nachrichten des Reichs-Versicherungsamts* 2/7 (1 April 1886), pp. 20–46.
[70] BArch: R1501: 100399: 150: Prussian Legation in Württemberg to Bismarck, 2 January 1881.
[71] BArch: R1501: 100401: 100–4: Vote of the Ministry of Agriculture, Domains and Forests, 6 February 1884.
[72] See Chapter 4.

serving on their boards, for the purposes of compiling safety measures that member firms should carry out. Their presence in the accident funds seemed so significant that some employers' organisations began to worry about workers colluding. Moreover, some worried that the funds could provide opportunities to 'turn' seemingly apolitical workers socialist. As a conference of industrialists in Alsace-Lorraine put it, 'the Alsatian worker is, to be sure, by nature peaceful, sensible and up to now untouched by socialist heresy'.[73] The corporatist organisation of social insurance could result in the demise of their dependability. Despite this fear, many employers' groups felt that it was necessary to include workers in administering the policy in order to give them a sense of ownership and responsibility for it. The Association of German Iron Foundries, for example, claimed that only this set-up would give workers a sense of 'real trust' in the policy. It would also mean that social insurance could 'avoid having the character of a police institution'.[74] Perhaps due to these mixed concerns, workers were involved in most aspects of administering accident insurance but did not supervise whether and how the safety measures outlined by the employers' liability funds were put into effect. The uneven role of workers and employers in governing occupational risk in Germany resulted in the impression that accident insurance was ultimately a means for employers to maintain a firm grip on their businesses while snuffing out popular complaints about the harms of industrialisation. Moreover, by organising employers into accident funds, it seemed that businesses could easily collude against workers.[75] For example, in order to monitor the law, the government required employers to report accidents. It supplied employers with a form that asked for details about each accident, including when it took place; the age, sex and profession of the worker involved; and its cause and consequences. Local police authorities collected this information, which was sent to the Imperial Insurance Office to tabulate statistics, and they also investigated accidents on the ground. Government therefore defined the terms of occupational risk by setting the categories used in accident statistics, but it was up to employers to police their businesses on a day-to-day basis. On balance, however, this corporatist arrangement could contribute to the sense of 'real trust' in social insurance and, by extension, the state, that the Association of Iron Foundries and, indeed, Bismarck, had sought. It appeared to shift the risk of workplace accidents away from individuals and towards a new form of collective, embodied immediately by the employers' liability funds and indirectly in the form of the Imperial Insurance Office in Berlin.

[73] 'Sitzungsprotokoll einer Konferenz Elsaß-Lothringischer Industrieller', 16 February 1884, quoted in Tennstedt and Winter, eds., *QS*, vol. II, part 1, pp. 494–500.
[74] BArch: R1501: 100394: 211–14: *Verein deutscher Eisengiesserein* to the Imperial Chancellory, 25 November 1881. See also: 59–60: Petition to the *Reichstag* from the Directorate of the *Central-Verband Deutscher Industrieller*, 15 March 1881.
[75] 'Die neueste Unfallvorlage und die Arbeiter', quoted in Tennstedt and Winter, eds., *QS*, vol. II.i, pp. 479–81.

However, the system was not without its detractors. Some workers' organisation were particularly sceptical about governing risks according to new 'risk classes' made up of discrete occupational groups when it seemed that all workers could be the victims of occupational accidents.[76]

Although the Italian system was based on both commercial insurance and the semi-private National Accident Insurance Fund, it relied on governmental supervision and involvement. Local, regional and national governments all played a role in this new system, which created a new network of public obligations and shared collective responsibilities that coursed throughout the peninsula. Workers, however, did not play a central role within this network. In contrast to Germany, where disputes about compensation were presented to tribunals and special courts at the regional and national accident insurance offices, in Italy, these cases were resolved primarily through the regular court system. In early discussions about the policy, officials considered using special tribunals for this purpose, along the lines of the labour tribunals that were created in 1893 for other industrial disputes.[77] Workers' groups lobbied for this kind of representation in the administration of the new law. For example, Florence's Chamber of Labour called for 'cooperation with workers' and 'public powers' in its May Day petition of 1896. They demanded that workers be able to act as arbitrators in industrial disputes and supervise factory labour and hygiene alongside other areas, including the labour of women and children.[78] The request was granted in that disputes about small amounts of compensation for short-lived injuries could be resolved through local tribunals. However, as in Britain, officials saw the policy as a substitute for liability law, and they decided that more serious cases should be adjudicated in courts of cassation, which were used for all cases involving private law. In Italy, unlike in Germany, therefore, some links were maintained between the earlier treatment of workplace accidents under the civil code and the new system of compulsory accident insurance. A key difference between the governance of accident insurance and earlier labour legislation was the central role afforded to government: courts of cassation were instructed to report cases involving the new law to the Ministry of Justice, which published volumes summarising important verdicts. These digests were available for courts throughout the country when making decisions, and they were used by the Ministry of Agriculture for internal discussions about revising the law.[79]

---

[76] 'Die neueste Unfallvorlage und die Arbeiter', at p. 479.

[77] 'Allegato B' (1889), pp. 62–3.

[78] ACS: PCM (1896 – Rudini). Bta. 195. Fasc. 122: Petition from the Chamber of Labour in Florence to the Prime Minister, 1 May 1896.

[79] Art. 70 of the Regulation of 25 September 2898, N. 411. The Ministry of Justice later sent reminders to local government: 'Istruzioni del ministro di grazia e giustizia ai cancellieri circa la redazoine delle copie dei verbali delle inchieste', *Bollettino ufficiale del Ministero di grazia e giustizia* 20 (14 May 1901).

Regional prefects, who acted on behalf of the Ministry of the Interior, over-saw the day-to-day supervision of the law, which reflected their continuing authority in the years following national unification and especially from the 1880s and 1890s, when the central state sought to maintain a degree of control over local and regional government.[80] According to both the new law and an ordinance several months later, all employers were required to use forms provided by central government to report all accidents within two days, and it was the responsibility of prefects to relay this information back to Rome. This aspect of the policy allowed for the first comprehensive and long-term compilation of accident statistics in Italy. The government hoped that this information – alongside the regular compilation of legal verdicts on accident cases – would establish a clearer understanding of occupational risk, which would have an impact on both insurance premiums and later extensions to the law. Employers filled out these forms in duplicate, forwarding them to both the local and provincial or circondarial offices of public security. Along with these forms, they were required to include a medical report from any doctor they selected, which would cause contention once the policy was in effect.[81] The Ministry of Agriculture planned to use this information in order to evaluate the 'degree of risk inherent in the various kinds of industries' and to devise effective measures for accident prevention.[82]

It is noteworthy that accident prevention and accident insurance were introduced in Italy as part of a unified policy for managing workplace risk. Through the accident law, the government in Rome aimed simultaneously to tackle three central concerns: addressing the inevitability of occupational risk and its harmful consequences for workers; making workplaces less dangerous and thereby potentially more efficient; and, creating an administrative apparatus that ensured its authority. Several months after the accident insurance law was enacted in 1898, a national decree therefore mandated that employers open their premises to inspections by government-endorsed inspectors. These inspectors came from a variety of backgrounds. The Ministry of Agriculture, the Ministry of Public Works, the Royal Mining Corps, the Genio Civile, which was in charge of public engineering works, and private accident prevention organisations, where a variety of specialists worked, all contributed. Neither national nor local government played a role in directly supervising this aspect of the new law, though the national government did create forms for these inspectors to use throughout the country. Inspectors were sent to workplaces

---

[80] Nico Randeraad, *Autorità in cerca di autonomia: I prefetti nell'Italia liberale*, trans. David Scaffei (Rome, 1997), p. 265.

[81] See Chapter 4. Art. 25 of the 17 March 1898 law and 'Circolare 30 novembre 1898, n. 18581, del MAIC ai signore prefetti del regno che dà istruzioni per le denunzie degli infortuni', *Annali del credito e della previdenza* 18 (1900), pp. 110–12.

[82] 'Per la statistica degli infortuni sul lavoro', *Bollettino di notizie sul credito e sulla previdenza* 19 (1901, 1st semester), pp. 525–59, at p. 525.

at least once every two years, and the Ministry of Agriculture could call for additional extraordinary inspections. They were allowed to enter workplaces; interrogate the management, owners, supervisors and workers; examine the payment books and insurance contracts; and examine the equipment and premises. If they encountered difficulty gaining access to workplaces, they could call on local authorities.[83] This joint effort to insure against accidents and prevent them seemed to garner support for central government, which was evidenced by the vote of confidence by socialist deputies in parliament in 1901 and again in 1902, shortly after the accident legislation was put into effect. To be sure, various socialist factions continued to oppose government, resulting in continued strike waves throughout the early 1900s and demands for revolution. Nonetheless, the accident policy was certainly a step towards addressing the minimum programme outlined by the Socialist Party Congress in 1900, which called for protective labour laws. To many workers, it seemed that the new Italian state could take on the role of protector, eradicating the need for revolution outlined by those members of the congress who embraced maximalism instead.[84]

In Britain, workmen's compensation was predicated on the commercialisation of occupational risk as a means for workers and employers to take responsibility for accidents into their own hands. Nonetheless, the policy relied on a central administrative role for the state. The Home Office continued to call on its factory inspectorate as the main source of information about safety at work under the new compensation regime, and it also used the court system to oversee appeals cases involving the new compensation law. Workmen's compensation allowed a great degree of involvement for local government, various agencies in national government and the regular court system, alongside commercial insurance bodies. Moreover, disputes about compensation could be resolved in the first instance through tribunals that represented workers and employers alike. These tribunals were convened by an arbitrator selected by both the worker and employer involved or by a representative appointed by the local county court judge.[85] The other option was settlement without formal arbitration. Only for appeals was the regular court system invoked. An important new role was created within this judicial system: the impartial medical referee, who was appointed locally by county courts but approved in Whitehall by the Home Office.

[83] MAIC, Uffico del lavoro, *L'ispezione del lavoro: Studi sull'organizzazione del servizio di vigilanza per l'applicazione delle leggi operaie* (Rome, 1904), pp. 10–14.

[84] Daniel L. Horowitz, *The Italian labor movement* (Cambridge, MA, 1963), pp. 51–2; Maria Sophia Quine, *Italy's social revolution: charity and welfare from liberalism to fascism* (Basingstoke, 2002), p. 69.

[85] In Scotland, which had a separate legal system, the local Sheriff would fill the role of the county court judge, and sheriffs' courts would fill the role of county courts under the new law.

The workmen's compensation policy did not alter the system for supervising workplace safety, nor did it establish a new schedule of safety measures. In this respect, it contrasted with Germany, where employers' liability funds were empowered to draw up their own safety provisions and see that they were carried out, and Italy, where the new accident insurance law called for the first thorough supervision of workplace safety through an expanded national inspectorate. Workmen's compensation was meant to operate in conjunction with the extensive safety practices already in place, including the country's renowned factory inspectorate that dated back to the 1830s.[86] The policy transformed workplace safety in one significant respect: by compelling employers to compensate workers for accidents, it provided them with an incentive to keep work safe. Moreover, if employers took up commercial accident insurance policies, they would be penalised for accidents by higher premiums. By linking safety with costs, the policy was able to imply a new form of responsibilisation for employers without mandating outright protective measures for workplaces. Officials saw that grappling with the consequences of insurance or out-of-pocket payments would bring employers to regulate themselves perhaps better than the factory inspectorate ever could.[87] Workmen's compensation appealed to workers in this respect. As the Amalgamated Society of Engineers claimed, the main issue in the eyes of workers was ensuring safety. The group called for making 'preventable accidents impossible', going as far as demanding that employers be held criminally liable for accidents at work. An editorial to its monthly journal cited an example of a steel fitter who was blinded after a stray piece of metal hit his eye and suggested that standard goggles would have saved his vision. It also recalled the case of a woodworker who was seriously injured after a plank came loose from a machine above and fell on his back. 'It is blasphemy to characterise such an occurrence as an "Act of God"', claimed the author. 'These things are no accidents. They are the inevitable result of a want of *due precaution*, and the direct outcome of the mad rush to accumulate profits at the risk of workmen's lives and limbs.' Accidents could only be prevented, it seemed, if employers were made to pay for them.[88]

Workmen's compensation and the accident insurance laws were predicated on diverse assumptions about individual responsibilities, collective burdens and the

---

[86] P. W. J. Bartrip and Sandra Burman, *The wounded soldiers of industry: industrial compensation policy, 1833–1897* (Oxford, 1983), pp. 202–4, 212–14; A. F. Young, *Industrial injuries insurance: an examination of British policy* (New York, 1964), p. 41; 4 *Hansard* HC vol. 48 (3 May 1897), cols. 1434–7, 1446–8, 1462–4.

[87] V. Markham Lester, 'The employers' liability/workmen's compensation debate of the 1890s revisited', *Historical Journal* 44 (2001), pp. 471–95.

[88] Author's italics. WCML: S11V/15: Amalgamated Society of Engineers: Yearly and Monthly Reports, 1897: 'Editorial', *Amalgamated Engineers' Journal and Monthly Record of Facts, Figures and Fancy relating to the Engineering Trade, Unionism, and Industrialism* (n.s.) 1/2 (February 1897), pp. 2–5, at p. 4.

role of the state as an arbiter in social relations. In Germany, leading civil servants, following Bismarck, saw 'state socialism' as the best means to deal with social issues and had opted for a policy of compulsory, state-organised social insurance. By contrast, officials in Italy aimed for a compromise between the left-liberalism that had dominated domestic politics in the 1870s and the reformist ideas of the 1880s and 1890s, and the Italian system of accident insurance reflected this thinking. Like Germany, Italy enacted a social insurance policy for workplace accidents. The Italian government did not, however, seek to play a significant role in the daily management of this system. It is noteworthy that Britain steered clear of legislation that required insurance. British officials were anxious to avoid departing radically from the status quo, and they looked to the treatment of compensation under the common law as a model for the new system under the Workmen's Compensation Act. As a consequence, ideas about fault remained explicit within the policy. In Britain, workmen's compensation was viewed as a means to address workplace accidents by drawing on solutions *within* civil society. The policy created an interpersonal form of responsibility for occupational risk by binding individual employers and workers through claims at court and payments provided out of pocket by employers or individual arrangements via commercial insurance or mutual funds. The interpersonal nature of this relationship was made clear by the fact that employers could still hold workers directly accountable for gross negligence, while workers could continue to sue employers at court under liability law.

In overseeing these diverse arrangements, each government could garner a special role, helping to win newfound allegiances amongst workers and employers alike. Workmen's compensation instituted a new form of liberalism in Britain in which workers and employers could solve their conflicts through a new form of social law that was governed from a distance in Whitehall. By contrast, in Italy, social insurance could serve as a testament to the country's national development and seeming status as a 'modern' state as well as a tool for economic advancement. In Germany, the policy was seen as a means to achieve national solidarity in light of the continued political upheaval following national unification. Social insurance and the building of *nation* states therefore went hand in hand, and occupational risk was redistributed on a social basis, whether through the employers' liability funds in Germany or the mixture of mutual schemes, commercial insurance and the National Accident Fund in Italy. Work was viewed as a national good that contributed to the growth of the new nation states, which legitimated spreading the costs of its potential harms to a broader collectivity. These views would soon be tested. In practice, as the following chapter shows, it was anything but clear which groups were likely to suffer workplace accidents and where responsibility for accidents lay. Nor was it apparent how government could best manage insecurities prompted by the new insurance and compensation laws. Could accident legislation forge social solidarity, or would it create new uncertainties and social fissures?

4

Taking Risks and Dismissing Fate

In 1902, civil servants, insurance experts, engineers and physicians from around the world flocked to the German city of Düsseldorf in order to attend the sixth meeting of the International Congress for Work-Related Accidents and Social Insurance. It was here that Pompeo Colajanni, the director of the Association of Sicilian Mine-Owners for the Prevention of Accidents and a member of the Chamber of Commerce in Caltanissetta, presented a paper about the substantial increase in the number of reported accidents since Italy introduced compulsory accident insurance. Colajanni explained that the statistics collected for 1899–1901 demonstrated the 'very serious burden of risk' associated with the new policy. Colajanni, who represented the Italian government at the congress, implied that the new social legislation had created a new kind of risk by altering the responsibilities of workers, employers and the state in the face of workplace accidents. He claimed that two factors had led to the apparent rise in accident numbers. First, the meaning of an 'accident' was difficult to interpret, and confusion over what counted as a *workplace* accident contributed to a variety of contentious requests for compensation. What exactly was an accident? Who or what established whether one had occurred, and on what criteria did they base their judgments? He argued that the ambiguity of the term had not only led to more claims, but it had posed serious problems for the effectiveness of the new policy. While the loose interpretation of an 'accident' by a lenient judge might overburden employers and insurance funds, a narrow interpretation could condemn an injured worker to a life of poverty. The second factor that Colajanni cited was fraud, and this, too, was an issue that lent itself to a variety of understandings. How would it be possible to distinguish between 'authentic' accidents and those which had been engineered to secure access to compensation? Colajanni noted that at least three different types of fraud had contributed to the increase in accident numbers in Italy since the law was enacted.[1] Whether a claim for compensation was fraudulent, however, was difficult to ascertain, which meant that it would be difficult to weed out those who were abusing social insurance.

It seemed that the accident insurance law had provoked new forms of moral hazard. Some compensation recipients appeared to be taking advantage of the social solidarity fostered by the legislation. On the surface, the system had failed: not only was accident benefit granted to 'undeserving' claimants, proving costly and inefficient; it also failed to create bonds within society and allegiance to the nation state. In order for the new policy to operate effectively, Colajanni argued, those involved in administering compensation would have to investigate individual cases, interpret the wording of the law and consult medical and technical experts. Only through careful management could the nature of occupational risk become clear, shedding light on whether accidents stemmed from workers' poor choices, 'Acts of God' and other forms of bad luck or from the manufacturing process itself. Colajanni's suggestion resonated with the other conference participants. The statistics collected by the British, German and Italian governments all demonstrated a jump in accident rates in the first several years after the insurance and workmen's compensation laws were enacted. For example, in Britain, the number of reported accidents rose from 79,000 in 1900 to over 124,000 just seven years later. In metal foundries alone, the rate of nonfatal accidents had gone up 46 per cent during the same period. Meanwhile, in Germany, the annual number of reported industrial accidents resulting in death went from 1,548 in 1886 to 5,569 20 years later – an increase of almost 360 per cent.[2]

Like Colajanni, officials in Britain and Germany feared that growing accident claims pointed to a larger problem, which is the subject of this chapter. It seemed that the new compensation systems gradually eroded workers' sense of agency in working safely and, when work went wrong, caring for themselves and their families. Moreover, technical and legal arguments employed in claims cases undermined the idea that accidents could be caused by misfortune or those ill-fated events known as 'Acts of God'. As a result, whether based in

---

[1] Pompeo Colajanni, 'Trois premières années d'application de la loi sur les accidents du travail aux ouvriers des mines de soufre de la Sicilie', in *Congrès international des accidents du travail et des assurances sociales. Sixième session tenue à Düsseldorf* (Berlin, 1902), pp. 731–47, especially p. 737.

[2] *PP* 1911 (Cd 5535) XXIII.1–70: 'Report of the Departmental Committee on Accidents in Places under the Factory and Workshop Acts', pp. 8–9, 15–16, 20, 22–3. See also Konrad Hartmann, *Schutz gegen Unfallgefahren in gewerblichen Betrieben* (Berlin, 1902), pp. 2–3; 'Resultati delle ispezioni eseguite nell'anno dal maggio 1906 al 30 giugno 1907, dal personale tecnico dell'Associazione degli industriali d'Italia per prevenire gli infortuni del lavoro con sede in Milano (Relazione del Direttore dell'Associazione a S. E. Il Ministro di MAIC)', *Bollettino di notizi sul credito e sulla previdenza* 25/9 (1907), pp. 1707–28, at pp. 1710–11; Henry J. Harris, 'The increase in industrial accidents', *Publications of the American Statistical Association* 13/97 (1912), pp. 1–27, at p. 6.

industrialised Britain, in rural Italy or in Germany, where the complex system of social insurance brought citizens into frequent contact with civil servants, workers appeared increasingly dependent on the state. Compensation seemed to damage both workers' autonomy and the higher authority of fortune. At the same time, the compensation laws seemed to become yet another strain on industrial relations, sparking lockouts and accusations of cheating insurance companies, employers and workers. In Britain, Germany and Italy, the policies were tested against a backdrop of regular clashes about labour. The 1900 Taff Vale verdict in Britain meant that trade unions could now be held liable for financial damage caused by strikes, while the Osborne judgment a few years later held that unions could no longer require members to back specific political parties and, in particular, the nascent Labour Party.[3] By 1911, Britain witnessed nationwide railway and dock strikes that seemed to bring traffic to a standstill. Meanwhile, Germany saw a boom in unrest that roughly mirrored the ebbs and flows of unemployment rates. In 1900, 1,469 strikes took place across Germany, rising to as many as 2,834 in 1912. And in Italy, a wave of labour unrest in 1906 provoked a backlash amongst employers, resulting in the founding of associations such as the Industrial League of Turin which declared general lockouts in response to general strikes.[4]

Social democratic parties rallied to address some of the concerns that brought workers to the street, becoming 'fixtures of their political systems' by 1914.[5] The Italian Socialist Party provided an outlet at a time when the majority of workers on the peninsula were still unable to vote, and the German Social Democratic Party took off in both the *Reichstag* and regional elections from 1890 after having been effectively banned over a decade earlier, becoming the largest party in Germany by 1912. The seeds of the British Labour Party took root over the course of the 1890s, paving the way for the 1906 election of 30 Labour MPs to the House of Commons alongside a new era of Lib-Lab politics in which the majority Liberal Party's 'new liberal' social reforms thrived.[6] In this context, any uncertainties about the accident policies seemed to highlight broader questions about workers' demands and rights. Should workers receive compensation for *all* occupational accidents? How could workers be held to account for their actions?

---

[3] Andrew Thorpe, *A history of the British Labour Party* (1997; 3rd edn, Basingstoke, 2008), pp. 17, 26–8.

[4] Dick Geary, *European labour protest, 1848–1939* (London, 1984), pp. 105–6; Franklin Hugh Adler, *Italian industrialists from liberalism to fascism: the political development of the industrial bourgeoisie, 1906–34* (Cambridge, 1995), pp. 37–9, 49.

[5] Geoff Eley, *Forging democracy: the history of the left in Europe, 1850–2000* (Oxford, 2002), at p. 5.

[6] Chris Cooke and John Stevenson, *A history of British elections since 1689* (London, 2014), p. 98; Jonathan Sperber, *The Kaiser's voters: electors and elections in Imperial Germany* (Cambridge, 1997), pp. 52–5.

WHAT IS AN 'ACCIDENT'?

Insecurities about the use and abuse of workmen's compensation and social insurance stemmed largely from the lack of a clear definition for an 'accident'. What was an 'accident'? Was it simply 'something that happens' (or 'falls'), as its Latin etymology suggests?[7] More importantly, under what conditions did a particular accident merit compensation in terms of the law?[8] Questions about fault, consent and intention had already been handled in early legislative discussions, but others remained after the compensation policies had been enacted. The ambiguities stemming from the wording of the law were similar in Britain, Germany and Italy – despite the differences in language, culture and legal systems. It was only the German government, however, that was involved to a great degree in taking a stand on these uncertainties. Evaluating claims cases was left to courts throughout the country in Italy and Britain. However, in Germany, administrators at the Imperial Insurance Office in Berlin adjudicated final appeals in disputes over claims for compensation. The major issue that they confronted pertained to questions about work and the workplace. Legal debates revolved around the question whether the law referred to accidents *'beim Betrieb'*, meaning accidents 'at the firm' or 'in the workplace'. Or was the law intended to apply to all accidents somehow related to work as an activity, that is, *'Betriebsunfälle'*? The concept *'beim Betrieb'* could also be understood as an accident caused 'in the process of making [something]', but there was initially no clear consensus on the issue. The difficulty of interpreting these core concepts emerged in numerous court cases which often found civil servants deciding between the arguments of injured workers and the employers' liability funds in which they were insured (*Berufsgenossenschaften*).

Over time, the Imperial Insurance Office gradually expanded the notion of 'occupational risk' which formed the basis of the new accident law so that it applied to all unintended incidents that harmed workers while they were carrying out their jobs. In doing so, the agency came head to head with the new employers' liability funds that had been set up throughout the country to insure workers covered by the 1884 policy. While workers sought compensation for injuries stemming from these ambiguous cases, the insurance funds looked for a variety of arguments to dismiss their claims. They instead sought to direct their limited resources to other expenses, including the rehabilitation of injured workers, factory inspection and, of course, the compensation of clear-cut workplace accidents. As a result of the natural opposition between the two groups, many cases reached the appeals court at the Imperial

---

[7] 'Accident, n.', *Oxford English Dictionary Online* (Oxford University Press, December 2015), www.oed.com.eresources.shef.ac.uk/view/Entry/1051?isAdvanced=false&result=1&rskey=YoS5sT&, accessed 11 January 2016.

[8] This conundrum has been handled intelligently by Karl Figlio for early tort debates in Britain: 'What is an accident?', in Paul Weindling, ed., *The social history of occupational health* (London, 1985), pp. 180–206.

Insurance Office. The incident involving the agricultural worker Heinrich Faßbender typified disputes around this issue. Faßbender was delivering a cart filled with wood near the city of Bonn when he was hit with a stone, causing him to lose his right eye. The stone was thrown by the owner of the house that Faßbender was passing. Faßbender was not the intended target; the stone thrower had been attempting to strike a neighbour with whom he was involved in a feud. The fund in which Faßbender was a member refused to compensate him for his injury, claiming that the loss of his right eye did not result from his work. The insurance fund lost its case on appeal, first to the regional insurance office and again to the Imperial Insurance Office in Berlin. The final court of appeal declared that the original wording of the 1884 law emphasised the compensation of accidents occurring 'at work' but that later legal discussions instead embraced a broader view of compensation that would apply to injuries encountered through a 'danger to which [a worker] is exposed through occupation with the industry'. According to this logic, any activity involving work might be compensable, regardless of its location or time.[9]

This thinking meant that even 'murder' could now be viewed as a kind of workplace accident, at least in the sensational headlines of a case that caught national attention. In Bavaria, a regional insurance office followed the precedents adjudicated in Berlin in deciding to award compensation to the widow and daughters of the painter Johann Glöckl. Mr Glöckl had been shot and killed by an unknown assailant while on the way to a job, and the regional insurance office declared his death the result of a '*Betriebsunfall*'. It argued that he was exposed to an 'elevated danger of attack' while acting on behalf of his employer by travelling to a job that took him to a dangerous area.[10] The Glöckl case reflected the finding of a parliamentary commission that debated the question of '*Betriebsunfälle*' and ultimately came to the same conclusion as the Imperial Insurance Office and the regional insurance offices in Bavaria, Württemberg and Baden.[11] The widespread reporting of court cases like that involving Glöckl's family also facilitated a national consensus about the meaning of 'workplace accidents' as unfortunate incidents related to work, regardless of where exactly they happened.

[9] BArch: R89: 15107: 252–61: Ia15022/12.5B: *Heinrich Faßbender of Hemmerick v. Rheinische landwirtschaftliche Berufsgenossenschaft*, 26 February 1914; similarly: 262–72: Ia20428/11.17BL: *Johann Liebche v. Posensche landwirtschaftliche Berufsgenossenschaft*, 26 February 1914.

[10] 'Mord als Betriebsunfall', *Vossische Zeitung* 455 (8 September 1913); 'Mord als Betriebsunfall', *Die Berufsgenossenschaft: Zeitschrift für die Reichs-Unfallversicherung* 28/21 (12 November 1913), p. 255.

[11] See, for example: BArch: R89: 10146: unnumbered: 'Geschäftsbericht des Reichsversicherungsamts' (1905), pp. 21–2; 'Geschäftsbericht' (1909), p. 20; 'Zum Begriff des Betriebsunfalls', *Arbeiterversorgung* 16/26 (12 September 1899), p. 453; 'Über die Versicherung der Unfälle auf dem Hinweg zur Arbeit und auf dem Heimwege', *Monatsblätter für Arbeiterversicherung* 4/7 (5 July 1910), pp. 89–92.

The question of what counted as a 'workplace accident' was finally clarified in the Imperial Insurance Ordinance of 1911, which attempted to consolidate the complex social insurance system that had been taking root in Germany since the 1880s. The Ordinance, like several key court cases, including Glöckl's, embraced a juridical view that 'work' could incorporate 'accidents of daily life' that happen to take place while one is working.[12] This finding had significant implications. On a fundamental level, it reflected a changing understanding of human and divine agency. According to this logic, a wide variety of 'misfortunes' or 'accidents' were now standard, 'daily' risks. However, these risks were not to be borne by workers alone. Workers injured by activities only marginally related to the tasks involved in their job could now claim compensation from their employers, via the employers' liability funds, and guaranteed by the state.

This transformation in thinking about the nature of accidents was most evident when the Imperial Insurance Office and regional courts of appeal began awarding compensation to workers struck by lightning while employed outdoors. The first major case of this kind occurred in 1888, just three years after the law was put into effect, when Johann Faust III was struck by lightning while working on a ship. The issue at hand was whether the cause of the accident could be attributed to Faust's job on board or whether death by lightning was merely an 'accident of daily life' unworthy of compensation, or even a stroke of fate and not an 'accident' at all. The insurance fund in which Faust had been a member argued that the 'danger' of being struck by lightning was not a '*Betriebsgefahr*', that is, a danger associated with the job, but a general danger that could strike anyone in a storm. Moreover, the possibility of being struck by lightning was not merely a danger associated with the activities of 'daily life', such as being struck by a stone while making a delivery for work. Instead, building on a variety of arguments in Roman Law, ranging from *casus fortuiti* to *vis major*, it was seen in legal and insurance circles as an event brought about by an 'Act of God', known as '*Höhere Gewalt*', or a 'higher force'. Weather events such as storms, earthquakes and flooding stood alongside other extraordinary occurrences such as ransacking by pirates in this special legal category. Sometimes, though, as in the case of medieval marine insurance, insurers were willing to assume this risk, which perhaps set a precedent for later decisions.[13]

Given the complexity of this case, the Imperial Insurance Office called on an expert witness to evaluate the evidence. The court consulted with the

12 *SBDR* 21 March 1912, p. 899; 5 February 1913, pp. 3486, 3494. See also: BArch: R89: 15107: 107–9: 'Betriebsunfall', Report by Drs Rabeling and Moll, governmental advisers, and President of the Senate at the Imperial Insurance Office, Dr Ludeweig, 25 March 1913, in conjunction with the development of the Reichsversicherungsordnung, *Handbuch der Unfallversicherung* (3 vols., 3rd edn, Leipzig, 1909–10), vol. I, p. 76; vol. III, p. 536.
13 BArch: R89: 15110: unnumbered: Ia 12166: *Dependants of Johann Faust III from Niederlahmstein v. Westdeutsche-Binnenschiffahrts-Berufsgenossenschaft*, 17 December 1888; Florence Edler de Roover, 'Early examples of marine insurance', *Journal of Economic History* 5

renowned physicist Hermann von Helmholtz, who was then the president of the Physical-Technical Imperial Institute in Berlin, about this case. Helmholtz's involvement in this instance pointed to increasing governmental reliance on expert explanations for a wide variety of injuries that were subjected to medical and technical scrutiny. He drew up a lengthy report on Faust's accident, concluding that, according to the 'famous law of electric currents', the surfaces above deep water have a 'higher attraction power for lightning' than surfaces of flat, dry land. The Imperial Insurance Office concluded that the widow and four children left behind by Johann Faust would be entitled to compensation, as he had been on board the ship as part of his job and was, therefore, 'compelled' to be in a location more likely to be struck by lightning. The 'causal connection to the workplace', argued the Imperial Insurance Office, precluded any arguments about Acts of God or about the dangers of 'daily life'. Following this logic, the family of a farmer struck by lightning while harvesting potatoes could also claim compensation from his insurance fund. The laws of physics seemed to strip away that 'higher force' that might take a worker's life, just as legal arguments about the location of workplace accidents undermined claims that workers had made bad decisions, for example, in choosing their route to work.[14]

In Italy and Britain, similar questions about causation, risk and fault confounded officials in charge of overseeing workmen's compensation and accident insurance and resulted in analogous verdicts on rights to compensation. In neither country, however, was central government involved in making decisions on individual cases. In Rome, the Ministry of Agriculture, Industry and Commerce regularly published anthologies of important cases from across the peninsula in an effort to highlight precedents and clarify confusion. As Vincenzo Magaldi, head of the credit and insurance department at the ministry, argued in the first of these collections, it was of the 'utmost importance' to observe how the law was implemented on the ground.[15] What Magaldi and others observed were cases such as that of Antonio Bernatti, who permanently lost the vision in his left eye while building a roof. The freezing temperatures in which he

---

(1945), pp. 172–200, at p. 188; Cornel Zwierlein, *Der gezähmte Prometheus: Feuer Sicherheit zwischen Früher Neuzeit und Moderne* (Göttingen, 2011), pp. 235–42.

[14] BArch: R89: 15110: unnumbered report from Hermann von Helmholtz, President of the Physical-Technical Imperial Institute in Berlin, to Dr Bödiker, President of the Imperial Insurance Office, 16 October 1888; unnumbered: Ia 12166. See also the decision discussed in *Amtliche Nachrichten des Reichsversicherungsamts* (1887), p. 132; BArch: R89: 15110: Ia806: *The widow of Johann Heinrich Bähnk of Malente bei Eustin et al.*, v. *the Hamburg Baugewerks-Berufsgenossenschaft*, 21 March 1887; 'Rekurs-Entscheidungen des Reichs-Versicherungsamts: Unfall durch Blitzschlag', *Arbeiterversorgung* 15/4 (1898), pp. 69–71; Dr Assmann, 'Zum Begriff eines im Dienste (durch Blitzschlag) erlittenen Betriebsunfalls', *Amtliche Nachrichten des Reichsversicherungsamts* (1903), pp. 554–7; 'Körperschädigungen durch Blitzschläge als Betriebsunfälle', *Monatsblätter für Arbeiterversicherung* 1/10 (15 October 1907), pp. 113–17.

[15] *Giurisprudenza giudiziaria*, vol. I, special issue of *Annali del credito e della previdenza* (Rome, 1906), p. i.

worked contributed to the sudden inflammation of his retina, bringing about lasting damage. Bernatti lost his case both at a local tribunal and again at the court of appeals in Turin. The final ruling declared that Bernatti's injury was not due to an 'accident', implying that it arose from a risk of 'daily life', in the nomenclature used in Germany at the time.[16] Cases such as Bernatti's led to a governmental commission that investigated whether special courts should administer disputes involving the accident insurance law. It found that 80 per cent of compensation disputes arose from questions of a technical nature. In response to this finding, commission members argued for the incorporation of state-sponsored medical experts in cases involving accident insurance. It seemed that technical expertise would be needed to resolve lingering questions about the nature of occupational risk.[17]

In claims cases, this distinction between 'work' and 'daily life' proved crucial for evaluating which accidents merited compensation. As the legal expert Francesco Carnelutti explained, there was a convincing logic behind the narrow interpretation of work in Bernatti's case. Like other jurists in Italy, Carnelutti was anxious to maintain a clear and universal framework that could be called upon in court cases throughout the peninsula. Without such an outline, that 'serious burden of risk' to which Pompeo Colajanni referred might take root. As Carnelutti argued in his guide to the accident insurance law:

[W]hen one says *in everyday language* that industry, that the factory, that work create a series of dangers or of risks, the thought runs right away to the idea of work as the complex of industrial movements and of a given factory, a given workshop, like the gathering of machines, explosives, of men, of mechanical and physical activities, which constitute what we call industry. But *this grand and quasi-metaphorical idea of work is not what corresponds to the technical capacity of the [legal] vocabulary.* Work, as it is meant in article 7 [of the law] is only the fulfilment of the function to which the worker is destined in the exercise of industry.[18]

This technocratic understanding of work had, however, led to much confusion in disputes involving accident claims. The problem was that a wide gulf lay between legal understandings of 'accidents' and popular notions of the concept. Carnelutti argued that judges should take a medical-legal view of accidents, drawing on expertise from the academic discipline of medical law, in order to stamp out spurious claims. The subject had slowly emerged in the seventeenth century and expanded considerably in the nineteenth century in Italy,

---

[16] '*Antonio Bernatti v. Assicuratrice Italiana e Ditta Passera e Boggi*, 3 feb. 1911', *Giurisprudenza giudiziaria nell'anno 1911* (2nd series), vol. IX, special issue of *Annali del credito e della previdenza* (Rome, 1915), pp. 232–6.

[17] *Atti della commissione incaricata degli studi concernenti la giurisdizione e la procedura per le controversie dipendenti dall legge per gli infortuni sul lavoro*, special issue of *Annali del credito e della previdenza* (Rome, 1906), pp. 10–11, 44.

[18] Author's italics. Francesco Carnelutti, *Infortuni sul lavoro* (Rome, 1913), pp. 225–7.

with its own university departments, making it an ideal mediator in disputes about workplace risk.[19]

In Britain, by contrast, judges played a key role in defining 'accidents', 'work' and the terms under which compensation would be awarded. In 1900, therefore, the Home Secretary, Matthew White Ridley, wrote to county court judges throughout the country to solicit reports on their experience with the law. What the judges found was almost identical to the conundrum identified in Italy and Germany. The word 'accident' had led to much consternation, claimed Judge W. J. Greenbow from the county court in Leeds. As he noted, the law granted compensation for 'injury by accident arising out of the course of … employment'. The problem was that courts had held that there must be 'some extraneous and fortuitous force or agency to constitute an "accident"', yet a workman 'merely performing his ordinary duties in ordinary ways does not incur one'.[20] Already by 1903, though, just six years after the policy had been adopted, the courts had arrived at an authoritative definition of the word 'accident': 'an unlooked-for mishap or untoward event which is not expected or designed'.[21] Like their counterparts on the continent, judges throughout Britain also faced difficulties in coming to a common understanding of the notion of 'work'.[22] The phrasing of the law precipitated particular confusion here. The first Workmen's Compensation Act, which was ratified in 1897, allowed for the compensation of accidents occurring 'in the course of employment', and the places of employment cited in the law were defined as 'on or in or about a railway, factory, [etc.]'. The first phrase, which emphasised temporal and causal links with the act of work, could enable judges to arrive at a broader understanding of the concept. Yet the latter phrase, which was physically delineated, could be read in rather restrictive terms. In fact, the restrictive potential of the clause was intentional. While revising the workmen's compensation bill in parliament before it was ratified as law, legislators inserted this latter phrase as a means to narrow possible interpretations of 'work' and limit the financial burden that the law might hold for employers.[23]

[19] Alessandro Pastore, *Il medico in tribunale: la perizia medica nella procedura penale d'antico regime (secoli XVI–XVIII)* (Casagrande Bellinzona, 1998), pp. 8–10; Silvia de Renzi, 'La natura in tribunale: conoscenze a pratiche medico-legale a Roma nel XVII secolo', *Quaderni Storici* 36 (2001), pp. 799–822; Francesco Puccinotti, *Lezioni medicina legale* (Milan, 1856), p. 11.

[20] TNA: PIN 12/1: unnumbered: Judge W. J. Greenbow of the County Court of Leeds to Sir Kenelm Digby, 19 November 1900.

[21] *Fenton* v. *Thorley* (1903) A.C. 443. See also: *PP* 1904 (Cd 2208) LXXXVIII.743: 'Home Office Departmental Committee on Workmen's Compensation: Report of the Departmental Committee', pp. 787–8.

[22] For example: TNA: PIN 12/1: unnumbered: Report of Judge Darcy Ayre, of the County Court at Winchester, to Matthew White Ridley, 3 November 1900; unnumbered: Report of Judge Charles Whitehorne of the County Court of Birmingham to Sir Kenelm Digby, 2 November 1900.

[23] 4 *Hansard* HC vol. 50 (1897), cols. 1400–2.

This complicated definition of 'work' led to a Home Office investigation soon after workmen's compensation was put into effect because it had led to confusion and dissatisfaction in courtrooms across the country. Judges were summoned to a Departmental Committee in 1904 which found that the wording of the policy had, in practice, led to a 'strong sense of injustice and inequality'.[24] As a consequence, many judges awarded compensation on a wider basis by reassessing the view that 'work' was an activity bound to a specific physical location. Judicial activism therefore led to a more redistributive policy because judges chose to define workplace risk broadly. As in Germany, judges in Britain granted compensation to workers killed in exceptional circumstances if there was a direct correlation between the accident and the 'course of employment'. Therefore, when a cashier was shot with a revolver and killed by a robber while delivering wages to a colliery, his family received compensation due to the causal link between the accident and his employment.[25]

Unlike the governmental committee that had met in Italy to discuss similar issues, that in Britain left the issue of interpretation to judges. It decided not to push for a rewording of the law or for the mandatory consultation of medical experts. Medical opinion about accidents was certainly sought in courtrooms, and by insurance companies, across the country.[26] And medical referees would play an enormous role in shaping a variety of discussions in Britain about uncertainties and problems with workmen's compensation. However, individual compensation cases would be dealt with on their own terms, rather than through mandates from Whitehall. Occupational risk was a matter left to courtrooms in Britain, not government. Courts would determine instances of fault, fate and probability, and it was through courts, alongside official memoranda and legislation, that workmen's compensation contributed to a sense that the state oversaw the world of work and individual woes related to that world.

OCCUPATIONAL ILLNESS AS AN 'ACCIDENT'

Since the nature of occupational risk was so ambiguous, courts regularly assessed whether compensation should be awarded to a larger range of ailments related to work. The most difficult challenge that judges encountered was ascertaining whether illnesses could count as consequences from an

---

[24] PP 1904 (Cd. 2208) LXXXVIII.743: 'Home Office Departmental Committee on Workmen's Compensation: Report', pp. 788–90, at p. 790.

[25] *Nisbet* v. *Rayne & Burn* [1910] Court of Appeal, 2 K.B. 689; 103 L.T. 178; 54 S.J. 719; 26 T.L.R. 632. See also: G. N. W. Thomas, *Leading cases in workmen's compensation* (London, 1913), pp. 21–43, 79–80; V. R. Aronson, *The Workmen's Compensation Act, 1906* (London, 1909), p. 67.

[26] M. A. Crowther and Brenda M. White, 'Property and the law in Britain, 1800–1914', *Historical Journal* 31 (1988), pp. 853–70, especially pp. 863–8. See also Marguerite W. Dupree, 'Other than healing: medical practitioners and the business of life assurance during the nineteenth and early twentieth century', *Social History of Medicine* 10 (1997), pp. 79–103.

'accident'. Was an 'accident' something that happened instantaneously, or could it be something that takes place over a longer period of time? Could multiple smaller 'accidents', such as daily exposure to toxic chemicals, contribute to a single disease, making the sufferer eligible for compensation? Answering these questions would require the combination of medical understandings of causation and jurisprudential arguments about time. Initially, courts decided that diseases which develop over a longer period were ineligible for compensation as 'accidents'; 'accidents' were thought to be instantaneous by nature. For example, the Imperial Insurance Office in Berlin rejected the appeal of a worker in 1889 when he claimed that his loss of hearing had resulted from working with explosives in mines and quarries. Doctors in Germany began calling for these kinds of injuries to be seen in court as the result of 'a great series of small accidents'. Nonetheless, they remained outside of the remit of the accident insurance law.[27] The 1900 revision to the policy later defined an accident clearly as a 'sudden' occurrence, 'an event included within a relatively short time period, due to which bodily damage is causally attributed'.[28] This definition resembled that cited in the Italian insurance law of 1898, in which accidents were declared the results of a 'violent cause'. In fact, this terminology was appropriated from the German legal context by Italian jurists, and counter-arguments about diseases as resulting from a 'series' of smaller accidents were also widespread in Italy.[29]

British officials came to a similar conclusion but were less dogmatic about defining accidents, again reflecting their reluctance to become involved in the daily operation of workmen's compensation. A Home Office committee that investigated revising the policy confirmed that an 'accident' should be understood as it would in 'everyday language'. The definition should not be complicated by over-interpretation. Tellingly, unlike in Germany and Italy, in Britain, 'accidents' were not defined explicitly in a revised version of the law or in an official circular.[30] As a result of these decisions, workers in all three countries

---

[27] Richard Müller, 'Unfall oder Gewerbekrankheit? Eine ohrenärztliche Erörerung', *Ärztliche Sachverständigen-Zeitung* 18 (15 September 1898).

[28] *Handbuch der Unfallversicherung*, vol. I, p. 69, n. 26 to section 1 of the *Gewerbliche Unfallversicherungs-Gesetz*.

[29] See Vicenzo Magaldi, 'Les accidents du travail en Italie: progrès legislatifs – applications de la loi', *Congrès international des accidents du travail et des assurances sociales*, pp. 681–99, at pp. 687–8; Lorenzo Borri, *Gli infortuni del lavoro sotto il rispetto medico legale* (Milan, 1910), pp. 196–7. On the connection to Germany: Carnelutti, *Infortuni*, pp. 140–2. See also: Lorenzo Borri, 'Causa violenta in occasione del lavoro', *Rivista infortuni* 1901, p. 166. On 'series of accidents', see Arnaldo Agnelli, *Infortuni sul lavoro e assicurazione* (Milan, 1908), pp. 27–8.

[30] *PP* 1904 (Cd 2208) LXXXVIII.743: 'Home Office Departmental Committee on Workmen's Compensation: Report', pp. 787–8. Similarly: *PP* 1907 (Cd 3495) XXXIV.1045: 'Departmental Committee on Compensation for Industrial Diseases', pp. 1072–3; *Marshall* v. *East Holywell Coal Col.*, *Sorley* v. *Backworth Collieries* (1905) 93 L.T. 360.

were denied compensation if they suffered from ailments that develop gradually such as lead poisoning and repetitive strain injuries.[31]

Since accidents were seen as instantaneous events, courts in each country recognised that sudden poisoning or infection related to work could be eligible for damages. In this light, blood poisoning or the inhalation of toxic fumes could be compensated.[32] Similarly, diseases that struck quickly were also compensated under the accident insurance or workmen's compensation laws. Malaria in Italy was the most common case of this kind of 'accident', yet occasional outbreaks of bubonic plague amongst dock workers also helped to expand legal interpretations of accidents.[33] According to the same reasoning, German sailors who contracted tropical diseases while working abroad were also awarded accident benefit.[34] So, too, were British textile workers who contracted the anthrax bacillus, which reflected the fact that connections between the illness and wool sorting had been well established by the late nineteenth century.[35] While the German Imperial Insurance Office played a direct role in these rulings, the British and Italian governments monitored the decisions of courts throughout the country when reflecting on the issue of occupational illness. These cases would prove crucial for later debates about whether and how to compensate related conditions.

Over time, it seemed obvious that workers could not be held accountable for diseases that had a clear and demonstrable connection to their job. In reaching this conclusion, officials in Britain, Germany and Italy drew on arguments from biology, medicine and physics. For instance, in 1907, the German government began hosting occasional presentations by doctors on medical questions related to accident insurance, while medical experts served in governmental commissions in Britain and Italy that investigated accident insurance and workmen's compensation.[36] Their findings had significant

---

[31] For example: *Steel v. Cammell, Laird and Co.* [1905] 2 K.B. 232; Alfred Henry Ruegg, *The Employer's Liability Act, 1880 and the Workmen's Compensation Act, 1906* (7th edn, London, 1907), p. 262; Lorenzo Borri, 'Le infezioni delle ferite rispetto alla legge degli infortuni sul lavoro', *Rivista infortuni* 1899, p. 152.

[32] For example: *Thompson v. Arlington Coal Company, Ltd* (84 L. T. 412); BArch: R1501: 100753: 266–7: IA 4780/12–15B: *Frieda Peukert v. Hamburg Baugewerks-BG*, 20 February 1913; 268–9: *Dependants of Karl Wüstefeld v. the Agricultural Berufsgenossenschaft for Saxony*, 22 February 1913.

[33] For example: *Rosa Esposito v. Mutua Infortuni*, Court of Appeal of Naples, 29 July 1904, cited in *Giurisprudenza giudiziaria*, vol. 1 (Rome, 1906), pp. 305–9.

[34] For example: BArch: R89: 343: unnumbered: Ia7071/01.18: *Dependants of Captain Heinrich Braue v. the See-Berufsgenossenschaft*, 13 December 1901. Relatedly: *Amtliche Nachrichten des Reichsversicherungsamts*, 1886, p. 251.

[35] *Brintons Ltd. v. Turvey* [1905] A. C. 230; P. W. J. Bartrip, *The Home Office and the dangerous trades: regulating occupational disease in Victorian and Edwardian Britain* (Amsterdam, 2002), pp. 233–66; Rosemary Wall, *Bacteria in Britain: 1880–1939* (London, 2013).

[36] *Geschäftsbericht des Reichs-Versicherungsamts*, 31 January 1908. For example, a collaborator with the Home Office was the doctor Thomas Oliver, who compiled what was at the time the major work on the issue: Thomas Oliver, ed., *Dangerous trades* (London, 1902).

implications for questions about applying accident insurance and workmen's compensation policies to occupational illnesses. For example, as the judge Sir Richard Harrington noted to a 1904 Home Office Departmental Committee on workmen's compensation: 'I can see no distinction in principle between the accidental entry of a spark from an anvil or the accidental squirting of scalding water or some poisonous liquid into the eye. The only difference is that, in those cases, the foreign substance will be so large as to be *visible*. In this case, the foreign substance is *microscopic*.'[37] For Harrington, the connection between an eye injury and an accident, even if its origins were not visible, seemed clear. The fact that an injury had been caused by a physical act – the entry of a foreign particle – meant that there could be no doubt about *when* the accident had occurred.

The connection between illnesses and work was less obvious in the case of diseases that developed over a long period of time, and it was in this instance that the findings of industrial medicine proved significant. The roots of the discipline lay in Bernardino Ramazzini's research on occupational illnesses that was first published in Italy in 1700. Ramazzini explored the topic by trade, which set the groundwork for evaluating industrial diseases under compensation law. Over the course of the nineteenth and into the early twentieth century, numerous scholars followed suit, including the Newcastle-based physician Thomas Oliver, the Florentine socialist Gaetano Pieraccini and the Viennese professor Ludwig Teleky, who spent much of his early working life in Germany.[38] For instance, in 1831, the physician Charles Thackrah published his influential *The effects of the principal arts, trades and professions and of civic states and habits of living on health and longevity*. Thackrah considered both occupational and lifestyle factors contributing to illnesses, devoting an entire section to 'bons vivants', for whom 'cookery becomes the minister of gluttony'! He also detailed at length the effects of drinking alcohol on workers and their families. For Thackrah, as for many early nineteenth-century writers on public hygiene, environmental factors and individual 'character' (and its moral failings), together with the specific circumstances related to work, all led to poor health. Cobblers, for example, suffered from poor posture while hunched over the shoes they mended. However, Thackrah claimed that their tendency to lounge around on Sundays and drink excessively on Mondays also contributed to their ailments, which ranged from digestive woes to the possibility of aneurysms. Nonetheless, for Thackrah, as for other early writers on occupational medicine, some ailments, such as the headaches associated with snuff

[37] *PP* 1904 (Cd 2334) LXXV.487: 'Home Office Departmental Committee on Workmen's Compensation: Minutes of Evidence with Index', p. 514.
[38] Bernardino Ramazzini, *Le Malattie dei lavoratori (De morbis artificum diatriba): testi delle edizioni del 1700 e del 1713*, ed. Francesco Carnevale (Florence, 2000); Francesco Carnevale and Alberto Baldasseroni, *Mal da lavoro: storia della salute dei lavoratori* (Rome, 1999), pp. 12–14.

making, seemed to stem entirely from work.[39] This connection became increasingly clear with further research. For example, a few years later, the pioneering Prussian physician Louis Pappenheim illuminated the link between long-term exposure and illness in his enormous *Handbook of the sanitation police*. The compendium detailed noxious chemicals and the ailments that they caused.[40]

Thus, the link between certain occupations, such as working with textiles or in mining, and the prevalence of particular diseases amongst workers in those industries was relatively well known by this time. However, legislative action on industrial diseases focused primarily on those conditions which were most *visible* and whose aetiologies were most clear. Even then, most illnesses remained out of the remit of accident insurance in Italy and Germany until the 1920s, including ailments such as weaver's acne and dyer's hand, whose effects were apparent for all to see.[41] The fact that some workers developed these conditions while others did not undermined arguments about their occupational origins. Instead, courts frequently resorted to what Dietrich Milles has called a 'biography of risk' when assessing the lives of individual workers and the origins of illnesses that could be attributed to the workplace.[42] For example, in 1887, the Imperial Insurance Office rejected the compensation claim of a matchmaker who had required surgery to remove half of her jaw after it had rotted from phosphorus necrosis, a condition related to phosphorus exposure. The court argued that her 'phossy jaw', as the horrific ailment has come to be known in English, was a form of 'chronic disease' (Figure 5). Moreover, it was an 'established fact' that 'not all workers who are exposed to phosphorus vapours to an equal degree' acquire the illness. The implication was the matchmaker's physical disposition was a determinant in her acquisition of the illness. In any case, the condition developed over a long period of time, meaning that it was difficult to prove that the disease stemmed from her current job.[43]

Beyond these arguments about time, character and causation, concerns about economic growth and international competition also militated against taking a legal stand against occupational illnesses. Financial considerations were, for example, significant in the handling of 'phossy jaw' in Britain. Even

[39] Thackrah's full title reveals his objective: *The effects of the principal arts, trades and professions and of civic states and habits of living on health and longevity, with a particular reference to the trades and manufactures of Leeds and suggestions for the removal of many of the agents which produce disease and shorten the duration of life* (London, 1831), p. 88, pp. 114–16, 22–3, 32–3.

[40] Louis Pappenheim, *Handbuch der Sanitäts-Polizei nach eigener Untersuchungen* (2 vols., Berlin, 1859).

[41] See Theodor Sommerfeld, *Handbuch der Gewerbekrankheiten* (Koblenz, 1898), tables 7–8, cited in Dietrich Milles, 'Produktivität schützen, Wachstum sichern: die Schweiz und der deutsche Arbeiterschutz im 19. Jahrhundert', in Historischer Verein des Kantons Glarus, ed., *Das Glarner Fabrikgesetz und der Arbeiterschutz im 19. Jahrhundert* (Näfels, 2015), pp. 79–116, at p. 91.

[42] Dietrich Milles, 'Medical opinion and sociopolitical control in the case of occupational diseases in the late nineteenth century', *Dyanmis* 13 (1993), pp. 139–53, at p. 152.

[43] Quoted in Milles, 'Medical opinion', p. 146.

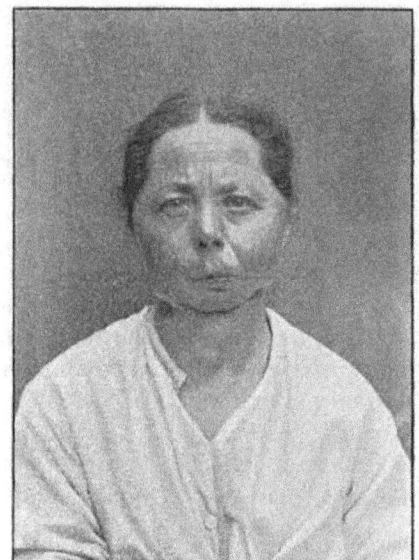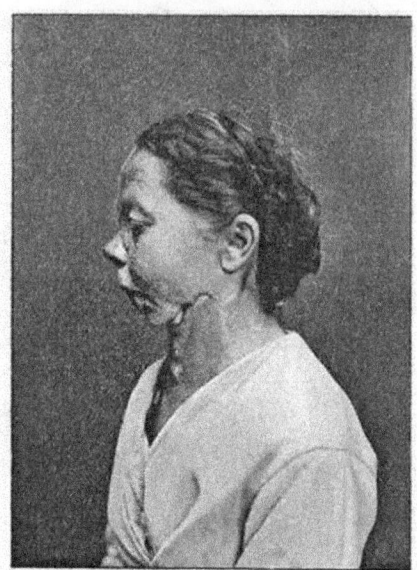

Margareth Trachsel, 43 Jahre alt.

Totalnekrose und Entfernung des Unterkiefers in ganzer Ausdehnung.

FIGURE 5. 'Phossy jaw'.
Source: Theodor Kocher, *Zur Kenntnis der Phosphornekrose* (Biel, 1893). Courtesy Bruno Müller, Hubert Steinke and Ulrich Woermann of the University of Berne.

Thomas Oliver, perhaps the most significant specialist in occupational medicine at the turn of the century, argued that 'it would be useless for Britain with her free trade to abolish yellow phosphorus, thereby crippling her own matchmaking industry and at the same time allow matches to be imported from other countries'.[44] On the same grounds, ancylostomiasis, the 'miners' anaemia' caused by hookworms which burrowed into the bare feet of miners working underground, was neglected by Italian legislators. Nonetheless, the condition was widely known to affect as many as 50 per cent of sulphur miners working in Sicily.[45] Similar economic considerations may also have led to the neglect of occupational illnesses in small industries and the home. Many of those who suffered did not fall into categories traditionally associated with 'dangerous trades', as was the case, for example, with predominantly female

---

[44] Thomas Oliver, 'Phosphorus and lucifer matches', in Oliver, ed., *Dangerous trades*, pp. 417–33, at p. 432. On the broader discussion, see Bartrip, *Home Office*, pp. 209–11.

[45] Gianfranco Tore, 'Miniere, lavoro e malattie nell'Italia postunitaria (1860–1915)', in Maria Luisa Betri and Ada Gigli Marchetti, eds., *Salute e classi lavoratrici in Italia dall'Unità al fascismo* (Milan, 1982), pp. 75–99, at pp. 80, 89.

domestic servants and workers in cottage industries. In any case, policy makers may have been reluctant to interfere in what seemed to be private spheres.[46] In each country, accident legislation was created to target the workplace and thereby benefit the national economy. In this way, the policy was within the natural remit of the state. What happened in private was another matter. To a certain extent, however, workers' own intransigence in the face of occupational risks may also have played a role in delaying regulation and compensation. For instance, British miners frequently took risks at work because risk taking was seen to be masculine and therefore desirable.[47] For all these reasons, numerous widespread conditions remained beyond the remit of legal intervention.

With continued research and the introduction of new protective legislation, especially from the turn of the century, specialists in occupational medicine called for the mandatory compensation of specific industrial diseases.[48] For example, in his 1906 *Pathology of labour and social therapy*, the physician Gaetano Pieraccini called for a move beyond 'practical medicine'. Instead, what was needed was 'social or political medicine'. By 1910, now as a member of parliament for the Socialist Party of Italy, he petitioned for the inclusion of occupational illnesses in accident insurance.[49] Not only industrial hygienists shaped thinking about occupational illnesses. Organised labour also noted the connections between ailments and certain trades and began calling for some degree of compensation. For example, the newsletter of the German Union of Christian Miners reported on nystagmus, a condition leading to blindness due to prolonged exposure to darkness underground. The group soon began lobbying the Imperial Insurance Office to make the illness eligible for compensation under accident insurance.[50] Political parties, including Social Democrats in

[46] Barbara Harrison, *Not only the 'dangerous trades': women's work and health in Britain, 1880–1914* (London, 1996), pp. 11–12, 106–19.

[47] Arthur McIvor and Ronnie Johnston, *Miners' lung: a history of dust disease in British coal mining* (London, 2007).

[48] For example: Dr. med. W. Hanauer, 'Gewerbekrankheiten und Reischsversicherungsordnung', *Die Arbeiter-Versorgung* 29/27 (21 September 1912), pp. 617–21. See also: Dietrich Milles, 'Industrial hygiene: a state obligation? Industrial pathology as a problem in German social policy', in W. R. Lee and Eve Rosenhaft, eds., *State, social policy and social change in Germany, 1880–1994* (1990; Oxford, 1997), pp. 164–202; Antonio Pagano and Gaetano Fara, 'Dalla soluzione imposta al consenso acquisito: la storia della prevenzione dalla polizia sanitaria alla promozione della salute', in A. Grieco and P. A. Bertazzi, eds., *Per una storiografia italiana della prevenzione occupazionale ed ambientale* (Milan, 1997), pp. 289–308, especially p. 301.

[49] Gaetano Pieraccini, *Patologia del lavoro e terapia sociale* (Milan, 1906), quoted in Francesco Carnevale and Alberto Baldasseroni, 'Gaetano Pieraccini e la medicina del lavoro in Italia nella prima metà del Novecento', *Medicina e Storia* 2 (December 2011), pp. 29–43, at pp. 32–3.

[50] For example: BArch: R1501: 100753: 163: *Zentralstelle des Gewerkvereins christlicher Bergarbeiter Deutschlands* to Secret Governmental Adviser Dr Würmeling, 7 August 1912; CdAs: Leg. XXII, Sess. 1904–9, Proposte di legge: Bta. 860: Representatives of the National League of Cooperatives et al., n.d. [c. 27 April 1908]; TNA: HO 157/6/280: E. Blackwell, Under-Secretary of State at the Home Office, to the Secretary of the Amalgamated Society of Railway Servants, 23 May 1911.

Germany, Labour in Britain and Socialists in Italy, also began invoking revisions to the accident insurance and workmen's compensation laws to take occupational illnesses into account.[51] In response, groups of industrialists called for narrower readings of compensation law.[52]

International organisations helped fuel these debates. At its 1897 meeting in Brussels, the International Congress on Labour Legislation sought to highlight 'trades dangerous to health' with a view towards legislative action. In 1900, the group formed a permanent organisation, the International Association for the Legal Protection of Workers, and both Germany and Italy had national organisations that were affiliated with it. In 1906, the Association put forward an international convention to ban night work for women and children as well as the use of white phosphorus, the chemical behind 'phossy jaw', in the match-making industry. Both Germany and Italy ratified it. Italy, in particular, had been involved in a long battle to address the issue, which had garnered attention in medical studies since the middle of the nineteenth century. The problem was highlighted again in an 1877 investigation by the Ministry of Agriculture, and it also contributed to a strike wave in the industry in the 1890s.[53] Britain did not sign the convention, which perhaps reflected long-standing governmental reluctance towards international cooperation in social politics alongside concern about possible economic consequences of the policy. It nonetheless participated in a variety of international congresses on occupational health, sending civil servants such as the chief medical inspector of factories, Thomas Legge.[54] Participants at these events debated for the next several years about how to address occupational diseases, and, by its eighth meeting in Rome, the International Congress on Social Insurance considered whether diseases, like accidents, merited compensation.[55] By 1912, the International Labour Office (ILO), an auxiliary organisation to the International Association for the Legal Protection of Workers, began pressuring governments on compensation

[51] 'Sociales: die Vergiftungen in Betrieben und das Unfallversicherungsgesetz', *Vorwärts*, 30 January 1902; 'Quecksilbervergiftung – Betriebsunfall oder Gewerbekrankheit?', *Vorwärts*, 18 August 1908; *SBDR* 23 January 1902, p. 3612; 11 March 1905, pp. 5173–4; 13 March 1908, p. 3857; *A.P. Cam.*, 27 March 1901, 9 March 1912; 4 *Hansard* HC vol. 154 (26 March 1906), cols. 900–6.

[52] For example: CdAs: Leg. XXII, Sess. 1904–9, Proposte di legge: Bta. 860: unnumbered: 'Relazione illustrativa dei voti del congresso degli industriali italiani per la riforma della legge sugli infortuni del lavoro, Roma 1908', p. 16.

[53] Paul Perigord, *The International Labor Organization* (New York, 1926), p. 70; Alberto Baldasseroni and Franco Carnevale, 'L'abbandono dell'uso del fosforo bianco nella produzione dei fiammiferi: un lungo processo per la realizzazione di un precoce esempio di vera prevenzione (1830–1920)', in Grieco and Bertazzi, eds., *Per una storiografia*, pp. 133–87.

[54] Bartrip, *Home Office*, pp. 209–13; Julia Moses, 'Policy communities and exchanges across borders: the case of workplace accidents at the turn of the twentieth century', in Davide Rodogno et al., eds., *Shaping the transnational sphere, 1830–1950* (New York, 2014), pp. 60–81.

[55] *Actes du VIII congrès international des assurances sociales … Rome 12–16 octobre 1908* (3 vols., Rome, 1909), vol. II.

for diseases. As part of its lobbying endeavours, the ILO published a booklet which listed toxins related to the workplace for which it sought protective legislation.[56] The group would continue to push for the acknowledgement of illnesses as a form of occupational risk, continuing after the First World War when it was absorbed into the International Labour Organization.

Court cases, industrial medicine and lobbying from various fronts all seemed to suggest that workers should not be held accountable for occupational illnesses which were due to their origins in work. However, it was less clear whether ill workers should be cared for by their employers and what role, if any, the state should play in mandating compensation or treatment. In Germany, the Imperial Insurance Office began considering this issue already in the mid 1880s, following the first claims for the compensation of industrial diseases. Yet, it decided to uphold the distinction between occupational illnesses and accidents, only to return to the matter again many years later. As Bernhard Würmeling, a long-time member of the department, noted, the liability law from which accident insurance stemmed did not address occupational illnesses. Liability law instead targeted specific events – 'accidents' – whose origins clearly lay in work. The implication was that employers, as the overseers and primary beneficiaries of the workplace, were responsible for remunerating injuries. Due to the complex origins of illness, it was more difficult to prove that a condition derived only from the workplace. A worker might, it was presumed, have a weak constitution or a poor lifestyle that rendered him susceptible to illness. Proving an employer's liability for illness seemed impossible, and occupational diseases had therefore never been the target of liability law. Würmeling also argued that it would be difficult to include illness in the accident insurance system because the policy was still in its infancy. It was being extended slowly to different categories of workers, and each of these risk classes would bring with them new uncertainties. For these reasons, government decided to leave the issue at rest when Gustav Roesicke, a conservative member of parliament and prominent member of the Agrarian League, demanded in 1902 the compensation of occupational illnesses under accident insurance. Roesicke's point was both moral and economic. Under German social insurance, workers suffering from long-term illnesses – whatever their origin – were eligible for a small pension under disability insurance. By contrast, accident benefit was substantially more generous. Moreover, it was entirely employer-funded. Claiming that he 'represent[ed] the interests of the workers', Roesicke called for shifting

[56] For example: BArch: R89: 15127: unnumbered: Director of the Office International du Travail to the Imperial Insurance Office, 18 November 1912; Prof. Dr Th. Sommerfeld and Dr R. Fischer, *Liste der gewerblichen Gifte und anderer gesundheitsschädlicher Stoffe, die in der Industrie Verwendung finden: nach den Beschlüssen des Komitees der Internationale Vereinigung für gesetzlichen Arbeiterschutz* (Jena, 1912). On the International Labour Office: Boutelle Ellsworth Lowe, *The international protection of labor* (New York, 1921), p. 39.

the burden of payment for occupational illnesses to the accident insurance scheme.[57] His demand, like others during this period, was unsuccessful. In fact, the issue remained so contentious in Germany that few of the claims for compensating ailments related to work succeeded until the late 1900s and 1910s.[58]

In Italy, a sticking point in the debate about occupational illness was also the question of liability: could employers – as overseers and primary beneficiaries of the workplace – be held financially accountable for illnesses that seemed to stem from work? Economic concerns, alongside anxieties about the lack of sufficient information, shaped these considerations. Fears about possible abuse of the system also hampered efforts to legislate on the issue. As a result, the Italian government investigated the matter for years without drawing a definitive conclusion. The first serious effort towards incorporating industrial diseases within the accident insurance law came in 1902, when the Ministry of Agriculture set up a commission on the matter. By this point, the question of covering occupational illnesses under accident insurance was well known. It had been discussed already in 1896 – before the accident insurance law was ratified. Although several members of parliament advocated their inclusion in the policy, the Minister of Agriculture, who was spearheading the legislative initiative, vetoed the possibility on the grounds that it would lead to too many uncertainties.[59] The Ministry of Agriculture investigated the issue further in 1901, when it requested information about industrial diseases from prefects, associations of industrialists, employers, mutual aid societies and cooperative societies. However, this information proved unhelpful. As the Prefect of Siena noted, it was difficult to obtain answers to the questions that government put forward because neither the heads of businesses nor many doctors had comprehensive records about industrial diseases.[60] The 1902 commission therefore decided to compile further data from provincial medical authorities. Only then, it saw, would government come to have comprehensive statistics about occupational illnesses, including information on their causes and consequences.[61]

However, the statistics it accumulated only complicated matters by revealing the numerous kinds of illnesses related to work. The commission advocated compensating infections and poisoning within the accident insurance scheme, but it was divided over how to proceed. It seemed clear that any policy on

---

[57] BArch: R1501: 100753: 2: Notes by Bernhard Würmeling on 'Sociales: die Vergiftungen in Betrieben und das Unfallversicherungsgesetz', *Vorwärts*, 30 January 1902; *SBDR* 23 January 1902, pp. 3611–12; BArch: R1501:100753: 3: Notes by Bernhard Würmeling of the Imperial Insurance Office on conservative Gustav Roesicke's comments in parliament.

[58] See 'Berufskrankheit und Betriebsunfall', *Soziale Praxis*, 12 November 1903.

[59] *Commissione per studiare le cause e i provvedimenti preventivi delle malattie professionali degli operai nelle industrie*, special issue of *Annali del credito e della previdenza – Anno 1902* (Rome, 1903), pp. 13–14.

[60] *Commissione per studiare le cause*, Allegato B: 'Informazione e proposte pervenute in risposta alla predetta circolare', p. 83.

[61] *Commissione per studiare le cause*, pp. 14–18, 21, 24–5, 27–8, 30, 33, 105–77.

occupational illness should include an explicit list of compensable conditions. Otherwise, it would be difficult to draw a line on where liability fell for an illness. To this end, the body identified eight instances which seemed to derive without a doubt from work. These included lead, mercury and phosphorus poisoning, asphyxiation from noxious fumes, as well as infections related to animal transport. How to compensate these conditions, however, remained unclear. Few countries had included industrial diseases in compensatory legislation at this point. As a consequence, officials in Italy, who often looked abroad in moments of uncertainty on social policy, found it difficult to resolve these debates. France and Switzerland were the only known precedents at the time of the commission. However, members felt that the Swiss policy on occupational illness might prove too generous to emulate, as the Italian insurance policy was still in its infancy. In Switzerland, at the discretion of judges, all occupational illnesses could be compensated under the law on workplace accidents. The French policy was unappealing because it remained untested: provision was made in the 1898 French accident insurance law for the later inclusion of diseases, but no illness had been incorporated by this time. Other possibilities might be the compensation of industrial diseases within a system of health insurance, which Italy still lacked.[62]

Moreover, members of the commission, and especially the Ministry of Agriculture, were concerned about burdening industry by insuring industrial diseases, not least because doing so could lead to a boom in compensation claims. Magaldi argued that including occupational illnesses within accident insurance

would undoubtedly introduce a disruptive element in the valuation of risk, facilitating and possibly promoting fraud. How to judge, in fact, whether a bronchial or pulmonary condition had really been caused by the inhalation of dust that had developed from an industrial matter or had derived [instead] from an ordinary cause, whether the effect of a contagion or [something] hereditary? How could one prevent a worker, with a natural predisposition or who had already contracted a kind of illness ... from being able to claim compensation in case of an accident? Is it possible to draw a strict dividing line between occupational illness and that which is not?[63]

According to Magaldi, industrial diseases seemed to threaten the consensus that had been reached on the meaning of occupational risk and its implications for the moral and financial responsibilities of employers, workers and the state. Moreover, the ambiguity of cause and effect in the case of occupational illness meant that calculating their likelihood and economic repercussions would prove difficult. Proposals to legislate on occupational illness had been made

---

[62] *Commissione per studiare le cause*, pp. 17–18; Luigi Rava and Vicenzo Magaldi, 'Congresso internazionale medico degl'infortuni sul lavoro tenuto in Liegi nei giorni 29 maggio a 3 giugno 1905', *Bollettino di notizie sul credito e sulla previdenza* 23/8 (1905), pp. 1411–39, at 1417.

[63] Rava and Magaldi, 'Congresso internazionale', p. 1417.

repeatedly in parliament in 1901 and 1902 by Angelo Celli, the malaria expert who was linked to radicals in the Chamber of Deputies, and by the socialist deputy Angiolo Cabrini, who was a long-standing advocate of social reform. Yet they withdrew their petitions, agreeing with the Ministry of Agriculture's commission that Italy was not yet ready for the compensation of occupational illness.[64]

In Britain, early legislative debates on the matter resembled those in Italy because they also focused on the question of liability. A 1904 Home Office Departmental Committee investigated industrial diseases, but it did not recommend including them in a revised version of the workmen's compensation law. The committee consulted with factory inspectors, employers' representatives, trade union representatives and medical experts and saw much evidence indicating the correlation between certain trades and diseases. It nonetheless concluded that, if occupational illnesses were to be addressed with legislation, they should be incorporated into a system of health insurance that would not require a causal link between the workplace and illness. Even Thomas Legge, who had been appointed the first medical inspector of factories in 1898, argued against applying workmen's compensation to diseases because proving the connection between work and illness was difficult. Legge was an expert on occupational health who was not only known in Britain but also had contacts on the continent, having studied in several western European countries as well as having been involved in a research project on anthrax hosted at the University of Siena.[65] In his position in the factory inspectorate, he had seen numerous cases of occupational illness that seemed to uphold Ramazzini's thinking: certain jobs were linked to certain diseases. Nonetheless, his testimony to the committee on lead poisoning, for example, suggested that 'it is extremely difficult … to say with any approach to certainty whether the symptoms observed are the result of poisoning contracted in the course of and arising out of occupation, or whether they arise from entirely different causes'.[66] The intellectual roots of workmen's compensation lay in liability law, meaning that causation and fault still played an implicit role in the awarding of compensation, even if the system was ostensibly based on a no-fault concept of occupational risk.

This tenuous consensus on occupational illness broke down a couple of years later, following the 1906 election of a new Liberal government which sought to differentiate itself not only from its Conservative predecessor but also from previous Liberal administrations. In order to achieve this goal, it advocated a new form of socially orientated legislation. Herbert Gladstone, the new Home Secretary, reopened discussions about revising the Workmen's

---

[64] Arnaldo Cherubini and Italo Piva, *Dalla libertà all'obbligo: la previdenza sociale fra Giolitti e Mussolini* (Milan, 1998), pp. 98–100.

[65] James F. Stark, *The making of modern anthrax, 1875–1920* (London, 2013), pp. 119–20.

[66] *PP* 1904 (Cd 2208) LXXXVIII.743: 'Home Office Departmental Committee on Workmen's Compensation: Report', pp. 787–8.

Compensation Law, and he pushed for the inclusion of industrial diseases in an amended version of the policy. Members of the Home Office looked to the findings of the report from the recent Departmental Committee in order to draw up a finite list of compensable diseases. It was, therefore, significant that the British government was in possession of ample information about occupational illnesses when it legislated on the matter. The resulting 1906 Workmen's Compensation Act not only applied to six occupational diseases, but it also enabled the Home Office to add further illnesses to the list. By 1907, another Departmental Committee met and added 18 diseases to the original list. The committee met again in 1913 and during the First World War, bringing the total number of illnesses compensable under the law to 30.[67] The British policy marked a radical reinterpretation of workplace accidents that sparked worldwide debate and attempts at emulation. It seemed that 'accidents' were no longer simply a matter of immediate cause and effect related to work. By bringing illnesses within the fold of workmen's compensation, Britain signalled a move away from linear thinking about occupational risk. The notion became more expansive and flexible, continuing the gradual shift that had begun during the discussions about the time and location of accidents 'at work'. As a consequence, the boundaries further blurred between what could be perceived as private and individual problems – for example, illnesses that might be associated with a worker's weak physical constitution – and those which seemed public and communal in nature.

By 1908, two years after Britain adopted its first schedule of illnesses that were eligible for workmen's compensation, the Imperial Insurance Office in Germany examined how to incorporate similar diseases into its accident insurance scheme. In a memorandum to the head of the Imperial Insurance Office, Bernhard Würmeling and Ludwig Lass outlined recent calls to reform the law in Germany and cited efforts abroad, including in Switzerland, France, Russia, Italy and Britain. They decided to consult the report from the Home Office Departmental Committee of 1907 on industrial diseases as well as numerous monographs on the issue. They also looked to findings of a variety of international conferences, such as the International Congress on Occupational Illnesses that met in Milan in 1906. Würmeling and Lass concluded that there were two options: either to include a list of scheduled diseases in the revised accident insurance law, which would emulate the British model, or to allow the *Bundesrat* to schedule diseases as cases arose.[68] Their findings led to the creation of a commission based at Prussia's Ministry of Trade that included several advisers from the Prussian government, the Imperial Office of the Interior

---

[67] *PP* 1907 (Cd 3495) XXXIV.1045: 'Departmental Committee on Compensation for Industrial Diseases'; *PP* 1913 (Cd 6956) XVIII.649: 'Departmental Committee on Compensation for Industrial Diseases'.

[68] BArch: R1501: 100753: 65–70: Dr Würmeling and Dr Lass, 'Aufzeichnung über Einbeziehung von Berufs- (Bewerbe-) Krankheiten in die Unfallversicherung', 21 April 1908.

and the Imperial Insurance Office.[69] Without much debate, the group decided
to include in the next revision of the accident insurance policy a list of illnesses
that seemed to stem clearly from work.[70]

Their easy resolution was, however, waylaid, as the Imperial Insurance
Office next turned to the employers' liability funds for guidance.[71] The department circulated Britain's recently enacted list of compensable ailments, and the
insurance funds conceded the prevalence of those conditions in their trades.
For example, the Mining Fund recognised ancylostomiasis and nystagmus as
work-related conditions, and its office in Waldenburg in Silesia had gone as
far as granting compensation to chronic strain injuries from work, including
inflammation of the hands, wrists and elbows. The Silesian section was in the
minority, though, and the few other funds that compensated occupational illness recognised only ailments that stemmed from one-time occurrences that
could be linked to a specific activity on a specific day.[72] As the Association
of German Employers' Liability Funds argued, for any condition to be compensated, it would have to be related to a 'definite professional activity' as its
'cause', with 'very specific symptoms' confirmed, and 'without objection', by a
'doctor experienced in this area'. Attaining such a clear and convincing diagnosis would, however, be difficult in Germany, they argued. Unlike in Britain,
whose workmen's compensation scheme incorporated state-certified medical
officers, in Germany, unwell workers could choose any doctor they preferred,
whether or not that doctor had experience with occupational illnesses and with
the specifics of the accident insurance law.[73]

The insurance funds argued that extending accident insurance to occupational illness in general would erode the moral foundation upon which accident
insurance was built. That foundation was based on clear and demonstrable
probabilities that seemed to trump fault: 'if this [policy] should be extended
to concepts which are neither limited in time or space, like the occurrence of
an accident, then the entire legislation must be transformed from the ground
up'. For example, the Association suggested that 'generally spread' illnesses like
tuberculosis, arthritis and asthma should not be covered by accident insurance
in any case.[74] The suggestion indicated that some workers were simply more

[69] BArch: R89: 15127: unnumbered: Secretary of the Interior to the Imperial Insurance Office,
4 April 1913. See also: BArch: R1501: 100753: 159–62: Imperial Office of the Interior to the
Minister of Trade and Commerce, 9 November 1912.
[70] BArch: R1501: 100753: 208–11: Minutes of Ministry of Trade Commission investigating industrial diseases, 16 January 1913.
[71] BArch: R89: 15127: unnumbered circular from the Imperial Insurance Office to the Committees
of the *Berufsgenossenschaften*, 3 May 1913.
[72] BArch: R89: 15127: unnumbered: *Knappschafts-Berufsgenossenschaften* to the Imperial
Insurance Office, 25 August 1913. See also: unnumbered: Section 1 of the *Süddeutsche Edel-
und Unedelmetall-Berufsgenossenschaft* to the Imperial Insurance Office, 30 June 1913.
[73] BArch: R89: 15127: unnumbered: *Verband der Deutschen Berufsgenossenschaften* to the
Imperial Insurance Office, 26 June 1913.
[74] BArch: R89: 15127: unnumbered: *Verband*, 26 June 1913.

prone to infirmity, for example by being asthmatic or susceptible to consumption, the scourge of damsels in distress and children in melodramatic novels of the nineteenth century. Their view also meant that workers suffering from ailments like silicosis, which stemmed from hammering away at silica-laden stone, could be turned away as suffering from 'asthma' or 'tuberculosis'.[75] The Association also cited 'fear' about 'unjustified claims' and the resultant financial 'burden' on industry as reasons to avoid a generous policy on occupational illness. It seemed that workers could take advantage of the insurance funds, making the funds into a new kind of victim of occupational health. In any case, as the Association argued, there was no need for employers to deal with the effects of occupational illness. The existence of mandatory disability insurance and health insurance in Germany, which Bismarck had enacted in the 1880s alongside accident insurance, meant that workers could turn elsewhere (and not at the expense of employers), should they fall ill.[76]

Government ultimately sided with the insurance funds by proposing a compromise: including occupational illnesses within a revised accident insurance law, but only at the discretion of the upper chamber of parliament, the *Bundesrat*, in conjunction with the insurance funds. The sentiments of a long-time official at the Imperial Insurance Office, Franz Caspar, reflected the rationale behind this decision. Not only was the cause of occupational illness often disputed in medical circles, but the cost of compensation could ruin the German economy. Not least, he noted, Germany did not have to include a list of diseases in its accident scheme just because Britain had done so. After all, social policy was not a competition, and Germany had done much in this arena anyway.[77] The fact that Britain was slowly catching up to German advances in social policy, not only with its generous provisions for occupational illness but also with its recent introduction of national old-age pensions (1908), health and unemployment insurance (1911), informed the nature of these discussions. However, these developments failed to push officials in Germany towards legislating on occupational illness. By the outbreak of the First World War, the *Bundesrat* had not proposed a single disease for coverage under the accident insurance law.

In Italy, employers, physicians and civil servants alike had earlier raised similar concerns about the possible abuse of accident insurance if occupational illnesses were to be incorporated into the scheme. For example, in his 1905 inspection of the Sicilian Mutual Fund for Workplace Accidents in Sulphur Mines, Lorenzo Borri, Professor of Legal Medicine at the University of Florence, claimed that the fund had been overwhelmed by the 'phenomenon of litigious contagion'. It seemed that litigiousness was a new form of occupational illness.

---

[75] See Paul-André Rosental, ed., *Silicosis: a world history* (Baltimore, 2017).

[76] BArch: R89: 15127: unnumbered: *Verband*, 26 June 1913.

[77] BArch: R1501: 100753: 63: Franz Caspar, Director in the Imperial Insurance Office, to Dr Würmeling and Dr Lass, 23 May 1908.

Borri nonetheless saw that miners in the fund suffered from ailments that were genuinely related to work and should be considered for compensation. He complained that the accident insurance law was not made in a 'humanitarian sense' but instead followed a different form of 'social logic'. That logic accorded with the fund's attempts to clamp down on 'fraud'.[78] It was perhaps out of these concerns, in conjunction with worries about burdening the peninsula's developing economy, that Britain's schedule of compensable diseases gained little traction in Italy. Like Germany, it failed to take a stand on compensation for occupational illness prior to the First World War.

Paradoxically, as was also the case in Germany, the health problems and science behind occupational illness were well researched in Italy.[79] The topic was the focus of a series of national and international congresses on industrial hygiene that met in the period between 1906 and 1913.[80] In fact, the first International Congress on Occupational Illnesses met in Milan in 1906 with a view to considering possible protective and compensatory legislation, and it was here that the International Commission on Occupational Health was founded.[81] At these meetings, participants debated the merits of the British and Swiss systems of compensation for occupational illnesses and, eventually, the compromise policy adopted in Germany. By 1907, the national congress in Palermo began calling for the compensation of industrial diseases. Participants at the meeting drew on the vast health problems of the nearby Sicilian sulphur mines in order to make a compelling case about the prevalence of specific health problems in particular trades.[82] Parliamentarians followed suit, putting forward numerous proposals following the enactment of Italy's accident insurance law.[83]

In the eyes of government, however, legislating on occupational illness could create new risks for the country that should be avoided. Before pursuing the

---

[78] 'Relazione presentata a S. E. il signor Ministro per l'agricoltura, l'industria e il commercio, on. Prof, Luigi Rava, dal Prof. Lorenzo Borri, incaricato di una ispezione al Sindacato obbligatorio siciliano di mutua assicurazione per gli infortuni sul lavoro nelle minierer di zolfo', *Bollettino di notizie sul credito e sulla previdenza* 23/10 (1905), pp. 1587–655, at pp. 1630, 1645, 1654.

[79] For an overview of these institutes: Alberto Baldasseroni et al., eds., *Alle origini della tutela della salute dei lavoratori in Italia: nascita e primi sviluppi dell'Ispettorato del Lavoro (1904–1925)* (Rome, 2009), p. 21.

[80] Palermo in 1907, Florence in 1909, Turin in 1911 and Rome in 1913. Relatedly, the topic was addressed at the International Congresses on Social Insurance, which met at the Hague in 1910, Dresden in 1911 and Zurich in 1912; at the International Technical Congress on the Prevention of Industrial Accidents, which met in Milan in 1912; at the International Congress for the Prevention of Accidents in Vienna in 1913; and at the International Congress for Occupational Illnesses that met in Vienna in 1914.

[81] The group continues to operate and works closely with the ILO and WHO.

[82] See Giovanni Berlinguer, 'La medicina del lavoro all'inizio del secolo XX. Riflessioni sul I Congresso Internazionale (1906) e sul I Congresso Nazionale (1907) per le malattie del lavoro', in Grieco and Bertazzi, eds., *Per una storiografia*, pp. 107–24, at pp. 121–2.

[83] On the parliamentary proposals: Cherubini and Piva, *Dalla libertà all'obbligo*, pp. 102–7, n. 20.

policy, more information would be needed. In 1902, the Office of Labour was established as a first step in this direction. In subsequent years, the Ministry of Agriculture continued to focus on obtaining more information about the nature of occupational illness. Under the liberal Francesco Cocco-Ortu, the Ministry of Agriculture finally set up a small factory inspectorate in 1906 as a means to achieve this. Over the next several years, government worked on extending the inspectorate and increasing its powers, especially in terms of gaining access to workplaces.[84] The problem of having insufficient information to act, along with what officials saw as the more pressing issue of extending insurance to the vast agricultural workforce, meant that Italy delayed legislating on occupational illnesses until 1929.[85] Until that point, only a few illnesses that were contracted suddenly at work (for example, malaria) counted as 'accidents' and received compensation.

TRAUMA, SIMULATION AND FRAUD

Debates about the meaning of an 'accident' revealed broader anxieties about the failure of individuals to take responsibility for their own circumstances and the failure of the state to manage social legislation. The rise in cases involving mental and nervous disorders, many of which were dismissed as fraudulent, seemed to epitomise this trend. The new diagnosis of 'pension neurosis' posited that accident benefit was making claimants physically ill from anxiety about whether and when they would receive their next payment. Over time, medics, civil servants and employers voiced increasing concerns about whether workers were becoming too reliant on compensation. The fact that a number of workers were found consciously maiming themselves in order to receive payment, and that some insurance funds had adopted dubious tactics to deprive claimants of accident benefit, seemed to indicate that the accident schemes had ceased to be socially beneficial. This discourse about fraud became elevated to a level of national panic in Germany, where the state, symbolised by the Imperial Insurance Office, was seen as the guarantor of the country's new social security system. To a certain extent, similar worries took hold in Italy, whose early adoption of accident insurance had seemed a premature stab in the dark for the new nation state. By contrast, in Britain, physicians and insurers investigated fraudulent and dubious cases of accident claims, but no national scandals erupted.

The legal and medical recognition of the physiological and psychological effects of 'traumatic accidents', a condition known as 'traumatic neurosis',

---

[84] On the Ministry of Agriculture's efforts to develop the factory inspectorate, see Baldasseroni et al., *Alle origini della tutela della salute dei lavoratori in Italia*, pp. 21–7.

[85] See the following chapter on these debates about extending accident insurance to new groups of workers. For a variety of reasons, occupational illnesses would only be granted compensation in 1929: Regio Decreto 13 May 1929, n. 928.

helped to fuel concern about whether the consequences of accidents were real or imagined and how best to compensate individuals who might be 'addicted' to compensation. The first cases of 'traumatic neurosis' following an accident were studied in Britain in the mid 1860s, following claims from train passengers against railway operators. Several British physicians began studying 'railway spine' and 'railway brain', which were neurological conditions associated with the traumas of railway accidents.[86] By the 1880s, the French neurologist Jean-Martin Charcot began studying the psychological effects of workplace accidents. His research both shaped and was influenced by German scholarship, in part, through translations of his teachings into German by Sigmund Freud. Meanwhile, German physicians linked neurological issues associated with trauma to the concept of 'traumatic hysteria'.[87] It seemed as though workplace accidents had sweeping consequences that went well beyond their immediate physical aftermath. Accordingly, physicians and workers began arguing for the state to protect individuals suffering from the psychological fallout of occupational accidents.

The consequences of accidental trauma – as well as the causes – were, however, by no means clear, which meant that claims about traumatic neurosis were often dismissed as bogus. It seemed that some workers were faking their ailments. Others were discounted as suffering from 'nervous dispositions' and therefore prone to neurosis, just as some workers seemed likely to develop occupational illnesses due to their fragile physical constitutions. For instance, Charcot claimed that 75 per cent of his hysterical patients had a hereditary predisposition to psychological disturbances. Children of alcoholic, epileptic and syphilitic fathers were more likely to suffer from hysteria, he argued, while 'hysteria in the mother frequently begets hysteria in the son'.[88] Since the eighteenth century, hysteria was most often associated with feminine frailty, which made the link from mother to son seem credible. However, this understanding of hysteria as a 'female malady' also complicated perceptions of male workers suffering from psychological symptoms following occupational accidents.[89] A German study from 1889 claimed that there were two main groups

---

[86] William Camps, *Railway accidents or collisions: their effects, immediate and remote, upon the brain and spinal cord* (London, 1866); John Eric Erichsen, *On concussion of the spine, nervous shock and other obscure injuries of the nervous system, in their medical and medicolegal aspects* (London, 1875). See Ralph Harrington, 'On the tracks of trauma: railway spine reconsidered', *Social History of Medicine* 16 (2003), pp. 209–23.

[87] R. Gnauck, 'Die Wandlungen in der Lehre von den Nervenerkrankungen nach Trauma', *Ärztliche Sachverständigen-Zeitung* 4/23 (1 December 1898), pp. 481–9, at pp. 481–2; Esther Fischer-Homberger, *Die traumatische Neurosen: vom somatischen zum sozialen Leiden* (Berne, 1975), pp. 120ff. On Charcot, see Christopher G. Goetz et al., *Charcot: constructing neurology* (Oxford, 1995), pp. 72–4, 225–6, 242–4.

[88] Quoted in Mark S. Micale, *Hysterical men: the hidden history of male nervous illness* (Cambridge, MA, 2008), p. 137.

[89] On gender and hysteria, see Micale, *Hysterical men*; Elaine Showalter, *The female malady: women, madness and English culture, 1830–1980* (New York, 1987).

of traumatic neurosis: one characterised by localised nervous disturbances, the other by the shaking of the whole body. No internal injuries seemed to cause these nervous movements; instead, it was the 'psychic condition' of the injured that caused these. Sometimes, traumatic neuroses developed 'the character of a melancholic and hypochondriacal tone' whereby the injured entered a form of depression. The study reported that workers suffering from a traumatic neurosis might also develop other symptoms, such as insomnia, hyper-sensitivity, headaches, backaches or finding that food has lost its flavour.[90] What caused these ailments was disputed. It was not clear whether they stemmed from physical trauma, as argued by some neurologists, or from shock, as contended by the psychiatrist Emil Kraepelin. German psychiatrists, following Charcot, also considered whether some people were predisposed to the condition.[91]

Despite these doubts about the origins of traumatic neurosis, insurers began awarding compensation to workers suffering from the condition. Several claims were made in the German accident insurance system already in the late 1880s. Based on the neurological and psychiatric research, government decided that claimants afflicted with the condition were eligible for compensation. For example, Julius Röhl, a worker on a private railway, was granted a full pension from his employers' liability fund when the Imperial Insurance Office declared him 'completely unable to work'. His physician submitted a report claiming that Röhl suffered from 'severe sickness of the nervous system – a so-called traumatic neurosis – which is exclusively the consequence of the accident that he had on 9 September 1886'. The court argued that it had come across a number of cases involving the 'simulation and exaggeration' of the psychological consequences of workplace accidents. Nonetheless, it determined that Röhl's condition was genuine. Moreover, it agreed that Röhl's illness stemmed from his occupational accident rather than a weak psyche or hereditary predisposition.[92] The decision of the Imperial Insurance Office reflected a sea change in thinking about the consequences of occupational risk. For example, the Italian accident insurance law of 1898 recognised 'mental alienation' and 'serious mental disturbance' following an accident as grounds for compensation.[93] The British Workmen's Compensation Law of 1897 did not specify compensation as related to specific kinds of injuries, so it did not mention 'traumatic neurosis' or related conditions as possible damages that might be compensated.

---

[90] Adolf Strümpell, *Über die traumatischen Neurosen*, vol. III in the series *Berliner Klinik: Sammlung klinischer Vorträge*, eds. E. Hahn and P. Fürbringer (Berlin, 1888), pp. 2–10.

[91] Hermann Oppenheim, *Die traumatische Neurose* (Berlin, 1889); Emil Kraepelin, *Compendium der Psychiatrie* (8th edn, Leipzig, 1909–15). See Fischer-Homberger, *Die traumatische Neurosen*, pp. 80–6, 93–7.

[92] BArch: R89: 343: unnumbered: Ia5868: *Julius Röhl* v. *Privatbahn-Berufsgenossenschaft*, 17 June 1889. See also: unnumbered: Ia8583/01.10: *Augusta Leuchtenberger* v. *Schlesische Textil-Berufsgenossenschaft*, 7 March 1902; BArch: R89: 342: unnumbered: Ia3008: *Heinrich Kehr* v. *Knappschafts-Berufsgenossenschaft*, 29 March 1889.

[93] Art. 74 of the Regulation of 25 September 1898, n. 411.

Yet, British courts acknowledged that workers suffering the mental effects of traumatic accidents could receive financial remuneration.[94]

As courts began granting accident benefit to cases like Röhl's, concerns about fraud became more prevalent. In Germany, and, to a lesser extent, in Britain and Italy, medics and insurance bodies targeted 'accident neurotics' and 'simulators' as symbols for a possible failure of the compensation laws. In all three countries, magistrates, insurance companies and medical experts saw small pensions for minor accidents as the root of much fraud committed either by opportunistic individuals consciously seeking financial gain or by 'pension addicts', as certain claimants came to be known in Germany. Eliminating smaller pensions altogether or distributing lump-sum payments instead of weekly pensions were seen as possible solutions.[95] For instance, a German study cited by critics of 'pension addicts' argued that 81.5 per cent of nervous ailments related to accidents were cured after the injured received a lump-sum payment.[96] Similarly, a British handbook on workmen's compensation claimed that symptoms tended to improve upon settlement of a case, even if the patient was not a 'schemer'. Instead, 'uncertainty and the excitement of legal procedure' could be to blame.[97]

Arguments along these lines were by far the most plentiful and the most potent in Germany, where claims for traumatic neurosis were seen as a testament to a bloated social insurance system that spurred abuse. A series of scientific and pseudo-scientific pamphlets and articles targeted problems associated with entitlement. As one author claimed, workers had become the 'victims of accident legislation, not of ... accident[s]', thereby inverting the usual rhetoric applied to injured workers at the time. He saw that workers had become 'victims' because they were becoming ill in their quest for pensions. The author even coined the term for a new kind of neurasthenia: that associated with complaining.[98] In a related inversion of language, all parties involved in this

[94] For example: *Pugh v. London, Brighton, and South Coast Railroad Company* (1896) 2 Q.B. See Aronson, *The Workmen's Compensation Act*, p. 49.

[95] For example: Ettore Vecchietti, *Rilievi ed appunti sulla esecuzione della legge infortuni* (Naples, 1912), pp. 10–11; Paul Lohmar, *Schattenseiten der Reichs-Unfallversicherung. Gesundeitlich, sittlich und volkswirtschaftlich nachteilige Begleiterscheinungen der Reichs-Unfallversicherung und ihre Bekämpfung* (Berlin, 1916), especially pp. 12–14, 29; BArch: R1501: 100522: 59–64: 'Anträge geschäftsführenden Ausschusses des Verbandes der deutschen Berufsgenossenschaften zu dem Entwurf einer Reichsversicherungsordnung', from the 24th annual meeting of the Association of German *Berufsgenossenschaften*, 10–11 May 1910.

[96] Prof. Dr Rumpf, 'Ueber nervöse Erkrankungen nach Eisenbahnunfällen', *Zeitschrift für Bahn- und Bahnkassenärzte* 5 (1913), p. 5.

[97] H. Norman Barnett, *Accidental injuries to workmen with reference to the Workmen's Compensation Act, 1906* (London, 1909), p. 280.

[98] Kurt Mendel, 'Über Querulantenwahnsinn und "Neurasthenia querulatoria" bei Unfallverletzten', special issue of *Neurologisches Centralblatt* 21 (1901), p. 4. Greg Eghigian has traced these discussions further, outlining a 'history of the modern form of political complaint' in his study of

discourse began ascribing the term 'accident neurosis' to individuals whose neurosis stemmed from their quest for compensation rather than to those individuals who suffered neurosis from an accidental trauma. Certain physicians made efforts to differentiate between 'pension neurosis' and 'accident neurosis' as a legitimate ailment. Yet, the language describing neurosis became muddled, highlighting widespread uncertainties about the consequences of social legislation.[99] Physicians brought together plenty of evidence that could support arguments about 'pension addiction' and link the problem directly to the German system of accident insurance. One study on 'the battle for pensions and suicide' gave a particularly vivid example of a case that began just two years after the adoption of the accident insurance law. Wilhelm Jung injured himself while working in the sugar industry, resulting in the loss of a testicle. By 1905, he was rendered entirely unable to work because he had developed 'hysterical disturbances and numerous hypochondriacal and paranoid movements'. Over the course of 19 years, he went to a court of arbitration ten times and confronted the Imperial Insurance Office on eight occasions. The report claimed that his accident insurance file alone contained 724 pages, pointing to the failure of the German government in dealing with such cases.[100]

The prevalence of accusations about individuals such as Wilhelm Jung reflected broader societal anxieties about social insurance. Not only had social insurance led workers astray, guiding them towards strange new addictions, but it had also failed in one of its most basic purposes: forging social solidarity, especially with the working classes. It is telling, therefore, that some doctors began looking beyond medical causes when citing the rise in cases of pension neurosis. A lecturer at the University of Leipzig claimed in the same year that the heart of the problem was not 'the lack of professional joy' that injured workers experienced after their accidents. Instead, it was that workers lacked 'the feeling of obligation' they should possess as a response to the rights they receive under social insurance. He saw the actions of the Social Democratic Party as to blame, as it had encouraged workers to claim 'their rights against civil society'.[101] This depiction of pension claimants did not go uncontested. For example, the Medical Director at the Berlin Accident Station of the Red

---

accident insurance and disability benefit: *Making security social: disability, insurance, and the birth of the social entitlement state in Germany* (Ann Arbor, MI, 2000), p. 21.

[99] Hugo Starsberg, *Unerwünschte Folgen deutscher Sozialpolitik? Eine Entgegnung an Prof. Ludwig Bernhard* (Bonn, 1913), p. 11.

[100] Ernst Schultze, 'Der Kampf um die Rente und der Selbstmord in der Rechtsprechung des Reichsversicherungsamts', *Sammlung zwangsloser Abhandlungen aus dem Gebiete der Nerven- und Geisteskrankheiten* 9/1 (1910), pp. 3–4. See also Dr Leopold Laquer, 'Die Heilbarkeit nervöser Unfallsfolgen: dauernde Rente oder einmalige Kapitalabfindung?', *Sammlung zwangsloser Abhandlungen aus dem Gebiete der Nerven- und Geisteskrankheiten* 9/5–7 (1912), especially pp. 5, 32–5.

[101] Dr Döllken, 'Wann sind Unfallneurosen heilbar', special issue of *Neurologisches Centralblatt* 25/23 (1906), p. 9.

Cross defended injured workers to the Imperial Insurance Office, stating that not every injured person who exaggerated his ailments was a 'pension neurotic'. Moreover, people of 'the middle class and higher classes' also tended to exaggerate their claims, possibly more so than members of the working class. The 'battle for pensions' was by no means unique to public insurance.[102] Some participants in this debate noted that doctors and insurance companies first recorded the desire for compensation in the early 1880s, with cases of middle-class claimants against commercial insurance funds.[103] Characterised by such conflicting 'scientific' information and unmediated opinion, the 'battle for pensions' became especially heated in the years leading up to the outbreak of the First World War. Those involved in administering social insurance saw it as such a significant development that it became the focus of discussions at international congresses already from the late 1880s. By 1909, the topic served as a running theme at the second International Congress for Health Care Related to Accidents, where speakers presented on research and cases from Germany, Italy and Switzerland.[104]

In response to the suggestions by medics involved in the treatment of accident neurotics, the Imperial Insurance Office debated whether to allow injured workers who received 20 per cent of their former salaries as a pension to obtain a lump-sum payment in order to encourage claimants to move on with their lives. The 1900 revision to the accident insurance law already entitled pensioners receiving 15 per cent of their former salaries as a one-off payment. Pushing up the cut-off to 20 per cent would not be a major change. Nonetheless, officials at the Imperial Insurance Office remained conflicted about whether to amend the policy further by increasing the cap on lump-sum payouts. As Paul Kaufmann, a socially orientated Catholic and the long-time head of the department, noted, lump-sum payments could provide a 'cure' for patients suffering from pension neurosis. However, he also saw that a one-off payment would mean that these pension recipients would not be entitled to further claims – even if their symptoms worsened.[105] The issue of lump-sum pensions was further complicated by the fact that many recipients of accident compensation preferred them. When considering the matter further, members of the Imperial Insurance Office turned to the numerous letters they received from pension

---

[102] BArch: R89: 15112: unnumbered: Dr Paul Frank to the Imperial Insurance Office, 2 September 1912. See also: Starsberg, *Unerwünschte Folgen*; Bernhard Würmeling, 'Zum "Kampfe um die Rente"', *Concordia: Zeitschrift der Zentralstelle für Volkswohlfahrt* 20/1 (1913); Friedrich Zahn, 'Besprechung', *Zeitschrift für die Gesamte Versicherungs-Wissenschaft* 2 (1913).

[103] Ludwig Bernhard, *Unerwünschte Folgen der deutschen Sozialpolitik* (Berlin, 1912), p. 47.

[104] Dr Blind, 'Internationale Erfahrungen in der Arbeiterfürsorge und deutsche Reichsversicherungsordnung', *Ärztliche Sachverständigen-Zeitung* 16/4 (15 February 1910); Bernhard, *Unerwünschte Folgen*, p. 49.

[105] BArch: R1501: 101120: 117–32: Minutes of Special Plenary Session of the Imperial Insurance Office, discussing the government proposal for an Imperial Insurance Ordinance, 6 May 1909; 133–54: Appendix; 201–14: Appendix.

recipients, who invoked genuine reasons for a single, final payout. Johan Peter Thiel's motive for writing was typical: he planned to move on with his life as a semi-retired construction worker by travelling to the Netherlands, England, Spain and Italy in order to study for a new profession within the industry.[106] Ultimately, government avoided taking decisive action on the issue, even though public discussions of social insurance continued to focus on curing 'pension neurosis'. Officials feared that succumbing to demands about 'pension neurotics' would undermine the purpose of compensation as a no-fault solution to the consequences of occupational risk. At the same time, they feared that becoming entangled in the debate might delegitimise the role of government as a neutral arbiter in social problems. After several pamphleteers submitted their arguments to the Imperial Insurance Office, it therefore consulted regional insurance offices and employers' funds for their views on 'pension addiction'. Kaufmann concluded from this investigation that there was not a serious problem with pension fraud. Instead, he argued that these pamphlets were 'exaggerated attacks on German social insurance' as an institution.[107] Critics of 'pension neurosis', he implied, thought that the state had become too expansive, making citizens reliant upon it.

In both Italy and Britain, the ambiguous border between 'simulation' and outright fraud provided a point of debate that resembled, yet was much more tempered than, the primarily German discourse about 'pension neurotics'. 'Simulation' was a form of 'malingering' that scientists in each country recognised as 'the natural tendency to exaggerate the consequences of rather minor injuries'. As Giovanni de Bury argued in his report on claims cases around Naples, injured workers caught simulating would complain about 'subjective' issues, such as pain and weakness, whose existence was difficult to disprove.[108] In Britain, John Collie, the president of the Special Medical Board for Neurasthenia and Functional Nerve Disease, drew a distinction between malingering as the 'conscious and deliberate simulation of disease or exaggeration of symptoms', which was a fraudulent activity, and '*valetudinarianism*', as 'the unconscious or subconscious simulation of symptoms'. His portrayal of the valetudinarian echoed German descriptions of accident neurotics: 'many of these unfortunate people are converted into chronic invalids, or can be induced to return to work, according to the attitude taken up by the medical man in attendance'. He was inspired by both French and German literature on the topic. Unlike German portrayals of 'pension neurotics' as feminised

---

[106] BArch: R1501: 101235: unnumbered folio: here, Nr.10421901: Johan Peter Thiel to the Imperial Insurance Office, 30 May 1910. See also: 2: Andreas Hack, 15 May 1911; 8: Karl Jost, 23 November 1909.

[107] BArch: R89: 15113: unnumbered: President of the Imperial Insurance Office to the Secretary of the Interior, 23 April 1913.

[108] Giovanni de Bury, *Relazione sul contenzioso della cassa nazionale infortuni, sede compartimentale di Napoli, dal gennaio 1900 al dicembre 1904* (Naples, 1905), pp. 75–83, at p. 75.

men, however, the British concept of the 'valetudinarian' often pointed to the hysteria of women, whose 'defective will power' led them to adopt subjective symptoms. Even male 'valetudinarians' were prone to 'auto-suggestion', though, such as lingering pain after a back injury that had healed.[109]

In order to differentiate between simulators and outright frauds, physicians began calling for the careful inspection of injured workers. The social legislation in each country meant that workers' bodies were now subjected to investigation as part of a broader project to care for those who were deemed genuinely in need and to shunt 'frauds' off compensation and back to productive work. Through social policy, it seemed that the state had taken on a new role as the physical guardian of the workforce. In turn, workers were expected to be honest about their ailments. Wounds were examined for signs of self-infliction, which could often be determined by their severity: self-inflicted injuries tended to be superficial, created simply for show, as John Collie argued in his tome on 'malingering'. Photographic evidence confirmed his arguments about fraudulent claims and demonstrated the need to inspect workers' bodies for signs of disability (Figure 6).[110] Workers were also tested physically to determine whether their seemingly injured body parts functioned and, if so, whether they were capable of labour. In Britain, physicians advocated using electrodes to test muscle capacity and nerve damage, while X-rays were used to assess other injuries (Figure 7).[111] Such testing was also typical in Germany and Italy, where the Imperial Insurance Office and other adjudicating bodies sent injured workers to specialist clinics for examinations.[112] Long seen as the cause of occupational risk, machines like Schall & Son's electric battery were increasingly employed as a means to combat its consequences.

In Britain and Italy, physicians and judges were aware of dubious claims from 'pension neurotics', 'simulators' who exaggerated or imagined their symptoms and 'malingerers' who continued to collect accident benefit after they had healed. However, these cases did not become the regular subject of public outcry, even if the occasional national scandal emerged in Italy. By contrast, in Germany, social insurance had initially come under attack as an etatist incursion into the economy, local and regional particularism and individual

[109] John Collie, *Malingering and feigned sickness, with notes on the Workmen's Compensation Act, 1906 and compensation for injury, including the leading cases thereon* (1913; 2nd edn, London, 1917), pp. 2–3, 199–200, 14. Specifically, he cites Walther Ewald, *Die traumatische Neurosen und die Unfallgesetzgebung*, special issue of *Medizinische Klinik* 12 (Vienna, 1908) and A. Brissaud's work on 'sinistrosis'.
[110] Collie, *Malingering*, pp. 356–64.
[111] Collie, *Malingering*, pp. 508–13.
[112] de Bury, *Relazione*, pp. 76–8; J. J. Scanlan, *The mutilated hand and the Workmen's Compensation Act, 1906: having special reference to 'missing' fingers* (London, 1913), pp. 60–4; BArch: R89: 342: unnumbered: Medical Report from Professor Dr Quincke, Secret Medical Adviser and Director of the Medical Clinic in Kiel, to the Imperial Insurance Office, 15 February 1890.

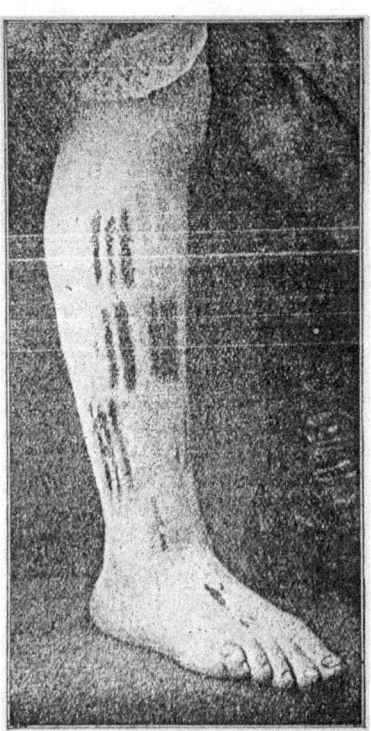

FIGURE 6. *Dermatitis artefacta*, a superficial, self-inflicted injury.
Source: Collie, *Malingering*, p. 360.

liberties, and it was later blamed for the weakening of workers' resolve to take care of themselves and their families. As a consequence, compensation claims that seemed to have little to do with workplace accidents and their immediate physical effects were routinely invoked as a testament to the failure of the state to manage its behemoth social legislation. The limited direct involvement of the Italian and British governments in administering accident benefit meant that it was difficult to implicate them in the potential failings of the policy. With few exceptions, physicians, insurance companies, employers and 'accident victims' never called upon government to participate in public debates about fraud and 'simulation'. Moreover, due to the lack of direct government involvement in adjudicating court cases, officials in Britain and Italy rarely noted problems with the daily practice of accident insurance and workmen's compensation. Only when they made special inquiries or were contacted by interested parties did they closely follow the issues of 'simulation' and fraud.

In Britain, concerns about fraud, and especially malingering, emerged in the discussions leading up to the enactment of the first Workmen's Compensation Act in 1897, and measures were put in place to address these, including

FIGURE 7. Battery for combined continuous and faradic currents, to test muscle activity. *Source*: Collie, *Malingering*, p. 513.

lump-sum payments and a 50 per cent cap on the total amount of salary that could be compensated.[113] Questions about fraud and 'malingering' surfaced again in discussions about revising the law, when government contacted county court judges to inquire about the effects of the 1897 Act. Certain judges were critical of workers for their 'unblushing perjury' and 'frivolous claims', yet few commented on the matter.[114] In 1907, a mining inspector responded to a Home Office inquiry about the general operation of Workmen's Compensation by stating that malingering was putting accident funds under considerable financial strain. The policy seemed to encourage workers to become dependent on compensation, and the result was harmful to British industry, which suffered from growing insurance premiums. The inspector pointed out that many workers insured themselves against accidents through friendly societies, even though

---

[113] TNA: HO 45/9867/B13816L/13: B. Huntsman to Fred Milner, MP, 10 May 1897; Home Office Memorandum, 15 May 1897.

[114] TNA: HO 157/3/232–3: Sir K. E. Digby to all County Court Judges, 15 October 1900; TNA: PIN12/1: unnumbered: Report of Judge Whitehorne, KC, 2 November 1900; unnumbered: Report from Dr F. Stevenson, 30 October 1900, to Sir K. E. Digby.

they were also eligible for compensation from their employers. As a result, they might receive payouts from both their employer and the friendly society in which they were a member. Claiming compensation could, therefore, prove more lucrative than working for regular wages.[115] These arguments about 'frivolous claims' and the lure of compensation were, however, ignored. Four years later, the Home Office Departmental Committee on Accidents in Places under the Factory and Workshops Act found that only a 'very small proportion' of compensation cases actually stemmed from malingering.[116]

In Italy, by contrast, fraud was the subject of several national scandals that seemed to reveal the failure of the state to manage social insurance because it was unable to tackle local collusion and clientelism. In the initial decade of the policy, employers, doctors, lawyers and workers were implicated in covering up a wave of self-inflicted injuries at the docks in Livorno. An investigative commission unearthed an 'epidemic of simulated cases' in which workers at the port of Livorno were attracted by the 'seduction of an easy earning'. The commission found that the way in which the dockworkers of Livorno organised themselves led to a 'spirit of fraud' because, by tradition, they took up jobs that were passed down from father to son. If workers preferred other jobs, they would hire replacements to fill their nominal positions and instead work in jobs that offered better pay or benefits. In this environment, the commission alleged, it was easy for more widespread fraud to develop. Moreover, the fact that only certain workers at the port were subject to the accident insurance law had bred feelings of jealousy and rivalry at the docks. The insured workers took advantage of their position and began simulating injuries, specifically, to the backs of their hands. The director of the Mutua Infortuni fund claimed that within his brief stay in Livorno, there were 39 cases of simulated injuries of this kind. Moreover, both employers and workers acted complicitly in reporting these 'accidents', while doctors and lawyers were involved in the whole affair. Insurance premiums were rising due to this 'moral risk'. By 1907, one by one, the private insurance companies operating in Livorno dropped their policies there, leaving only the National Accident Insurance Fund to cover the risks of these simulating workers. When the National Fund raised its premiums in 1908, employers instituted a lockout that put hundreds of workers out of employment.[117]

[115] TNA: PIN 12/3: unnumbered: 'Summary of Replies of H.M. Inspectors', January 1907.
[116] *PP* 1911 (Cd 5535) XXIII.1–70: 'Report of the Departmental Committee on Accidents in Places under the Factory and Workshops Act', p. 23.
[117] 'Relazione a S.E. il Ministro della Commissione d'inchiesta sul servizio dell'assicurazione infortuni nel porto di Livorno composta dall'ing. Luigi Pontiggia e dall'avvocato Ulrico Aillaud', *Bollettino di notizie sul credito e sulla previdenza* 26 (1908), pp. 53–66; ACS: PCM (1908). Cat. 10. Fasc. 6: unnumbered: Telegram from the Prefect of Livorno to Prime Minister Giovanni Giolitti, 1 February 1908. See also Italo Giudici, 'Un caso di truffa in materia di assicurazione contro gli infortuni sul lavoro', *Bollettino della Cassa nazionale per gl'infortuni degli operai sul lavoro* 1/3 (March 1914), pp. 25–31.

Insurance companies had noted the potential for such fraud already in a governmental inquiry from 1906 into judicial procedure for the accident insurance law. They claimed that the 'roots' of insurance abuses lay in the 'moral character of certain categories of persons', since these individuals were predisposed to corruption. The insurance companies questioned suggested changing the system for making insurance claims, because workers had become increasingly attracted by litigation. They suggested that the appeal of compensation had led workers to consult with each other in order to learn how to benefit from the insurance system. As one doctor put it in his report to the 1907 National Congress on Occupational Illnesses at Palermo, genuine 'schools of simulation' had begun to spring up across the country, 'in which worker[s are] directed in the technical-medical nature of fraud'.[118] Moreover, these workers were able to find medical professionals who were willing to assist in their deceit for small financial gains.[119] The nature of this situation appears to have been unique to Italy, as no similar cases were uncovered by the German or British governments. It is possible that the fears of Italian officials could, at least in part, be justified: the new government, and its system of social insurance, lacked authority and did not inspire compliance. On a more pragmatic level, the fact that German liability funds used their own medical examiners and that the British government certified a select number of doctors for the examination of accident cases meant that both systems were less susceptible to this form of fraud.

The Italian government and parliament realised that the system needed reform, but it had not materialised by the point when the Livorno incident erupted. In the aftermath of Livorno, employers argued for insurance reform to ensure that premiums remained equitable. They also sought to counteract fraudulent actions by implementing more regulatory measures: routine medical examination by trustworthy practitioners and harsh sanctions for those caught simulating illness or assisting simulators.[120] It was left to local

---

[118] Domenico Mirto, 'La simulazione negli infortuni del lavoro', in *Atti del I Congresso per le malattie del lavoro (malattie professionali), Palermo, 19–21 ottobre 1907* (Palermo, 1908), pp. 23–54, quoted in Berlinguer, 'La medicina del lavoro', p. 121.

[119] 'Allegato C: Proposte presentate dalle società di assicurazione "Alleanza" di Genova – "Anonima italiana infortuni" di Milano – "Assicuratrice italiana" di Milano – e "Ausonia" di Genova', *Atti della commisssione incaricata degli studi concernenti la giurisdizione e la procedura per le controversie dipendenti dalla legge per gli infortuni sul lavoro*, special issue of *Annali del credito e della previdenza* (Rome, 1906), pp. 207–10.

[120] ACS: PCM (1908). Cat. 10. Fasc. 6: unnumbered: Telegram from Chamber of Commerce in Livorno to Prime Minister Giolitti, 10 February 1908. See also: Camera di Commercio ed Arti di Livorno, *Relazione sulle modificazioni alla legge per gl'infortuni degli operai sul lavoro: approvata dalla Camera di commercio nell'adunanza del 2 marzo 1908* (Livorno, 1908); ACS: PCM (1908). Cat. 10. Fasc. 6: unnumbered: Minister of Agriculture, Industry and Commerce Cocco Ortu to Prime Minister Giolitti, 31 December 1907; unnumbered: Telegram from the Sindacato sugli infortuni nella solfare di Sicilia to the Chamber of Deputies, n.d. [May 1908].

authorities to work in conjunction with insurance bodies to prevent scams. In 1914, the National Fund noted a new case of serious fraud, this time at the port of Naples. The coal loaders at the docks were 'systematically' injuring themselves and aggravating their injuries in order to receive compensation. The president of the National Fund considered turning to the Ministers of Justice, Agriculture and the Interior to aid the Fund in snuffing out these 'abuses'. Ultimately, however, the Fund dealt with local authorities in Naples, where the port authority agreed to construct a wooden pavilion to monitor the situation at the docks. The local police arrested several individuals whom the local branch of the National Fund denounced. The police also confiscated some of the tools used to create the injuries in question. According to the local branch, more than 200 people were involved in this incident.[121]

In Italy, as in Germany and Britain, accident compensation was predicated on honesty. As a no-fault system, it relied on workers, employers and insurers to honour their responsibilities: working, preventing accidents and paying for their consequences if they arose. This web of mutual responsibility depended on the state as a guarantor, which meant that officials were often as concerned about preventing everyday forms of deceptive behaviour stemming from employers and insurance companies as they were about self-harming and malingering amongst workers. The entire systems of compensation in Britain and Italy hinged on the just behaviour of insurance companies and employers, which led central government in each country to monitor these groups closely by despatching factory and workplace inspectors and compiling accident statistics. The failure of either employers or insurers to act according to the principles of the compensation policies would point towards the failure of the legislation. It would also reveal the incompetence of government in having entrusted the management of a key flank of social legislation to those groups. In Germany, by contrast, central government was not especially concerned about fraud amongst employers or the employers' funds. The structure of the German funds lent itself to self-policing and made it more difficult for employers and insurers to commit acts of fraud. Moreover, as Germany had a federal system of government, factory inspectors existed on both national and member-state levels. By 1913, there were 256 inspection districts in the country, and this division of labour was further complicated by the fact that Germany operated a 'dualist' system of factory inspection whereby the employers' liability funds as well as the federal states were responsible for overseeing workplace safety.[122]

---

[121] *Atti della Cassa nazionale di assicurazione per gli infortuni degli operai sul lavoro: verbale delle sedute d'insediamento del nuovo Consiglio Superiore* (n.s. 1914–15) 8 (27 July 1914), pp. 11–12.

[122] Peter Hennock offers a helpful comparison of the German and British factory inspectorates: E. P. Hennock, *The origin of the welfare state in England and Germany, 1850–1914: social policies compared* (Cambridge, 2007), pp. 128–9, 135–8. On the dualist system: Rolf Simons, *Staatliche Gewerbeaufsicht und gewerbliche Berufsgenossenschaften: Entstehung und*

Against this context, in Germany, central government was not concerned about fraud amongst employers or the insurance funds. Instead, officials were anxious that the corporative and federal system as a whole seemed to operate in a way that was fair to all parties involved.

In Italy, the Minister of Agriculture asked factory inspectors to examine whether employers had followed through with their obligation to take out insurance for workplace accidents. Evidence that construction firms had failed to insure their workers led him to order regional prefects to investigate.[123] When the Palermo branch of the National Accident Insurance Fund notified him that employers in the Sicilian sulphur mines had misrepresented the number of workers they were required to insure, let alone their wages and hourages, the government investigated again.[124] Similarly, government investigated whether insurance companies were properly paying out compensation.[125] It is noteworthy that the Minister of Agriculture emphasised the 'good application of the laws' to regional authorities when investigating these issues, revealing central government's objective to create a uniform system throughout Italy in a period of administrative expansion and the construction of the Italian nation state.[126]

In Britain, government monitored unscrupulous insurance companies and employers, but found few cases. Discussions about the unethical practices of insurance companies and employers sometimes transformed into invectives against the poor behaviour of compensation recipients. When preparing a revision to the 1897 Workmen's Compensation Act, the Home Office inquired with county court judges about the Act's implementation. Certain judges noted that the system for collecting compensation needed to be improved, as there was no means to enforce payment, which sometimes resulted in compensation not reaching injured workers or their families.[127] Others pointed to unethical insurance companies and employers that induced workers to accept small lump-sum payments instead of the weekly payments to which they were entitled. Both judges and Home Office officials were particularly concerned about

Entwicklung des dualen Aufsichtssystems im Arbeitsschutz in Deutschland von den Anfängen bis zum Ende der Weimarer Republik (Frankfurt a. M., 1984), p. 114.

[123] 'Circolare 15 agosto 1900, n. 21725, del Ministero di agricoltura ai signori prefetti del regno circa l'esecuzione della legge', *Annali del credito e della previdenza* (1904), pp. 184–6.

[124] 'Cassa nazionale di assicurazione contro gli infortuni degli operai sul lavoro: Rendiconto dell'essercizio 1899 e notizie statistiche', *Bollettino di notizie sul credito e sulla previdenza* 19/2–3 (1901), pp. 167–92, at p. 168. See also 'Ispezioni eseguite nelle miniere e nelle cave nel 1911', *Bollettino di notizie sul credito e sulla previdenza* 30/5 (1912), pp. 493–500.

[125] 'Circolare ministeriale 17 maggio 1905, n. 6, di protocollo 14257, diretta agli Istituti di assicurazione contro gli infortuni sul lavoro, intorno al pagamento agli aventi diritto per infortuni seguiti da morte', *Bollettino di notizie sul credito e sulla previdenza* 23/6 (1905), pp. 901–2; ACS: PCM (1903). Bta. 305. Cat.11. Fasc. 1–2: unnumbered: Antonio Tedeschi to 'Eccellenza' (the Prime Minister), 9 September 1902.

[126] 'Circolare 15 agosto 1900', p. 186.

[127] TNA: PIN 12/1: unnumbered: Report of Judge Whitehorne, KC, 2 November 1900.

the practice of awarding lump-sum payments, which they considered detrimental to claimants. They were especially worried about widows using the money to open businesses that were doomed to fail![128]

The Home Office Departmental Committee which investigated revising workmen's compensation found that payouts were 'squandered or dissipated or getting into the wrong hands', especially in claims cases involving women. Several members of the committee doubted women's ability to manage money. One witness cited the case of a woman whose character was known to be poor. She was the mother of two or three children and received a lump-sum compensation award, which she wasted, leaving her children without subsistence. Another mother spent her lump-sum settlement within three months, leaving her four children to starve. She was sentenced to prison. Some committee members therefore recommended entrusting lump-sum payments to trustworthy men from the community, such as other miners, if the deceased husband had worked in a colliery. The committee ultimately concluded that funds for dependants should instead be invested by a neutral authority, the county courts, and paid out with discretion. The 1906 revision to the Act did, in fact, adopt this amendment. However, committee members also resolved that the commutation of compensation into a single lump-sum payment should be discouraged in general, as workers and their families should have been capable of managing their own affairs.[129] These discussions about the problems with compensation involving deceptive employers and insurers did not persist after the 1904 meeting of the Home Office Departmental Committee on Workmen's Compensation. As one judge remarked already in 1900, he could recall only one case in which an insurance company sought to settle for a lump-sum payment that went against the interests of the compensation recipient. The reason why there were so few instances like this, he argued, was that workers knew their 'rights' under the law and had grown 'accustomed' to it.[130] Since workers helped to oversee compensation in this way, government rarely needed to intervene.

The issue of fraud, in its various forms, revealed nationally specific anxieties about social legislation and its effects on the relationship between individuals and the state. Judge Whitehorne's argument suggested that, for the most part, workmen's compensation functioned well and could run smoothly without daily involvement from Whitehall. The assumption was that citizens could be

---

[128] TNA: HO 157/3/232–3: Sir K. E. Digby to all County Court Judges, 15 October 1900; TNA: PIN 12/1: unnumbered: Report of Judge Whitehorne, KC, 2 November 1900; unnumbered: Report from Dr F. Stevenson, 30 October 1900, to Sir K. E. Digby. See also: TNA: PIN 12/3: unnumbered: C. E. Troup from the Home Office to H.M. Inspector of Mines, 2 March 1904.

[129] *PP* 1904 (Cd 2208) LXXXVIII.743: 'Home Office Departmental Committee on Workmen's Compensation: Report', pp. 827–31, at p. 831.

[130] TNA: PIN 12/1: unnumbered: Report of Judge Whitehorne, KC, 2 November 1900.

trusted with their role in the compensation system – even if workers would need to be subjected to the occasional electric shock to see whether they were faking an injury. In light of these views, it is not surprising that fraud never reached the level of national scandal in Britain that it did in Germany and, to a certain extent, in Italy. By contrast, German discussions of fraud reflected the constant anxieties within government and society at large about the success of social insurance. Were accident beneficiaries now dependent on the state? Would German industry suffer from substantial payouts to 'malingerers'? In Italy, unlike in Germany or Britain, officials never took comfort in the notion that accident insurance would be able to function without careful monitoring. They recognised that the policy lacked both substance, in the form of certified doctors, and the loyalty of citizens.

As this chapter has shown, the compensation policies in Britain, Germany and Italy gave rise to new questions about the responsibilities of workers, employers and the state. Individual court cases and new jurisprudential and scientific developments gradually expanded the meaning of an 'accident'. As a result, in all three countries, workers were no longer held accountable for injuries that occurred while making deliveries or involved in other activities located outside their physical workplace, and arguments about ill-fated 'Acts of God' became less credible. The concept of 'occupational risk' was stretched to allow for 'invisible' accidents as well, and workers could even claim compensation for certain illnesses that were contracted suddenly, for example, by inhaling microscopic anthrax spores embedded in wool. Nonetheless, doubts about causation and the culpability of workers remained, as was most evident in the discussions about weak physical dispositions and the contraction of occupational illnesses and about poor heredity and the propensity to nervous disorders following accidents. Debates about 'malingering' and fraud began to highlight widespread anxieties about the abuse of social legislation. To some, it seemed that accident compensation had not only failed to forge social solidarity. It had also led to new forms of moral hazard, as certain individuals and businesses used the system for their own deceptive ends.

The contours of these discussions were similar across Europe, in part due to the regular international conferences on industrial hygiene and occupational accidents. Nonetheless, individual governments perceived and handled these issues in different ways that reflected distinct concerns about the role of the state in governing risk. Officials in Germany saw that any form of abuse involving compensation could be viewed as an indictment of the whole system of social insurance, let alone the state. As the final court of appeal in accident claims, the Imperial Insurance Office in Berlin was directly responsible for any controversial decisions. As a consequence, government, with the aid of a team of legal advisers, technical experts and workers' and employers' representatives, played a substantial role in overseeing compensation on a daily basis.

Officials at Whitehall and in Rome, by contrast, saw that their authority rested on the behaviour of those outside government who were involved in implementing accident compensation every day, whether commercial insurance firms or county court judges. Over time, as new groups of workers claimed entitlement to compensation, could these various arrangements endure? Would each government see that accident benefit, more than ever before, was a matter for the state?

5

Workers, Citizens and the State

On a crisp spring night in 1912, a passenger ship that was 'designed to be unsinkable' collided with an iceberg on its starboard side. The hull buckled in several places, and the ship's compartments filled with saltwater. The vessel began to sink. With only 20 lifeboats to carry passengers and crew and no nearby ships to rescue the sinking ship, most passengers onboard were left to the frigid Atlantic. The sinking of the *Titanic* off the southern coast of Newfoundland resulted in the deaths of 1,514 people, including 696 crew members. One of the most infamous maritime disasters in history, the destruction of the *Titanic* was also a workplace accident of international significance. Almost 77 per cent of the crew on board, ranging from sailors and engineers to musicians, perished that night. By the following year, the first International Convention on the Safety of Life at Sea was drawn up in London. It prescribed requisite numbers of lifeboats and other safety equipment as well as emergency procedures for merchant vessels. It also led to the development of an International Ice Patrol. International collaboration in preventing future disasters was not the only result of the *Titanic*'s demise. The families of crew who died in the accident expected compensation from the British White Star Line that owned the sunken ship. The magnitude of the catastrophe led governments around the world to inquire with Britain about remuneration for the families of deceased crew members. As it happened, their survivors were eligible for workmen's compensation because the policy applied to all workers employed by British companies – regardless of whether they were British citizens or whether their families were resident in the United Kingdom.[1] From the perspective of other countries, this conclusion was anything but obvious, and

[1] TNA: HO 157/6/777: E. Blackwell, Under-Secretary of the Home Office to the Under-Secretary of the Foreign Office, 3 June 1912.

these doubts about eligibility for workmen's compensation take us to the heart of this chapter's subject.

Like other countries, Britain, Germany and Italy saw their systems of accident compensation expand considerably in the years immediately following the enactment of the new policies. The extension of compensation to new groups of workers reflected a broader movement to address various individual woes, from old-age poverty to unemployment, with social legislation that would later come to be seen as the seeds of modern 'welfare states'. While Germany had already introduced old-age pensions, disability insurance and health insurance for manual workers in the 1880s, by the late 1900s, it began new initiatives to consolidate this system and to grant white-collar workers pensions for old age and disability. Parallel to these social security programmes were a myriad of local and increasingly coordinated efforts such as clinics focused on tuberculosis (from 1899), dispensaries for infants (from 1905) and an increasingly comprehensive network of labour exchanges.[2] In Britain, new social legislation also took off in the early 1900s, from a national school milk scheme in 1906 to old-age pensions (1908) and national insurance for unemployment and health (1911). Following the insights of Seebohm Rowntree and other social investigators, officials in Britain had begun to regard cycles of poverty and poverty-related ill health due to old age, youth, unemployment and disability as predictable risks, akin to occupational risk, that could be managed by the state. To be sure, however, various factors led to these efforts, beyond concerns about the inadequacy of the Poor Law as a means to address swings in the labour market or vulnerable periods in one's life. Growing popular demand for a 'right to work' played a role, as did anxieties about infant mortality and population health that were fuelled in part by the British army's near defeat in South Africa in the Boer War (1899–1902).[3] In Italy, too, new national policies were introduced at the turn of the twentieth century that focused on various problems encountered throughout the lifecycle, including maternity insurance (1912) and a state-subsidised old-age and disability pension fund (1898). In his blueprint for a 'new historical era', Prime Minister Giovanni Giolitti declared that government would need to create effective 'social laws' that would help to ease the poverty, excessive taxes and ill treatment of workers that had been brought to national attention by a recent general strike in Genoa.[4]

---

[2] Paul Weindling, 'The medical profession, social hygiene and the birth rate in Germany, 1914–18', in Richard Wall and Jay Winter, eds., *The upheaval of war: family, work and welfare in Europe, 1914–18* (Cambridge, 1988), pp. 417–38, at p. 419; E. P. Hennock, *The origin of the welfare state in England and Germany, 1850–1914: social policies compared* (Cambridge, 2007), pp. 310–14.

[3] Michael Hanagan, 'Citizenship, claim-making, and the right to work: Britain, 1884–1911', *Theory and Society* 26 (1997), pp. 449–74; *The solidarities of strangers: the English Poor Laws and the people, 1700–1948* (Cambridge, 1998), pp. 233–58; Jose Harris, *Unemployment and politics: a study in English social policy, 1886–1914* (Oxford, 1972), pp. 12–13.

[4] Giovanni Giolitti, 'Il nuovo indirizzo della political liberale' (4 February 1901), *Discorsi parlamentari di Giovanni Giolitti* (4 vols., Rome, 1953), vol. II, pp. 632–3. Nonetheless, few

Against this backdrop, officials in Britain, Germany and Italy began to question their handling of workplace accidents. Should the state ensure that *all*
accidents at work were taken care of – regardless of the injured's occupation,
social status, nationality or even physical location? As we saw in Chapter 1,
an earlier shift in thinking along these lines had already taken place in the mid
nineteenth century. Governments followed jurists and 'scientists of work' alike
in rejecting liberal understandings of risk which suggested that workers consented to job-related hazards because they were free agents in the labour market who could choose any job, knowing that they might be paid higher wages
for dangerous employment. Instead, it seemed that some jobs were so dangerous that they were likely to cause accidents to which no one was in a position to consent. The idea of occupational risk upon which the compensation
laws were based suggested that accidents stemmed from work, not workers,
and not their employers or managers. Gradually, officials considered whether
compensation was a kind of social right to which all workers should be entitled, and not just those in the most dangerous trades or even those working
in manual labour. As the *Titanic* disaster reveals, citizens or workers located
within national borders were not the only targets of these discussions, which
considered nationals employed at home and overseas, itinerant foreigners, such
as the 350,000 Polish workers dotted along the German banks of the Rhine
and throughout the coalfaces of the Ruhr valley, as well as colonial subjects
in outposts abroad.[5] In different ways, Britain, Germany and Italy grappled
with the meaning of statehood through addressing these conflicts about entitlement: did the social state exist only within the sovereign territory of the nation
state?[6] And was the social state inclusive, bringing all workers into its fold?

At the turn of the twentieth century, these questions about entitlement and
its relationship to statehood were informed by the context of global migration,
imperial expansion and a related movement for international norms in social
legislation.[7] For officials in Britain, Germany and Italy, protecting national
diaspora abroad was an important aspect of social statehood, as was fostering
economic growth through extending or limiting benefits to migrant workers

substantive policies emerged from his vision, and many of the reforms, such as compulsory
disability and old-age pensions for public employees, seemed a testament to clientelism and corruption rather than a concerted effort at addressing social risks. See Maria Sophia Quine, *Italy's
social revolution: charity and welfare from liberalism to fascism* (Basingstoke, 2002), pp. 80–2.
[5] Volker R. Berghahn, *Imperial Germany, 1871–1918: economy, society, culture and politics* (rev.
edn, Oxford and New York, 2005), pp. 100–4.
[6] Perhaps as the mirror to the state's 'monopoly on the legitimate use of physical force' within its
sovereign territory: Max Weber, *Wirtschaft und Gesellschaft*, ed. Johannes Winckelmann (5th
edn, Tübingen, 2002), p. 29.
[7] Martti Koskenniemi, *The gentle civilizer of nations: the rise and fall of international law, 1870–
1960* (Cambridge, 2001), pp. 3–4, 14, 18, 42–6. For example, the 1906 international conventions on the abolition of white phosphorus in the production of matches and the abolition of
female and child night labour. See: Vittorio Manfredi, 'La conferenza diplomatica di Berna sulla
protezione internazionale del lavoro', *Nuova antologia* (4th series) 201 (1905), pp. 155–64.

or domestic companies operating overseas. Statistics on migration for the late nineteenth and early twentieth centuries are unreliable and, for certain aspects, unavailable. Nonetheless, several general patterns can be found, including the fact that European labour emigration declined steeply with the outbreak of the First World War.[8] German emigration was extensive throughout this period but peaked in the 1880s, and the vast majority of emigrants went to the United States. By the late nineteenth century, officials were mainly concerned to manage the vast immigration to Germany from across Europe, such as the hundreds of thousands of agricultural workers recruited through organisations like the Prussian Farm Workers' Agency, which could register up to 10,000 new recruits per day from its many offices in Galicia and elsewhere. By 1907, there were over 100,000 Dutch workers just in Prussia.[9] Britain, too, attracted many workers from abroad, such as the approximately 60,000 Germans living in Manchester, London and Liverpool before the outbreak of the First World War. While the 1905 Aliens Act attempted to reduce the flow of migrants to Britain, its effects were limited, and the policy even opened the door to a new category of immigrant: asylum seekers. As in Germany, British emigration continued throughout this period, and it targeted the United States as well as colonies and dominions. In 1910, for example, 157,000 Britons left for Canada, while 132,000 moved to the United States, 46,000 to Australia and 27,000 to South Africa.[10]

Italian labour migration was more varied, and it also prompted different attitudes within government about the social state. Over 14 million Italians emigrated between 1876 and 1915, and 44 per cent of these individuals sought work in other European countries. About 250,000 workers left Italy every year in search of jobs located north of the Alps. However, many more migrated around the peninsula in search of work rather than going abroad. Italian migration also differed from that in Germany and Britain, as a particularly high percentage of these emigrants returned home, and as the geographical origins of migrants varied considerably.[11] As a result of the large proportion of the population working abroad, the valuable remittances they sent home and their intention to return at a later point, the Italian government was especially keen to ensure that its citizens would be treated well abroad. It also saw that protecting emigrant Italians could encourage their sense of national belonging.

[8] Walter Nugent, *Crossings: the great transatlantic migrations, 1870–1914* (Bloomington, 1995), pp. 43, 64; Klaus J. Bade, *Migration in European history*, trans. Allison Brown (Oxford, 2003), p. 184.
[9] Bade, *Migration*, pp. 55, 159–61.
[10] Bade, *Migration*, p. 176; Nugent, *Crossings*, p. 43; Alison Bashford and Jane MacAdam, 'The right to asylum: the 1905 Aliens Act and the evolution of refugee law', *Law and History Review* 32/2 (2014), pp. 309–50; Brian R. Mitchell, *Abstract of British historical statistics* (Cambridge, 1971), p. 50.
[11] Rudolph J. Vecoli, 'The Italian diaspora, 1876–1976', in Robin Cohen, ed., *The Cambridge survey of world migration* (Cambridge, 1995), pp. 114–22, at 114, 116.

Following unification, many Italians only began to embrace a feeling of *itali-anità* after they left their hometowns and found themselves in communities elsewhere with other Italians. This consciousness of *italianità* might bring emigrant workers to help fund economic growth by sending home remittances. It could also foster Italian world power, in the form of a 'Greater Italy' that reached far beyond the peninsula, let alone a sense of Italian cultural ties that extended across the globe.[12] This sense of a 'Greater Italy' informed the treatment of workers in Italy's North African colonies, who were included within the country's accident system. In Britain and Germany, by contrast, the social state seemed to stop at the national border, even if officials in both countries aimed to help citizens overseas by signing reciprocity treaties for accident benefits. Despite J. R. Seeley's 1883 claim that the British Empire constituted part of a 'Greater Britain', imperial statehood was more of a dream than a reality for Britain, whose imperial ties were fragmented and largely cultural rather than legal.[13] In Germany, too, the push for an overseas empire resulted in new colonies that were governed by the 'rule of colonial difference', which was carefully defined in legal terms about the territorial limitations of the state and, within the administration, in cultural terms about the specific nature of the local population.[14]

As this chapter shows, the impact of these considerations about the relationship between entitlement and social statehood was uneven. It proved difficult to shed earlier thinking that accidents were a problem of the workplace alone and should be handled accordingly. Moreover, other priorities, such as economic growth and maintaining clear distinctions between social classes and different races, meant that not all workers would become equally eligible for compensation. Despite growing claims about rights to social provisions, from milk dispensaries to old-age pensions, it remained unclear whether accident benefit was an entitlement to which all could lay claim. And, in spite of the increasing visibility of the state – through court rulings, official publications

[12] Mark I. Choate, *Emigrant nation: the making of Italy abroad* (Cambridge, MA, 2008), pp. 25, 49–56, 101–28, 155; Donna R. Gabaccia and Fraser M. Ottanelli, 'Introduction', in Donna R. Gabaccia and Fraser M. Ottanelli, eds., *Italian workers of the world: labor migration and the formation of multiethnic states* (Urbana and Chicago, 2001), pp. 1–20, at pp. 3–4; Donna R. Gabaccia, *Foreign relations: American immigration in global perspective* (Princeton, NJ, 2012), pp. 2–4.

[13] David Armitage, '"Greater Britain": a useful category of analysis?', *American Historical Review* 104/2 (1999), pp. 427–45; Anthony Pagden, 'The empire's new clothes: from empire to federation, yesterday and today', *Common Knowledge* 12/1 (2006), pp. 36–46. Nonetheless, colonies around the empire emulated aspects of political and legal conventions in the metropole, but they remained distinct and, in the case of law in India, were based on entirely different assumptions about the role of law in society. See for example: Elizabeth Kolsky, *Colonial justice in British India: white violence and the rule of law* (Cambridge, 2009).

[14] Partha Chatterjee, *The nation and its fragments: colonial and postcolonial histories* (Princeton, NJ, 1993), p. 26; George Steinmetz, *The devil's handwriting: precoloniality and the German colonial state in Qingdao, Samoa and Southwest Africa* (Chicago, 2008), pp. 47–8, 61–2.

and responses to individual letters – what part it would play in addressing workplace accidents continued to be anything but certain. The existence of unified lobbies of employers, workers and insurers fed into these considerations, as did the specific nature of national economies and workforces. However, attitudes within each government about the state's role in managing social problems also proved decisive, informing daily interactions with groups that demanded access to compensation and shaping efforts to overhaul each system. As a consequence, by the start of the First World War, almost three-quarters of the working population in Britain and Germany were eligible to receive accident benefit. By contrast, in Italy, just under 15 per cent of the population could claim the same privilege.

RISKY WORK?

Ideas about rights to compensation were repeatedly tested in court cases, challenged in pleading letters from workers and trade unions and questioned in the investigations of physicians, civil servants and jurists. Over time, trades that were less obviously dangerous were gradually incorporated into the compensation systems. The extension of accident benefit to the bulk of the population in Britain and Germany and to a substantial group of new workers in Italy pointed to new ways of thinking about who was at risk. Despite broad agreement about the issue across national borders, however, there were striking differences in how each country extended accident benefit to new groups of workers. In Germany, for example, new groups of workers were gradually incorporated into the accident insurance system, as the civil service systematically thought through which trades were particularly dangerous. Government in Berlin was reluctant to apply the policy to workers in trades that lacked a clear element of occupational risk. As a consequence, officials painstakingly debated the minutiae of various jobs in order to ascertain whether they were so risky that neither workers nor employers could be held accountable for accidents. A complicating factor in these considerations was the corporative structure of social insurance in Germany for workplace accidents. Granting the right to compensation to new groups meant finding existing or creating new insurance funds to cover them. As a result, officials saw that they could not simply open the floodgates of accident benefit to all workers without reforming the system as a whole. Instead, they would need to enact specific pieces of legislation that would enable certain categories of workers, bit by bit, to enter the complex system of German social insurance. Another factor played into these considerations: the concern that some workers were fundamentally different from others and should be offered different kinds of protections by the state.

As a consequence, government in Berlin gradually saw that more and more jobs were dangerous, whether or not they fitted within traditional conceptions of 'dangerous employment', but many workers were initially excluded from the accident scheme. This process of extending compensation began already in the 1880s, shortly after the first accident insurance law was enacted. For example, those involved in writing the early accident laws, including various Prussian ministries and the People's Economic Advisory Board, recognised that there were risks associated with agricultural labour that could not be avoided, meaning that accidents stemming from these risks merited compensation on an obligatory, no-fault basis. The main problem that law-makers saw in including agricultural labourers in the social insurance system was the transitory nature of their work. They tended to change jobs and locations frequently, following the demands of each season, and the distinction between employers and workers was often ambiguous. This concern was not, however, insurmountable, and agricultural workers were made eligible for accident insurance in 1886 through regional, rather than industry-based, funds.[15] By contrast, these early debates about entitlement to compensation came to a standstill over the question of handicrafts and 'small' industries. The Berlin Bookbinder Guild petitioned the Imperial Insurance Office within months of the ratification of the first accident insurance law. The guild argued that the restriction of the policy to factories with more than ten workers was illogical because 'the danger of accidents in small industries is, if not greater, then in any case not less' since a worker was required 'to go from one machine to another in order to finish his work'.[16] Others involved in handicrafts instead pointed to more specific dangers inherent in their occupations, such as using butchers' equipment.[17] The Imperial Insurance Office responded reluctantly to these petitions, eventually sending out a questionnaire to the employers' liability insurance funds (*Berufsgenossenschaften*) to ask which industries should be covered.[18]

By 1893, the long-standing head of the Imperial Office of the Interior, Karl Heinrich von Boetticher, declared that 'all working classes as long as

[15] BArch: R1501: 100651: 12–14: President of the Imperial Insurance Office to Secretary of the Interior von Boetticher, 8 October 1884; BArch: R1501: 100653: 85–8: Secretary of the Interior von Boetticher to the Kaiser, 17 October 1884; BArch: R501: 100656: 2–7: Petition from the Committee of the *Deutsche Landwirthschaftsrath* to the *Bundesrath*, March 1885. See also Chapters 2 and 3 above.

[16] BArch: R1051: 100694: 8–9: Berlin Bookbinder Guild to the Imperial Insurance Office, 1 December 1884; 10–11: Petition of the League of German Bookbinder Guilds to the Imperial Insurance Office, n.d. [June 1885].

[17] BArch: R1501: 100695: 21–2: Locksmiths' Guild of Cologne to the Imperial Insurance Office, 9 April 1885; BArch: R89: 948: unnumbered: Committee of the German Butchers' Guild League to the Imperial Insurance Office, 13 November 1886.

[18] BArch: R1501: 100694: 40–2: 'Die soziale Gliederung der kleingewerblichen Bevölkerung in Preussen', *Statistische Korrespondenz* 12/36 (25 September 1886); BArch: R89: 948: unnumbered: Imperial Insurance Office to the Secretary of the Interior, 2 November 1885; unnumbered: Secretary of the Interior to the Imperial Insurance Office, 18 April 1887. See also Ernst Wickenhagen, *Geschichte der gewerblichen Unfallversicherung: Wesen und Wirken der gewerblichen Berufsgenossenschaften* (Munich, 1980), vol. II, pp. 323–8.

they encountered dangers at work' should be entitled to accident compensation.[19] Before proposing more legislation, Boetticher solicited further opinions on the issue, and it was arguments about the practicality of including new groups of workers that prevented him from putting forward a law proposal for the next several years. He was uninterested in deviating from a traditional idea of occupational risk that focused on heavy industry and saw that the two main drawbacks to including small industries were the economic depression that Germany had been facing since the stock market crash in 1873 and the difficulty of organising the multitude of small trades into accident funds.[20] He also reflected on the point made by the Central Association of German Industrialists, which noted that it would be difficult for many smaller firms to bear the financial burden of accident insurance.[21] The 1900 law that emerged from these debates was a compromise, as it included several smaller professions that were perceived to be especially dangerous, such as butchers, smiths and locksmiths, but it did not extend accident insurance to all small firms and handicraft trades in general.

The Commercial Accident Insurance Law of 1900 explicitly cited new forms of technology, including automobiles used for commercial purposes, as dangerous tools which would require special intervention by the state.[22] Officials were particularly concerned about the risks associated with the many new inventions of the 1890s and 1900s, and they questioned whether workers using this equipment merited specific arrangements within the social insurance system. Automobiles, in particular, provoked a mixture of anxiety and optimism, and governmental debates about automotive accidents reflected broader discussions about dealing with the risks of new technologies.[23] By 1908, the *Reichstag* began discussing whether all workers using vehicles as well as animals for transportation should be covered by the accident insurance law. The issue first arose in a discussion about Germany's new civil code, which had been introduced in 1900 in order to codify the country's many diverse legal systems. The code included liability clauses that applied to all accidents to third parties

---

[19] GStAPK: I. HA. Rep. 77. Tit. 923. No. 1. Vol. 7: 309–10: Imperial Office of the Interior, to the Royal (Prussian) Minister of the Interior and the other Royal (Prussian) Ministries, 23 December 1893.

[20] GStAPK: I. HA. Rep. 84a:5295: 181: Vote of the Ministry of Agriculture, Domains and Forests on the 1893 law proposal for extension of accident insurance to all 'dangerous' small industries, 16 January 1894; 176–9: Vote of the Ministry of State, 10 January 1894; 221–6: Summary of the minutes from the Prussian Royal State Ministry, 11 June 1894; GStAPK: I. HA. Rep. 77. Tit. 923: No. 1. Vol. 7: 314–16: Minister of Trade and Commerce to the Imperial Office of the Interior, 8 December 1893.

[21] G. A. Bueck, *Der Centralverband deutscher Industrieller, 1876–1901* (2 vols., Berlin, 1905), vol. II, pp. 478ff.

[22] *RGBl* 30 June 1900, p. 573.

[23] Uwe Fraunholz, *Motorphobia: anti-automobiler Protest in Kaiserreich und Weimarer Republik* (Göttingen, 2002); Bernhard Rieger, *Technology and the culture of modernity in Britain and Germany, 1890–1945* (Cambridge, 2005), pp. 4, 16.

which involved animals. It was a reflection of ongoing debates in Germany about responsibility for harms to others. Should car owners or the keepers of animals be held liable for accidents that stemmed from an untried new technology and from unruly beasts? When did holding individuals accountable for accidents that affected others no longer make sense?

These discussions about liability shaped thinking about workers' eligibility for accident insurance. By 1911, the Imperial Insurance Office and the Imperial Ministry of the Interior responded by enacting the expansive Imperial Insurance Ordinance. The policy, which consolidated the various strands of social insurance, was remarkable in that it broke down the earlier distinctions between industrial and agricultural dangers. Instead, all workers using certain kinds of technologies were now subject to special treatment. The law required employers who used vehicles to join a special fund to provide accident insurance for any workers who operated them. This clause applied specifically to individuals such as medical doctors who might use automobiles as part of their work and employed assistants in order to operate and maintain them. It is noteworthy that the clause also applied to workers in other non-commercial activities related to 'luxury, sport or science', such as the maintenance of automobiles, riding animals, motorboats, air balloons and aircraft.[24] In response to the new policy, members of the German Auto-League, the Royal Automobile Club and the Association of German Motor Vehicle Industrialists successfully petitioned government for a new accident fund for these non-commercial groups that would be run separately from the existing funds that applied to transportation industries. Similarly, users of Zeppelins fell within the accident fund that included fine mechanics and electronics industries rather than those specialising in iron and steel, revealing the increasing movement of accident insurance away from traditional industry to different labour practices and kinds of workers.[25]

This extension of accident insurance to users of new technologies demonstrated a shift in thinking about what constituted 'dangerous' work. However, it reified class divisions through the risk classes that comprised – or were excluded from – the accident funds. Germany's many white-collar workers continued to be omitted from the policy, regardless of their exposure to occupational risks. In this way, Boetticher's earlier emphasis on extending social insurance to the 'working classes' proved revealing. Officials consistently

---

[24] Ludwig Lass, *Reichsversicherungsordnung*, vol. II: *Unfallversicherung* (3rd and 4th edns, Berlin, 1914), sect. 537, no. 17; *DDR* 12/1 (1907–9), Nr. 1250: 'Bericht der Kommission von 10. März 1909'.

[25] BArch: R89: 15051: unnumbered: Report on 'Sport-Unfallversicherung: Bildung einer unabhängigen Versicherungsgenossenschaft', n.d. [April 1912]; BArch: R89: 11458: unnumbered: *Luftschiffbau Zeppelin* in Friedrichshain to the Imperial Insurance Office, 3 January 1910; unnumbered: Minutes from Meeting with the Imperial Insurance Office and Representatives of the Fine Mechanics *Berufsgenossenschaft* and the Northwest Iron and Steel *Berufsgenossenschaft*, 16 March 1910.

claimed that the occupational risks encountered by white-collar workers were fundamentally different from those seen by manual labourers. When it came to social insurance in prewar Germany, a 'worker' was not middle class. Nonetheless, the number of lower-middle-class employees (*Angestellten*) had increased significantly since the last years of the nineteenth century in response to demands for office clerks, telephonists and salespeople. By the 1890s, several associations of these salaried workers began a movement for statutory accident insurance and old-age pensions that echoed claims made in the 1880s by those employed in handicrafts. The broader significance of the lower middle classes had increased dramatically in Germany in the early twentieth century, where there were approximately 2 million salaried workers to the 13,700,000 wage-earners in 1907. One third of these salaried employees belonged to an association that represented their interests.[26] The Central Association of German Salespeople, for example, petitioned the *Bundesrat* for accident insurance because the increased use of ladders and stairs in shops had caused many accidents.[27] The German Association of Mining and Factory Employees went as far as creating a special committee on pensions for salaried workers in 1901. Two years later, this group had expanded to 24 organisations with more than 300,000 members across the country. Government responded to these demands for compensation with an investigation of its own. In 1907, the Imperial Office of the Interior compiled information from salaried workers throughout Germany and wrote a report on their inclusion within the existing system of accident insurance. It found that most of these workers were unable to afford private insurance; it seemed that their demands for social insurance were justified.[28]

Despite this finding, the 1911 law on social insurance for white-collar workers did not include compensation for occupational accidents. Instead, it required salaried employees to contribute to insurance funds for old age and disability alone. It is noteworthy that these pension funds were kept entirely separate from those used for industrial and agricultural workers. To be sure, the question whether to include white-collar workers within the existing system of social insurance provoked enormous debate throughout Germany. Associations of heavy industry argued against a separate insurance organisation for white-collar workers. It seemed more equitable to bring all employees into the fold of a single social insurance system, which would help to redistribute risks (and the costs of those risks) more widely. Similar arguments had, of

[26] *Statistisches Jahrbuch für das Deutschen Reich* (Berlin, 1914), pp. 14ff; Jürgen Kocka, 'The First World War and the "Mittelstand": German artisans and white-collar workers', *Journal of Contemporary History* 8/1 (1973), pp. 101–23, at p. 103; Arno J. Mayer, 'The lower middle class as historical problem', *Journal of Modern History* 47/3 (1975), pp. 409–36, at pp. 419–20.

[27] GStAPK: I. HA. Rep. 84a:5303: 23–5: Proposal to the *Bundesrat* from the Committee of the Central Association of German Salespeople, 10 November 1895.

[28] Tanja Anette Glootz, *Geschichte der Angestelltenversicherung des 20. Jahrhunderts* (Berlin, 1999), pp. 16–20.

course, been put forward before. In early discussions about whether to introduce a policy on accidents in the first place, mine owners played a key role in
lobbying for a broad system of social insurance in Germany that would help to
spread the costs of accidents in the most dangerous industries.[29] Others were
unpersuaded by the idea that salaried employees faced the same kinds of risks
that manual labourers faced every day in their jobs. The separate organisation
of old-age and disability pensions for white-collar workers revealed this kind
of reasoning. It seemed that the working life – and, as a consequence, the entire
lifecycle – of a white-collar worker was simply different from that of a manual labourer. Moreover, it seemed that wage labourers and salaried employees
came from two different worlds that should be kept separate. Placing all of
Germany's workers in the same social insurance scheme could encourage them
to think about labour as a common plight, with common political and economic demands. As the head of the National Liberal Party, Gustav Stresemann,
argued, white-collar workers needed to be kept separate within the organisation of social insurance, lest they be tempted by the 'siren calls' of social
democracy.[30]

The case of the salesgirl Else Anarée exemplifies this complex thinking
about occupational risk and its treatment by the state. The young woman, who
was represented in court by her father, worked at the sales counter of a factory in Berlin that specialised in picture frames. Part of Anarée's job required
her to go to the factory floor to collect material or show clients around, and
she suffered injuries to her nose and eye one day when a piece of wood sprang
from a turning machine and hit her in the face. The case reached the Imperial
Insurance Office as the last court of appeal. It rejected Anarée's claim for compensation because she did not work in the 'industrial technical part of the
firm'. In any case, it declared that she was a 'sales employee' and, therefore,
uninsured. Although a variety of salaried employees, and especially shop assistants, made similar demands for compensation, they remained excluded from
the accident insurance system in prewar Germany.[31] Of course, most workers
within Germany had become eligible for the policy by this point, but it was
still unclear whether accident benefit was a social right that *all* workers could
claim. And it was still not entirely obvious who was a 'worker' anyway. It
seemed that members of the middle classes – beyond those few doctors driving
cars or engineers working on Zeppelins – were part of a separate order who
would need to be handled differently.

[29] See Chapter 3.
[30] GStAPK: I. HA. Rep. 84a.201: 7–10: Imperial Office of the Interior to the Collective State
Ministers of Prussia, 28 June 1909; *DDR* 1907, Nr. 226; 1907/9, Nr. 986; Glootz, *Geschichte
der Angestelltenversicherung*, pp. 21–2.
[31] For example, BArch: R89: 15107: 48–51: Ia16245/119a: *Else Anarée* v. *the Glas-
Berufsgenossenschaft*, 14 June 1913; BArch: R89: 15052: 32: Director of the *Verein junger
Kaufleute von Berlin* to the Imperial Insurance Office, 11 November 1911.

As in Germany, in Britain, white-collar workers were also left without recourse to accident benefit, but the two countries otherwise differed substantially in how they determined entitlement. In Britain, only two major revisions to the Workmen's Compensation Act of 1897 took place in the several years preceding the outbreak of the First World War. Officials sought to avoid revising the policy bit by bit, which reflected their long-standing concerns about becoming too involved in its daily management. Instead, government opted to act on questions such as who was a 'worker' and what constituted 'occupational risk' rarely but to great effect. In 1900, the Home Office reconceptualised the principle of occupational risk that underpinned the first Workmen's Compensation Act and, under widespread political pressure, extended the policy to several new groups, including rural labourers. Lobbying by both the TUC and by Conservative MPs representing rural constituencies played a role in the 1900 extension. For example, at its 1897 meeting in Birmingham, the TUC Parliamentary Committee spoke out against the exclusion of many trades from the workmen's compensation policy. It supported a bill to extend the scheme to all types of employment that had been listed in the Factory and Workshop Act of 1891.[32] Two years later, a Conservative bill in parliament made the case for including agricultural workers, even though official statistics seemed to prove that rural labour was not especially prone to occupational risks, and even though individual farmers protested against the prospect of having to pay compensation to their workers. For instance, Thomas Judge, who owned a couple of hundred acres of land in Northamptonshire, complained to the Home Office that he did not see how an employer could be held either financially or morally liable for farmhands out in the fields. He cited the case of a man who came to work 'giddy' before falling to his death from the top of a haystack. As Judge argued, 'formerly, it was considered praiseworthy to find employment for your fellow man. Now, under this fiendish Act, an employer as such is a criminal. Such is now our boasted liberty!'[33] However, his claims about freedom and the relative obligations of both workers and employers no longer seemed as convincing as they might have been several decades earlier. And with the continued lobbying efforts of groups such as the Central Associated Chambers of Agriculture, but, more importantly, in light of concerns about upcoming elections, government decided to expand the workmen's compensation policy considerably by extending it to rural labour.[34]

[32] *Proceedings*, TUC Congress (1897), p. 34; TNA: HO 45/9936/B27239: Home Office memorandum on the Workmen's Compensation (1897) Amendment Bill, written by Sir Edward Troup, 28 June 1898.

[33] 4 *Hansard* HC vol. 80 (21 March 1900), cols. 1406–7; TNA: HO 45/9943/B29142A: unnumbered: Thomas Judge to Matthew White Ridley, 2 April 1900. See also P. W. J. Bartrip, *Workmen's compensation in twentieth-century Britain: law, history and social policy* (Aldershot, 1987), pp. 27–31.

[34] TNA: HO 45/9943/B29142A: Home Office memorandum, n.d.; 4 *Hansard* HC vol. 84 (27 June 1900), col. 122; 4 *Hansard* HL vol. 86 (16 July 1900), col. 37; 122 (13 May 1903), cols. 626,

After this initial step, officials considered whether accident benefit should be an entitlement for all workers, regardless of trade. In contrast to Germany, debates in Britain about the specifics of occupational risk focused less on eligibility. This difference may have reflected the broader political context in Britain at the time. The TUC played a major role in pushing for the general extension of workmen's compensation, which it suggested at its annual meeting in 1900, and a cross-party consensus in parliament began to share this thinking.[35] By 1903, the Home Office decided to investigate further, creating a Departmental Committee that included representatives from insurance companies and the British Medical Association alongside workers' and employers' organisations.[36] The results of the investigation were inconclusive. The minority, led by Charles Edward Troup, an assistant under-secretary of state at the Home Office, argued that the 1900 extension of workmen's compensation to agriculture and gardening meant that the law had now 'abandoned the idea that the act should only apply to dangerous industries'.[37] Troup saw that the fundamental principles behind workmen's compensation had already been redrawn when the 1900 revision was introduced. Accordingly, accident benefit should now be a right to which all workers could lay claim. Echoing government in Germany, however, the majority of the Home Office Departmental Committee decided that a reform to workmen's compensation should focus on rectifying technical issues and clarifying definitions. Its recommendation revealed lingering concerns that only some forms of work actually encountered risks that were grave enough to warrant special protection by the state. The final report suggested extending the policy only to select groups such as sailors and transport workers. The committee's rationale for a limited extension of the law echoed that of the German government: it would be difficult to address the issues of casual labour and the financial viability of smaller employers. Not least, the report claimed that the law should apply only to those occupations of a 'dangerous character associated with a number of accidents'.[38] The concept of occupational risk still sat at the heart of workmen's compensation. The government bill that followed in 1905 roughly heeded the committee's findings and ignored the demands of the most recent TUC congress as well as the views of officials such as Troup

636; TNA: HO 45/9943/B29412A: unnumbered: Central Chamber of Agriculture to Secretary of State for the Home Office, 5 May 1900.

[35] *Proceedings*, TUC Congress (1899); (1900), p. 74; (1901), p. 76; 4 *Hansard* HC vol. 122 (13 May 1903), cols. 620–46.

[36] TNA: PIN 12/3: Home Office memorandum, 18 September 1903; *PP* 1904 (Cd 2208) LXXXVIII.743: 'Home Office Departmental Committee on Workmen's Compensation: Report', p. 749.

[37] *PP* 1904 (Cd 2334) LXXV.487: 'Home Office Departmental Committee on Workmen's Compensation: Minutes of Evidence', p. 494. A similar view: TNA: PIN 12/1: unnumbered: Darcy Ayre to Henry Cunynghame at the Home Office, 13 December 1903.

[38] *PP* 1904 (Cd 2208) LXXXVIII.743: 'Home Office Departmental Committee on Workmen's Compensation: Report', pp. 863–6, 853.

who thought that all workers should be included within a revised workmen's compensation law.[39]

The following year, the new Liberal government proposed another bill that was based on the Home Office Departmental Committee's findings, but it took up Troup's position on a mass extension of the law to the majority of the British workforce. While the bill reflected long-standing thinking from officials like Troup, it also pointed to the shift in the politics of the Liberal Party that had been occurring since at least 1902, which informed the new Prime Minister, Sir Henry Campbell-Bannerman, and his Home Secretary, Herbert Gladstone.[40] Their proposal succeeded in parliament, and the 1906 Workmen's Compensation Act that resulted broadened the remit of the law enormously. It applied to all workers involved in manual labour who earned less than £250 per year,[41] with a few exceptions that targeted the groups about which the Departmental Committee had been most reluctant – casual workers and outworkers – in addition to the police and family members working from home. This swift extension in 1900 and again in 1906 to the majority of the British workforce reveals the fact that British officials, unlike those in Germany, did not need to worry about the logistical details of where and how to include these workers in the system of accident compensation. In Germany, the civil service debated at length how new groups of workers would fit within the complex corporative arrangement of social insurance. In Britain, however, government legislated only on compensation; organising insurance – or choosing to go without it – was left entirely to employers. It was ostensibly a matter for civil society, and not within the remit of the social state.

In Italy, in contrast to Britain, officials were uneasy about including various different kinds of workers within the country's accident scheme, and they made little headway in expanding entitlement before the outbreak of the First World War. Italian employers were required to pay for insurance, and, as in Germany, it was unclear how this would work in practice for the country's many itinerant and seasonal rural workers. Moreover, Italy was still predominantly agricultural, and sharply divided between an industrialising and increasingly wealthy north, exemplified by the booming factories dotted around Lombardy and Piedmont, that contrasted with rural Sardinia and the *Mezzogiorno*, which had become the ongoing focus of the 'southern question'. By 1901, over 63 per cent of the workforce was based on the land. In Germany, just under a third of the population still worked in agriculture, while only 8 per cent of Britons did the same (Appendix, Table 3). In this context, it seemed that requiring employers to pay for compensation could be yet another potential burden for the fragile and still developing national economy.

[39] *Proceedings*, TUC Congress (1905), p. 71.
[40] H. V. Emy, *Liberals, radicals and social politics, 1892–1914* (Cambridge, 1973), pp. 127–41, 147.
[41] Approximately £24,000 p.a. income value in 2014. See www.measuringworth.com/m/calculators/ukcompare/relativevalue.php, accessed 10 January 2016.

These concerns reflected a broader intellectual movement that had taken hold in the country since the middle of the nineteenth century. It seemed that the 'real' Italy had failed to live up to expectations about its potential. The reality was that only 25 per cent of the population was literate when Italy unified, and the south was still characterised by vast landed estates, peasants and corrupt rule by local mafia. Not least, few had the right to vote, and those who did often chose to boycott elections anyway because the Catholic Church had effectively ruled the new Kingdom of Italy illegitimate through various means including the *non expedit* formula and Pope Pius IX's *Syllabus of errors*.[42] Officials had initially viewed accident benefit as the kind of policy that could address some of their disillusionment about the contrast between the Italy of their aspirations and the country they actually governed. It seemed that social insurance could help modernise the peninsula, making it akin to its northern European neighbours, but government also feared that taking the policy too far could be financially ruinous, undermining economic growth and national prosperity. As a consequence, while industrialists, trade unions, cooperatives, insurance bodies and social-reform organisations alike argued for the extension of the law, especially in the case of rural labourers, legislative proposals repeatedly failed in parliament due to the lack of governmental support. When government eventually decided to back a proposal on the extension to agriculture, its efforts failed, along with the collapse of individual administrations. As a result, the dominant sector of the Italian economy remained largely ineligible for accident benefit until 1917.

Officials anticipated the need to extend accident insurance soon after introducing the initial policy, and they focused on groups who encountered obvious dangers at work. By 1903, parliament agreed to the Ministry of Agriculture's bill that required accident insurance for a wide variety of manual trades and almost doubled the remit of compulsory accident insurance, incorporating 1.5 million workers into the system.[43] The proposal, like its failed predecessors, followed the logic of occupational risk, and the Ministry of Agriculture drew on comprehensive accident statistics and the precedents of foreign legislation to argue in favour of extending insurance to specific trades that could be proved dangerous, such as fishing and shipping. It also drew on evidence and arguments from a variety of sources, including socialist parliamentarians, municipal chambers of labour, trade unions and congresses and insurance

---

[42] Richard Bellamy, *Modern Italian social theory: ideology and politics from Pareto to the present* (Cambridge, 1987), ch. 1.

[43] *A. P. Cam.*, Doc., Leg. XXI, Sess. 1 (1900–1), Nr. 298: 'Disegno di legge per modificazioni alla legge 17 marzo 1898, n. 80, sugli infortuni degli operai sul lavoro, presentato alla camera dei deputati nella seduta dell'8 giugno 1901, dal presidente del Consiglio, Ministro (ad interim) di agricoltura, industria e commercio (Zanardelli)'; *A. P. Sen.*, Doc., Leg. XXI, Sess. 2 (1902), Nr. 22; *Gazzetta ufficiale* 151 (29 June 1903); Arnaldo Cherubini and Italo Piva, *Dalla libertà all'obbligo: la previdenza sociale fra Giolitti e Mussolini* (Milan, 1998), p. 22.

companies as well as the National Accident Insurance Fund.[44] A significant aspect of this law was its inclusion of agricultural labourers who worked with machines, and the fact that the majority of the workforce was employed in agriculture made their inclusion particularly salient.[45] Already in 1900, the first national congress of the Federation of Land Workers called for a general extension of accident insurance to agriculture.[46] Employers and workers, especially in northern Italy, responded to concerns about the dangers of agricultural work by creating private insurance funds such as the two mutual insurance schemes for the areas surrounding Lodi and Milan and the noted fund in Vercelli, near Turin. By 1907, Senator Emilio Conti spearheaded a bill for a general extension of accident insurance to agriculture that proved popular with agricultural associations across the north.[47]

Despite the growing lobby to extend insurance to this major sector of Italy's workforce, the progressive Minister of Agriculture, Francesco Cocco-Ortu, rejected the proposal. He cited practical grounds, and especially the potential economic burden that the new law might bring. Cocco-Ortu had headed the Ministry of Agriculture at the time that the first accident insurance law was adopted, and he argued that the policy should continue to focus only on those groups who were most at risk of accidents, also because it was easier to organise and monitor compensation for them. While Conti suggested that the extension would add a further 18 million people to the system of compulsory accident insurance, government calculated that as many as 30 to 40 million new workers would be covered.[48] The bill fell in parliament, and the senate committee investigating the matter charged the Office of Labour to continue studying the issue. The Office of Labour found that 95 per cent of the agricultural assemblies in central and northern regions of Italy favoured obligatory accident insurance, but southern landowners opposed it. The lack of organised labour on southern estates meant that landowners there were not particularly concerned about assuaging workers' demands for compensation in any case. In 1909, Conti's second bill fell, largely due to the continued lack of governmental support. Cocco-Ortu again cited the pragmatic difficulties and economic

---

[44] Alessandro Cabrini, 'La riforma della legge sugli infortuni', *Avanti* 19 (April 1902). On insurance funds: *A. P. Sen.*, Doc., Leg. XXI, Sess. 2 (1902), Nr. 22: 'Disegno di legge per modificazioni alla legge 17 marzo 1898, n. 80, per gli infortuni degli operai sul lavoro, approvato dalla camera dei deputati il 23 aprile 1902, presentato al senato dal ministro di agricoltura, industria e commercio (G. Baccelli), nella tornata del 30 aprile 1902'.

[45] 'Atti della commission consultiva sugli istituti di previdenza e sul lavoro', 3 December 1903, *Annali del credito e della previdenza* 26 (1903), pp. 16–18.

[46] Cherubini and Piva, *Dalla libertà all'obbligo*, p. 51.

[47] 'Disegno di legge presentato al Senato del Regno dal presidente del Consiglio dell'Interno, Luzzatti, di concerto col ministro di MAIC, Raineri, e col Ministro delle Finanze, Facta, nella tornata del 5 dicembre 1910, sull'infortuni del lavoro nell'agricoltura', *Bollettino di notizie sul credito e sulla previdenza* 28/12 (1910), pp. 1163–273, at p. 1165.

[48] Cherubini and Piva, *Dalla libertà all'obbligo*, p. 53.

strains that would be involved in insuring rural workers. It is likely that, following his Prime Minister and long-time ally, Giovanni Giolitti, Cocco-Ortu was also anxious to appeal to southern landowners and stave off public anxieties about the rise of left-wing politics.[49]

While the Office of Labour was undertaking its investigation, numerous workers' organisations petitioned government for a general extension of accident insurance to all industries, or at least those that involved dangerous tasks. The Tuscan Glass Workers' Federation, for example, argued for access to accident benefit because glass workers were 'very exposed to accidents' due to the nature of their work, which involved moulding 'tons' of glass in 'very hot ovens', day and night. Since making glass was intrinsically dangerous, the Federation argued that it was 'unjust' that they were excluded from the law simply because they did not employ machines.[50] Similarly, the National Cooperative League convened a meeting in Milan in 1907 where they called for the 'radical reform' of the accident insurance law so that it would apply to all categories of workers. Their resolution was spurred by two events: the recent convention of industrialists in Rome, which discouraged any amendment to the law out of financial concerns, and the recent vote of the Società Umanitaria in Milan, which called for a general extension of the policy.[51]

Yet, government prioritised the issue of rural labour, and not a general extension of the law, in the next several years. There were three reasons for this narrow focus: the early acknowledgement in parliament that rural workers were unfairly disadvantaged by current legislation; the numerous and repeated lobbying efforts of various agricultural and insurance bodies; and, especially, the Ministry of Agriculture's continued anxieties about the particularities of the primarily rural Italian economy. By 1910, the year following Conti's last attempt with a bill on accident insurance for agricultural workers, the new Prime Minister Luigi Luzzatti presented a legislative proposal together with the Minister of Agriculture. Government support for the policy under Luzzatti stemmed from the new administration's lack of concern for navigating a middle way between socialism and conservatism. The Ministry of Agriculture therefore dropped the earlier policy of non-intervention that was upheld under Giolitti and Cocco-Ortu. Nonetheless, government continued to prioritise economic

[49] Cherubini and Piva, *Dalla libertà all'obbligo*, pp. 58–9, 63; Alexander de Grand, 'Comment on Corner: Giolitti's Italy: *Sonderweg* or well-travelled road?', *Contemporary European History* 11 (2002), pp. 296–300.

[50] CdAs: Leg. XXII, Sess. 1904–9, Proposte di legge: Incarti delle commissioni incaricate dello studio dei disegni di legge e delle proposte d'inizative parlamentare: Bta. 860: President of the Glass Workers of the Federation of the Tuscan *Bufferie* to President of the parliamentary commission for the revision of the accident law (Ferraro di Cambiano), 12 May 1908.

[51] CdAs: Leg. XXII, Sess. 1904–9, Proposte di legge: Incarti delle commissioni incaricate dello studio dei disegni di legge e delle proposte d'inizative parlamentare: Bta. 860: National Cooperative League to Cocco Ortu, Minister of Agriculture and President of the Upper Labour Advisory, 9 April 1908.

arguments – rather than reasons solely linked to occupational risk – when justifying the extension of compensation to agriculture. The proposal conceded
the difficulty of legislating on agricultural workers in Italy, noting that there
were no comparable foreign laws to draw upon because other economies had
not dealt extensively with the problem of share-croppers. It claimed that foreign agriculture had 'assumed more modern and industrialised forms' than that
in Italy. As a result, 'the character of the employer presents itself as distinct'
from that of the worker, which was not the situation in Italy.[52] In this respect,
governmental anxieties about economic backwardness worked against extending accident insurance, which is especially surprising in light of the fact that
worries about remaining the 'least of the great powers' had, in part, spurred
officials to advocate the policy in the first place.[53]

Government saw that the only solution to this conundrum would be creating a novel system of social insurance that addressed the specific context of
Italy's rural economy. And a proposal to this end was put forward in 1913 by a
special commission set up by the prominent Neapolitan economist and current
Prime Minister, Francesco Saverio Nitti. The commission was appointed in the
wake of lobbying efforts by workers' organisations and insurance companies
alike. A few months earlier, members of the General Confederation of Labour
had met with insurance companies in Rome to call for extending the policy
to agriculture and introducing a law on health insurance, too. And in early
1913, the First National Workers' Congress for Insurance against Accidents at
Work convened in Milan, supported by the General Confederation of Labour
and the Federation of Cooperatives. Not only did it argue for the extension of
obligatory accident insurance to agriculture, but it anticipated the movement
towards a 'global' insurance for all social issues.[54] In the face of these broad
proposals, Nitti's commission focused instead on the lingering question about
agricultural workers. It claimed that the inclusion of rural labour had been
carried out in every country as a 'logical evolution' of the law on accident compensation. Moreover, one of the main reasons to extend compulsory insurance
to agriculture was 'justice', not 'opportunity, not … sentimentalism', as workers in industry already benefited from compensation for accidents. Taking note
of recent workers' congresses, the commission claimed that 'a spirit of solidarity united industrial workers with agricultural ones'. It was not only these
lobbying efforts that proved persuasive. The commission argued for the extension of compulsory accident insurance to agricultural workers out of concerns

---

[52] 'Disegno di legge presentato al Senato del Regno', p. 1199.
[53] See Chapter 2 on these discussions. These anxieties also drove administrators to a variety of
other initiatives, not least in foreign policy. See Richard J. B. Bosworth, *Italy, the least of the
Great Powers: Italian foreign policy before the First World War* (Cambridge, 1979).
[54] Giovanni Allevi, 'Le assicurazioni sociali', *Il Secolo*, 17 July 1917; Luigi Bernacchi, 'Il Congresso
nazionale operaio per l'assicurazione contro gli infortuni sul lavoro, Milano, 23–25, II, 1913',
Medicina delle Assicurazioni 4 (1913), p. 104. See also Filippo Virgilii, *L'assicurazione degli
infortuni sul lavoro agricolo* (Turin, 1913), pp. 45–8.

about the changing nature of agricultural work, let alone its significance for
the Italian economy. As Nitti argued, the current legislation was 'out-dated'.
Industrialisation within agriculture had profoundly transformed the nature of
rural work, making it into 'almost a kind of [industry]'.[55] Although the commission saw that rural workers were subject to occupational risks, it sought to
handle those risks differently. It claimed that worker numbers in agriculture
were always fluctuating, making minimum requirements for workers in a given
firm, which served as a basis for the existing accident insurance law, an impossible standard for this sector of the economy. When debating how to proceed,
the group considered numerous foreign models of agricultural accident insurance. However, it decided that policies plucked from other countries could not
adequately address the unique nature of Italian agriculture. The Ministry of
Agriculture noted that there were 700 agricultural zones throughout the peninsula. Foreign legislation would be unable to account for the peculiar nature
of these various regions. The commission put together a law proposal that
took into account these considerations, but it was shelved in 1914 when Nitti's
administration fell.[56]

The limited remit of Italian social legislation became increasingly contentious in the year leading up to Italy's entry into the First World War in 1915,
as more and more workers' organisations began mobilising to demand access
to accident insurance. In May of 1914, for example, 6,000 farmers from Assisi
and Perugia and 8,000 farmers from the Organised Catholic United Congress
of Jesus congregated to demand the right to compensation for rural workers.
A few weeks earlier, the Workers' Mutual Society of Brescia wrote to the new
Prime Minister, Antonio Salandra, to inform him of their recent resolution to
address this 'urgent problem'.[57] It was not, however, only the issue of insurance
for agricultural workers that remained pressing. Other organisations petitioned
government for a general extension of accident insurance to 'all labouring
classes of the land'.[58] No further extension of social insurance succeeded, however, until 1917, when the majority of agricultural workers were made eligible. The Italian government's long-standing reservations about burdening the

[55] *L'assicurazione obbligatoria contro gli infortuni sul lavoro*, special issue of *Annali del credito
e della previdenza* (2nd series) 18 (1916), pp. 169–70, 5, 199; Choate, *Emigrant nation*, pp.
97–100.

[56] *L'assicurazione obbligatoria*, pp. 26–7, 199, 47.

[57] ACS: PCM (1914): Bta. 478: Fasc. 5: n. 295: Telegram from the President of the Federation of
Catholic Agriculture to Prime Minister Antonio Salandra, 24 May 1914; n. 204: Telegram from
President of Federazione Cappanni to the Prime Minister, 4 May 1914; n. 295: Telegram from
President Ferici of the Workers' Mutual Society of Brescia to the Prime Minister, 27 April 1914.
See also n. 132: President of the Agricultural Association of Catania to Prime Minister Salandra,
13 April 1914.

[58] ACS: PCM (1914). Bta. 478. Fasc. 5: unnumbered: President of the Liberal Society of Workers'
Mutual Insurance 'di Sandra' in Regio Castelnuovo Veronese to the Minister of the Interior, 20
July 1914.

economy, along with the lack of parliamentary approval and governmental stability towards the end of this period, meant that Italy diverged sharply from Britain and Germany by 1914 in terms of the scope of its system of compensation. Reluctant about extending accident benefit to rural workers at home, the Italian government found more success during this period in making the policy available to its millions of workers abroad.

CITIZENS AND ALIENS

While officials in Britain, Germany and Italy contemplated eligibility for compensation for various kinds of professions, they also considered whether and how to cover migrant workers as well as indigenous labour based in overseas colonies and protectorates. Officials in each country sought to ensure that citizens abroad were guaranteed accident benefit, and they signed reciprocity treaties to this end. Other considerations, however, also informed these agreements. In Germany, in particular, the guarantee of social provision was seen as an important means to attract labour from neighbouring countries to supply local businesses. Reciprocity treaties made it easier to extend compensation to foreigners employed temporarily in Germany who might later choose to return home to retire. These agreements were also seen as a means to ensure that Germany's economy would not be overburdened by paying too much money in accident benefit. Many German companies operated across borders, for example, those straddling the Rhine. As a consequence, it was unclear whether these firms would be subject to social-security laws in multiple jurisdictions, which could prove expensive, and reciprocity treaties could help to solve this problem. The push for reciprocity raised broader questions about whether all social legislation was equally valuable: were some countries stingier in their provisions for workers? Should government ensure that businesses abided by – and workers were guaranteed – certain standards of care, regardless of their physical location? These concerns about entitlement were complicated when it came to the question of compensation for workers in overseas colonies and protectorates, where other logics often prevailed. Officials in Berlin determined that some – but not all – indigenous workers were eligible for accident insurance. They saw that the social state was limited to a specific territory over which Germany was sovereign. Government in Britain also claimed that the social state was territorially bounded. It extended across the globe to protect citizens abroad who had suffered injuries at work. However, when it came to providing for aliens, including Britain's numerous colonial subjects, the social state stopped abruptly at Albion's borders. By contrast, in Italy, the social state saw no clear geographical boundaries. Officials in Rome sought to establish Italian hegemony over the country's new North African protectorates. They saw that granting foreign workers accident insurance could help to achieve this goal by ensuring both that indigenous workers were satisfied with Italian rule and that Italian workers would be attracted to job opportunities in the developing empire. Policy makers such as Leopoldo Franchetti also saw the empire as an outlet for Italy's unemployed and impoverished workers. Making the North African protectorates appealing could, therefore, help to ease social tensions, and especially the question of southern poverty, at home.[59] In these various ways, guaranteeing accident benefit for workers abroad reflected the purpose – and limits – of the social state in each country.

For the German government, social statehood meant ensuring that workers were protected from risks, but it also meant protecting the national economy and implied territorial limits on state sovereignty. It was with this perspective in view that officials handled questions about eligibility for accident benefit. In the 1890s, when German shipping firms operating on the Belgian, Luxemburg and Dutch borders were notified that they should join the countries' national insurance schemes, officials in Berlin focused on how they could protect these businesses from new costs.[60] These firms and the funds in which they were members demanded that the German government do something to prevent them from paying accident insurance contributions twice – once at home, and again abroad.[61] This problem arose because the German accident insurance laws were based on a territorial logic. Branches of German businesses were required to contribute to the accident insurance scheme as long as they were deemed to be 'dependent radiations' of a company. 'Independent' branches of German firms, however, were not obligated to contribute to the German national scheme. These included business outlets that were operated primarily with local equipment and workers and remained established abroad for more than six months. However, businesses that were constantly in motion, such as transportation industries, railways and the German post, were required to pay insurance contributions in Germany.[62] At around the same time, German

[59] Choate, *Emigrant nation*, pp. 34–9; Stephen C. Bruner, 'Leopoldo Franchetti and Italian settlement in Eritrea', *European History Quarterly* 39 (2009), pp. 71–94.
[60] For example: GStAPK: I. HA Abt. VIII. Fach. 4. No. 1. Vol. 8: 40: Chamber of Commerce at Frankfurt a.M. to the Prussian Minister for Trade and Commerce, 17 March 1894; BArch: R1501: 100486: unnumbered: from the Dutch Steamship Shipping Firm administration in Rotterdam to the *Bundesrath*, 14 November 1891.
[61] For example: BArch: R1501: 100486: 59–60: *Verein zur Wahrung der Rheinschiffahrts-Interessen* to the Secretary of the Interior, 27 August 1901; BArch: R1501: 100484: 45–6: *Südwestdeutsche Eisen-Berufsgenossenschaft* to the Imperial Insurance Office, 20 July 1903; BArch: R1501: 100487: 3: *Westdeutsche Binnenschiffahrts-Berufsgenossenschaft* to the Secretary of the Interior, 29 June 1905. Occasionally, firms with outlets in Italy expressed similar concerns: BArch: R89: 11267: unnumbered: Amme, Giesecke & Koneger to the Imperial Insurance Office, 11 May 1905.
[62] Ernst Wickenhagen, 'Das Territorialitätsprinzip und seine Ausnahmen in der gesetzlichen Unfallversicherung', *Die Berufsgenossenschaft* 2 (February 1954), pp. 66–70, and 3 (March 1954), pp. 106–9; Ernst Wickenhagen, 'Gedanken zum Territorialprinzip in der Sozialversicherung', in Arbeitsgemeinschaft der Knappschaften der Bundesrepublik Deutschland and Bundesverband der Betriebskrankenkassen, ed., *Beiträge zur Sozialversicherung: Festschrift*

firms, including state industries, began calling on government in Berlin to draw up some kind of agreement with other countries that would allow for migrant workers to receive compensation upon returning home. The Saxon State Railway Industry, for example, was especially concerned about its workers based in neighbouring Austria.[63] A few years later, social-reform organisations such as the Society for Social Reform and the German section of the International Association for the Legal Protection of Workers petitioned for reciprocity treaties that would protect the right of migrant workers, including Germans abroad, to compensation.[64] By the early 1900s, officials began negotiating agreements with other countries that allowed foreign firms to go without German social insurance as long as the same was possible for German firms operating in those countries. These accords also made stipulations for paying pensions from the German accident insurance scheme to foreign workers living abroad. The 1900 revision and consolidation of all preceding accident insurance laws had granted the *Bundesrat* the power to make such agreements, which were eventually arranged between Germany and Luxemburg, Belgium, the Netherlands and Italy in the 1905–12 period.[65] Throughout this period, therefore, the German government closely monitored new foreign legislation on accident insurance and workmen's compensation, often with an eye towards possible treaties of this kind.

Government was nonetheless reluctant to sign reciprocity treaties with other countries, because it often seemed that their social provisions were so stingy that they would not be of much benefit to German workers in the first place. As the German Consul in Lima claimed when forwarding information about Peru's new accident insurance policy, 'the law presents a cursory, pale imitation

für den Herrn Präsidenten des Bundesversicherungsamts Kurt Hofmann aus Anlaß seines 60. Geburtstages (Berlin, 1964), pp. 83–97, especially pp. 93–4.

[63] BArch: R1501: 100490: 5–12: Austrian-Hungarian Embassy in Berlin to Secretary Marschall of the Foreign Office, 22 April 1892; 33: Austrian-Hungarian Embassy in Berlin to Secretary Marschall of the Foreign Office, 7 December 1892; 58–9: Secretaries of the Interior, Railways and Justice to the Secretary of Foreign Affairs, 9 October 1896; 127–9: Imperial Insurance Office to the Secretary of the Interior, 5 October 1903. Similarly: BArch: R1501: 100491: 6: Royal Bavarian State Ministry of the Royal House and of External Affairs to the Imperial Ministry of the Interior, 1 July 1908.

[64] BArch: R1501: 100495: 152–4: Petition from the *Gesellschaft für Soziale Reform* to the Chancellor, 31 August 1909.

[65] Negotiations with Austria-Hungary and Switzerland began not long before the outbreak of war, but fell apart amidst the wartime upheaval. A helpful overview: 'Die Stellung der Ausländer in der deutschen Arbeiterversicherung', *Soziale Praxis: Zentralblatt für Sozialpolitik* 8/43 (21 July 1904), pp. 1124–7. Luxemburg: *RGBl* 1905, p. 753; Netherlands: *RGBl* 1907, p. 763; Belgium: *RGBl*, 1913, p. 23; Italy: *RGBl* 1913, p. 171; Ernst Wickenhagen, *Zwischenstaatliches Sozialversicherungsrecht* (Bonn-Bad Godesberg, 1957), p. 41. These agreements foreshadowed the long-standing wave of reciprocity treaties that would follow in the wake of the First World War: Christoph Rass, *Institutionalisierunsprozesse auf einem internationalen Arbeitsmarkt: bilaterale Wanderungsvorträge in Europa zwischen 1919 und 1974* (Paderborn, 2010).

of the European models'.[66] European social states, it seemed, operated on a different level, and the Ministry of the Interior declared that foreign legislation needed to be of 'equal value' to German accident insurance in order for any reciprocity treaties to be negotiated. In particular, compensation amounts abroad had to be comparable to those in Germany, and eligibility had to be drawn on a similar basis. Moreover, officials argued that implementing these treaties had to be practicable.[67] Their main concern was whether foreign legislation required insurance, which would guarantee that workers received benefit. As we saw in Chapter 2, officials in Germany saw that insurance was a moral good because it was guaranteed to provide for the consequences of known risks. Not making provisions for known risks would be unethical. Since the British Workmen's Compensation Acts of 1897 and 1906 mandated only compensation, and not insurance, the German Secretary of the Interior and future Chancellor Theobald von Bethmann Hollweg decided against opening negotiations for a treaty with Britain.[68] Similarly, officials decided against concluding a reciprocity treaty with Russia. Although Russia had adopted an accident insurance law in 1912, it was limited in scope and excluded foreign workers in any case. Germany did, however, make an exception for certain villages on the porous Russian border of Eastern Prussia that supplied numerous workers to German firms.[69]

Officials saw a further moral problem with reciprocity: policies on accident compensation in some countries included explicit clauses on fault. Germany's social state was founded on the assumption that blame for hardships should not be attributed to individuals. Instead, responsibilities for social problems, whether injuries from workplace accidents or old-age poverty, should be shared. However, some laws on accident compensation included fault clauses for workers' actions. For example, the British Workmen's Compensation Acts allowed employers to opt out of compensation if they could prove that workers had acted with 'serious and wilful misconduct' when an accident occurred. The 1906 Workmen's Compensation Act slightly revised this stipulation by granting compensation to permanently and totally disabled workers and the

---

[66] BArch: R1501: 100452: 3: Royal German Legation in Lima, Peru to Chancellor Bethmann Hollweg, 28 February 1911.

[67] For example: BArch: R1501: 100479: 50–2: Report on possible reciprocity treaty with Belgium by governmental adviser Beckmann, n.d. [*c.* March 1904]; BArch: R1501: 100481: 7–10: Report on possible reciprocity treaty with France by governmental adviser Gabel, 15 April 1902.

[68] BArch: R1501: 100482: 6–8: Secretary of the Interior to the Foreign Secretary, 3 August 1908; 10: German Foreign Office to Ambassador Frank Cavendish Lascelles in Berlin, 20 August 1908; 3: Frank C. Lascelles to the German Foreign Secretary, 27 May 1908; 5: British Embassy in Berlin to the German Foreign Secretary, 25 July 1908; 13–14: General Consulate for Germany and Great Britain and Ireland in London to the German Foreign Secretary, 6 November 1909.

[69] BArch: R89: 11274: 18–29: Report of the Imperial Insurance Office, n.d. [May–June 1913]; BArch: R89: 11248: 13: Imperial Insurance Office to the Secretary of the Interior, 20 September 1913.

families of workers who died due to accidents, whether or not 'serious and wilful misconduct' was involved. Yet neither the revised version of this clause, nor the 1898 French law's stipulation about '*faute inexcusable*', which reduced compensation amounts if workers had contributed to an accident, satisfied the German government that either policy was comparable to the entirely no-fault system of German accident insurance.[70]

For officials in Germany, the social state was not only obliged to protect the vulnerable in times of hardship. It was also a manager of the national economy and should ensure that German economic well-being thrived. A major concern voiced by German firms, after their opinion on the matter was solicited by the Imperial Insurance Office, was that they had many foreign workers from countries such as Italy, but there were not many Germans working for Italian firms.[71] Some argued that it might not be just for German industry be burdened with paying accident benefit that would go back to Italians and their families abroad, with no particular gains for German workers. The Imperial Insurance Office agreed with this thinking and made a similar point with regard to Russian workers.[72] While officials agreed with the economic arguments made by German companies, they did not, however, support claims that foreign workers were especially prone to fraud and should be banned from social insurance. For instance, the German mining accident fund pointed out that there had to be a good way to prove that Italians truly had dependants back in Italy. Otherwise, miscellaneous relatives or friends of deceased workers might receive insurance benefit not otherwise owed to them.[73] Moreover, local doctors in Italian towns might feel pressured to exaggerate the severity of injuries so that workers would receive a higher pension. It argued that this was especially likely due to the 'national character of revenge'.[74] Not least, it would be difficult to ascertain in the first place whether the injuries suffered by Italian workers were genuine or had been faked.[75]

---

[70] The only form of workers' fault that the German law conceded was criminal acts. BArch: R150 1: 100482: 10: German Foreign Office to Ambassador Frank Cavendish Lascelles in Berlin, 20 August 1908; BArch: R1501: 100481: 7–10: Report on possible reciprocity treaty with France by governmental adviser Gabel, 15 April 1902.

[71] BArch: R1501: 100478: 94–7: *Südwestdeutsche Eisen-Berufsgenossenschaft* to the Imperial Insurance Office, 21 April 1911. Relatedly: GStAPK: I. HA: Rep. 120BB. Abt. VIII. Fach. 8. No. 1. Vol. 1: 175–6: Petition from the *Verband der deutschen Berufsgenossenschaften* to the *Bundesrat*, 30 December 1913. On '*faute inexcusable*': François Ewald, *L'État providence* (Paris, 1986), p. 305.

[72] BArch: R89: 11274: 18–29: Report of the Imperial Insurance Office, n.d. [May–June 1913].

[73] BArch: R1501: 100478: 59–63: Committee of the *Knappschaftsberufsgenossenschaft* to the Imperial Insurance Office, 11 June 1911.

[74] BArch: R1501: 100478: 70–9: Report from Section I of the *Knappschaftsberufsgenossenschaft*, 11 June 1911. See also: BArch: R1501: 100491: 22–8: *Westdeutsche Binnenschiffahrts-Berufsgenossenschaft* to the Imperial Insurance Office, 21 September 1909.

[75] Constantin Kaufmann, *Handbuch für Unfallmedizin: mit Berücksichtigung der deutschen, österreichischen, schweizerischen und französischen Arbeiter- und der privaten Unfallversicherung: für den akademischen und praktischen Gebrauch* (3rd edn, Stuttgart, 1907), pp. 124ff.

The German government dismissed these concerns, arguing that the economic benefits that could be gained from attracting foreign workers to Germany outweighed any potential costs. It reached this decision by 1901, when the Imperial Office of the Interior received a petition from two migrant labourers along the Russian border area of Upper Silesia.[76] The problem that these workers, like other immigrants, encountered was that they were unable to receive accident benefit if they left Germany. Moreover, if foreign workers died as a consequence of an accident, their families would not receive an accident pension if they lived abroad. In 1911, the Imperial Insurance Office inquired with the accident funds about their reliance on foreign workers, asking whether it was important to attract immigrants with insurance benefits. Many funds declared that a substantial part of their membership consisted of workers from abroad. For example, the Southwest German Iron Employers' Liability Fund paid approximately 10 per cent of its annual compensation payments to Italians and argued that an agreement with Italy would be important for guaranteeing the well-being of these individuals and their families.[77] While several funds made this argument from an economic standpoint, others pointed to humanitarian grounds of caring for their workers.[78] On both economic and moral grounds, it seemed that the social state in Germany was responsible for foreign workers.

However, the social state reached only so far, and, in many cases, it stopped short at German lands. For example, Germany's consulate in St Thomas in the Virgin Islands contacted the Imperial Insurance Office on behalf of the Hamburg-America shipping line to request that compulsory accident insurance should not apply to 'coloured' workers, including Japanese, Chinese, Malaysians, 'blacks' and other labourers on board its ships. By German law, however, ships registered in Germany were obliged to provide social insurance because they were a kind of extension of German territory, regardless of whether they were currently located. The consulate argued that accident benefit would be unnecessary because these workers almost never entered Germany; they instead joined and left crews during a ship's passage. Moreover, it pointed out that some of these workers were exempted from other forms of social insurance in any case. It is noteworthy that the Imperial Insurance Office did not take a stance on the issue, instead ruling that the business could decide for

---

[76] GStAPK: I. HA. Rep. 120BB. Abt. VIII. Fach. 4. No. 1. Vol. 9: unnumbered: Royal Ministry of Foreign Affairs to the Prussian Ministry of the Interior and the Prussian Ministry of Agriculture, Domains and Forests, 9 February 1901.

[77] BArch: R89: unnumbered: *Südwestdeutsche Eisen-Berufsgenossenschaft* to the Imperial Insurance Office, 21 April 1911.

[78] For example: BArch: R1501: 100478: 51: *Südwestdeutsche Eisen-Berufsgenossenschaft* to the Secretary of the Interior, 6 February 1911; 64–7: *Oberschlesischer Berg- und Hüttenmännischer Verein* to the Committee of Section VI of the *Knappschafts-Berugsgenossenschaft*, 12 May 1911.

itself.[79] The government accepted another argument when it came to denying accident insurance to workers in Germany's African colonies and protectorates. The German Colonial Society began lobbying for the extension of social insurance to German protectorates in the early 1900s, as it sought to promote settlement abroad, in particular, in south-west Africa.[80] However, the President of the Imperial Insurance Office, Otto Gaebel, argued that German protectorates were not considered 'domestic' for the purposes of social insurance. No permanent residents there would receive accident benefit. He claimed that these areas were not yet suitable for the general introduction of social insurance; moreover, the special conditions in the protectorates meant that insurance would need to be regulated rather differently once introduced there.[81] The industries that were operated out of Germany's African colonies, such as the East African Railway Society, would be considered 'independent' branches of German firms. The only way to circumvent this ruling would be to change the political standing of individual protectorates so that they were placed in a similar position to Alsace-Lorraine, which Germany held in special status since 1871.[82] The loss of Germany's colonies in 1919 finally resolved the issue of social insurance in German Africa.

For officials in Italy, in contrast to those in Germany, the boundaries of the social state were expansive, extending not only to the country's many emigrant workers abroad but also to its colonial subjects. In 1891, the Minister of Foreign Affairs contacted all Italian embassies and consuls in order to compile statistics on the number of Italians resident outside the peninsula, and some of the information he received suggested that Italian workers were being treated poorly in their host countries. The vice-consul in Vienna, for example, claimed that workers came from Italy unprepared and ignorant about the labour situation in Austria. Although Austrian labour legislation treated Austrian and Italian workers equally, Italians often ended up worse off.[83] One way to tackle this problem was informing Italian workers abroad of their rights in

---

[79] BArch: R89: 15426: 12–14: German consulate at St Thomas to the Imperial Insurance Office, 15 December 1906; 20: Imperial Insurance Office to the German Consulate in St Thomas, 7 May 1907.

[80] BArch: R1501: 101255: 29: Foreign Office to the Secretary of the Interior, 9 September 1904; 'Die Invalidenversicherung und die Schutzgebiete', *Deutsche Kolonialzeitung: Organ der Deutschen Kolonialgesellschaft* 21/39 (29 September 1904).

[81] BArch: R1501: 101255: 33–5: President of the Imperial Insurance Office to the Secretary of the Interior, 14 October 1904. See also Paul Laband, *Handbuch des öffentlichen Rechts der Gegenwart in Monographien*, vol. II: *Das Staatsrecht des Deutschen Reichs* (3rd edn, Tübingen, 1902), sect. 70: IV.2; BArch: R1501: 101120: 22–4: Secretary of the Imperial Colonial Office to the Secretary of the Interior, 30 March 1909.

[82] BArch: R1501: 101255: 86–7: Secretary of the Imperial Colonial Office to the Secretary of the Interior, 29 July 1914; 95: President of the Imperial Insurance Office to the Secretary of the Interior, 12 November 1914.

[83] *Emigrazione e colonie: Rapporti di RR. Agenti diplomatici e consolari publicati dal R. Ministero degli affari esteri* (Rome, 1893), pp. 5–7, 92.

specific countries. As a result, the government drew up brochures on topics such as workplace accidents in France and sent them to the Royal General Commission for Emigration, consular agents in France and regional prefects, who distributed these to mutual aid societies.[84] In situations where Italians were not guaranteed equal treatment under the labour legislation of their host countries, the government sought to agree treaties that would ensure their rights abroad, as was the case with Germany. By 1901, the two countries had reached an agreement. Several years later, in 1913, a formal treaty was signed that enabled Italian workers to receive compensation from German funds even after they returned to Italy. Annuities to this end would be set up at the Italian National Accident Insurance Fund.[85] Italy concluded a similar treaties with France (1904/7), Hungary (1911) and Sweden (1911).[86] The thinking behind these agreements was made apparent in a 1912 royal decree that enabled government to sign international conventions on social insurance, but also to *revoke* social insurance privileges from 'citizens from those states that make less favourable conditions to Italians than those made to nationals'.[87] In Italy, it seemed that the social state would aim to protect its citizens, whatever the cost.

This view meant that officials intervened frequently to resolve the problems that Italian workers encountered in the Americas. Between 1890 and 1910, over 2.5 million Italians emigrated to the United States alone.[88] Due to its federal system of government, labour laws differed from state to state, making the protection of Italian workers throughout the country particularly difficult to guarantee. A treaty on commerce and navigation that the United States and Italy signed in 1871 called for the equal treatment of citizens and property from both countries. However, later American laws and proposed legislation that related to liability and compensation did not uphold these terms. In 1912, the 'Sutherland Bill' on interstate railways sought to exclude compensation to families of foreign workers if they were not resident in the United States. The bill did not succeed in Congress, but a number of state laws undermined the

---

[84] 'Circolare del 27 novembre 1907, n. 29578–13', *Bollettino di notizi sul credito e sulla previ-denza* 25 (1907), pp. 1927–8.

[85] Vicenzo Magaldi, 'Gli operai stranieri nelle leggi concernenti le assicurazioni sociali', *Nuova antologia* (4th series), 203 (16 September 1905), pp. 277–86, at pp. 281–2; Regio Decreto 28 March 1913, n. 376, *Gazzetta ufficiale* 111 (13 May 1913).

[86] France: Regio Decreto 30 June 1907, n. 546, *Gazzetta ufficiale* 182 (1 August 1907); Hungary: Regio Decreto 6 July 1911, n. 713, *Gazzetta ufficiale* 169 (20 July 1911); 'La legge svedese sugli infortuni del lavoro e gli operai italiani', *Gazzetta ufficiale* 52 (3 March 1911), p. 4157; 'Internationaler Arbeiterschutz', *Bulletin des internationalen Arbeitsamtes* 10/6 (June 1911), p. 10.

[87] 'Legge 19 giugno 1913, n. 736, che converte in legge il R. Decreto 6 luglio 1912, n. 1067, recante provvedimenti per le assicurazioni sociali nei riguardi degli italiani emigrati e degli stranieri residenti nel regno', *Gazzetta ufficiale* 155 (4 July 1913).

[88] Riccardo Faini and Alessandra Venturini, 'Italian emigration in the pre-war period', in Timothy J. Hatton and Jeffrey G. Williamson, eds., *Migration and the international labour market* (London, 1994), pp. 72–90.

1871 agreement. For example, New Hampshire, Oregon and New Jersey all passed legislation between 1911 and 1913 that denied non-resident 'aliens', in the nomenclature of Anglo-American immigration law at the time, equal compensation following workplace accidents. Even in California, where the law on accident compensation did not discriminate between foreign and American workers, the Italian consul at San Francisco noted that procuring compensation for dependants of Italian workers had been difficult. He called for Italy to adopt some sort of agreement with the United States along the lines of those that had been drawn up with European governments.[89] Italy concluded a treaty with the US federal government in 1913 in order to rectify this situation. In theory, the treaty should have proved effective. However, the agreement with the federal government went unenforced, as a report by the Italian ambassador argued the following year.[90]

Italian consulates throughout the United States, as elsewhere, therefore, continued to offer legal aid, monitor cases involving workplace accidents and collect related statistics on incidents involving Italian workers abroad. For example, when Giovanni Lattanzio di Ignazio died in a workplace accident at the Watertown Arsenal in Massachusetts shortly before Christmas in 1914, the Emigration Commission at the Foreign Office attempted to secure benefits for his pregnant widow, Assunta, and their children. Upon learning about the death, it was Assunta's father who contacted government from his home in Aquila. As a consequence, she was able to receive weekly workmen's compensation payments through the local Italian consulate in Boston. The Emigration Commission made similar investigations following the death of a railway worker based in Buenos Aires, Fidele Prina di Pio, which was reported by a family that had repatriated from Argentina back to Italy, and following the death of a worker in Saskatoon in Canada.[91]

[89] Ministero degli affari esteri: Archivio storico: Commissariato generale dell'emigrazione (1901–27): Bta. 17: unnumbered: Consul in San Francisco, California to the Royal Commissioner General of Emigration, 7 June 1912. See also 'Cronaca dell'emigrazione', *Rassegna contemporanea* (2nd series) 11/2 (25 January 1913), pp. 335–40.

[90] MdaeAs: Commissariato generale dell'emigrazione (1901–27): Bta. 17: unnumbered: Commissioner General of the Commission on Emigration to the Marquis Cusani, Ambassador in Washington, DC, 16 July 1913; unnumbered: General Commission on Emigration, Ambassador at Washington, DC, Director General of Private Affairs, Consul General of the of the Commission on Emigration, Royal Consul for Foreign Affairs, 'Inefficacia del trattato del 25 febbraio 1913 fra l'Italia e gli Stati Uniti', to the Marquis of San Giuliano, Minister of Foreign Affairs, 22 July 1914.

[91] MdaeAs: Commissariato generale dell'emigrazione (1901–27): Bta. 88: unnumbered: Domenico Mastrodomenico to to the Emigration Commission, 14 Jan 1915; unnumbered: Società umanitaria, Brescia branch, to the Emigration Commission, 20 October 1915. See also: unnumbered: Consul General in Denver, Colorado to the Royal Commissioner of Emigration, 24 September 1914; Royal Consulate of Italy at Montreal to the Emigration Commission, 7 December 1914. On statistical collection: unnumbered: Consul in Montreal, Canada to the Commissioner of Emigration, 18 February 1914. On legal aid: 'Circolare 20 novembre 1909,

The Italian government's interest in promoting equal social rights for workers extended to foreign labourers in its African protectorates, where it was eager to plant roots as the sovereign authority.[92] In 1913, the Ministry of Colonies and the Ministry of Agriculture, Industry and Commerce convened a commission with members of the National Accident Insurance Fund in order to investigate extending insurance to Tripolitania and Cyrenaica. Italy had acquired the Libyan regions in 1911 following a war with the Ottoman Empire, though the new protectorates would not be fully conquered for years to come. Members of the commission claimed that introducing accident insurance for workers in Libya would help to integrate Italy's new 'subjects' and encourage a 'coordinated collaboration' with Italian workers there. Introducing the policy, and especially medical assistance following an accident, would be a 'humanitarian' gesture which could help to address some of the ailments of the local population, such as widespread visual impairments. Commission members also drew on economic arguments, suggesting that requiring employers to provide accident insurance for the 'natives' would make North African workers, including migrants from neighbouring Tunisia, no more desirable than their Italian counterparts. To support the claim, they cited French Tunisia's introduction of accident insurance just a few years before, in 1908. If all workers in Libya were eligible for social insurance, regardless of their citizenship or ethnicity, then Italian workers would not need to fear unfair competition from a less expensive labour supply. Not least, the commission noted all foreign workers within mainland Italy were treated equally, so African workers should be entitled to the same privilege in Libya.[93] Ultimately, however, entitlements differed for 'natives' and Italians in the colony. The official policy documents even contained separate sections for 'Italian workers' and 'indigenous workers', alongside a list of universal provisions that would apply to both.[94]

Ideas about race and religion informed this division within the policy. The commission declared that indigenous workers would be less reliant on accident pensions because they had a different form of 'family solidarity' which meant that multiple earners helped to support a single household. The fact that Tripolitania and Cyrenaica were home to various ethnic groups, each with

n. 7, del ministero di agricoltura, industria e commercio ai Regi Agenti consolari italiani in Francia, intorno all convenzione italo-francese per gl'infortuni del lavoro', *Bollettino di notizie sul credito e sulla previdenza* 28/11 (1909), pp. 971–3.

[92] Choate, *Emigrant nation*, pp. 180–3.

[93] INAIL: 'Relazione della Commissione nominata dal Ministro delle Colonie, di concerto col Ministro di MAIC, coll'incarico di procedere agli studi per l'estensione dell'assicurazione infortuni alla Tripolitania e alla Cierenaica', *Atti della Cassa nazionale di assicurazione per gli infortuni degli operai sul lavoro: verbale delle sedute d'insediamento del nuovo Consiglio Superiore* (n.s.) 5 (1913), pp. 3–21, at pp. 4–5, 7–9.

[94] INAIL: 'Norme relative agli infortuni degli operai sul lavoro nella Tripolitania e nella Cirenaica', *Atti della Cassa nazionale di assicurazione per gli infortuni degli operai sul lavoro: Verbale delle sedute d'insediamento del nuovo Consiglio Superiore* (n.s.) 5 (1913), pp. 69–75.

their own familial traditions, was beside the point. In the case of a worker's death, the commission argued, his dependants would rely on inheritance rules laid out in Islamic law, which addressed the particularity of Libyan family structures. Personal status law, above all, should dictate the treatment of the indigenous population in the colony, and social insurance should not conflict with that order. This decision reflected the nature of Italian rule in the colony: upon declaring its authority over Tripolitania and Cyrenaica, the Italian government had granted both freedom of religion and deference to existing Muslim traditions.[95] In any case, though, the commission argued that workers in Libya would not need much assistance following accidents because members of the 'native' population had 'less sensitivity to pain'! They were likely to go on working even after being injured.[96] And perhaps indigenous workers should feel obliged to continue working in the face of pain because it was likely that they had caused the injurious accident in the first place. Unlike Italian workers, colonial subjects were not blameless: they disregarded safety guidelines and were prone to duplicity. Since North African workers might be more likely to commit fraud than Italians, and since insuring them could be very expensive, the National Fund lobbied for exclusive rights to accident insurance in Italy's African protectorates, which was granted.[97] In line with a more general strategy of distinguishing Italian settlers from the indigenous inhabitants of its North African protectorates,[98] government conceded that foreign workers might merit ostensibly equal but rather different rights than Italians when it came to compensation. In this way, the state would serve as a protector for both groups, but its role was also to distinguish between different kinds of subjects and to ensure that those distinctions held.

In Britain, as in Italy, government saw entitlement to accident benefit as a tool for social inclusion (and concomitant exclusion), but it adopted different strategies to this end. Unlike officials in Germany and Italy, those in Britain were not interested in extending workmen's compensation to the colonies. They rejected the German understanding of 'dependent' branches of domestic businesses and instead decided that the reach of workmen's compensation simply ended beyond British shores.[99] The decision reflected a broader strategy of British imperial rule that could also be found in other legislative domains

---

[95] Anna Baldinetti, *The origins of the Libyan nation: colonial legacy, exile, and the emergence of a new nation state* (London, 2010), pp. 39–40.

[96] INAIL: 'Relazione della Commissione', pp. 9–11.

[97] INAIL: 'Relazione della Commissione', pp. 7–8, 14–15. On its operations in Africa: Cassa nazionale d'assicurazione per gl'infortuni sul lavoro, sede centrale in Roma, *Organizzazione del servizio di assistenza agli infortuni* (Rome, 1922), p. 5.

[98] Aliza Wong, *Race and the nation in Liberal Italy, 1861–1911* (Basingstoke, 2006), pp. 79–112.

[99] TNA: PIN 11/8: unnumbered: Home Office memorandum on the amendment bill with regard to extension to workmen employed abroad otherwise than on a British ship, 16 April 1923. On the British legal understanding of the geographical limits to compensation: Peter Benson Maxwell, *On the interpretation of statutes* (4th edn, London, 1905), p. 212.

such as family law: colonies were subject to their own laws, while 'native' subjects could turn to personal status law. Meanwhile, British common law by no means extended seamlessly throughout the empire.[100] In the case of workplace accidents, the only exception to this rule was the 1906 extension of workmen's compensation to maritime workers, which meant that British ships abroad were covered by the law. Parliament had debated whether workmen's compensation should be extended more generally through the Empire, though the discussion did not go very far. Already in 1893, in the early discussions about enacting a workmen's compensation policy, parliament considered whether to set Indian workers and businesses on equal footing with those in Britain. The rationale behind this suggestion was similar to that behind Italy's policy on social insurance in Libya. By ensuring that Indian workers were entitled to accident benefit, Britain could prevent disadvantaging British workers and firms in the face of cheap Indian labour. This proposal was dropped already with an early draft bill. The parliamentary committee debating the bill decided that it would be premature to extend the new law beyond British soil. Moreover, members of the committee claimed that it would be difficult to implement the law in India, given that the infrastructure for it was not yet in place. Legislation for workmen's compensation only reached the colony in 1923 – after a wave of violent political unrest, the growing threat of Indian nationalism and the rising pressure of the new International Labour Organization, in which India was an early and vocal member.[101] Significantly, government never pushed for an extension to India during this period, maintaining its stance that workmen's compensation should not apply beyond British soil (or ship decks).

Officials sought, however, to create standard practices in accident compensation throughout the Empire where laws on compensation existed, which reflected both their concern to protect Britons who had emigrated to colonial outposts and their interest in encouraging common practices throughout 'Greater Britain'. Numerous dominions had enacted workmen's compensation laws since the early 1900s.[102] And by the 1911 Imperial Conference, participants agreed to New Zealand's proposal that there should be greater uniformity and reciprocity in workmen's compensation law throughout the British Empire. The Home Office responded by drawing up a memorandum that compared the law in Britain with its counterparts in British colonies and

---

[100] See, for example, Rebecca Probert, 'English exports: invoking the common law of marriage across the empire in the nineteenth century', in Julia Moses, ed., *Marriage, law and modernity: global histories* (London, 2017), pp. 168–83.

[101] TNA: RAIL: 1124/136: Minutes from the Standing Committee on Law and Courts of Justice and Legal Procedure on the Employers' Liability Bill (*PP* 1893–4 (C 284) XI.907), at pp. 162, 164.

[102] For example: New Zealand: 1900; South Australia: 1900; Western Australia: 1902; New South Wales: 1905; British Columbia: 1902; Ontario: 1914.

dominions.[103] In the end, the department argued against creating identical legislation throughout 'Greater Britain': it would be impracticable due to the 'wide diversity of the industrial and social conditions and the administrative and legal machinery in the different parts of the Empire'. Nonetheless, officials praised New Zealand's proposal to aim for reciprocity and encouraged the adoption of agreements that would allow for the dependants of British subjects to receive compensation regardless of where they resided. However, it was only in 1927 that Britons were granted the right to transfer compensation payments throughout the Empire.[104] Although the British government was reluctant to embrace identical social legislation throughout 'Greater Britain', it saw that common standards for the collection of accident statistics would be beneficial: unlike legislation or even compensation payments, knowledge could be transferred easily and used as a source of information to guide practices – but not dictate them – throughout the Empire.[105] For officials in Britain, the social state was *not* an imperial state: it was specific to the British Isles.

Although not imperial, Britain's social state did expand beyond British shores when it came to protecting citizens abroad, and it also encompassed foreigners working in Britain. However, officials continued to worry about the question of equivalence: was social legislation elsewhere fundamentally different from that in Britain? Did it operate according to other assumptions? Not least, was it more expensive? For example, the 1904 Home Office Departmental Committee on revising workmen's compensation approved of the treatment of migrant workers under the law because it was 'substantially in accordance with the laws of France and Germany', and it encouraged parliament to 'recognise the principle of reciprocity' for accident insurance and workmen's compensation in these cases. To this end, the committee decided to find ways of securing compensation for British workers abroad, which later resulted in a Foreign Office report on the effects of the European accident laws on Britons.[106] By 1907, the Home Office decided that, at least in the case of France, some sort of reciprocity agreement would be necessary to ensure that Britons received the same rights to accident benefit as their French counterparts.[107] For the

---

[103] TNA: HO/157/6/584: Under-Secretary of the Home Office to the Under-Secretary of the Colonial Office, 2 January 1911.

[104] TNA HO/157/7/567: Home Office to the Colonial Office, 15 March 1913. On the 1927 Act, see Bartrip, *Workmen's compensation*, p. 146.

[105] *PP* 1911 (Cd 5745) LIV.03: 'Minutes of the Proceedings of the Imperial Conference of 1911', pp. 259, 261. Relatedly, see: Jean-Pierre Beaud and Jean-Guy Prévost, 'Statistics as the science of government: the stillborn British Empire Statistical Bureau, 1918–20', *Journal of Imperial and Commonwealth History* 33 (2005), pp. 369–91.

[106] *PP* 1904 (Cd 2208) 743: 'Home Office Departmental Committee on Workmen's Compensation: Report', p. 800; TNA: HO/157/4/935: Under-Secretary of the Home Office to Under-Secretary of State in the Foreign Office, 28 November 1908.

[107] TNA: HO/157/4/19: H. Cunynghame in the Home Office to the Under-Secretary in the Foreign Office, 17 April 1907; Workmen's Compensation (Anglo-French Convention) Act, 9 Edw. 7. ch.16, 3 July 1909.

same reason, government attempted to negotiate an agreement with Austria-Hungary, and it persuaded Sweden to enact a Royal Ordinance that would improve the position of Britons under Swedish accident insurance.[108] Despite these various arrangements, however, to officials in Britain, the social state was something that they governed within British shores, following what they saw as British traditions in law and governance. The social state would not extend to 'Greater Britain', nor would it become all-encompassing at home.

BUILDING SOCIAL STATES

The extension of accident benefit to new groups of workers at home and abroad posed new questions about the reach of the social state. Should the compensation systems in each country be unified, and perhaps run directly by government? And were accidents no longer simply a matter of the workplace, but rather a kind of social risk that should be shared by all? At the turn of the twentieth century, officials in Britain, Germany and Italy debated restructuring their compensation systems. However, the way in which the risk of accidents was shared remained essentially the same in each country. Only Italy adopted a new type of insurance scheme that placed mining companies for the first time in a common fund. Officials in Germany never seriously considered moving away from the corporative system that they had created over the last several years. Civil servants in Whitehall contemplated requiring employers to purchase accident insurance, but ultimately decided against it. By the outbreak of the First World War, therefore, officials in Britain, Germany and Italy decided to maintain – at least for the next several years – the systems of compensation that had been created in the 1880s and 1890s. Behind this intransigence to change lay officials' conviction that their social states had already taken form in particular ways that could not be undone. Transforming the structure of social legislation would seem to erode the values upon which it was based. Rather than enacting grand projects to redesign the accident laws – beyond, of course, redefining entitlement – officials instead focused on communicating with the public about the policies. In doing so, they demonstrated how the state cared for citizens and aliens alike.

---

[108] TNA: HO/157/5/69: Home Office to Under-Secretary of State of the Foreign Office, 17 March 1909; 638–40: Under-Secretary of State of the Home Office to Under-Secretary of State of the Foreign Office, 22 April 1910; TNA: HO/157/6/664–5: Under-Secretary of State of the Home Office to Under-Secretary of State of the Foreign Office, 1 March 1912; TNA: HO/157/8/145: Home Office to Foreign Office, 23 June 1914; TNA: HO/157/4/759–61: Herbert Samuel of the Home Office to the Under-Secretary of State in the Foreign Office, 11 June 1908; TNA HO/157/5/350: Henry Cunynghame in the Home Office to the Under-Secretary of State in the Foreign Office, 24 August 1909. Relatedly, see TNA: FO/115/1655/5–6: Under-Secretary of State of the Home Office to the Under-Secretary of State of the Foreign Office, 21 February 1911; 28: British embassy at Washington, DC to Edward Grey, 24 April 1911; 41: E. Blackwell to the Under-Secretary of State of the Foreign Office, 31 May 1911.

In Germany, questions about entitlement seemed to indicate that accident benefit needed to be granted on a universal basis since all professions encountered some kind of occupational risk. In turn, it seemed that social insurance in general might need to be restructured to reflect changing assumptions about universal rights to social provision and the role of the state in ensuring those rights. Accordingly, a movement to reform the policy began shortly after its introduction in the 1880s. However, the proposals were seen as too radical to be taken further. For example, some argued that both the general community and state taxes should pay for every branch of social insurance – that is, it should become truly universal rather than contributory.[109] Others called for some sort of universal scheme that would unify accident, sickness, disability and old-age pensions rather than running each fund separately. The most far-reaching proposal was perhaps that given at the 1895 meeting of the Congress of German Commercial Associations, which suggested a universal insurance system that would provide a 'minimum of existence' that would effectively replace 'public poor care' under the guidance of community authorities.[110] Officials in Berlin took these suggestions seriously and began collecting information on 'shortages' in social insurance with a view to 'melding' the system as a whole.[111] The plan did not go very far. The employers' liability funds lobbied to maintain their independence, especially in resolving disputes about accident benefit, and the Imperial Secretary of the Interior, Karl Heinrich von Boetticher, along with Tonio Bödiker, the long-standing head of the Imperial Insurance Office, ultimately resolved that 'complaints about the level of the administrative costs [associated with the existing social insurance system] are exaggerated'.[112] The system did not need to be simplified in order to become more efficient, let alone to provide a kind of universal basis of social assistance. As a consequence, the 1900 revision to the accident insurance policy broadened entitlement, but it did not produce any change in how risk was redistributed or managed.

[109] Dr Lange, 'Die positive Weiterentwicklung der deutschen Arbeiterversicherungsgesetzgebung', *Archiv für soziale Gesetzgebung und Statistik* 5 (1892), p. 383.

[110] BArch: R1501: 101110: 247–82: Memorandum from the Imperial Office of the Interior: 'Die Vorschläge zur Vereinfachung der Arbeiterversicherung', 1906.

[111] BArch: R1501: 101098: 55: Imperial Office of the Interior to the Collective Federal States and *Statthalter* for Alsace-Lorraine, 4 October 1895.

[112] For example: BArch: R89: 929: unnumbered: Memorandum from the committee of the *See-Berufsgenossenschaft*: 'Bemerkungen zu den Gesetzentwürfen betreffend die Abänderung der Unfallversicherungsgesetze und die Erweiterung der Unfallversicherung', 15 June 1894; GStAPK: I. HA. Rep. 77. Tit. 923. No. 1. Vol. 1: 469: *Süddeutsche Edel Unedelmetall-Berufsgenossenschaft*, Section IV to the Minister of the Interior in Prussia, 15 May 1900. BArch: R1501: 101098: 7–8: Minister of Agriculture, Domains and Forests to Chancellor Hohenlohe-Schillingsfürst, 8 April 1895; 9–26: Secretary of the Interior to the Prussian Minister of Agriculture, Domains and Forests, 6 May 1895; BArch: R1501: 101098: 98–103: Tonio Bödiker, President of the Imperial Insurance Office, 'Vorschläge zur Vereinfachung der Arbeiterversicherung', 1 November 1895.

Despite continued proposals to unify or simplify social insurance such as those made at the International Workers' Congresses,[113] government maintained its stance against reforms that would transfer authority from the employers' liability funds to the state. Under the long-standing Minister of the Interior, Arthur Graf von Posadowsky-Wehner, it nonetheless considered whether the various branches of social insurance could be 'melded' internally, with their goal as solidarism in the face of risk, or the 'common bearing of danger'. The Ministry of the Interior also considered whether the different policies on old age and disability, sickness and accidents could be connected externally through 'common administration' which would be overseen by an 'administrative community'.[114] However, it was clear that the insurance funds, alongside the Central Association of German Industrialists, would not budge in their resistance to centralisation of any kind. Under the new Minister of the Interior and future Chancellor, Theodor von Bethmann Hollweg, plans to restructure social insurance were finally shelved.[115] Bethmann Hollweg argued that accident insurance should be linked with the other branches of social insurance through a 'common substructure' in order to make the whole system more 'uniform and transparent'. However, due to the different kinds of dangers associated with work, accident insurance should be administered separately through the employers' liability funds and the Imperial Insurance Office.[116] This was the same line of thinking behind the decision to exclude white-collar workers from accident insurance: the policy targeted the working classes and was essentially a matter of industry, even if it was overseen by the state in what Bismarck, and government in his wake, claimed was an act of 'state socialism'. The Imperial Insurance Ordinance of 1911 reflected this thinking. It called for a greater degree of cooperation between the accident and sickness funds, and it created regional insurance offices that managed all branches of social insurance on the state level. Nonetheless, social insurance in Germany remained far

[113] F. von Iagwitz, *Die Vereinheitlichung der Arbeiter-Versicherung und der VII. Internationale Arbeiter-Versicherungs-Kongress* (Berlin, 1906).

[114] BArch: R1501: 101110: 247–82: Memorandum from the Imperial Office of the Interior: 'Die Vorschläge zur Vereinfachung der Arbeiterversicherung', 1906.

[115] GStAPK: I. HA. Rep. 77. Tit. 923. No. 19. Vol. 1: 63: Chancellor/Imperial Office of the Interior to the Minister of the Interior of Prussia, 6 October 1908; BArch: R1501: 101106: 22: Secretary of the Interior to the Committee of the *Glas-Berufsgenossenschaft*, etc., 25 May 1908; BArch: R1501: 101111: 59–61: *Verband der Deutschen Berufsgenossenschaften* to Chancellor von Bülow, 3 November 1906; 196–7: Head of the Standing Committee of the German Agricultural *Berufsgenossenschaften* to the Secretary of the Interior Bethmann Hollweg, 6 November 1907; 250–1: Resolution of the Congress of the *Centralverband deutscher Industrieller*, 28 October 1907.

[116] GStAPK: I. HA. Rep. 77. Tit. 923. No. 19. Vol. 1: 1–6: Chancellor Bethmann Hollweg/ Secretary of the Interior to the Collective State Governments and Alsace-Lorraine, 5 March 1908; 63: Chancellor/Imperial Office of the Interior to the Minister of the Interior of Prussia, 6 October 1908: appendix: 73–5: 'Leitsätze', 6 October 1908.

from unified, and the distribution and basic management of workplace risk remained exactly as it had been for the last two decades.

As in Germany, in Britain, the extension of workmen's compensation to new groups of workers provoked enormous debate about creating a unified system that would apply to all workers and involve a greater role for the state. However, it was unclear what that system would be: would employers, for the first time ever, be required to pay for insurance to cover their workers? If so, what would happen to workers' right to seek more lucrative payouts for injuries under liability law? And would Britain create some sort of social insurance fund, or would it continue to rely on commercial insurance companies to provide an institutional basis for social legislation? These questions arose, in part, because the Workmen's Compensation Acts allowed workers *either* to make a claim under the policy *or* to try their chances for a bigger settlement at court under the Employers' Liability Law of 1880. This choice was unique to Britain. Both the Italian and German accident insurance policies forbade workers to sue employers for compensation. They instead compelled employers to pay for insurance that would cover all accidents – no questions asked (in theory, if not in reality). The idea behind the policies was that accidents were always the result of occupational risk, and it would be immoral not to insure against them, hence state-mandated insurance. In Britain, by contrast, it seemed that workplace accidents could be seen as *both* an outcome of occupational risk, which accorded with the thinking behind the workmen's compensation policy, *and* the consequence of individual negligence or incompetence. The logic behind the policy was paradoxical, which made it difficult to proceed with any kind of reform that required the sharing of risk via insurance. It also meant that the state's role as risk manager was uncertain. Accordingly, the Home Office resolved that the liability law should not be repealed for those eligible for workmen's compensation. For example, when the department asked county-court judges about the overlapping goals of the two laws, it heard that repealing the Employers' Liability Act could be seen as 'a step taken in ... employers' interests and against [workers']'.[117] It was significant that the standard for compensation under liability law differed from that under workmen's compensation. Under liability law, one could sue for pain and suffering, disfigurement and other negative effects of a workplace accident that had no direct bearing on earnings lost and earning potential – as well as, of course, for lost earnings. Liability law understood 'damages' broadly, while workmen's compensation was based on the idea that damages were only related to one's ability to earn money.[118] Officials saw that the two policies could not be consolidated, because they operated according to entirely different principles: while workmen's compensation was based on the idea of occupational risk, liability law

---

[117] TNA: PIN 12/1: unnumbered: Report of Judge Charles Whitehorne, 10 December 1903.
[118] *PP* 1904 (Cd 2334) LXXV.487: 'Home Office Departmental Committee on Workmen's Compensation: Minutes of Evidence', p. 495.

was predicated on the notion of fault.[119] Denying workers the right to make a claim under the liability act would amount to implicating the workplace in all accidents. While employers would have to bear the entire cost of accidents under workmen's compensation, the policy at least ensured that the cost of payouts would be limited.

To officials, this dual system seemed most equitable to workers and employers alike – and least expensive. Nonetheless, the system was not entirely equitable, as ideas about fault also crept into the workmen's compensation policies. As the German government had noted with unease, in Britain, employers could refuse to pay out accident benefit to workers who were harmed as a result of their own 'serious and wilful misconduct'. For example, a number of cases in Britain hinged on workers' involvement in 'horseplay' following a visit to the pub or 'disobedience' by venturing to places at work where they had 'no right to be'.[120] And employers' organisations such as the Federation of Master Cotton Spinners pushed to bring these cases to trial, ensuring that 'serious and wilful misconduct' remained on the agenda.[121] Of course, it was clear to trade unions that this system did not work well in practice, and groups like the Amalgamated Society of Engineers lobbied to make accident insurance both compulsory and available through a national fund as a way to clamp down on these kinds of verdicts.[122] As the secretary of the National Amalgamated Union of Enginemen argued, a national accident insurance policy would be the only way to ensure that injured workers were not let off at the insistence of unscrupulous insurance companies or employers.[123] While factory inspectors sometimes agreed with this view, the Home Office ultimately decided against requiring employers to buy insurance or creating a national fund.[124] And officials even rejected the idea put forward in the House of Commons to let the

---

[119] *PP* 1904 (Cd 2208) LXXXVIII.743: 'Home Office Departmental Committee on Workmen's Compensation: Report ', p. 835.

[120] For example: *Mullen* v. *Stewart & Co., Lim.* (1908) 45 Sc. L. R. 729; [1908] S. C. 991; 16 S. L. T. 172; 1 B. 204 – Ct. of Sess.; *Traynor* v. *Robert Addie & Sons* (1911) 48 Sc. L. R. 820; 4 B. 257 – Ct. of Sess.; *Lanarkshire Steel Co., Lim.* v. *Powell* (1904) 42 Sc. L. R. 231; 6 F. 1039; 12 S. L. T. 656 – Ct. of Sess., both cited in Frank Beverly, ed., *A digest of cases decided under the Workmen's Compensation Acts, 1897–1909 of the House of Lords Court of Appeal in England and Ireland, Division and High Courts in England and Court of Session in Scotland* (1910; 2nd edn, London, 1912), pp. 33 and 36.

[121] Arthur McIvor, *Organised capital: employers' associations and industrial relations in northern England, 1880–1939* (Cambridge, 1996), p. 80.

[122] *PP* 1904 (Cd 2208) LXXXVIII.743: 'Home Office Departmental Committee on Workmen's Compensation: Report'; Memorandum from G. N. Barnes., n.d. [1904].

[123] *PP* 1904 (Cd 2208) LXXXVIII.743: 'Home Office Departmental Committee on Workmen's Compensation: Report', p. 782.

[124] *PP* 1904 (Cd 2208) LXXXVIII.743: 'Home Office Departmental Committee on Workmen's Compensation: Report', pp. 785–6; *PP* 1904 (Cd 2334) LXXV.487: 'Home Office Departmental Committee on Workmen's Compensation: Minutes of Evidence', p. 493; TNA: HO 157/5/70: E. Blackwell of the Home Office to the Under-Secretary of State of the Foreign Office, 19 March 1909. See also Emy, *Liberals, radicals and social politics*, p. 148.

Post Office offer an accident insurance policy for purchase that would resemble the life insurance scheme it already sold to the public. As the overseeing body for workmen's compensation, the Home Office had long insisted on maintaining a limited role in the daily management of the policy, and officials were reluctant to create a national fund or oversee an initiative that would require employers to provide insurance. As a compromise, local post office branches were eventually allowed to provide literature to their customers so they could make an informed choice about whether to insure against workplace accidents. However, the Post Office was not granted a licence to sell its own accident policies as a form of quasi-social insurance that would be analogous to that offered through Italy's National Accident Fund. Instead, it was only allowed to disseminate information about the main providers of *commercial* accident insurance that were already on the market.[125] Only gradually did government begin to shift its attitude towards the role of the state in overseeing workmen's compensation. The 1911 National Insurance policies on health and unemployment proved an influential first step in this direction. And in 1914, the Home Office planned to form a committee that would investigate the possibility of adding accident insurance to some sort of unified system of National Insurance.[126] Although plans for the committee were dropped with the outbreak of war, they were not forgotten.

In Italy, in contrast to Britain, entitlement to accident benefit was narrowly circumscribed, but it was nonetheless clear to officials that the policy should be handled through some sort of universal system that granted the state a central role. Following the thinking outlined in Giolitti's 1901 speech on social law, government came to reject the principles of free choice and economic liberalism that had guided earlier Italian administrations in opting to maintain an open market for accident insurance. As a consequence, soon after the introduction of the accident insurance law in 1898, officials in Rome began pushing to insure all workers under the National Accident Insurance Fund or under one of several specialised funds along the lines of those in Germany. The Ministry of Agriculture and Industry played a key role in setting the new agenda. After a decade of observing the vast dangers associated with the Sicilian sulphur mines, as well as the difficulties of providing insurance to workers there, it seemed that the only way forward was a new system. The mine owners protested against the government's proposal, but the department continued to press for a policy reform along these lines because local corruption involving the Sicilian mines had often resulted in workers not receiving accident

---

[125] *PP* 1907 (Cd 3568) LXVIII.163: 'Report of the Departmental Committee Appointed to Consider whether the Post Office Should Provide Facilities for Insurance under the Workmen's Compensation Acts', p. 172.

[126] TNA: PIN 12/10: unnumbered: Home Office to Sir Robert Morant of the National Health Insurance Commission (England), 11 June 1914; unnumbered: Note from Robert Bannatyne of the Home Office, 28 May 1914.

benefit.[127] Following the same agenda, the Ministry of Agriculture also began negotiating with the National Accident Insurance Fund about the possibility of moving towards some sort of state monopoly. As an initial and symbolic step to this end, its headquarters were relocated from the financial capital of Milan to the government's seat in Rome.[128] The Ministry of Agriculture saw the move as a means towards increased cooperation between the two national insurance funds, which separately handled accident benefit and old-age and disability pensions. However, officials also recognised that a move to the capital might lend legitimacy to the National Accident Insurance Fund, whose membership numbers paled beside those of commercial and mutual insurance providers.[129] With a new law, the status of the National Accident Insurance Fund was altered slightly, from a semi-public body to an 'institution of the state', and operations were placed not far from the main governmental ministries in the capital. Officials presented the relocation as the 'harmonic expression of converging tendencies, under the vigilance of the state, towards the humanitarian ends of the institution'.[130]

It took almost a decade before the move went ahead, which reflected the vast intransigence towards any kind of reform that would shift further authority to the state. For example, critics condemned Senator Luigi Luzzatti's attempt to create a national monopoly on life insurance as a form of 'statali[sation]'. Although that policy was eventually approved in parliament, the National Accident Insurance Fund saw no similar success in creating a monopoly. The only exception was its control of the small market in Italy's North African colonies.[131] And while the Ministry of Agriculture was able to push through

[127] 'Circolare 13 luglio 1903, n. 18, del Ministero di agricoltura, ai signori prefetti del regno, agli istituti assicuratori, ecc., ecc., circa la legge 29 giugno 1903, n. 243, e circa la compilazione del regolamento per l'esecuzione di essa', *Infortuni degli operai su lavoro: Legge (testo unico), regolamento, studi preparatori del regolamento, regolamenti preventivi, regi decreti, circolari, ecc., ecc.*, special issue of *Annali del credito e della previdenza* (1904), pp. 213–42; Direzione generale dell'agricoltura, *Pubblicazioni del Corpo reale delle miniere. Studio sulle condizioni di sicurezza delle miniere e delle cave in Italia* (Rome, 1894), p. 7; CdAs: Leg. XXI, Sess. 2. 1902–4, Proposte di legge: Incarti delle commissioni incaricato dello studio dei disegni di legge e delle proposte d'iniziativa parlamentare: Bta. 756: Minister of Agriculture to the President of the Chamber of Deputies, 14 February 1901.
[128] *Atti del Consiglio superiore del lavoro, 1. Sessione ordinaria dell'anno 1903*, p. 54; *Atti della Cassa nazionale di assicurazione per gli infortuni degli operai sul lavoro* (1904), pp. 36–8.
[129] *Atti del consiglio superiore del lavoro, 1. Sessione ordinaria dell'anno 1903*, p. 53; *Atti della Cassa nazionale di assicurazione per gli infortuni degli operai sul lavoro* (1904), p. 32.
[130] A. P. Sen., Doc., Leg. XXII, Sess. 1 (1912–13), Nr. 731: 'Disegno di legge presentato dal Ministro di agricoltura, industria e commercio, Nitti, nella tornata dell'11 marzo 1912', p. 2; 'Legge fondatori della Cassa nazionale d'assicurazione per gli infortuni degli operai sul lavoro', *Gazzetta ufficiale* 94 (19 April 1912).
[131] ACS: PCM (1911). Bta. 417. Fasc. 16: unnumbered: Petition from the *Fascio assicuratori ed impiegati di assicurazioni della provincia di Parma e circondario di Guastalla*, n.d. [c. 25 May 1911]; unnumbered: Telegram from insurers based in Savoy to the Ministry of the Interior, 18 May 1911; unnumbered: 'Open letter to Giovanni Giolitti' from the Advisory Committee of the Tuscan Association of Insurance, 28 June 1911; ACS: Arch. Nitti. Bta. 9. Fasc. 17. Subfasc.

its requirement for the Sicilian mining funds to join a single, state-mandated insurance fund in 1903, it was unable to build on the precedent by requiring further industries to join comparable funds.[132] Similarly, a decade after the first accident law was enacted, officials made a failed attempt to create a supreme court of appeal for accident insurance that would be operated along the lines of the Imperial Insurance Office in Berlin.[133] Despite these efforts at centralisation, however, government was reluctant to take reforms too far. For example, it rejected the proposal of the League of Italian Cooperatives to unite the National Accident Insurance and National Old-Age and Disability Insurance Funds in order to create a 'real institution of social insurances'. As the Ministry of Agriculture argued, each body was 'governed by different mathematical laws' and, in any case, both were still too new to reorganise.[134] Moreover, in light of the vast opposition against creating any kind of monopoly for the National Accident Insurance Fund, officials shelved further proposals along these lines until after the First World War.

Instead, the Italian government, like those in Britain and Germany, focused on other activities that would highlight the central role of the state as a risk manager – even if, in reality, its authority was rather limited. Officials in each country recognised, to varying degrees, the importance of communicating about the new legislation with the general public and with those involved in implementing the law, including jurists, physicians and actuaries, as well as workers' organisations and employers' organisations. Journals, pamphlets and monographs, social museums and congresses, as well as public competitions provided various means of publicising the court rulings on key issues such as whether a particular kind of incident was an accident in terms of the law or

2: unnumbered: Petition from the *Società di assicurazioni e le federazione fra gli industriali in Monza*, n.d. [*c.* 29 June 1911]; unnumbered: 'Order of the Day' for the Chamber of Commerce in Venice, 3 June 1911.

[132] CdAs: Leg. XXI, Sess. 2 (1902–4), Proposte di legge: Incarti delle commissioni incaricato dello studio dei disegni di legge e delle proposte d'iniziativa parlamentare: Bta. 756: Resolution of the Chamber of Commerce in Milan, 18 April 1902; ACS: PCM (1908). Cat. 10. Fasc. 6: Petition from the *Associazione di mutua assicurazione contro gli infortuni*, n.d. [*c.* December 1908]; unnumbered: Telegram from the *Associazione laniera italiana* and the *Lega industriali Biellese* to the Prime Minister, 27 November 1908; unnumbered: Chamber of Commerce and Arts for the Province of Caltanissetta to the Prime Minister, 11 December 1908; CdAs: Leg. XXI, Sess. 2 (1902–4), Proposte di legge: Incarti delle commissioni incaricato dello studio dei disegni di legge e delle proposte d'iniziativa parlamentare: Bta. 860: unnumbered: Petition from the *Unione delle camere di commercio italiano*, 12 December 1908; Camera di commercio ed arti in Firenze, *Osservazioni e rilievi al progetto parlamentare degli infortuni sul lavoro* (Florence, 1908), pp. 4–8.

[133] *Atti della commissione incaricata degli studi concernenti la giurisdizione e la procedura per le controversie dipendenti dalla legge per gli infortuni sul lavoro*, special issue of *Annali del credito e della previdenza* (1906), pp. 39, 41–2.

[134] ACS: PCM (1903). Bta. 305. Cat.11. Fasc. 1/2: Secretary General of the *Lega delle Cooperative italiane* to Prime Minister Zanardelli, 5 June 1903; *Atti del consiglio superiore del lavoro*, 1. *Sessione ordinaria dell'anno 1903*, pp. 50, 51, 54.

whether a particular kind of individual was eligible to receive compensation. In addition to these public forms of communication, officials in each country were in direct contact with individuals. These outlets provided important means of consolidating interpretations of the new laws, but they also enabled each government to legitimise its actions in administering compensation. For officials in Germany, the possibility of self-legitimation through publicity was especially significant because they were particularly involved in overseeing the day-to-day operation of accident compensation. By contrast, for the British and Italian governments, publishing and attending conferences related to accident compensation was less significant because neither administration was particularly implicated in the interpretation or the supervision of the law. While each government shared several means of communicating about the compensation policies, the tone and frequency differed greatly from country to country. For officials in Berlin, it seemed imperative to justify Germany's comprehensive programme of social insurance to citizens at home and observers abroad. Germany had adopted the system before any other country had embarked on a similar venture and against the wishes of a substantial part of the population, ranging from Social Democrats to left-liberals. As the final court of appeals for accident cases, the German government also saw the need to publicise the outcomes of key court cases. By contrast, in Britain, government did not seek to become substantially involved in the daily operation of workmen's compensation, and not publicising about the policy served this goal. In Italy, the Ministry of Agriculture sought to create a cohesive system by publicising key court cases, but it also hosted several international and domestic congresses as a means to highlight the progressive nature of Italian social politics. Over time, each government became more involved in communicating publicly about its compensation policies, which revealed the increasingly widespread and international interest in issues related to accidents, insurance and industrial hygiene. In Germany, the intensification of publishing efforts also revealed officials' concern to encourage other countries to adopt something analogous to Germany's comprehensive and expensive system of social insurance.

The most direct means of public contact was also the first: circulars to local officials and industries affected by the new laws, which outlined the framework of the legislation. It is noteworthy that only in Italy did these circulars beg for cooperation from their recipients. For example, the Minister of Agriculture, Industry and Commerce instructed Italian consuls posted abroad to assist in overseeing the new law with regard to Italians working in other countries, instructing them to fulfil this 'noble and pious mission with the tender loving zeal that inspires the humanitarian goal of the legislation'. To employers, he instead emphasised the obligatory nature of the accident insurance policy; workers were told that they should abide by their 'duties' to follow the workers' protection measures that were put into effect along with the accident insurance law. It was clear that both workers and employers were responsible for making sure that accident insurance worked.[135] This emphasis on cooperation became a repeated theme in government publications in Italy, where anxieties about fraud were widespread after the law had been enacted. Initially, however, the issue of cooperation spoke to concerns in Rome about applying national legislation throughout the recently unified country. Many perceived Italy to be almost lawless in parts, and especially in the south, for the first several years after unification. Against this backdrop, Italy appeared schizophrenic, divided between its 'real' self and its 'legal' counterpart. While the state held authority on paper, in reality, local elites often seemed to rule the show. In order to manage accident insurance at all, central government found that it had to cultivate the loyalty of powerful local notables, and communicating effectively through official publications was an important tool in this regard.[136]

While official circulars laid out the laws, they did not explain what they meant or how they would work in practice. Much was left to individual interpretation, sparking a wave of confusion about how the laws should be implemented. The German government attempted to redress this issue by publishing a variety of administrative guidebooks targeted at local officials, jurists and physicians. Italian and British officials, by contrast, relied on what Janet Horne has identified as a 'parapolitical sphere' of individuals involved in the administration of the law to publish exegeses based on their own experiences.[137] While government in Berlin saw that the state had to appear as unified, consistent and official, the administrations in Italy and Britain were less concerned about keeping up appearances in this way. Given reluctance in Italy about 'statalisation' and in Britain about even offering a basic insurance policy through the Post Office, suggesting that the state was omnipresent in its handling of workplace accidents would have been taboo. By contrast, officials in Germany were prolific in their endeavours to convey what the social state had achieved for its citizens. The sentiment was repeated to various audiences, sometimes by reiterating the rationale behind social insurance that Bismarck gave when introducing the first proposal for the policy in 1881:

That the state, more than before, embraces its needy members is not merely a duty of humanity and Christianity that should infuse state institutions. It is also a means to

[135] 'Circolare del 27 novembre 1907, n. 28578-13', *Bollettino di notizi sul credito e sulla previdenza* 25 (1907), pp. 1927–8; 'Circolare 5 maggio 1904, n. 1, del MAIC ai prefetti, con la quale si dànn istruzioni per l'esecuzione della legge e del relativo regolamento, no. 5', *Bollettino di notizi sul credito e sulla previdenza* 22 (1904), pp. 803–26, at p. 813.

[136] John Davis, *Conflict and control: law and order in nineteenth-century Italy* (Basingstoke, 1988), part II, especially pp. 262–3, 271–4 and p. 5; Nico Randeraad, *Autorità in cerca di autonomia: I prefetti nell'Italia liberale*, trans. David Scaffei (Rome, 1997), 268–9; Raffaele Romanelli, *Sulle carte interminate: un ceto di impiegati tra privato e pubblico: i segretari comunali in Italia, 1860–1915* (Bologna, 1989), pp. 30–1.

[137] Janet Horne, *A social laboratory for modern France: the Musée social and the rise of the welfare state* (Durham, NC, 2002), p. 5. See also Daniel Béland, 'Ideas and social policy: an institutionalist perspective', *Social Policy and Administration* 39 (2005), pp. 1–18.

preserve the state by cultivating the view, also in the propertyless classes of the population, which at the same time are the most numerous and the least educated, that the
state is not merely necessary, but that it is a benevolent institution.

Within the first few years after the law was enacted, the German government
produced little literature of this kind, instead focusing primarily on circulars and a
single journal. By the late 1890s, however, and largely spurred by its participation
in domestic and international conferences, it began publishing a series of detailed
brochures and monographs about social insurance.

The establishment and effect of German workers' insurance, which the
Imperial Insurance Office wrote for the 1900 Exposition Universelle in Paris, is
typical of these publications and, indeed, cited that 1881 rationale behind social
insurance.[138] The book outlined the three branches of social insurance in 243
pages and four appendices, with general overviews of each followed by discussions of the 'foundations' of each branch of insurance. It explained not only what
was meant by the debated terms 'work-related accident' (*Betriebsunfall*) and the
'inability to earn' (*Ewerbsunfähigkeit*), but it also gave a detailed description of
how the insurance system worked. A final section on the effects of social insurance gave a statistical analysis of the policy's effects. Similar texts on social insurance were published with greater frequency in subsequent years, especially with
major reforms of the law in 1900 and again in 1911–13. The 832-page volume
on the accident insurance law that followed the Imperial Insurance Ordinance of
1911 demonstrated the increasing importance of these kinds of administrative
guides as the law and possible interpretations of it became more complex. It also
reflected officials' compulsion to legitimate governmental activities by laying out
potential secrets for a seemingly 'democratic public sphere'.[139]

The development of a variety of legal analysis in Britain and Italy resulted
in a portrayal of the new laws in each country that was less homogeneous
than that in Germany. Some of these tracts focused on an explanation of legal
verdicts that had served as important precedents for accident cases throughout
the country. Arnaldo Agnelli, a lawyer and representative in the lower chamber
of the Italian parliament, wrote one such exegesis, which was first delivered
as a speech to the Practical School of Social Legislation for workplace inspectors, secretaries of labour associations, arbitrators and others. In addition to
these audiences, the labour office of the Milan-based Humanitarian Society
was the kind of readership this piece targeted. Although Agnelli's paper seemed
an objective and narrow reading of the accident insurance law, he still opined
that judges ought to interpret the law generously due to the variety of uncertainties about it.[140] Other authors were more direct in suggesting particular

---

[138] Ludwig Lass and Friedrich Zahn, *Einrichtung und Wirkung der Deutschen Arbeiterversicheru
ng: Denkschrift für die Weltausstellung zu Paris, 1900* (Berlin, 1900), at p. 125.

[139] For example: Lass, *Unfallversicherung*. Oz Frankel, *States of inquiry: social investigations and
print culture in nineteenth-century Britain and the United States* (Baltimore, 2006), p. 69.

[140] See Arnaldo Agnelli, *Infortuni sul lavoro e assicurazione* (Milan, 1908), especially pp. 32–3.

kinds of juridical interpretations.[141] This variety of sources also emerged in Britain, where barristers and high-level physicians wrote elaborations on workmen's compensation. Several published case books that organised important court rulings into categories that dealt with themes such as 'what is an accident' and 'injury due to "horse-play"', while others wrote detailed analyses of the wording of the Workmen's Compensation Acts of 1897 and 1906.[142] Physicians focused on particular issues such as recognising industrial diseases or neuroses.[143] While these sorts of works were also widespread in Germany, they lacked the authority and uniformity of opinion that was concomitant with official publications.

The Italian government redressed this lack of communication in the form of brochures and monographs by publishing journals that dealt with the new accident insurance law. In Britain, by contrast, officials did not found new periodicals that dealt explicitly with issues of insurance in general or workmen's compensation in particular. Instead, they relied on the *Parliamentary Papers* as a forum to publish the findings of Home Office committees that dealt with matters related to workmen's compensation, such as occupational illnesses and legal questions. They also turned to the Board of Trade's *Labour Gazette*, which was first printed in 1893, to place occasional announcements about court rulings related to accident insurance and about upcoming congresses related to occupational hygiene and accidents. The journal was produced 'for the use of workmen and of all others interested in obtaining prompt and accurate information on all matters specially affecting labour', which included articles on lockouts, wages and related issues.[144] Producing detailed collections on court cases or exegeses of the law was, however, left to specialists involved more directly in its administration, which pointed to government's uneasiness about becoming implicated in the daily running of the policy.

The administration in Rome played a central role in setting up Italy's semi-public National Accident Fund and in overseeing it, and it began publishing two major periodicals about the Fund following its creation in 1883. Each journal served as a voice for the department of insurance and credit within the Ministry of Agriculture. The *Bollettino di notizie sul credito e previdenza*, was, as its name suggests, a bulletin with updates on insurance and banking. It

---

[141] For example: Giovanni de Bury, *Relazione sul contenzioso della cassa nazionale infortuni, sede compartimentale di Napoli, dal gennaio 1900 al dicembre 1904* (Naples, 1905); Francesco Carnelutti, *Infortuni sul lavoro* (Rome, 1913).

[142] Two of the categories examined in G. N. W. Thomas, *Leading cases in workmen's compensation* (London, 1913). A detailed analysis of the law: V. R. Aronson, *The Workmen's Compensation Act, 1906* (London, 1909).

[143] John Collie, *Malingering and feigned sickness, with notes on the Workmen's Compensation Act, 1906 and compensation for injury, including the leading cases thereon* (1913; 2nd edn, London, 1917); J. J. Scanlan, *The mutilated hand and the Workmen's Compensation Act, 1906: having special reference to 'missing' fingers* (London, 1913).

[144] 'The objects of the "Labour Gazette"', *Labour Gazette* 1/1 (May 1893), p. 1.

published statistical tables on premium rates, governmental circulars and brief articles on matters such as hygiene congresses and reports from workplace inspectors. The *Annali del credito e previdenza* complemented the *Bollettino* by publishing the minutes of the Advisory Board on Insurance, which was founded in 1869, as well as the minutes on consultative commissions about more specific issues, such as the compensation for workers suffering from occupational illnesses. This journal also produced numerous special issues with more detailed discussions of topics such as the operation of social insurance abroad. Amongst these special issues was the only official source of information on court rulings for questionable accident claims. Between 1904 and 1915, the Ministry of Agriculture produced seven volumes of this kind, which were organised around specific categories of disputes.[145] Both journals served as founts of information for civil servants and jurists, but they were not directed to a wider audience. Only in 1914, with the publication of the semi-public National Accident Insurance Fund's *Bollettino* was a more popular source of information on the accident insurance law available. With numerous images and longer articles on issues such as the treatment of injured workers, retraining and medical debates about the causes of injuries, this journal appealed to a relatively wide but expert audience involved with the administration of accident insurance.[146]

The German government predominated in publishing official periodicals in this field. The first major publication came in 1886, a year after the establishment of the Imperial Insurance Office. It was the official report of that department (*Amtliche Nachrichten des Reichsversicherungsamts*), and it provided monthly reviews of recent court cases, statistics, reminders of government circulars and announcements of events relevant to social insurance aimed at officials in the regional insurance offices and employers' liability funds. In 1907, the bureau began publishing the more popular *Monatsblätter für Arbeiterversicherung*, which discussed similar themes along with longer articles on issues such as accident prevention. This publication was explicitly aimed at the employers' liability funds, medics, legal advisers, trade unions and individual workers and, therefore, offered at an inexpensive subscription rate of only 1 mark per year.[147] The *Reichsarbeitsblatt* was published by the Imperial Statistical Office from 1903. Targeting a general audience, it dealt with issues relating to labour, including news on labour exchanges and strikes, but it also focused on

---

[145] *Infortuni sul lavoro: Giurisprudenza giudiziaria* (7 vols., Rome, 1905–15).

[146] This underwent several title changes in its first few years: *Rassegna di assicurazioni e previdenza sociale: bollettino mensile della Cassa nazionale d'assicurazione per gli infortuni degli operai sul lavoro* from 1916 to 1917, and *Rassegna sociale: assicurazioni e previdenza, infortuni e igiene del lavoro: rivista mensile della Cassa nazionale di assicurazione per gl'infortuni degli operai sul lavoro* from 1918.

[147] 'Zur Einführung', *Monatsblätter für Arbeiterversicherung* 1/1 (15 January 1907), p. 2.

social insurance. In addition to these journals, several others that had links to government dealt with questions relating to the new accident insurance law. *Die Arbeiter-Versorgung*, first published by the Central Association of Health Insurance Funds in 1884, was the most significant of these. It reported on matters relating to the administration of the accident insurance law, not least the treatment of the injured.

In Italy and Germany, these journals and guides did not, however, provide the most salient forum for communicating about social insurance. Nor did they provide the most explicit examples of governmental self-legitimation in adopting and administering the new laws. Congresses, social museums and the occasional public competition instead fostered widespread communication amongst those involved in the accident insurance systems. Both governments sponsored social museums, following the model first developed in France, which were based in Milan and Berlin and offered visitors explanations of the new social legislation and glimpses of efforts to prevent accidents and rehabilitate the injured and ill. Milan's Industrial Museum, established in 1886, built on a long tradition of municipal institutions of this kind. In 1862, an Italian senator returned from London with the goal of emulating the materials on display at the International Exhibition put on by the Royal Society of Arts, Manufactures and Trade. The result was a boom in museum building across the peninsula.[148] Berlin's Permanent Exhibition on Workers' Welfare was created in 1903 and became one of the most important museums of its kind. It attracted 16,000 visitors in its first year, rising to as many as 35,000 by 1914. It had a long heritage, going back to the German General Exhibition on Hygiene and Emergency Services that had been established two decades earlier, in the wake of a related international exhibition.[149]

This link between the museums and international exhibitions on hygiene and safety was significant, also giving rise to the influential Dresden Hygiene Museum in 1912 following the first International Hygiene Exhibition. The motivation behind the technical and hygiene museums and the international exhibitions was similar: education mixed with commerce. Business owners, workers and officials, in addition to students in technical colleges, came to learn about safety techniques, as well as safety equipment on the market that might be relevant for particular workplaces. At both domestic and international congresses, delegates from each government, along with a host of experts employed at universities, insurance offices, courts and elsewhere, gave papers on accident insurance, alongside safety at work and other issues affecting

---

[148] 'Relazione al ministro d'Agricoltura, Industria e Commercio dei Regii Commissari generali del Regno d'Italia presso l'Esposizione Internazionale del 1862', quoted in Monica Amari, *I musei delle aziende: la cultura della tecnica tra arte e storia* (Milan, 2001), p. 31.

[149] Stefan Poser, *Museum der Gefahren: die Gesellschaftliche Bedeutungen der Sicherheitstechnik: das Beispiel der Hygiene Austellugen und Museen für Arbeiterschutz in Wien, Berlin und Dresden um die Jahrhundertwende* (Münster, 1998), pp. 95–6, 124.

workers' health such as tuberculosis.[150] The German government also hosted
official displays and produced numerous brochures for these meetings, such
as Zahn and Lass' book for the 1900 Exposition Universelle in Paris and the
elaborate display it put on for the 1904 World's Fair in St. Louis, Missouri.
Officials in Germany were especially keen to demonstrate that social insurance
was not only a success, but that the German state was benevolent, yet fair to all
members of society, including employers and workers alike.[151] Visual aids were
used in these exhibits, some of which toured German schools as a means to
educate citizens in the benefits of social insurance.[152] Typical images included
the maternal Germania benevolently presiding over male workers from various regions and industries in Germany, characterised by mountains, forests,
fields and rivers; or an oak tree, which was a common symbol for Germany,
flanked by shields that highlighted the numbers of workers insured and the
contributions to social insurance paid by employers and workers (Figures 8
and 9). This ideal of social integration through state-operated social insurance even informed government's actions with its *own* employees. The Imperial
Insurance Office encouraged officials involved in the accident insurance system
with special medals for their contributions. While the Italian government was
less regular and less dogmatic in conveying similar messages, it employed a
similar means of public affirmation by hosting international competitions for
innovative devices to prevent work-related accidents.[153]

It is noteworthy that the British government, by contrast, never hosted one
of the congresses specifically on workplace hygiene or social insurance, nor
did it offer a system of awards for those involved in the administration of
workmen's compensation.[154] To be sure, though, through the Royal Society
of the Arts, it played a key role in promoting world's fairs in which safety

[150] See, for example, the papers listed in: *Exposition universelle internationale de 1889. Congrès
international des accidents du travail ... Rapports* (Paris, 1889); *Congrès international des accidents du travail. Deuxième session tenue à Berne ... 1891. Rapports et procès-verbaux* (Berne,
1891); *Congrès international des accidents du travail et des assurances sociales. Troisième session tenue à Milan ... 1894 ... Rapports* (Milan, 1894); *Congrès international des accidents
du travail et des assurances sociales. Quatrième session tenue à Bruxelles ... 1897. Rapports*
(Brussels, 1897).

[151] For example: Georg Zacher, *Leitfaden zur Arbeiterversicherung des Deutschen Reichs* (Berlin,
1893). First published for the 1893 Chicago World's Fair, this reached a thirteenth edition
by 1908.

[152] BArch: R1501: 101093: 370: President of the Imperial Insurance Office to the Secretary of the
Interior, 21 July 1900.

[153] 'Risultati delle ispezioni eseguite nel biennio 1904–5 dal personale tecnico dell'associazione
degli industriali d'Italia per prevenire gli infortuni del lavoro, con sede in Milano (relazione
del direttore dell'associazione a s.e. il ministro di MAIC)', *Bollettino di notizie sul credito e
sulla previdenza* 24/8 (1906), pp. 1349–489; 'Decreto ministeriale 1. dicembre 1909 che ban-
disce cinque concorsi a premi per congegni e sistemi di prevedenza degli infortuni del lavoro',
Bollettino di notizie sue credito e sulle previdenza 28/12 (1909), pp. 1099–101.

[154] An exception: TNA: HO 157/7/841–3: Under-Secretary of the Home Office to the Secretary of
the Treasury, 13 October 1913.

Die Arbeiterversicherung
des Deutschen Reichs

1885–1899 Gesammtentschädigungen
= 2,4 Milliarden Mark =
961 Tausend Kilogramm gemünztes Gold,
als Obelisk Grundfläche 7,4 qm, Höhe 14,0 m.
🦅 = Reichszuschuss, U = Unternehmer, A = Arbeiter.

FIGURE 8. Germania watching over a realm of workers ('A'), supporting their employers ('U').
Source: Lass and Zahn, *Einrichtung*.

devices, amongst many other goods, from statues to exotic wares from the empire, were for sale. Nonetheless, Britain's first attempt at creating a social museum was only in 1928, following in the wake of the Safety First Movement that had gained traction following the First World War.[155] In sum, Whitehall's public engagement with workmen's compensation was relatively remote after the law was enacted.[156] In fact, the Home Office, which oversaw the policy, generally refused to participate in even the most direct form of communication about the law: interpersonal letters. When lawyers, employers or injured workers asked for advice about particular cases or questions of interpretation, it declined to comment, suggesting instead that they contact specialists such as physicians, lawyers or judges. For example, in reply to a machine manufacturer from Ludgate, the Home Office declared that it '[could] not undertake to

[155] MRC: MSS 292/146/21/2: unnumbered leaflet: 'Home Office Industrial Museum', n.d. [1929].
[156] Although Britain's increasingly large and well-trained factory inspectorate monitored industrial hygiene and safety on the ground, it did not focus on the workmen's compensation policy.

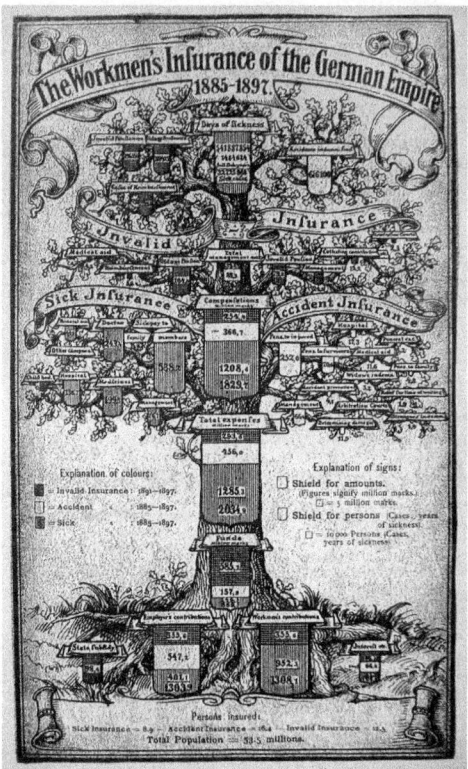

FIGURE 9. 'The workmen's insurance of the German Empire'.
Source: Georg Zacher, *Guide to the workmen's insurance of the German Empire* (Berlin and London, 1900).

advise individual employers as to the application of the workmen's compensation act to their works. The act applies to all "Factories" within the definition in section 93 of the Factory and Workshop Act of 1878. *You* should examine that definition and see whether it applies to your works.'[157] Despite its massive Blue Books related to workmen's compensation, the British government generally sought to keep a safe distance from the policy, instead delegating its interpretation and implementation to those in the 'parapolitical sphere'. As it seldom advocated particular views of the policy, Whitehall also saw little need to legitimate its actions in administering it.

---

[157] Author's italics. TNA: HO 157/1/79: Charles S. Murdoch to Messrs C. W. Burton Griffiths and Co., 6 July 1898. See also: TNA: HO 157/1/274: Charles S. Murdoch to Messrs Peter Lawson and Son, Ltd, 16 July 1898; TNA: HO 157/2/181: Charles S. Murdoch to H. S. Whitfield, Esq., 9 August 1898.

As this chapter has shown, the scope of social legislation had changed substantially in the several years following the introduction of compulsory accident insurance in Germany and Italy and workmen's compensation legislation in Britain. These policies had been introduced with the specific goal of combating social ills associated with occupational risk in heavy industry. Yet officials soon recognised the need to extend the policies to new groups of workers across the social spectrum. It seemed that workplace accidents were no longer a matter linked only to occupational risk; they were part of a broader range of social risks for which individuals began claiming assistance from the state. Yet it was not only the idea of risk underpinning these laws that had changed. The concept of entitlement, too, changed form. The initial compensation laws targeted national citizens within particular industries and from a particular social class. Gradually, however, the particularism of accident compensation eroded with regard to both domestic and foreign workers. The emergence of an idea of social risk not only had an impact on the remit of compensation laws. It also provoked new ways of thinking about the administration and distribution of risk through the state. To be sure, by 1914, officials in each country had decided against fundamentally changing how they managed the risk of workplace accidents. And none of the proposals for a major push to centralisation or for new systems for redistributing costs were taken up. To officials, it often – but not always – seemed that their country had developed a particular kind of social statehood that could not be undone. Moreover, understandings of the inclusiveness and expansiveness of the social state differed in each country, as evidenced in the varying provisions for different groups of workers, whether foreign or domestic, metropolitan or colonial. Nonetheless, over time, it became clear that most individuals could not be held accountable for various kinds of accidents, regardless of whether they worked in heavy industry or were citizens. And it seemed that the state was responsible for ensuring that injured workers and their dependants were provided for, even if government was not involved on a daily basis in adjudicating appeals cases or handing out accident pensions. Through regular publications and presentations at schools, fairs and conferences, officials, sometimes in conjunction with the broader parapolitical sphere upon which they relied, offered guidance on safety, accidents and their consequences. In doing so, they not only addressed questions about accidents, but they signified how the state served as a risk manager, whether symbolised through Germania looking down maternally at farmers in the field or through dry official summaries of court rulings. In the next decade, this process of renegotiating the meaning of risk and, in turn, the role of the state as its manager would see dramatic change, as the First World War and its aftermath marked a decisive turning point for each country as a social state.

6

Risk Societies as 'People's Communities'

Between 1914 and 1924, most of Europe experienced a 'world turned upside down' by a global war and rampant inflation.[1] The First World War led millions of men to the battlefield and women, the elderly and youths into the factory, as was the case in Britain and Germany between 1914 and 1918 and in Italy from 1915. In Germany alone, the rate of female participation in industry jumped 17 per cent during the conflict.[2] And the deaths of spouses on the battlefield left families without breadwinners, wives without husbands and children without fathers. Just over one in ten Italian and British recruits perished during the conflict, while Germany lost approximately 15 per cent of its soldiers.[3] Many of the soldiers who returned home came back as broken men, some without limbs, others with psychological damage that would never be cured. Moreover, the monetary inflation that struck all three countries during the war and continued in the several years following compromised living standards, bringing mass hunger to the home front. It also 'destroyed savings and eroded real incomes', demonstrating 'in countless everyday transactions that the fixed relationships of the prewar world had been destroyed'.[4] The political authorities and economic and social institutions that had once seemed so stable and enduring were transformed within just a few years.[5] The postwar era ushered in new forms of democracy and shooed out the old aristocracy,

---

[1] Martin H. Geyer, *Verkehrte Welt: Revolution, Inflation und Moderne: München, 1914–1924* (Göttingen, 1998).

[2] Roger Chickering, *Imperial Germany and the Great War, 1914–1918* (3rd edn, Cambridge, 2014), pp. 137–8.

[3] Jay Winter, 'Demography', in John Horne, ed., *A companion to World War I* (Chichester, 2012), pp. 248–62, at p. 249.

[4] Richard Bessel, *Germany after the First World War* (Oxford, 1993), p. 31.

[5] The scholarship on this issue is extensive. Meaningful starting points on political and social change and the question of 1914–18 as a possible caesura: Belinda Davis, 'Review: experience, identity, and memory: the legacy of World War I', *Journal of Modern History* 75/1 (2003),

revolutionising the hierarchies of prewar society and relations between both generations and genders.[6] Revolution in Germany in 1918 and 1919 and the derailing of democratic politics in Italy between 1919 and 1922 provoked the collapse of each country's political system. The German Empire came to an end, giving way to the Weimar Republic, and the Kingdom of Italy fell into the hands of Benito Mussolini's Fascist government. Meanwhile, Britain witnessed the 'strange death' of political liberalism at home and the rise of new nationalist movements across the Empire, from Ireland to India, in search of independence. Not least, European dominance across the globe began to wane, as the First World War marked out the United States as the new leader on the world stage.[7]

The Great War had not only resulted in mass death, alongside mass suffrage and a shift in the balance of power in geopolitics. Mobilisation affected every aspect of German, British and Italian society throughout the war, while shortages of food and raw materials, especially in Germany, meant that the state became more than ever a 'guarantor of the social existence of its citizens'.[8] As a consequence, each government, despite sometimes significant losses in its own administration due to military service,[9] monitored and responded to the marked rise in work-related accidents throughout the war and reacted to the depreciation of accident benefit in the wake of inflation. As a 'total war', the conflict touched civilians and soldiers alike. Crucially, as Michael Geyer has noted, the conflict made 'war into work', with the state as the presumed employer of soldiers and, later, veterans, who returned from the battlefront with new claims about social rights. Across class divides, regions and confessions, the war had mobilised both soldiers and workers to serve their nation. In turn, it seemed, the state should serve those who had fought, on the home front

---

pp. 111–31; John Horne, ed., *State, society and mobilization in Europe during the First World War* (Cambridge, 1997), especially introduction, part IV.

[6] Even if they continued to haunt social circles and political projects throughout the interwar era. For example: Dina Gusejnova, *European elites and ideas of empire, 1917–1957* (Cambridge, 2016); Stephan Malinowski, *Vom König zum Führer: der deutscher Adel und Nationalsozialismus* (Frankfurt, 2004).

[7] Adam Tooze, *The deluge: the Great War and the remaking of global order, 1916–1931* (London, 2014).

[8] Even if those states lacked the funds and agencies necessary to deliver on those expectations: Marc Allen Eisner, *From warfare state to welfare state: World War I, compensatory state building and the limits of the modern order* (University Park, PA, 2000). Geyer, *Verkehrte Welt*, pp. 37–47, at p. 41. See also: Jürgen Kocka, *Facing total war: German society, 1914–1918* (Cambridge, MA, 1984); Adrian Gregory, *The last Great War: British society and the First World War* (Cambridge, 2008); Antonio Gibelli, *La Grande Guerra degli Italiani, 1915–1918* (Milan, 1998).

[9] For example, the Imperial Insurance Office lost 59 of its members to military service already by August 1914. By the winter of 1914/15, three of these had died in battle. BArch: R89: 10151: unnumbered: President of the Imperial Insurance Office to the Secretary of the Interior, 5 August 1914; 'Statistik und Volkswirtschaft: der Geschäftsbericht des Reichsversicherungsamts für das Jahr 1914', *Reichs und Staatsanzeiger* 69 (23 March 1915).

and the battlefront, for that nation.[10] In various ways, the war had contributed
to the idea that individuals were members of broader 'people's communities'
who shared an 'ideology of sacrifice' and national belonging long before the
concept of *Volksgemeinschaft* had come to provide the racial organising principle for National Socialism.[11]

How did the dramatic consequences of the war shape expectations about
the role of the state in governing social risks? And how did patriotic feelings of
national community forged during wartime, in turn, shape expectations about
individuals – as workers, employers and citizens – in contributing to their societies? As we saw in the previous chapter, at the turn of the twentieth century,
the view that workplace accidents were solely a problem for dangerous industry slowly gave way to new understandings about risk as a general social problem. It seemed that individuals could encounter all sorts of predictable risks
throughout their life time, from infant mortality to old-age poverty. Not only
workers in heavy industry seemed likely to face occupational risks. Even locksmiths or gardeners could suffer the same, as could both citizens and colonial
subjects employed in distant lands. In various ways, by 1914, Britain, Germany
and Italy had become what Ulrich Beck has called 'risk societies': languages
of risk abounded, as did the acceptance that the state should manage many
of the problems associated with those risks.[12] As this chapter shows, the long
sequence of shocks experienced by European societies during and immediately
following the First World War placed enormous pressure on social provision
and posed new questions about the obligations of workers, employers and
the state.

To be sure, the experiences of war, economic crisis and, in the cases of
Germany and Italy, regime change between 1914 and 1924 were complex
and differed from country to country and region to region. Mobilisation
in Germany was regimented and planned in detail after an initial boom in
voluntary enlistment in the summer of 1914. In Italy and Britain, however,
it was comparatively uneven, affecting certain regions and economic sectors
more than others. Unlike Italy and Germany, Britain initially relied exclusively on voluntary recruits, for example, through the 'Pals battalions' from

---

[10] Michael Geyer, 'Ein Vorbote des Wohlfahrtstaates: die Kriegsopferversorgung in Frankreich,
Deutschland und Grossbritannien nach dem Ersten Weltkrieg', *Geschichte und Gesellschaft* 9/2
(1983), pp. 230–77, at pp. 236–7.

[11] Alexander Watson and Patrick Porter, 'Bereaved and aggrieved: combat motivation and the
ideology of sacrifice in the First World War', *Historical Research* 83 (2010), pp. 146–64;
Jörn Retterath, *Was ist das Volk? Volks- und Gemeinschaftskonzepte der politischen Mitte in
Deutschland, 1917–1924* (Oldenbourg, 2016); Michael Wildt, *Hitler's* Volksgemeinschaft *and
the dynamics of racial exclusion: violence against Jews in provincial Germany*, trans. Bernard
Heise (New York and Oxford, 2012); Martina Steber and Bernhard Gotto, eds., *Visions of community in Nazi Germany: social engineering and private lives* (Oxford, 2014).

[12] Ulrich Beck, *Risk society: towards a new modernity*, trans. Mark Ritter (Thousand Oaks,
CA, 1992).

northern cities like Manchester and Glasgow. Conscription began only two years into the war, in March 1916.[13] While food shortages and rationing were a common feature of war in each country, the naval blockades against Germany meant that hunger became widespread, resulting in low-calorie diets and low morale, epitomised by the miserable 'turnip winter' of 1916/ 17.[14] Not least, Britain ultimately won the conflict, while Germany lost not only a war but also an empire, and Italy joined the action at a later point, only to win a victory that most Italians perceived as 'mutilated'. These differences mattered for understandings about the nature and treatment of workplace accidents, and they helped to transform Britain, Germany and Italy as social states.

Despite these differences, across national borders, the risk of workplace accidents had come to be seen as normal in the context of the First World War. To varying degrees, and with diverse effects, officials in Britain, Germany and Italy shifted away from their former preoccupation with occupational risk and its effects on individual workers. They instead focused on ministering to the needs of what were seen as *national communities* beleaguered by war and economic crisis. Preventing accidents, rather than compensating them, became crucial to ensuring that economic and military mobilisation continued. Moreover, efforts to rehabilitate disabled soldiers and veterans, as workers on the battlefront, held important implications for the treatment of workers on the home front, who were increasingly expected to return to work rather than subsist on pensions. At the same time, officials began to question whether some workers were especially accident-prone or particularly liable to abusing accident benefit; it seemed that certain individuals were a threat to social solidarism. In the wake of the First World War, ideas about mutual obligations in the face of shared risks became more important than ever before, testing the foundations upon which each country's social state was built.

WORK AT WAR

Economic and military mobilisation for war collapsed the divide that delineated the sphere of work as a unique realm within civil society and daily life that was separate from the state. Work became the driving force of the war,

---

[13] Roger Chickering, 'World war and the theory of total war: reflections on the British and German cases, 1914–1915', in Roger Chickering and Stig Förster, eds., *Great War, total war: combat and mobilization on the western front, 1914–1918* (Cambridge, 2000), pp. 35–56; Keith Grieves, 'Lloyd George and the Management of the British War Economy', in Chickering and Förster, eds., *Great War, total war*, pp. 369–88; Paul Corner and Giovanna Procacci, 'The Italian experience of "total" mobilization, 1915–1920', in Horne, ed., *State, society and mobilization*, pp. 223–40.

[14] Tammy M. Proctor, *Civilians in a world at war, 1914–1918* (New York, 2010), pp. 84–97; Belinda J. Davis, *Home fires burning: food, politics and everyday life in World War I Berlin* (Chapel Hill, NC, 2000).

both on the home front and in the field, leading to what some have seen as a new 'organised' form of capitalism in which businesses and government worked together to ensure that mobilisation ran smoothly.[15] In various ways, this phenomenon emerged in Britain, Germany and Italy, as the unskilled and infirm became workers, and workers became soldiers. The mass employment of labour towards the war effort meant that work took on a new significance. It also meant that officials attempted to address new risks at work that were specifically related to the war and not inherent in industry. These included the threat of attacks on factories and other workplaces from foreign enemies, but also the increased rate of accidents caused by inexperienced workers and illnesses caused by manufacturing hazardous materials employed on the front. The elevation of work to a national good meant that these risks were viewed during the war more than ever before as social risks that members of a national community faced together. Gender, age and class divisions often – but not always – seemed to subside as each government responded to the risks of war with novel measures.

On the home front, one of the effects of wartime that most concerned officials was the skyrocketing number of workplace accidents. For example, in Düsseldorf, the number of fatal accidents jumped from 226 in 1913 to 409 in 1917, with 0.41 fatal accidents per thousand workers in the year before the war and 0.69 per thousand towards the end of the war. Similar increases occurred throughout Germany, Britain and Italy.[16] Munitions factories, in particular, were vulnerable to this wartime increase: workers in the industry were four times more likely to suffer an accident, sometimes with catastrophic consequences. For example, the chemical works Brunner, Mond & Co. on the Thames in London witnessed a massive explosion in January 1917, injuring over 400 and killing 69, many of whom were women. The same year, 40 women were killed in a munitions factory in Fürth and 30 in Cologne.[17] And in Italy, explosions in 1917 and 1918 entirely destroyed two munitions factories, and another in the summer of 1917 killed 41 workers and injured a further

---

[15] An issue that has been much debated, most often under the heading of 'corporatism' but also in conjunction with the related concept 'organised capitalism': Heinrich August Winkler, ed., *Organisierter Kapitalismus: Voraussetzungen und Anfänge* (Göttingen, 1974); Gerald D. Feldman, *Army, industry, and labor in Germany, 1914–1918* (Princeton, NJ, 1966); Stephanie Tilly, *Arbeit – Macht – Markt: industrieller Arbeitsmarkt, 1900–1929: Deutschland und Italien im Vergleich* (Berlin, 2006); Alberto Caracciolo, 'La crescita e le trasformazioni della grande industria durante la prima guerra mondiale', in Giorgio Fuà, ed., *Lo sviluppo economico in Italia*, vol. III (Milan, 1969), pp. 195–248; Keith Middlemas, *Politics in industrial society: the experience of the British system since 1911* (London, 1979).

[16] 'Betriebsunfälle nach den Jahresberichten der deutschen Gerwerbeaufsichtsbeamten für das Jahr 1920', *Reichs-Arbeitsblatt* (n.s.) nichtamt. Teil 1/27 (15 November 1921), pp. 1139–45, at pp. 1139–40.

[17] Angela Woollacott, *On her their lives depend: munitions workers in the Great War* (Berkeley, CA, 1994), pp. 84–8; Chickering, *Imperial Germany*, pp. 137–8.

200 at the Sutter and Thevenot factory in Milan.[18] However, the primary reason for the rise in accidents was not explosions. A postwar study on British labour found that the increased speed of production was the major factor for the boom in accidents during the war. As evidence, it cited a fuse factory in Britain that saw a 27 per cent increase in the rate of production by male workers between 1916 and 1917 that resulted in a shocking 48 per cent increase in the frequency of accidents.[19] This finding reflected the growing consensus that workplace accidents could and should be prevented. As Horace Vernon, a chemical physiologist at Oxford who worked for Britain's wartime Health of Munitions Workers Committee, put it: 'nearly all the factors [behind workplace accidents] are ultimately *human* in origin'. However, he claimed 'it is useful to draw a distinction between those which are due directly to the subject who suffers the accident, because of his own carelessness, lack of knowledge, or lack of skill, and those which are caused indirectly by his employer or someone else in authority because of the dangerous conditions under which he is compelled to carry on his work'. Vernon was sympathetic to the inhospitable conditions that might cause carelessness, having spent a summer working in a Birmingham shell factory: 'no industrial worker can concentrate all his mental energies on his task for the whole of his working hours. His attention is bound to wander at times, and the more monotonous the task the more will his attention tend to scatter. In many types of industrial work such daydreams are harmless.' But, as Vernon argued, 'exhaustion and general fatigue' at work could prove fatal.[20] The increase in workplace accidents during the war was seen as both a humanitarian problem, characterised by the hundreds of women lost in explosions at munitions factories, as well as a pragmatic concern: accidents were disruptive, and production needed to match demand to support the war. The state seemed implicated in solving both problems. However, as a result of the tension between humanitarian and productive imperatives, safety regulations would need to be flexible – at times made more lax, at others more stringent.

Before the war, Britain, Germany and Italy had enacted a range of safety legislation as a counterpart to their policies on accident compensation. In fact, safety provisions, including factory inspection, stood at the heart of early policy on workplace accidents. It was only in the period between the 1870s and 1890s that officials in Britain, Germany and Italy began to suggest that

---

[18] ACS: Maem. Ccmi. Bta. 47: unnumbered: 'Sinistri e attentati'; unnumbered: Report of the Comitato regionale mobilitazione industriale, 22 November 1918. Similarly: ACS: Maem. Ccmi. Bta. 230: unnumbered: 'Relazione Comando militare del 10.3.1917' from Genoa. See also Bruna Bianchi, 'Salute e rendimento nell'industria bellica (1915–1918)', in Maria Luisa Betri and Ada Gigli Marchetti, eds., *Salute e classi lavoratrici in Italia dall'Unità al fascismo* (Milan, 1982), pp. 101–28.

[19] H. M. Vernon, 'The human factor and industrial accidents', *International Labour Review* 13 (1926), pp. 673–716, at p. 682.

[20] Author's italics. Vernon, 'The human factor', pp. 674–5, 712; Thomas Bedford, 'Obituary: H. M. Vernon', *Occupational Medicine* 1/1 (1951), pp. 47–8.

workplace accidents could never be prevented entirely and should be eligible for compensation as a remedy. By the early 1900s, reformers in industrial hygiene like Vernon began concentrating on efficiency, fatigue and management practices, and it was this new emphasis that shaped wartime policy on accident prevention. Britain took up the perspective of 'scientific management' that was inspired by the American Frederick Winslow Taylor at the turn of the twentieth century, while Germany and Italy increased regulations on safety.[21] For Britain, the movement towards 'scientific management' was manifested in the efforts of the Health of Munitions Workers Committee founded by the Ministry of Munitions in the summer of 1915. It aimed to investigate industrial fatigue, work hours and other factors influencing the physical health of munitions workers.[22] By 1918, it relied on a workforce of 800 factory inspectors.[23] Members of the committee realised that their findings had implications for British industry in general, and their work led to the creation of the Industrial Fatigue Research Board in 1918.[24] The committee found that long working hours, poor working conditions and the monotony and speed of production had all contributed to fatigue in general and 'primarily and almost wholly problems of fatigue in the nervous system'.[25] The issue was seen to be particularly grave amongst female and young workers. One study conducted in the autumn of 1917 found that, amongst 1,183 women and children in eight munitions factories, 42 per cent demonstrated signs of fatigue and nerve problems.[26] The Board ultimately recommended limiting work to eight hours a day, banning nocturnal labour and work on holidays and instituting regular breaks. It also suggested preventative medical exams.

In a striking rejection of nineteenth-century rhetoric about workplace accidents, the Health of Munitions Workers Committee concluded that there had

---

[21] For example: BArch: R89: 10151: Circular from the President of the Imperial Insurance Office to the Collective Commercial and Agricultural *Berufsgenossenschaften*, 10 August 1914; BArch: R89: 11308: 72: Circular from the Imperial Insurance Office to the Committees of the Agricultural *Berufsgenossenschaften*, 13 February 1917; A. P. Cam., Doc., Leg. XXVI, Sess. 1921–3, Nr. 21, vol. 2: 'Relazione della Commissione parlamentare di inchiesta per le spese di guerra presentata il 6.2.1923', pp. 9–10; ACS: Maem. Ccmi. Bta. 93: unnumbered: Circolare 52944.

[22] *PP* 1914–16 (Cd 8056) XXIV.1–36: 'Home Office Interim Report of an Investigation of Industrial Fatigue by Physiological Methods by A. F. Stanley Kent', pp. 3–4. See also *PP* 1914–16 (Cd 8335) XI.9–96: 'Home Office Interim Report of an Investigation into Industrial Fatigue by Physiological Methods by A. F. Stanley Kent', especially pp. 51–2, 73. On the origins and significance of the Committee: Arthur J. McIvor, 'Employers, the government and industrial fatigue in Britain, 1890–1918', *British Journal of Industrial Medicine* 44 (1987), pp. 724–32.

[23] H. M. Vernon, *The health and efficiency of munitions workers* (Oxford, 1940), p. 2.

[24] Ministry of Munitions, Health of Munitions Workers Committee, *Final report* (London, 1918).

[25] H. M. Vernon, *Industrial fatigue and efficiency* (London, 1921); Health of Munitions Workers Committee, *Final report*, p. 16.

[26] Janet Campbell, *A further inquiry into the health of women munitions workers*, Appendix B in Health of Munitions Workers Committee, *Final report*, pp. 132–45. See also T. H. Agnew, *Relation of general health to length of employment hours and nature of work* (London, 1917), pp. 142–3.

been a substantial shift in thinking about dangers of industrial work in the last 50 years, with a movement away from 'humanitarian reasons' for regulation and towards 'scientific and economic evidence'. It was this emphasis on science, and especially industrial psychology, that characterised the work of the Health of Munitions Workers Committee and related bodies.[27] A hallmark of this thinking was the suggestion to remove 'unsafe people' from work altogether. A 1919 publication by two members of the Industrial Fatigue Research Board claimed that 'the bulk of accidents occur to a limited number of individuals who have a special susceptibility to accidents and suggests that the explanation of the susceptibility is to be found in the personality of the individual'.[28] The idea was significant, as it implied that accidents did not emerge from abstract occupational risks; instead, individuals played a role in bringing them about. In order to address the accident problem, a new style of workplace regulation – one that focused on individuals – would need to be developed. Paradoxically, that focus on individuals meant 'play[ing] for the team' by promoting a healthy workplace for all.[29]

In Germany and Italy this thinking about accident proneness did not influence wartime policy, although similar concerns about special threats to women and children workers were shared. Karl Marbe had developed a concept of 'accident proneness' using statistics from social insurance cases, but his work did not filter into governmental investigations of workplace accidents or policy decisions during the war.[30] Although several German researchers like Marbe investigated workplace management in the years preceding and during the war, most remained distant from politics and business and predominantly focused on workers' psychology rather than industrial efficiency.[31] Similarly, in Italy, new ideas about scientific management – with its implications for managing accident-prone workers – did not become significant until after the war and, even then, employers remained reluctant to implement them because they seemed ill-suited to the particular nature of the Italian economy.[32] Nonetheless,

---

[27] Health of Munitions Workers Committee, *Final report*, p. 16; Steven Kreis, 'Early experiments in British scientific management: the Health of Munitions Workers Committee, 1915–20', *Journal of Management History* 1 (1995), pp. 65–78.

[28] Quoted in John C. Burnham, 'Accident proneness (*Unfallneigung*): a classic case of simultaneous discovery/construction in psychology', *Science in Context* 21/1 (2008), pp. 99–118, at p. 107. On the origins and development of this idea: John C. Burnham, *Accident prone: a history of technology, psychology and misfits of the machine age* (Chicago, 2009).

[29] Vicky Long, *The rise and fall of the healthy factory: the politics of industrial health in Britain, 1914–60* (Basingstoke, 2010), p. 209.

[30] On Marbe, see Burnham, 'Accident proneness'.

[31] Joy Campbell, *Joy in work, German work: the national debate, 1800–1945* (Princeton, NJ, 1989), pp. 73–106, 131–57.

[32] And even then, it seems never to have held the same authority that it would have in Germany and Britain: Tobias Abse, 'Italian workers and Italian fascism', in Richard Bessel, ed., *Fascist Italy and Nazi Germany: comparisons and contrasts* (Cambridge, 1996), pp. 40–60; Victoria de Grazia, *The culture of consent: mass organization of leisure in Fascist Italy* (Cambridge, 1981), pp. 64–5.

both the Italian and German governments attempted to address the substantial new issues with workplace safety that emerged during the war, especially as they related to what were seen as vulnerable populations. For example, German studies cited gynaecological difficulties, including pelvic problems, malfunctioning ovaries and miscarriages, as a consequence of excessive work. A gynaecologist working in three munitions factories based in Spandau, just north-west of Berlin, found that 'war production ... will be paid for by society with a complete exhaustion of the female labour force'.[33] The Imperial Insurance Office responded by reminding the employers' liability funds, which remained in charge of accident prevention during the conflict, to enforce strict standards of workplace safety and, in particular, to ensure that female clothing and hair-styles should be kept out of the workplace, as both were liable to cause accidents. The department suggested that female workers should instead wear men's work clothes and protective caps.[34]

The Italian government was ambivalent about intervening in industry with safety regulations but recognised the need to make special provisions when it came to young workers and women. A decree in 1916 dramatically changed the prewar regulations governing the labour of these two groups, allowing both to work in dangerous industries. The following year, the Ministry of War sent out a circular on improving the supervision of women and children in the munitions industry. The Ministry also called for the training of women and children for factory work.[35] The Italian government recognised, however, that its efforts in protecting these workers would be limited due to the haphazard implementation of safety regulations in Italy at the time. The chief labour inspector decried the lack of extra hygiene and safety measures in war-related industries and argued that doctors in Italy were not properly trained in social medicine, while others did not perceive the 'moral, social and economic importance' of hygiene regulations at work. He was particularly concerned that,

---

[33] Ernst Brezina, *Internationale Übersicht über Gewerbekrankheiten nach den Berichten der Gewerbeinspektionen der Kulturländer über die Jahre 1914–1918* (Berlin, 1921), pp. 14, 16, 23.

[34] BArch: R89: 11308: 2: Circular from the Imperial Insurance Office to the Committees of the *Berufsgenossenschaften*, 20 December 1916. See also: 'Unfallversicherung: Vaterländischer Hilfsdienst, Beschäftigung von Kriegsbeschädigten und Unfallschutz', *Montatsblätter für Arbeiterversicherung* 11/1 (15 January 1917), pp. 12–13.

[35] 'Il lavoro delle donne e dei fanciulli', *Rassegna di assicurazioni e previdenza sociale* 3/9 (September 1916), pp. 1454ff.; 'Il lavoro delle donne e dei fanciulli', *Rassegna di assicurazioni e previdenza sociale* 3/10 (October 1916), pp. 1721–31; 'Circolare n. 409819, 30 apr. 1917, del Ministero della guerra – sottosegretariato per le armi e munizioni (Comitato centrale per la mobilitazione industriale – ufficio segreteria) – sulla tutela delle maestranze femminili e minorili, diretta a tutti I comitati regionali di mobilitazione industriale e, per conoscenza, a tutte le commissioni di collaudo d'artiglieria', *Rassegna di assicurazioni e previdenza sociale* 4/9 (September 1917), pp. 1658–61.

without any inspections, it was unlikely that factories would adopt the most basic preventive measures.[36]

The Italian government, like those in Germany and Britain, began to argue that many of the accidents that happened during the war could not be prevented through safety measures alone or even predicted as arising from known dangers. They saw that many wartime accidents stemmed from causes extrinsic to the process of work. These were the accidents related directly to war. In a testament to the wartime collapse in the divide between work and other activities, all three countries allowed for the compensation of workplace accidents that had resulted from 'danger[s] of war'.[37] The term gained prominence during the conflict both as a description for the likelihood of war erupting (including its possible 'eugenic' or 'civilising' consequences!), but also as an international actuarial category used for war risks insurance that was especially administered by national governments.[38] However, governments compensated war risks in slightly different ways. The Imperial Insurance Office in Germany, which also served as the last court of appeal for accident claims, dealt with a variety of cases involving war risks and set a precedent in 1916 that would require employers to pay compensation for all industrial accidents caused by the war. The Italian government, which did not serve as a court of appeal for accident cases, enacted a special wartime decree to achieve the same goal. By contrast, officials in Britain came to the decision that workplace accidents caused by the war should receive compensation, but, significantly, they concluded that compensation should be granted on a case-by-case basis, with the burden of proof on the injured worker. In this respect, the British government both preserved traces of the common-law origin of the workmen's compensation policy and avoided becoming involved in compensation decisions.

In all three countries, the problem of war risks was complicated by the fact that it extended to several different kinds of cases. A typical incident involved air strikes on munitions factories, which was a concern for government, especially

---

[36] Quoted in Bianchi, 'Salute e rendimento', p. 114; Luigi Carozzi, 'Diciotto mesi di vigilanza igienico-sanitaria sugli stabilimenti ausiliari', *Bollettino dell'Ispettorato del lavoro* 9/9–12 (September–December 1918), p. 302.

[37] The formulation 'dangers of war' is explicitly articulated here: 'Unfallversicherung: Recht und Rechtsübung auf dem Gebiete der Unfallversicherung mit Bezug auf den Krieg', *Monatsblätter für Arbeiterversicherung* 10/8–9 (15 September 1916), pp. 101–32, at p. 105. In Italy, the formulation 'risks of war' was used instead. For example: 'Decreto luogotenenziale 31 ottobre 1915, n. 1577, riguardante i soprapremi pei rischi di guerra nelle assicurazioni degli opreai contro gli infortuni sul lavoro', *Gazzetta ufficiale* 275 (10 November 1915). In Britain, the Home Office cited extra liability for employers in certain industries that were subject to 'special risks' associated with the war. For example: TNA: HO 157/9/483: Under-Secretary of State in the Home Office to London Line Mills, Ltd., 16 July 1917.

[38] For example: Friedrich von Bernhardi, *Germany and the next war*, trans. Allen H. Powles (New York, 1914), p. 18; Alfred Rosenblatt, 'The civilizing influences of war', *Current History* 5/1 (1916), pp. 103–5; Thomas B. Love, 'The social significance of war risks insurance', *Annals of the American Academy of Social and Political Science* 79/1 (1918), pp. 46–51.

in Britain and Germany. The case of the builder Adam Schuster in Germany reveals the contested nature of this work-related risk during the war. Schuster was killed by a French air strike just outside his place of employment, which had been made into a munitions factory during the war. The accident fund in which he was a member argued that it was not obligated to compensate his family, as his death was the consequence of a risk of war, and not a work-related risk. The Imperial Insurance Office ruled in favour of Schuster's dependants, arguing that his death was a work-related accident because he would not have been subjected to the danger of an air strike in that instance had he not been based at a munitions factory.[39] Yet, air strikes were one of several problems that the war presented workers on the home front. Therefore, an agricultural accident fund in Germany would also be required to pay accident compensation to a farmer if he were injured while defending cattle from foreign troops.[40] The Home Office and legal experts in Britain came to similar conclusions in a variety of cases that involved workers killed or injured in air raids. In Britain, however, a worker's right to compensation for this 'special risk' associated with the war, as the Home Office saw it, was more difficult to claim than it was in Germany. Workers were required to show that, 'by reason of their employment, they were exposed to a special risk not shared by the public at large'.[41] Thus, judges and the central government alike dealt with questions of these special risks on a case-by-case basis, instead of applying a general edict on compensation for war-related injury 'in the course of work', which was the basis of accident compensation in British law. By this token, the Home Office suggested that workers in munitions factories should receive accident compensation in air raids due to the 'special liability of munitions workers to attack'.[42]

The British government's treatment of these accidents contrasted with the approaches in Germany and Italy. The German government, through the Imperial Insurance Office, approved compensation to all workers operating within 'danger areas'. The appeals senate of the Imperial Insurance Office came to this decision because it upheld the concept of *Betriebsunfall*, that is, an accident related to one's place of work, that had governed the concept of work-related risk before the outbreak of war.[43] The Italian government required

---

[39] BArch: R89: 11158: 291–3: Summary of the decision of the fifth appeal senate of the Imperial Insurance Office for the case Ia218/16: 1 April 1916; 'Unfallversicherung: Recht und Rechtsübung', p. 105.

[40] 'Unfallversicherung: Recht und Rechtsübung', p. 106.

[41] TNA: HO 157/9/483: Under-Secretary of State in the Home Office to London Line Mills, Ltd., 16 July 1917.

[42] TNA: HO 157/8/757: Under-Secretary of State in the Home Office to the Secretary of the Ministry of Munitions of War, 8 October 1915. See also: TNA: HO 157/9/34: Under-Secretary of State of the Home Office to the Ministry of Munitions, 31 July 1916.

[43] For example: BArch: R89: 11158: 302: *Verband Südwestdeutscher Industrieller* to the Imperial Insurance Office, 31 March 1916; 357–8: *Berufsgenossenschaft der Feinmechanik und Elektrotechnik* in Karlsruhe to the Imperial Insurance Office, 6 May 1916.

insurance companies to honour compensation for injury due to risks associated with the war and mandated employers to pay extra insurance premiums to account for these added risks.[44] It also provided insurance for war risks to maritime workers and shipped merchandise even before Italy entered the conflict, and it offered reinsurance for war risks through the National Accident Insurance Fund.[45]

Unlike attacks from foreign aircraft, certain war-related risks sat more ambiguously between those intrinsic to and extrinsic from normal activities of work, and each government's handling of these risks had powerful implications for conceptions of national community and social rights. In particular, occupational illnesses related to manufacturing explosives[46] provoked particular concern from all three governments, due both to their role in worker absenteeism and to the efforts of trade unions and medical experts to have these investigated. This war-related risk was particularly grave in the eyes of administrators, as it had the potential to paralyse economic mobilisation on the home front. In Turin, approximately 20 to 25 per cent of female workers in munitions factories were absent from work on any given day, and this number occasionally increased to an immobilising 50 per cent. The local Office of Disciplinary Supervision explained to the Ministry of Arms and Munitions that working with various toxic powders and acids had severely damaged their health and made it difficult to work.[47] By 1918, the Italian Federation of State Workers demanded the inspection of a munitions factory in order to prevent future poisoning. The government responded to the issue of poisoning and related ailments on a case-by-case basis by instituting factory inspections.[48] It did not, however, decree that occupational illnesses related to the munitions industry should be compensated. Italy did not provide for the compensation of industrial diseases other than those which patently stemmed from an instantaneous event that could be construed as an accident. While malaria infections could be compensated as accidents, dermatitis from working with explosives could not.[49]

---

[44] 'Decreto luogotenenziale 31 ottobre 1914, n. 1577', *Gazzetta ufficiale* 275 (10 November 1915); *Atti della Cassa nazionale di assicurazione per gli infortuni degli operai sul lavoro: verbale delle sedute d'insediamento del nuovo Consiglio Superiore* (n.s.) 1914–15/13 (30 August 1915), pp. 30–2.

[45] 'Regio decreto 30 agosto 1914, n. 903', *Gazzetta ufficiale* 208 (31 August 1914); 'Decreto ministeriale 15 ottobre 1914', *Gazzetta ufficiale* 254 (23 October 1914); 'Decreto ministeriale 7 dicembre 1914', *Gazzetta ufficiale* 299 (15 December 1914).

[46] A helpful overview: Ludwig Teleky, 'La guerre et les maladies industrielles', *Revue Internationale du Travail* 3 (July–August 1921), pp. 53–5.

[47] ACS: Maem. Ccmi. Bta. 159: unnumbered: Report of the Office of Disciplinary Supervision in Turin, 15 July 1917.

[48] ACS: Maem. Ccmi. Bta. 93: unnumbered: *Federazione italiana dei lavoratori dello stato* to the Director General of the Mobilitazione industriale, 24 August 1918.

[49] On malaria and the Italian jurisprudential understanding of 'accidents', see Chapter 4.

By contrast, in Germany, the government decided to compensate occupational illnesses related to the manufacture of explosives. Complaints from the General Commission of German Trade Unions brought the imperial government to investigate the issue with the employers' liability funds involved in the manufacture of chemicals. As a result, the *Bundesrat*, the upper house in parliament, declared poisoning from compounds used in explosives a workplace accident that could be compensated. Two aspects of this development were particularly significant. On the one hand, this was the first occupational illness which the *Bundesrat* acknowledged as worthy of compensation, although it had been granted the authority in 1913 to make diseases eligible for compensation through accident insurance. On the other hand, the *Bundesrat* only declared these illnesses workplace accidents under the Enabling Act of 1914 and only allowed for the compensation of dependants of workers who died while manufacturing chemicals for the war effort.[50]

Unlike Germany or Italy, Britain had required employers to compensate workers for occupational illnesses several years before the outbreak of war, and the emphasis on similar conditions during wartime was an outgrowth of this development. In 1916, for example, the Medical Inspector of Factories, Thomas Legge, called on the Home Office to extend the schedule of conditions that could be compensated under the Workmen's Compensation Act of 1906 in order to address conditions like the dermatitis which afflicted workers manufacturing TNT.[51] The Home Office extended the policy to cover the ailment, but it was anxious to avoid broadening workmen's compensation greatly during the war, even though the new Home Secretary, Herbert Samuel, was a longstanding social reformer and advocate of Britain's 'new liberalism'. As Samuel put it, the department should, at least for the time being, maintain the policy of 'not going beyond the needs of the present emergency'.[52] The department soon broke with Samuel's informal edict, however, when forging a special compensation scheme in 1919 for silicosis, a lung disease associated with mining, after completing a longer study of the condition and after observing South Africa's successful adoption of a similar programme.[53]

---

[50] BArch: R3901: 4232: 79–80: Director of the General Commission of German Trade Unions to Chancellor Bethmann Hollweg, 28 June 1917; 98–100: Imperial Office of the Interior to the Committee of the *Berufsgenossenschaften* for chemical industries, 14 August 1917; *RGBl* 1917, p. 900: 'Bekanntmachung über die Gewährung von Sterbegeld und Hinterbliebenenrenten bei Gesundheitsschädigung durch aromatische Nitroverbindungen von 12. Oktober 1917'.

[51] TNA: PIN 12/4: unnumbered: Thomas Legge, Medical Inspector of Factories, to Herbert Samuel at the Home Office, 23 March 1916; unnumbered: Thomas Legge to the Under-Secretary of State of the Home Office, 23 March 1916; Deborah Thom, *Nice girls and rude girls: women workers in World War I* (London, 1998), pp. 122–43.

[52] TNA: PIN 12/4: unnumbered: Memo from Herbert Samuel, 6 May 1916. Samuel, like a number of British new liberals, was also a product of Balliol College, Oxford. See Bernard Wasserstein, *Herbert Samuel: a political life* (Oxford, 1992).

[53] TNA: PIN 12/11: unnumbered: Home Office Memorandum on compensation for miners' phthisis, 6 February 1917; unnumbered: Home Office memorandum, 18 June 1917; Mark W. Bufton and Joseph Melling, 'Coming up for air: experts, employers, and workers in campaigns

As prior conceptions of occupational risk were reformulated, so, too, were understandings of the consequences of workplace accidents. In particular, workers in Germany who were injured in accidents and classified as having long-term disabilities could nonetheless be conscripted as soldiers. These workers could serve in the military so long as they were not entirely disabled, and their compensation for workplace disability was forwarded to their dependants while they served.[54] Moreover, the German government encouraged individuals who were injured in workplace accidents to participate in the war effort at home by joining in the harvest – again, without any reduction in their compensation amounts.[55] It made similar stipulations for workers in other industries after various employers and regional governments claimed that the 'shortage of work forces in agriculture and industry' needed to be addressed by removing the 'mistrust' of compensation and pension recipients that they would lose their rights to compensation if they participated in work during the war.[56]

It is noteworthy that voluntary helpers in the harvest were eligible for accident compensation if they were 'workers' but ineligible if they were 'helpers of a higher class (*Stand*) who offer[ed] help merely out of national spirit (*Begeisterung*) and without economic compulsion'.[57] This class-based division in the treatment of workers confirmed earlier judgments about excluding white-collar employees from accident insurance. Yet, class politics in approaching accident compensation fell apart – at least on a rhetorical level – with the enactment of the Auxiliary Service Law, which provoked the *Bundesrat* to propose social insurance for all voluntary workers involved in the war effort. The law, passed on 5 December 1916, required all German men between the ages of 17 and 60 to work in the war effort if not serving as soldiers and encouraged women, children and the elderly to participate voluntarily. In official publications, the Imperial Insurance Office urged readers to believe that the Auxiliary Service Law, or, literally, the Law on the Aid to Service for the Fatherland, 'knows little about differences between levels and classes, just as

to compensate silicosis sufferers in Britain, 1918–1939', *Social History of Medicine* 18/1 (2005), pp. 63–86.
[54] 'Unfallversicherung: Recht und Rechtsübung auf dem Gebiete der Unfallversicherung mit Bezug auf den Krieg', *Monatsblätter für Arbeiterversicherung* 10/8–9 (15 September 1916), pp. 101–32, at p. 107. Greg Eghigian discusses these developments, in conjunction with a thorough analysis of the blurred boundaries between war, work and social insurance, in his *Making security social: disability, insurance, and the birth of the social entitlement state in Germany* (Ann Arbor, MI, 2000), pp. 159–90.
[55] 'Statistik und Volkswirtschaft: der Geschäftsbericht des Reichsversicherungsamts für das Jahr 1914', *Reichs und Staatsanzeiger* 69 (23 March 1915); BArch: R89: 11158: 440: President of the War Nutrition Office to the Imperial Insurance Office, 16 August 1916.
[56] BArch: R89: 11159: 22–3: Rudolf Rieck, city council member, architect and master builder at Stettin-Westend to the Chancellor Bethmann Hollweg, 21 August 1916; 431: Ministry of the Interior of the Great Archduchy of Hessen to the Imperial Insurance Office, 26 April 1917.
[57] 'Unfallversicherung: Recht und Rechtsübung', p. 107.

it is with [those under] the obligation to military service'.[58] In public speeches, the long-time president of that office, Paul Kaufmann, emphasised that 'social insurance', and not 'workers' insurance', as it was commonly called prior to the war, had contributed to the 'inner fortress of the Empire' by forging a unified national community. He testified to the importance of social insurance in creating national solidarity by pointing out that the 'the land of "militarism"' had spent 950 million marks on social insurance in 1913, and only 230 million marks more than that on defence.[59] In an attempt to fulfil its earlier declaration that social insurance could provide a 'work of peace' throughout the war, the government paid directly for social insurance for these conscripted workers if they worked in 'independent' branches of German firms that were located in foreign territories. As a consequence, earlier legal distinctions about obligations to insure beyond German borders fell by the wayside.[60]

The Italian government made a similar attempt to forge a national community during the war by extending accident insurance to all individuals working for the war effort in 'zones of war'. Yet, it conceded that classes still existed within this national community. The Ministry of War offered to provide compensation through the National Accident Insurance Fund specifically for 'middle-class workers', as these would not otherwise have been granted compensation due to their salary levels.[61] The British government avoided the issue of class entirely by leaving compensation for workers involved in the war effort open for individual employers to address. Moreover, it did not provide for a temporary exception to the maximum salary levels for workers eligible under workmen's compensation law, meaning that 'middle-class workers', let alone all 'helpers of a higher class', would not be entitled to accident benefit. Yet, the limited use of compensation in wartime Britain did not indicate the government's reluctance to intervene in the issue of civilian injury due to the risks of war. It was instead the continuation of the limited stipulations of workmen's compensation law regarding the role of the state, the sphere of work and the possibility for a worker's culpability, which were all residua from the treatment of liability under common law. In fact, the British government interpreted workmen's compensation, and its role in guaranteeing the policy,

---

[58] 'Die vaterländische Hilfsdienst und die Arbeiterversicherung', *Monatsblätter für Arbeiterversicherung* 3/6 (15 June 1917), pp. 70–9, at p. 71.

[59] Paul Kaufmann, *Was dankt das kämpfende Deutschland seiner sozialen Fürsorge?* (Berlin, 1917), pp. 5, 10. See also Paul Kaufmann, *Soziale Fürsorge und deutscher Siegeswille*, 12th repr. (Berlin, 1915), p. 24.

[60] *RGBl* 1917, p. 171: 'Verordnung über Versicherung der im vaterländischen Hilfsdienst Beschäftigten'.

[61] 'Liquidazione e pagamento per conto del Ministero della Guerra delle indennità di infortunio dovute a operai borghesi addettii ad opere e servizi in zona di guerra', *Atti della Cassa nazionale d'assicurazione per gl'infortuni sul lavoro: Sede centrale in Roma: verbale* (n.s.) 1919–20/23, pp. 85–9.

rather expansively when it came to another situation effected by the war: sudden inflation and the consequent devaluing of accident benefit.

INFLATION, *SOCIAL* INSURANCE AND THE MEANING OF COMPENSATION

The war had brought the governments in each country to see workers, more than ever before, as essential resources for the nation. Moreover, workers who had previously been denied access to accident benefit, such as the majority of agricultural labourers in Italy, also became increasingly valued in the war effort. Over 2.5 million agricultural workers were taken into the Italian army, endowing not only these individuals with an elevated status, but also forcing government and society at large to recognise the importance of the older men, women and youths who were left to work the fields.[62] When severe inflation hit during the middle of the conflict, wiping out the real value of accident benefit and leaving many pensioners without enough money to live, each government therefore felt compelled to act. The British and German governments introduced fixed pension increases that continued until shortly after the armistice. As a result, the premise upon which each country's compensation system was founded, compensation valued against known occupational risks, was shaken. The Italian government, by contrast, never considered the option of countervailing the actuarial principles underlying accident insurance. Instead, it exploited the financial hardships brought on by the war to extend accident insurance to the millions of agricultural workers who had been excluded from the law since its inception. With a special military decree, the Italian government was able to push through the contentious policy of agricultural accident insurance about which it had been so ambivalent before the war. In these ways, the economic crisis ensured, at least in part, that the wartime languages of solidarism in each country became a reality. Just as workers had risked their lives in the workplace during the war, it seemed that the state would need to guarantee compensation for their hardships.

Nonetheless, with the exception of Italy's new law on agricultural accident insurance, these decrees – like many of the wartime measures on workplace accidents – were provisional and short-lived. The first law on subsidies for recipients of accident compensation was passed in 1917 in Britain and in 1918 in Germany and granted additional pension payments only to the most severely disabled workers, with no additional allowance for dependants. In Britain, unlike in Germany, the law on subsidies for recipients of accident compensation was a particularly remarkable development. Given the limited involvement of central government in Britain's workmen's compensation law, wartime subsidies marked a particularly novel move. Both laws came as a response to demands in

[62] Martin Clark, *Modern Italy, 1871–1995* (London, 1996), p. 193.

parliament, as well as those made directly by pension recipients, that accident pensioners could not afford to keep up with the rapidly rising cost of living during the war.[63] In Britain, the additional lobbying efforts of trade unions and the Labour Party also were a crucial impetus for adopting such a policy, as was the agreement of employers' organisations.[64] In both countries, officials agreed with the pleas of these various groups and pushed for temporary relief – even though the policy undermined the principles behind accident compensation and despite the fact that, in the case of Germany, it ran against the interests of insurers. The British and German laws on pension subsidies were remarkable in that they called for insurance bodies to pay for subsidies from their own funds. Before drafting a bill on the subsidy, the Home Office in London met with the main insurance companies, which did not object to providing the extra payments to pension recipients.[65] Only the Secretary of the Treasury and a Unionist MP spoke out adamantly against the new law, on the grounds that it undermined the principles of workmen's compensation policy by 'transfer[ring] to a past employer part of the burden resulting from the present high prices'. The Treasury was particularly annoyed about not being consulted about the new law, given that government itself employed thousands of workers and would now need to pay out this upsurge in accident benefit. However, the Home Office was able to push through its proposal.[66] The British policy on subsidies is all the more noteworthy given that employers in Britain were not obliged to provide insurance for workmen's compensation; as a result, workers who were not in receipt of compensation through an insurance policy were not granted financial assistance under the special wartime provision.

In Germany, government had already made numerous demands on the employers' liability funds as a result of the war, including providing medical and rehabilitative facilities for injured soldiers and veterans and donating funds and supplies to support the home front.[67] When the *Bundesrat* enacted

---

[63] *RGBl* 1918, p. 31; 'Die Rentenzulagen der Unfall- und der Invalidenversicherung', *Monatsblätter der Arbeiter-Versicherung* 12/3–4 (15 March 1918), pp. 19–27; 7 & 8 Geo. V, c.42; 5 *Hansard* HC vol. 86 (9 December 1916), cols. 942–3.

[64] TNA: HO 157/9/514: Under-Secretary of State in the Home Office to the Minister of Shipping, 7 August 1917; TNA: PIN 11/4: unnumbered: Under-Secretary of the Home Office to A. C. Young, Esq., of the Accident Offices Association, 14 August 1919; TNA: PIN 11/2: W. Cole of the Legal Department of the Iron and Steel Trades Confederation in London to William Brace, Under-Secretary of State at the Home Office, 15 August 1917; unnumbered: Home Office notes from a meeting with between George Barnes of the War Cabinet with a deputation of MPs, representatives of trade unions, the Labour Party executive and the standing council of the Labour Party, 29 August 1917.

[65] TNA: PIN 11/4: unnumbered: Under-Secretary of the Home Office to A. C. Young, Esq., of the Accident Offices Association, 14 August 1919.

[66] TNA: PIN 11/2: unnumbered: D. L. Heath to the Under-Secretary of State at the Home Office, 10 November 1917; 5 *Hansard* HC vol. 96 (13 August 1917), cols. 1013–14.

[67] For example: 'Statistik und Volkswirtschaft'; BArch: R89: 10151: President of the Imperial Insurance Office to the Committees of the State Insurance Institutes and to the

an ordinance on subsidies, therefore, officials did not consult the accident funds. The funds soon objected to the burden of extra payments. The League of German Employers' Funds pointed out that the law on workplace accident insurance had been introduced to replace liability claims, meaning that it was based on the principle of compensation for specific harms, *and not* on that of 'welfare'. The funds claimed that the subsidy, therefore, '[stood] in no legal or moral connection with the duty to compensate'.[68] It appeared that the war had led the government to depart – temporarily – from that founding principle. The impact of inflation on accident pensions became particularly salient after Germany's defeat on the battlefield in November 1918, when an acrimonious debate ensued throughout the country. There was widespread confusion about who was responsible for assisting recipients of accident compensation in light of quickly increasing prices and a lack of basic provisions throughout the country. Following a request from the imperial government, local and state governments attempted to aid pension recipients with firewood and basic supplies soon after the war had ended.[69] By the following year, local and state governments petitioned the federal government for assistance, insisting that the rising poverty of pension recipients was an imperial matter and not an issue for local poor boards and tax payers. The administrations in Saxony, which had already spent 25 million marks on support for 'worker pensioners' by 1921, and Thuringia, amongst others, took this stand against the central government in Berlin. In industrialised Saxony, the lobbying efforts of trade unions for more assistance proved crucial for bringing the state government to seek federal aid.[70] Trade unions also petitioned the federal government directly

Berufsgenossenschaften, 3 August 1914. Further discussed in Eghigian, *Making security social*, pp. 159–90.

[68] GStAPK: I. HA. Rep. 120BB. Abt. VIII. Fach. 8. No. 1. Vol. 1: 275–6: Petition from the *Verband der deutschen Berufsgenossenschaften* to the *Reichstag*, 5 March 1918. See also Geheim Oberregierungsrat Düttmann, 'Die Verordnung vom 3. January 1918: Bericht erstattet in der Vollversammlung der Landesversicherungsanstalten zu Leipzig am 19. Januar 1918', *Die Arbeiter-Versorgung* 35/5 (11 February 1918), pp. 3–12; Dr Ostern, 'Bericht zur Frage der Kriegsrentenzuschläge (Bundesratsverordnungen vom 3. und 17. Januar 1918) erstattet in der Vollversammlung der landesversicherungsanstalten am 19. Januar 1918 in Leipzig im Auftrage des Verbandes der Deutschen Berufsgenossenschaften', *Die Berufsgenossenschaft* (15 February 1918), pp. 1–6.

[69] GStAPK: I. HA. Rep. 120BB. Abt. VIII. Fach. 8. No. 1. Vol. 1: 304: Imperial Labour Minister to the Collective Governments and to the Prussian Minister of the Interior, 26 November 1918.

[70] BArch: R3901: 4533: 56: The Thuringian Economic Ministry, Division for Labour and Welfare in Weimar, to the Imperial Labour Minister, 24 February 1921; 143: Saxon Legation to the Imperial Labour Ministry, 18 March 1922; BArch: R3901: 4532: 31: Magistrat des Stadtkreises Guben to the Government President in Frankfurt, 29 May 1920; 41: Baden Labour Ministry to the Imperial Ministry of Labour, 30 July 1920; BArch: R3901: 4547: 453: Saxon Minister of Labour to the Imperial Labour Ministry, 15 October 1921; BArch: R3901: 4529: 360: Saxon Ministry of Foreign Affairs to the Imperial Labour Office, 12 May 1919; 466: Mayor of Elberfeld to the Imperial Office of the Interior, 26 May 1919.

with the request for some sort of pension assistance, possibly through national funds.[71]

This confusion was further exacerbated by questions about whether all of Germany's citizens should receive equal treatment or whether certain pensioners, such as the war-disabled, the generally disabled or the accident-disabled, were more needy or possibly more worthy. Recipients of accident benefit began elevating the fact that they received compensation to an essential component of their identities and began articulating their demands to government as 'accident pensioners' who were entitled to assistance. Many organised in associations of pension recipients and began calling for the equal treatment of accident-disabled, war veterans and other pension recipients. Others claimed a special status as 'victims' of a government that refused sufficient funds to accident pensioners and of a society that prioritised war veterans over workers. Many, such as the 'accident pensioner Franz Grimm', petitioned the *Reichstag* with a 'scream of need'.[72] Accident pensioners also petitioned local or central government directly for assistance. For instance, Robert Nagel wrote to the local government in Mörs am Rhein and claimed that, as a 'mining disabled', he did not wish to seek 'foreign help' from charity or the local poor board. Due to the 'unfortunate war', however, he and his wife were now unable to survive on his pension alone. The government in Düsseldorf forwarded his correspondence to the Imperial Labour Minister when it became clear that Nagel and his wife would under no circumstances accept support for the indigent, even if it were given a euphemistic name. Nagel was 75 years old and his wife 71, and they lived in a single room and could not afford to buy milk, butter or even the 'cheapest margarine'.[73]

The Imperial Labour Minister offered Nagel hope by informing him of plans for a new law on pension subsidies. Yet, the demand made by some other compensation recipients for the equal treatment of all pensioners, including the war-disabled, elderly and chronically ill or disabled, was rejected. Instead, the government supported a version of the self-interested argument put forward by the accident funds: different kinds of pension recipients had different needs.

---

[71] BArch R3901: 4529: 359: *Generalkommission der Gewerkschaften Deutschlands* to the Imperial Labour Office, 6 May 1919.

[72] For example: BArch: R3901: 4533: 36–7: Josef Kohl of Regensburg, 'former machine master and current accident pensioner', to the *Reichstag*, 6 July 1920; BArch: R4530: 274: 'Anfrage Nr. 531' to the National Assembly from Frau Zietz, 27 November 1919; 170: Franz Grimm to the Reichstag, 30 March 1919. For more information, especially on the 'victimisation' of accident pensioners, see Eghigian, *Making security social*, pp. 191–233.

[73] BArch: R3901: 4547: 125: Robert Nagel to the 'welfare minister' in Mörs am Rhein, 1 September 1921; 127: Nagel to the 'welfare minister', 30 September 1921; 129: Government President in Düsseldorf to the Minister for Volkswohlfahrt in Berlin, 14 October 1922; 130: Imperial Labour Minister to Nagel, 3 November 1921. The Imperial Labour Ministry was established in 1919, having been founded in 1918 as the Imperial Labour Office. It took over several of the competences of the Imperial Ministry of the Interior, including labour and social-security policy.

These insurance bodies argued, however, that only local authorities or poor boards were in a position to offer pension recipients the 'individual' support they required.[74] By contrast, the government decided to maintain a policy of standard accident subsidies rather than granting general relief to all categories of the disabled or instructing accident pensioners to seek individualised assistance through poor boards. The first subsidy granted after the war came in 1919 with a law aimed at workers who were disabled by at least two-thirds of their full capacity to work.[75] In the next several years, further orders for pension subsidies were issued in response to the changing ratio of compensation amounts to bread prices as inflation continued. The subsidies ended only after the *Reichsmark* fell following the hyperinflation of 1922–3.[76] By the end of this period, though, confidence in maintaining subsidies began to falter. The Imperial Ministry of Labour, which was now headed by Heinrich Brauns, a socially orientated Catholic theologian and Centre-Party member, began arguing for accident insurance subsidies to be guaranteed on a more individualised basis. In a radical shift from the principles of social insurance, the Imperial Labour Ministry suggested granting subsidies as a form of 'damage equalisation' (*Schadensausgleich*) rather than a general top-up that was still in keeping with the actuarial model on which accident insurance was based.[77] His proposal was never enacted but demonstrated the powerful impact of the war and its aftermath on conceptualising compensation, social insurance and the role of government as a guarantor of social peace.

The disagreement over pension subsidies following the war unfolded in Germany with an intensity unparalleled in Britain. Since workmen's compensation was overseen in Whitehall but administered locally through a myriad of private mutual and insurance funds, tribunals and courts, it was clear to administrators *and* pension recipients where the jurisdiction for issues related to subsidies lay: outside government. The fact that Whitehall did not play a significant role in overseeing compensation also meant that the policy was rarely conflated with general social provisions; unlike in Germany, discussions in Britain were never able to question what was *social* about social insurance. The genuine problem of poverty amidst inflation did, however, lead officials and pension recipients alike to question whether compensation should also be granted to needy groups who had been overlooked in the initial policy. In the context of the war, should compensation be treated as a social right guaranteed by the state and extended to all as a form of solidarism? The question of

---

[74] BArch: R3901: 4532: 91–2: Head of the *Verband der deutschen Berufsgenossenschaften*, 28 August 1920.

[75] The decision to take this step is outlined here: BArch: R3901: 4530: 137: Proposal of the Imperial Labour Minister in the *Reichsrat*, 25 October 1919.

[76] BArch: R3901: 4547: 20–5: Imperial Labour Minister to the Chancellor and the Imperial Minister of Finance, 15 September 1921.

[77] BArch: R3901: 4536: unnumbered: Imperial Labour Ministry to the Württemberg Agricultural Chamber, 6 April 1923.

accident payments for dependants, in part, sparked this discussion. Towards the end of the war, the Miners' Federation of Great Britain began its lobby for an amendment to the War Additions Act for workmen's compensation that would allow for extra assistance for dependants.[78] George Cave, the Home Secretary and a member of the Conservative Party, took on the suggestion and consulted with employers, trade unions, government agencies and accident insurance companies about the proposal.[79] Yet, employers, insurers and, crucially, the Treasury saw creating a special wartime provision for dependants as a breach in the tenets of the compensation law.[80] The Treasury was again concerned about the costs of the proposal for the government, given its numerous employees.[81] In the end, the Home Office spearheaded a bill that would increase the overall amount of compensation payable to workers, rather than one that differentiated pension amounts by family size. As a consequence, a 75 per cent rise in compensation levels was granted to workers who were entirely disabled, and a 100 per cent rise to workers who earned less than £20 a week.[82] The major British insurance companies, organised in the Accident Offices Association, agreed to the government's recommendation and provided subsidies for compensation recipients without aid from government funds and without charging employers additional premiums.[83]

The question of providing for dependants of injured workers and generally improving the standard of living for pension recipients was not resolved with the various postwar laws on subsidies for workmen's compensation. It became a matter of considerable debate in a committee appointed by the Home Office in 1919 to investigate revising workmen's compensation law. The Home Office appointed the Departmental Committee, which was headed by the Liberal MP and barrister Henry Holman Gregory, in order to resolve long-standing questions about workmen's compensation that had arisen already before the outbreak of war, as well as new issues, such as the effect of inflation upon

---

[78] TNA: HO 157/11/217–18: Under-Secretary of the Home Office to the Secretary of the Board of Agriculture, 9 August 1919; 287: Under-Secretary of the Home Office to the Secretary of the Miners' Federation of Great Britain, 20 August 1919.

[79] TNA: HO 157/11/183: Under-Secretary of the Home Office to the National Confederation of Employers' Organisations, 7 August 1919; TNA: PIN 11/4: unnumbered: Home Office memorandum, untitled, 7 October 1919.

[80] TNA: PIN 11/4: unnumbered: National Confederation of Employers' Organisations to Sir Ratcliffe-Ellis of the Mining Association of Great Britain, 3 July 1919; unnumbered: Home Office memorandum, 7 October 1919; unnumbered: Home Office memorandum, n.d. [October 1919].

[81] TNA: PIN 11/4: Malcolm G. Ramsay of the Treasury Chambers to the Under-Secretary of State of the Home Office, 21 September 1919.

[82] TNA: PIN 11/4: unnumbered: Home Office memorandum, 7 October 1919.

[83] Though they reserved the right to increase premiums by up to 10 per cent for new policies. TNA: PIN 11/4: unnumbered: Under-Secretary of the Home Office to the Secretary of the British General Insurance Company, Ltd., 20 December 1919. See also: Guildhall MS: 29198: vol. 1: Minutes: 1920-1:31: Accident Offices Association General Purposes Committee Meeting Minutes, 25 October 1920.

compensation amounts. The war delayed addressing various problems inherent in the law, including the matter of compensation for dependants. The committee met for two years and concluded in 1920 that 'compensation for the loss of the bread-winner shall not be fixed on previous earnings, but to some extent on the needs of the dependants'.[84] The government took no action on the committee's suggestions, largely due to a difference of opinion between the reformist Home Office and the Cabinet, and instead persisted with subsidies to address the more immediate issue of inflation.[85] By 1921, the Miners' Federation again sought an answer to the problem of pension recipients and claimed that there were several cases of entirely disabled workers who were now having to seek relief from local authorities or their parish council. It was particularly concerned about the low compensation levels for widows and children of deceased workers, which had remained set at an inadequate limit of £300 by the 1906 Workmen's Compensation Act.[86] By the same token, the Union of Post Office Workers lobbied government for an increase in the maximum salary limit of £250 per year for workers eligible for accident compensation.[87] Wartime and postwar inflation had dramatically depreciated the value of these set amounts. After discussions involving employers' organisations, trade unions, the Accident Offices Association and the government, workmen's compensation law was finally revised in 1923 with increased maximum salaries for eligible workers and increased maximum compensation amounts for dependants. The most significant aspect of the new law was its recognition of degrees of dependency and allowance for varying amounts of compensation to partial and full dependants of injured workers. The 1923 Workmen's Compensation Act also marked the end to subsidies for inflation.[88]

In wartime and postwar Italy, unlike in Britain and Germany, the government focused on workers who were ineligible for accident insurance rather than on the issue of pension subsidies. Officials never seriously considered enacting a system of subsidies, perhaps because they sought to maintain the actuarial basis on which Italian accident insurance was based. Yet, they did not push the issue, because they were instead concerned about the more pressing problem of agricultural workers. Rural labour constituted nearly 60 per

---

[84] Quoted in TNA: PIN 12/15: unnumbered: Transcript of the notes of the deputation from the Miners' Federation Executive Committee to the Secretary of State for the Home Office, 7 January 1921. The findings of the committee: *PP* 1920 (Cd 816) XXVI.908: 'Departmental Committee on Workmen's Compensation: Report and Evidence'.

[85] For a thorough discussion of the committee, see: P. W. J. Bartrip, *Workmen's compensation in twentieth-century Britain: law, history and social policy* (Aldershot, 1987), pp. 88–119.

[86] TNA: PIN 12/15: unnumbered: Transcript of the notes of the deputation from the Miners' Federation Executive Committee to the Secretary of State for the Home Office, 7 January 1921.

[87] TNA: PIN 11/5: unnumbered: Under-Secretary of the Home Office to the Secretary of the Treasury, n.d. [December 1923].

[88] Workmen's Compensation Act, 1923, 13 & 14 Geo. V., c. 42. On the background: TNA: PIN 11/5: unnumbered: 'Workmen's Compensation, Memorandum A', 14 December 1923.

cent of the Italian workforce at this time, but remained outside the scope of accident insurance law. On a pragmatic level, the economic repercussions of the war were particularly difficult for these workers. Italy relied on imports of raw materials and food, and inflation as well as the closure of the Dardanelles and the Bosporus had made both difficult to attain during the war.[89] The fact that agricultural workers were not only suffering financially but also serving in large numbers on the front lines of the war, along with the fact that these workers were particularly well organised in Italy, meant that granting them accident insurance became an imperative in government. It seemed that if the state were to honour the contributions of these workers both in the field and on the battlefield, it would need to offer a token of solidarism in return. Officials in Rome not only promised 'land to the peasants' when they came home from the war. They also offered insurance for accidents that happened while working that land. Moreover, amidst the mass wave of wartime strikes in factories and the profound unpopularity of both the war and the government that had led Italy into combat, extending accident insurance to these workers seemed a necessary conceit.[90] Yet, the issue of accident insurance for workers in agriculture had much deeper roots: the matter was debated in government and parliament from the early 1900s, with a series of law proposals that floundered at first due to a lack of support in government and later due to parliamentary division over the matter. The issue emerged again after Italy had entered the war, with a series of failed law proposals in 1915 and 1916. By 1917, the policy was finally pushed through via a special military decree. As the Commission on Labour Legislation, Emigration and Social Insurance explained several years later, the war had made agricultural accident insurance a matter of urgency.[91]

For members of the Commission, the policy served as a means of domestic peace-keeping, aimed at 'that imposing mass of citizens which, during the war, provided the most intense labour in order to guarantee national agricultural production, in the most difficult moments and with a diminished workforce'.[92] The decision to act came in response to the claims of individuals such as the mayor of the Piedmontese town of Vespolate, who wrote to the Prime Minister in 1917. He argued that the policy was necessary 'at this moment', especially

---

[89] Vera Zamagni, *The economic history of Italy, 1860–1990* (Oxford, 1993), pp. 214, 217.

[90] On land reform and the nature of Italian agricultural labour: Charles S. Maier, *Recasting bourgeois Europe: stabilization in France, Germany and Italy in the decade after World War I* (Princeton, NJ, 1975), pp. 47–52. An overview of the social unrest: Giovanna Procacci, 'Popular protest and labour conflict in Italy, 1915–1918', *Social History* 14 (1989), pp. 31–58.

[91] 'Relazione della Commissione "Legislazione sul lavoro – emigrazione – previdenza sociale" presentata alla Camera dei Deputati nella Seduta del 29 giugno 1922', *Rassegna della previdenza sociale* 9/9 (September 1922), pp. 17–21.

[92] 'Relazione della Commissione "Legislazione sul lavoro – Emigrazione – Previdenza Sociale"', p. 17. A view shared by Fiorenzo Girotti, *Welfare state: storia, modelli, critica* (Rome, 1998), p. 179.

in light of the work of the elderly, children and women in cultivating the harvest, to introduce compulsory accident insurance for agricultural workers. The mayor was concerned that the land had been 'abandoned by valid arms', that is, men of working age, which meant that these new workers were not only more likely to suffer accidents but also, possibly, more worthy of financial support.[93] In Italy, as in Germany, the rhetoric of social solidarism became more significant during the war and helped to elevate accident insurance to what was perceived as a social good. Wartime rhetoric facilitated lobbying efforts by endowing agricultural accident insurance with a national imperative.

It was the Ministry of Industry, Commerce and Labour, which had been indecisive in its support of agricultural accident insurance in the years before the war, which embraced the arguments that a variety of groups put forward in favour of the policy.[94] The lobbying efforts of associations of agricultural workers and the Socialist Party, which had continued from the prewar era, played an important role in making the plight of these workers and their social rights more visible.[95] At the same time, protest against a failed rationing system, which included a clash in Turin in 1917 with 50 dead and 100 injured, gave greater credence to these demands.[96] Yet, the most significant contributor to the wartime debate about agricultural accident insurance came from insurance businesses. The semi-public National Accident Insurance Fund, in particular, was keen to expand its remit further by gaining a monopoly for the insurance of agricultural workers. It pointed out its plan to the Prime Minister in late 1916, not long after it decided to create a branch specialising in agricultural accident insurance.[97] Other insurance bodies, such as the Milan-based Insurance and Aid Fund for Accidents at Work called for agricultural accident insurance as a 'measure of social reparation of the character of high national

---

[93] ACS: PCM (1917). Bta. 530. Fasc. 5. No. 2: 213: Mayor of the Comune di Vespolate to the Prime Minister, 19 April 1917.

[94] The Ministry of Industry, Agriculture and Commerce was renamed in 1916 when a separate Ministry of Agriculture was founded. It was reconstituted again in the next few years. In 1920, it became the Ministry of Industry and Commerce, and in 1923, the Ministry of Labour and Social Insurance. For a thorough discussion of the lobbies for and against agricultural accident insurance during the war, as well as the legislative proposals, see Arnaldo Cherubini and Italo Piva, *Dalla libertà all'obbligo: la previdenza sociale fra Giolitti e Mussolini* (Milan, 1998), pp. 219–35.

[95] For example, on prewar lobbying: ACS: PCM (1914). Bta. 478. Fasc. 5: 295: President of the Federation of Catholic Agriculture to the Ministry of the Interior, 24 May 1914; unnumbered: *Società liberale operaia mutuo soccorso di Sandra* to the Minister of the Interior, 20 July 1913. See also Chapter 4.

[96] Zamagni, *The economic history of Italy*, p. 217. See also Giovanna Procacci, 'Repressione e dissenso nella prima guerra mondiale', *Studi storici* 22 (1981), pp. 119–50; Giovanna Procacci, 'La protesta delle donne nelle campagne in tempo di guerra', Istituto Alcide Cervi, *Annali* 13 (1991), pp. 57–86.

[97] ACS: PCM (1916). Bta. 514. Fasc. 12. No. 2: 840: *Cassa nazionale d'assicurazione per gl'infortuni degli operai sul lavoro, sede centrale in Roma* to the Prime Minister, 30 December 1916.

solidarity', a point on which they agreed with representatives of the municipality of Milan and local parliamentary deputies.[98]

The liberal Minister of Agriculture, Giuseppe De Nava, played a key role in pushing the policy through. He stemmed from an aristocratic family in Calabria, in the deep south of the peninsula, and had long been an advocate of reforms that would benefit the south, including measures to assist agriculture.[99] De Nava attempted to overcome some of the resistance encountered by earlier bills in 1915, put forward by several liberal members of parliament, and, in 1916, by Senator Emilio Conti, who was one of the most vocal advocates of the policy.[100] The main point of contention against these proposals was how to organise insurance for rural labour. De Nava solved the puzzle by latching onto the National Fund as a relatively easy way to extend social insurance to Italy's millions of itinerant and occasional agricultural workers.[101] As De Nava explained when presenting the bill to the senate, those working the land should not be 'considered less than the class of workers based in industrial manufactures'. If Italy was going to recognise the contributions of rural labour, it needed to introduce agricultural accident insurance. The policy was an 'inescapable necessity of justice towards a numerous class of workers that contribute[d] in an enormous way to the national wealth'. It should be introduced even though, as he put it, the 'risk of accidents' in agriculture was lower than in industry.[102] The 1917 law that resulted from his proposal increased the number of insured agricultural workers from 700,000 to over 8 million in one step, provoking a major reorganisation of the National Fund and the administration of accident insurance in general.[103] Overnight, it seemed, the National Fund had gained a notable place of prominence.

---

[98] ACS: PCM (1916). Bta. 514. Fasc. 12. No. 2: 160: *Patronato d'assicurazione e soccorso per gli infortuni del lavoro* to the Prime Minister, 24 March 1916.

[99] ACS: PCM (1916). Bta. 514. Fasc. 12. No. 2: unnumbered: Minister of Agriculture to Paolo Boselli, Prime Minister, 28 September 1916. Measures to assist the south's economic development later became a central tenet of the postwar economic recovery: Edoardo Pantano, *I problemi economic urgenti: voti e proposte per il passaggio dallo stato di guerra allo stato di pace* [report of the *Commissione per il dopoguerra*] (Rome, 1919), pp. 23–4.

[100] On these and earlier proposals: Ministero per il lavoro e la previdenza sociale, direzione generale della previdenza sociale, *L'assicurazione obbligatoria contro gli infortuni sul lavoro in agricoltura: Prima relazione sull'applicazione del decreto-legge 23 agosto 1917, n. 1450* (Rome, 1922), pp. 11–19; Bortolo Belotti, 'Per l'assicurazione obbligatoria degli infortuni sul lavoro agricolo', *Nuova antologia* 269 (1 October 1916), pp. 344–50.

[101] For example: ACS: PCM (1917). Bta. 530. Fasc. 5. No. 2: 213: Telegram from the President of the *Accademia reale di agricoltura di Torino* to Paolo Boselli, Prime Minister, 15 July 1917; SdAs: Sessione 1917: *Numero del Progetto* 360: unnumbered: *Comizio agrario di Firenze* to the President of the Senate, 3 July 1917.

[102] A. P. Sen., Doc., Leg. XXIV, Sess. 1 (1913–17), Nr. 360a: 'Progetto di legge presentato nella tornata del 26 marzo 1917 dal ministro dell'industria, commercio e lavoro: assicurazione obbligatoria contro gli infortuni sul lavoro in agricoltura, iniziato in senato', pp. 1, 11–12.

[103] CTNAIL, *Organizzazione del servizio di assistenza agli infortuni* (Rome, 1922), p. 12.

There were no other wartime or immediate postwar provisions that specifically targeted accident pensioners suffering from the consequences of inflation in Italy. However, as elsewhere, the central government rationed food and encouraged voluntary organisations and local governments to assist with providing basic supplies during the war. In addition, it supported the endeavours of industrialists to stave off workplace unrest at the beginning of the tumultuous *biennio rosso* of strikes in 1919–20 by implementing minimum wage levels and an eight-hour work day.[104] In 1919, government also spearheaded initiatives to make unemployment insurance and insurance for old-age and disability pensions compulsory. Together with workers brought under the new accident insurance law, there were over 15 million Italians who were affected by the new insurance policies, leading several historians to claim that the First World War 'effectively opened a new phase in the evolution of the Italian social state'.[105] As Vincenzo Magaldi, a senior civil servant in the Ministry of Agriculture, claimed on the eve of Italy's entry into the war, the 'modern concept of insurance' had finally taken root in Italy. This concept was predicated on social solidarism in which risks were shared – at least, financially.[106]

Magaldi's aim of extending social insurance in Italy as a means to foster solidarism resembled Heinrich Brauns' conception of subsidies for accident insurance as a form of 'damage equalisation'. Both Magaldi and Brauns saw social insurance as uniquely able to bind members of national communities together – even if, as in the case of Germany, doing so meant departing from the actuarial principles upon which the policies were based. During a time of crisis in the First World War, social insurance provided both governments with a means to foster patriotism and encourage compliance in a way which was not possible, and perhaps not desired, in other countries where social insurance did not exist. In Britain, officials felt the need to act on the issue of inflation, not only legislating on subsidies for compensation but extending compensation to dependants. Yet, they did not tap the rhetoric of national community that was widespread in both German and Italian representations of accident insurance during the war. This essential divergence between British workmen's compensation, on the one hand, and Italian and German accident insurance, on the other, reflected each government's initial goals when adopting these policies. For Germany and Italy, creating legitimacy while encouraging economic growth and social stability were at the core of considerations in government

---

[104] Maria Concetta Dentoni, '"Questioni alimentare" e "questione sociale" durante la prima guerra mondiale in Italia', *Società e Storia* 37 (1987), pp. 612–46. Or, in fact, to stave off the problems with strikes that had been brewing since the beginning of the war as part of a *quadrennio rosso*. See Procacci, 'Popular protest and labour conflict'.

[105] 'Il convegno della Confederazione del Lavoro per le Assicurazioni Sociali', *Rassegna della previdena sociale* 7/2 (February 1920), pp. 49–69, at p. 50. Gianni Silei, *Lo stato sociale in Italia: storia e document* (Manduria, 2003), p. 181.

[106] Vincenzo Magaldi, 'Il concetto moderno della previdenza', *Il Rinnovamento* (30 April 1915), p. iv.

about whether and how to act on workplace accidents. In Britain, by contrast, officials had sought to address the legal loopholes in liability law and the common law, while allowing individuals to resolve the consequences of workplace accidents on their own.

FROM WAR TO WORK

In the period between 1914 and 1918, occupational risk ceased to be a significant problem in the eyes of officials in each country. Instead, addressing the risks of war – including the employment of new groups of workers and the manufacturing of dangerous materials – and preserving peace in fragile national communities became priorities. The experience with workplace accidents had begun by this time to filter into broader considerations about risk and its social consequences. On the one hand, debates about environmental hazards, automobiles and other new technologies that had begun at the turn of the century continued to occupy officials after the war as they reflected on whether and how to legislate on the complex relationship between fault, danger and consent. On the other hand, each government came to deal with the new problem of war veterans by tapping some of their experiences with accident compensation. Injured soldiers, who were seen to be workers on the battlefront, became the subject of military psychiatrists, who applied ideas about traumatic neurosis in the form of 'shell-shock', 'hysteria' or 'trauma'. The concept of traumatic neurosis – a category first applied to railway accidents – migrated easily from describing the consequences of occupational accidents to characterising the psychological aftermath of war.[107] Addressing the effects of the war on returned soldiers became imperative, and a crucial issue for all three governments was how veterans could be reincorporated into the workforce in spite of their physical disabilities and mental anguish.

At the same time, considerations about the treatment of veterans flowed back into debates about injured workers and their role in the explicitly national communities that had been forged in war. This last development was manifested most clearly in Germany and Italy, where each government had embraced the rhetoric of social solidarity during the war and increasingly approached accident pensioners with expectations about contributing towards their national communities. The British government, by contrast, focused exclusively on

---

[107] For example: G. Benassi, 'Le neurosi traumatiche e l'esperienza della guerra', *Rassegna di assicurazioni e previdenza sociale* 8/6 (June 1921), pp. 27–57. These developments have been written about extensively. Meaningful starting points: Andreas Killen, *Berlin electropolis: shock, nerves and German modernity* (Berkeley, CA, 2006), pp. 127–61; Mark S. Micale and Paul Lerner, eds., *Traumatic pasts: history, psychiatry and trauma in the modern age, 1870–1930* (Cambridge, 2001), especially the chapters by Paul Lerner, Bruna Bianchi and Peter Leese; Peter Leese, *Shell shock: traumatic neurosis and the British soldiers of the First World War* (Basingtoke, 2002), ch. 2; Paul Lerner, *Hysterical men: war, psychiatry, and the politics of trauma in Germany, 1890–1930* (Ithaca, NY, 2003), chs. 1–2.

the retraining of injured soldiers in the war and the immediate postwar era. The dual focus on retraining both soldiers and veterans in Germany and Italy effectively continued the experience of economic mobilisation during the war. It also revealed the expectations of both governments and their societies for workers to participate in society as members of a national community who held certain obligations. These expectations led to a renewed backlash against 'pension neurotics', frauds and simulators and recipients of small pensions, indicating that the generous reframing of social risk during the war would soon come to an end.

Both during and after the war, the German and Italian governments began calling for injured workers and war veterans to be treated in similar ways, with a view to reinstating both in the workforce. Officials looked to new technologies to address physical problems, as well as surgical methods and orthopaedic devices to assist with recovery.[108] While the employers' liability funds and doctors in Germany had focused on the rehabilitation of injured workers before the war, in Italy, the new emphasis on retraining was revolutionary. Before the war, no institution in the peninsula focused on retraining for workers injured in accidents or disabled soldiers. The experience of the First World War brought medics, the National Accident Insurance Fund and the government to focus on rehabilitation for both groups. The new National Agency for War Invalids (the *Opera nazionale per gli invalidi di guerra*), which was created in 1917 as a means to organise rehabilitative work that had previously been carried out by various local and charitable institutions such as the Florentine Committee for the War Blind and Riccardo Galeazzi's Retraining School for War Disabled, also played a key role here. The National Fund was especially active in encouraging retraining and advocated applying the newest methods in rehabilitation, such as prostheses (Figure 10).[109] In Germany, physicians and the government

[108] 'Die Nachbehandlung von Unfallverletzten und Kriegsbeschädigten', *Monatsblätter für Arbeiterversicherung* 14/3–4 (15 March 1920), pp. 21–31, at p. 22; Heather R. Perry, 'Rearming the disabled veteran: artificially rebuilding state and society in WWI Germany', in Katherine Ott et al., eds., *Artificial parts, practical lives: modern histories of prosthetics* (New York, 2002), pp. 75–101; 'La Cassa nazionale infortuni alla Terza conferenza interalleata per lo studio delle questioni interessanti gli Invalidi di guerra', *Rassegna della previdenza sociale* 6/9–10 (September–October 1919), pp. 1201–17.

[109] Cassa nazionale d'assicurazione per gl'infortuni sul lavoro, sede centrale in Roma, *Organizzazione del servizio di assistenza agli infortuni* (Rome, 1922), p. 18; ACS: PCM (1917). Bta. 530. No. 2: unnumbered: *Convegno tra i cultori di medicina sociale* to Paolo Boselli, Prime Minister, 15 June 1917; Dr A. Zumaglini, 'La nuova protesi italiana per gli arti', *Rassegna di assicurazini e previdenza sociale* 4/3 (March 1917), pp. 500–24; INPS, 'Il lavoro agricolo e gli invalidi di guerra', *Rassegna di assicurazioni e previdenza sociale. Bollettino mensile della Cassa nazionale d'assicurazione per gli infortuni degli operai sul lavoro* 3/8 (August 1916), pp. 1356–8. On local efforts, see Martina Salvante, '"Thanks to the Great War, the blind gets recognition of his ability to act": the rehabilitation of blinded servicemen in Florence', *First World War Studies* 6/1 (2015), pp. 21–35; Anna Debè and Simonetta Polenghi, 'Assistance and education of mutilated soldiers of World War I: the Italian case', *History of Education and Children's Literature* 11 (2016), pp. 227–46. The revolutionary impact of the First World War

Mutilato di braccio destro con mano prensile,

FIGURE 10. 'Man with disabled right arm with a prehensile hand'.
Source: *Rassegna di assicurazione della previdenza sociale* 4/3 (March 1917), table IX.

now emphasised 'work therapy', retraining through learning new work-related skills and through sport, which was supposed to be helpful to both mind and body. The idea of individuals' 'joy in work', which was a remnant from the prewar era, guided the practices of retraining programmes and served as a harbinger of the revolution in workplace management in the 1920s.[110] In Italy, as in Germany, physicians and insurers alike emphasised understanding the individual psyche of the injured worker or war veteran as a means of finding the most appropriate solution in terms of rehabilitation.[111] Just as efforts

on the treatment of disability and welfare more generally in Italy resembles the experience of the USA at the same time: Beth Linker, *War's waste: rehabilitation in World War I America* (Chicago, 2011).

[110] 'Werkstätten für Ewerbsbeschränkte (Unfallverletze, Invalide, Kriegsbeschädigte)', *Monatsblätter für Arbeiterversicherung* 10/10 (15 October 1916), pp. 151–5.

[111] Gustavo Pisenti, 'Autolesionismo', *Rassegna di assicurazione e previdenza sociale* 6/12 (December 1919), pp. 1477–531; Benassi, 'Le neurosi traumatiche e l'esperienza della guerra', p. 57.

to prevent accidents had become individualised during the war, so, too, had efforts at rehabilitation and redeployment. By addressing the needs of individuals, it was hoped that those individuals could contribute back to their national communities that had been forged during the conflict.

Each government supported the efforts of workers and physicians involved in rehabilitation by calling for employers to improve safety measures so that rehabilitated workers and veterans could return to work without bringing further damage to themselves or others.[112] For the first time, Italian and German administrations articulated that they expected injured workers and soldiers to return to work rather than rely on pensions. As Heather Perry has persuasively shown, during the First World War, understandings of disability were transformed in light of advances in rehabilitation programmes and prosthetics. With proper assistance, it seemed that even disabled bodies could somehow be 'recycled'.[113] Accordingly, echoing the rhetoric of economic mobilisation on the home front, the German government now emphasised that 'accident insurance [would hold] a higher population-political value' if it focused on the reintroduction of workers into employment rather than compensation.[114] As a means to facilitate joining the workforce and as a gesture of gratitude, both governments, like their British counterpart, devised laws that encouraged the employment of injured soldiers and made dismissing them difficult. In 1921, Italy set quotas for employers on the number of war veterans to be hired, and Germany did the same the previous year with its 'Law of the Severely Disabled' (*Schwerbeschädigtengesetz*).[115] Neither government, however, enacted similar legislation for injured workers.

---

[112] 'Beschäftigung von Kriegsbeschägten und Unfallschutz', *Monatsblätter für Arbeiterversicherung* 9/10 (25 October 1915); 'Unfallverhütungsmaßnahmen während der Kriegszeit', *Monatsblätter für Arbeiterversicherung* 11/7–8 (15 August 1917), pp. 90–6; Cassa nazionale d'assicurazione, *Organizzazione del servizio di assistenza agli infortuni*, p. 18.

[113] Heather R. Perry, *Recycling the disabled: army, medicine and modernity in WWI Germany* (Manchester, 2014).

[114] Paul Kaufmann, *Zur Umgestaltung der deutschen Sozialversicherung* (Berlin, 1924), p. 21; 'Die Nachbehandlung von Unfallverletzten und Kriegsbeschädigten', *Monatsblätter für Arbeiterversicherung* 14/3–4 (15 March 1920), pp. 21–31, at p. 21; 'Werkstätten für Ewerbsbeschränkte (Unfallverletze, Invalid, Kriegsbeschädigte)', *Monatsblätter für Arbeiterversicherung* 10/10 (15 October 1916), pp. 151–5; Paul Kaufmann, *Wiederaufbau und Sozialversicherung. Vorschläge zur Änderung der Reichsvericherungsordnung* (2nd improved edn, Berlin, 1920), pp. 16–17; 'La Cassa nazionale infortuni alla Terza conferenza'; 'Insegnamento professionale e rieducazione degli invalidi di guerra', *Rassegna della previdenza sociale* 6/9–10 (September–October 1919), pp. 1219–22.

[115] 'IV. Conferenza interalleata per lo studio delle questioni riguardanti gli invalidi di guerra', *Rassegna della previdenza sociale* 8/1 (January 1921), pp. 147–56, at pp. 150–1; Christopher R. Jackson, 'Infirmative action: the Law of the Severely Disabled in Germany', *Central European History* 26/4 (1993), pp. 417–55. On the contrast between British and German policies on re-employment, see Deborah Cohen, *The war come home: disabled veterans in Britain and Germany, 1914–1939* (Berkeley, CA, 2001).

This legislation emerged in a context in each country in which the experience of shell-shock and male hysteria amongst soldiers had incited a backlash against what was perceived to be weak and feminine behaviour.[116] By contrast, work, and especially industrial labour, was associated with masculine attributes and constituted the way in which men contributed to their societies. This view was especially strong in Germany, where official policy prioritised putting veterans back to work as a counterpoint to receiving war pensions.[117] Accordingly, the Law of the Severely Disabled, which had introduced quotas on hiring injured veterans, was enacted the same year as Germany's Imperial Maintenance Law (*Reichsversorgungsgesetz*) for war pensions. The name of the latter policy reflected this emphasis on returning to work: it was a law on set *Versorgung* (maintenance) for the period of one's disability, and not a means-tested form of *Fürsorge* (welfare) or contributory *Sozialversicherung* (social insurance), which constituted the other two planks of German social law.[118] As Phillipp Jolly, a psychiatrist based at the military hospital in Nuremberg, claimed, the only way to deal with hysterical men was to remove them from the battlefield and gradually put them back into work. The main problem was that, when men had become wounded at war, after taking on a 'short or a long battle for a pension', they would 'mostly become dishabituated from work and would sit around at home or take on entirely unmanly work in the family, while the wife would have to earn money [to subsidise] the meagre pension'. It was imperative, he argued, to put men back to work doing things that would be of use for their 'current and future career', and not occupy them with 'playing games and pointless work'.[119] Similarly, a doctor in Baden claimed that 'The goal of treatment can always only be to make the neurotics' capacity for work useful to the community.' Simply surviving the war was not enough; men needed to be redeployed on the home front as a form of 'economic rehabilitation'. Out of this belief grew the 'Baden system', in which workers were deployed in a make-shift munitions factory next to a military hospital in southern Germany after first undergoing a week of treatment such as therapeutic gymnastics. Doctors at the facility aimed to send soldiers in their care to undertake either this kind of factory work or agricultural labour, and they avoided deployments to work in handicrafts because they were seen as 'feminine' and 'tasteless'.[120]

In the eyes of critics, the problem with veterans receiving pensions rather than returning to work was not simply about a reversal of gender norms. As

---

[116] George L. Mosse, 'Shell-shock as a social disease', *Journal of Contemporary History* 35/1 (January 2000), pp. 101–8.

[117] Deborah Cohen, 'Will to work: disabled veterans in Britain and Germany', in David A. Gerber, ed., *Disabled veterans in history* (2000; rev. edn, Ann Arbor, MI, 2012), pp. 295–322, at p. 301; Geyer, 'Vorbote', p. 245.

[118] Raimund Waltermann, *Sozialrecht* (8th edn, Heidelberg, 2009), pp. 35–7.

[119] Phillipp Jolly, 'Kriegsneurosen', *Archiv für Psychiatrie* 56/2 (1916), pp. 385–444, at pp. 392, 411–12, 438–9.

[120] Quoted in Lerner, *Hysterical men*, p. 127, 151. On the Baden system, see pp. 150–5.

one psychiatrist put it, there was a link between 'the nervous and psychopaths'. Veterans seeking out pensions on psychological grounds were not only 'work-shy'; they were 'antisocial' (*asozial*) and a 'failure in the face of the community'.[121] The fact that the German economy was in complete disarray made this claim especially poignant. Over 6 million soldiers and their family members were eligible for war pensions, which rose as a percentage of the national budget eight times between 1919 and 1922 alone, in part to keep apace of hyper-inflation. By the late 1920s, war pensions accounted for 20 per cent of the national budget (in contrast to just 7 per cent in Britain).[122] Like workers, veterans were meant to return to work as soon as possible in order to fulfil their obligations to society, and the state would help them in this goal through its system of quotas. The impact of this policy – and the expectation upon which it was founded – was significant: at the highpoint of the Great Depression, war veterans were almost twice as likely to retain their jobs because of the special protection afforded to them by the Law of the Severely Disabled.[123]

The backlash against veterans becoming comfortable on pensions, rather than returning to hard labour, extended to the treatment of injured workers in both Germany and Italy. Both governments agreed with insurers and physicians that recipients of accident pensions, and especially those suffering from psychological or neurological impairments, should return to work as soon as possible. In the case of injured workers, concerns about fraud, whether conscious or unconscious, lay at the heart of decisions about limiting access to compensation. Abusing accident benefit meant taking advantage of the social solidarism built up during the war, indicating just how easily citizens could scrounge off the state, as well as each other. In Germany, physicians and insurance bodies had been concerned about this possibility already before the conflict. The conflation of 'accident neurosis', the psychological consequence of accidental trauma, with 'pension neurosis', or the so-called 'battle for pensions', had pointed to anxieties about accident benefit gone wrong.[124] The imperial government previously dismissed calls to cut back pensions for 'accident neurosis'. However, by 1920 it began considering limiting the availability of small pensions for the long-term and partially disabled, which had long been demanded by insurance bodies and physicians as a means to prevent 'pension neurosis'.

[121] Quoted in Stephanie Neuner, *Politik und Psychiatrie: die staatliche Versorgung psychisch Kriegsbeschädigter in Deutschland, 1920–1933* (Göttingen, 2011), pp. 124–5.

[122] David Stevenson, *1914–1918: the history of the First World War* (London, 2004); David Reynolds, *The long shadow: the legacies of the Great War in the twentieth century* (New York, 2014), pp. 209–10. On the ebbs and flows of the monetary crisis in Germany: Gerald D. Feldman, *The great disorder: politics, economics, and society in the German inflation, 1914–1924* (New York, 1996).

[123] Deborah Cohen, 'The war's returns: disabled veterans in Britain and Germany, 1914–1939', in Roger Chickering and Stig Förster, eds., *The shadows of total war: Europe, East Asia and the United States, 1919–1939* (Cambridge, 2003), pp. 113–29, at p. 119.

[124] See Chapter 4.

The Ministry of Labour and the Imperial Insurance Office consulted with the sanitation offices, medical officers and medical experts on neurosis about the question of small pensions on the grounds that accident insurance would need some administrative and financial changes in light of deflation.[125] The accident funds soon began lobbying government on this issue. Along with members of the medical community and the government, they called to reduce the availability of appeals for cases involving small pensions and to grant insurance providers the option to commute lump-sum payments without the agreement of pension recipients in cases involving small pensions. In 1925, the Imperial Insurance Order, which revised social insurance legislation, incorporated both proposals.[126]

The new policy ran against arguments put forward by local governments, trade unions and pensioners' associations, which claimed that most pension recipients relied on this money to live.[127] Significantly, the policy also overlooked the fact that the military had broached the topic of lump-sum payments for neurotic soldiers and, on the evidence of military psychiatrists, decided against adopting them.[128] In this respect, official distinctions between soldiers and workers as deserving and undeserving groups became clear and supported some of the claims made by accident pensioners about their unfair treatment in light of their contributions to the national economy. The new policy on cutting off small pensions for 'accident neurotics' was enacted in 1920, after the Imperial Insurance Office consulted with commercial insurance firms throughout Germany and also considered foreign precedents. Switzerland proved especially instructive, as compensation for 'neurotics' under sickness and accident insurance was only granted as a lump-sum payment following a law in 1911.[129]

---

[125] Erwin Lowey-Hattendorf, *Krieg, Revolution und Unfallneurosen* (Berlin, 1920); BArch: R89: 15113: Erwin Lowey-Hattendorf, 'Die Kapitalabfindung bei Unfallneurosen', 25 November 1920.

[126] 'Das zweite Gesetz über Änderungen in der Unfallversicherung', *Reichs-Arbeitsblatt* (n.s.) nichtamtl. Teil 5/29–30 (8 August 1925), pp. 491–7.

[127] For example: BArch: R3901: 69: Thuringian Economic Ministry, Department for Work and Welfare to the Imperial Labour Minister, 17 January 1924; BArch: R3901: 4508: 189: *Verband der Arbeits-Invaliden* in Düsseldorf to the Imperial Labour Ministry, 17 March 1924; BArch: R3901: 4511: 318–19: *Bezirkskartell der christlichen Gewerkschaften Dortmund-Hörde* to the Imperial Labour Minister, 6 April 1925.

[128] BArch: R3901: 4511: 306–14: Report of Department IB to Department II of the Imperial Labour Ministry, 7 March 1925.

[129] BArch: R3901: 4590: 116–31: Chamber of Trade in Chemnitz to the Imperial Labour Minister, 8 February 1924; BArch: R89: 15114: 1–2: *Verband der Deutschen Berufsgenossenschaften* to the Imperial Labour Minister, 24 November 1924; 3–4: *Verband der landwirtschaftlichen Berufsgenossenschaften*, 10 December 1924; BArch: R89: 15113: unnumbered: Imperial Supervisory Office for Private Insurance to the Imperial Insurance Office, 16 August 1919; Paul Kaufmann, *Neue Ziele der Sozialversicherung* (München-Gladbach, 1921), pp. 9–10; Kaufmann, *Wiederaufbau und Sozialversicherung*, pp. 14–15; Kaufmann, *Zur Umgestaltung der deutschen Sozialversicherung*, pp. 19–20; BArch: R3901: 4511: 306–14: Report of Department IB to Department II of the Imperial Labour Ministry, 7 March 1925; 'Die Kapitalabfindung

This shift to lump-sum payouts was the hallmark of a longer-term movement against the expansion and possible abuse of social insurance. The year after the small-pension issue was decided, therefore, 'accident neurosis' ceased to be a compensable ailment. A ruling of the appeals court based at the Imperial Insurance Office overturned a policy that had been in place – and contested – for over a quarter of a century.[130]

In Italy, insurers, physicians and the government, by way of the semi-public National Accident Insurance Fund, were also concerned about the psychological ailments of injured workers and their effects on rehabilitation and redeployment in the workforce.[131] As in Germany, many who sought to limit fraudulent or spurious claims to compensation from workers employed derogatory languages of race and class to argue that these pension claimants possessed 'degenerate' intellects and morality. Such criticisms also echoed the moral and racial discourses that were widespread in criminology and military psychiatry in Italy.[132] However, in contrast to Germany, fraud provided the main focus of Italian discussions on shifting accident pensioners back to work. These concerns about self-injury and simulation predated the war, when scandals such as the ring of self-harmers in the docks of Naples were brought to light. Moreover, the rhetoric of abuse in Italy and Germany differed slightly, even if criticisms of pension fraud and malingering pointed to a common concern: a betrayal of one's community. While German criticisms of 'neurotics' pointed to their 'anti-social' tendencies, in Italy, suspicious and fraudulent claimants were sometimes seen as 'vampires' who were sucking the metaphorical lifeblood out of pension funds.[133] The reference was a possible hint at anti-Semitism and indicated pension frauds' marginalisation in predominantly Catholic Italy.[134]

---

bei Unfallneurosen', *Monatsblätter der Arbeiterversicherung* 14/11–12 (15 December 1920), pp. 88–95.

[130] BArch: R89: Rep. 322: Nr. 2373: unnumbered: *Morsbach and Betriebskrankenkasse Firma Geb. Hillers v. Nahrungsmittel-Industrie-Berufsgenossenschaft*, Senate of the Imperial Insurance Office, 24 September 1926; Eghigian, *Making security social*, pp. 250–5; Andreas Killen, 'From shock to *Schreck*: psychiatrists, telephone operators and traumatic neurosis in Germany, 1900–26', *Journal of Contemporary History* 38/2 (2003), pp. 201–20.

[131] Cassa nazionale d'assicurazione per gl'infortuni degli operai sul lavoro, sede centrale in Roma, *Assicurazioni e previdenza sociale: per la riforma della legge infortuni* (Rome, 1915), pp. 15, 24–5, 115; Benassi, 'Le neurosi traumatiche e l'esperizena della guerra'.

[132] Kaufmann, *Zur Umgestaltung der deutschen Sozialversicherung*, p. 19; Cesare Biondi, 'Simulazione e provocazione di lesioni e di malattie – conferenze pratiche', *Rassegna d'assicurazione e previdenza sociale* 5/7 (July 1918), pp. 658–68; Benassi, 'Le neurosi traumatiche e l'esperizena della guerra', pp. 52, 54; Bruna Bianchi, *La follia e la fuga: nevrosi di guerra, diserzioni e disobbedienza nell'esercito italiano (1915–1918)* (Rome, 2001); Daniel Pick, *Faces of degeneration: a European disorder, c. 1848–1918* (Cambridge, 1993), pp. 109–54.

[133] 'I vampiri: alcuni documenti', *Rassegna di assicurazioni e previdenza sociale* 5/4 (April 1918), pp. 390–1.

[134] For example: A. Lizier, 'Intorno alla questione giudaica nel medio evo', *Rivista internazionale di scienze sociali e discipline ausiliarie* 19/75 (1899), pp. 381–401, at p. 399. See Angela Connolly,

Yet, it also drew on an established discourse about financial abuses, broadly conceived, whether they stemmed from 'gypsies' in the nineteenth century or various aspects of the 'social question' in the early twentieth, from real-estate speculators preying on the poor, to overreliance on foreign food imports and the mistreatment of Italian emigrants abroad.[135] As in Germany, the small-pension question stood at the centre of discussions about how to prevent bogus claims. It seemed that 'schnapps and cigarette pensions', as they were sometimes called in insurance circles, were merely a bonus to the regular earnings of partially injured workers rather than a necessary and earned recompense for one's injuries.[136] While the backlash against recipients of small pensions was less pronounced than in Germany, it nonetheless resulted in a 1922 revision to the accident insurance law. As a result, compensation was now limited only to individuals who were deemed at least 10 per cent disabled.[137] Unlike in Germany, however, the crackdown on recipients of small pensions did not result in the banning of 'accident neurosis' as a compensable condition. As Italian physicians noted, psychological ailments required treatment on an individual basis, meaning that no general edict would be suitable for all psychologically disturbed workers.[138]

These Italian and German experiences with postwar rehabilitation differed markedly from those in Britain, where the government's expectations for retraining were limited to injured servicemen. And the main concern about war veterans was whether employers would hire them, given the lack of available jobs in the postwar economy and the possibly increased risk of workplace

---

'Psychoanalytic theory in times of terror', *Journal of Analytical Psychology* 48 (August 2003), pp. 407–41; Ken Gelder, *Reading the vampire* (London, 1994), p. 22. On the turn to racial anti-Semitism in Italy during this period, see: Cristina M. Bettin, *Italian Jews from emancipation to the racial laws* (Basingstoke, 2010).

[135] For example: Pietro Ellero, *La questione sociale* (Bologna, 1874), p. 40; Adriano Colocci, *Gli zingari: storia di un popolo errante* (Turin, 1889), p. 43; Luiei Caissotti di Chiusano, 'Il problema degli alloggi popolari: soluzioni', *Rivista internazionale di scienze sociali e discipline ausiliarie* 31/124 (1903), pp. 513–43, at p. 528; Pietro Pisani, 'I problemi dell'emigrazione italiana (continuazione)', *Rivista internazionale di scienze sociali e discipline ausiliarie* 46/184 (1908), pp. 508–18, at p. 508; Giovanni Lazzerini, 'Facciamo da noi!', *Bollettino della R. Società di Orticultura* (4th series) 4/8–9 (1919), pp. 81–4.

[136] Gustavo Pisenti, 'Le piccole indennità d'infortunio innanzi al Consiglio Superiore della previdenza', *Rassegna della previdenza sociale* 8/7 (July 1921), pp. 41–52, at p. 47.

[137] Benassi, 'Le neurosi traumatiche e l'esperienza della guerra', p. 36; 'Proposte di riforma alla legge 31 gennaio 1904, n. 51 (testo unico) per gli infortuni degli operai sul lavoro secondo la discussione svoltasi nel consiglio superiore', *Atti della Cassa nazionale di assicurazione per gli infortuni degli operai sul lavoro: Verbale delle sedute d'insediamento del nuovo Consiglio Superiore* (n.s.) 1914–15/11, pp. 27–35: appendix, p. 6; Pisenti, 'Le piccole indennità'; Vincenzo Magaldi, 'Provvidenze sociali post-belliche', *Rassegna di assicurazioni e previdenze sociale* 5/6 (June 1918), pp. 539–84.

[138] Gustavo Pisenti, 'Autolesionismo', *Rassegna d'assicurazione e previdenza sociale* 6/12 (December 1919), pp. 1477–531; Benassi, 'Le neurosi traumatiche e l'esperienza della guerra', p. 57.

accidents caused by injured soldiers. Officials devised a 'scheme for disabled men' that addressed both issues. They came to an agreement with insurance companies not to increase premiums for workmen's compensation insurance covering injured soldiers, which would make them attractive workers in the eyes of employers. The government agreed to pay insurers directly for any additional cost associated with insuring war veterans against workplace accidents, and it offered to pay uninsured employers the difference in the cost of compensation for these workers.[139] In this regard, the British government's treatment of war veterans emulated its experience with workmen's compensation. Employers and workers alike had contacted the Home Office repeatedly after the enactment of workmen's compensation law on the subject of where 'physically defective workmen' could be insured or whether they could 'contract out' of workmen's compensation law due to the lack or affordability of insurance for them. This question arose, in particular, in cases involving epileptics, but it was also an issue in the employment of the elderly, who were sometimes dismissed due to the expense associated with the risk of their employment. By 1910, the Home Office contacted major insurers to request that they cover higher-risk categories of workers, and the large insurance companies agreed to offer employers contracts for these groups.[140]

In Britain, unlike in Germany and Italy, the government's experience with rehabilitating war veterans did not contribute to a backlash against small pensions and related fraud or neurosis. Small pensions were perhaps not a heated topic in postwar Britain because they were never a widely perceived problem before the war, although doctors treating injured workers came across cases of fraud, malingering and neurosis and although physicians treating soldiers focused on rehabilitating those with psychological ailments such as shellshock. Physicians and insurers in Britain, unlike those in Germany, therefore never called on government to clamp down on cases involving partially injured workers. The primary reason behind the government's lack of interest in small pensions lay, however, within the structure of workmen's compensation law, not with interest-group politics and not with concerns about rehabilitating a war-torn and economically devastated society. Unlike in Germany and Italy, the commutation of accident benefit with lump-sum payments was already

---

[139] TNA: LAB 2/225/ED17097/175/1918: unnumbered: Herbert Austin, 'Scheme for Employment of Disabled Men', 19 November 1918; TNA: PIN 15/2665: unnumbered: Under-Secretary of State at the Ministry of Pensions to the Minister of Pensions and National Insurance, 16 April 1919; *PP* 1919 (Cd 154) XLI.763: 'Disabled Men (Facilities for Employment) Bill: Proposed Expenditure: Memorandum on Expenditure Likely to be Incurred under the Disabled Men (Facilities for Employment) Bill'.

[140] TNA: HO 157/5/659: Under-Secretary of State in the Home Office to the Secretary of Lloyd's Insurance, 2 May 1910; 888: Under-Secretary of State in the Home Office to C. Nash, 21 September 1910; *PP* 1904 (Cd 2208) LXXXVIII.743: 'Home Office Departmental Committee on Workmen's Compensation: Report', p. 782; TNA: HO 157/11/451: Under-Secretary of State in the Home Office to the Clerk to the Guardians, Barnstable, 13 October 1919.

common in Britain. The lack of a set scale of benefit levels in Britain also meant that the amount of compensation payable for injuries targeted the needs of individual workers in accordance with their actual earned salaries. Small pensions and the partial incapacity to work did, however, land on the political agenda in Britain several years later, amidst the economic crisis of the Great Depression.[141]

CODA: THE END OF 'OCCUPATIONAL RISK'?

War experiences transformed understandings of risk. Military and economic mobilisation meant that new categories of workers were exposed to workplace dangers, but it also meant that the divide between the spheres of work and daily life dissolved. The blurring of boundaries between war and work only bolstered the idea that workers were participating in the war effort as members of an explicitly national community. Accidents at work no longer seemed to be about occupational risk; they instead undermined the security of that national community. As a means to address the new risks of this period, all three governments intervened similarly during and after the conflict, and their efforts extended to problems caused by wartime and postwar inflation. The war and its aftermath revealed how much each government had begun to move away from the paradigm of occupational risk and towards seeing workplace accidents as one of many social risks that it would need to manage. And the conflict showed the extent to which individuals had come to see the state as a guarantor in a moment of crisis. In the cases of Britain and Germany, managing the new risks associated with the war meant departing from the principles that had long guided compensation, instead offering injured workers and their families subsidies that had no direct relation to accidents at work. At times, managing these risks also meant excluding certain groups from access to benefits when they seemed to undermine the well-being of the national community, as was the case with accident neurotics in Germany and Italy. Each government's policies towards accidents and compensation during this period seemed to herald a new era in the treatment of risk that was predicated on a national form of social solidarism. However, the measures that each country adopted during the war and its immediate aftermath were either provisional or had their roots in the early 1900s, if not before, as was the case with both agricultural insurance in Italy and accident neurosis in both Italy and Germany. In the wake of the First World War, ideas about occupational risk, individual responsibility and the role of the state in addressing social problems which had earlier guided the accident insurance and workmen's compensation laws remained in place.

Despite rhetoric about social solidarism and caring for national communities forged in the war, therefore, each government proved reluctant to agree to

---

[141] Bartrip, *Workmen's compensation*, pp. 94, 153–7.

new international norms in social legislation that were, for the first time, being comprehensively developed through the auspices of the new International Labour Organization. The ILO was set up in 1919 as a stipulation of the Treaty of Versailles. Its objective was fostering international cooperation in labour relations in order to promote world peace through 'social justice'.[142] The organisation would oversee the 'protection of the worker against sickness, disease and injury arising out of his employment' and effectively take over from the International Labour Office, a smaller international organisation that had ceased activity during the conflict.[143] Over the next decade, the new agency proposed four international conventions on workplace accidents, and Britain, Germany and Italy responded to the proposals with ambivalence. For example, each country signed the 1921 ILO convention that extended to agricultural workers the same right to accident compensation provided to industrial workers in the country where they worked. Britain, Germany and Italy already granted accident benefit to rural labour, meaning that the ILO's 1921 proposal was uncontroversial.[144] On similar grounds, each country agreed to the ILO's 1925 conventions on the equal treatment of migrant workers and the compensation of occupational illnesses.[145] However, all three governments decided to reject the ILO's more expansive 1925 convention on international norms in workmen's compensation.[146] The original proposal had included a clause on compulsory social insurance, a heated topic, especially in Britain.[147] Although the clause was scrapped from the 1925 convention, the agreement nonetheless proved unappealing. In its final format, the convention provided for a minimum standard of compensation for all countries that signed it. Its regulations were extensive: it would allow for the compensation of almost all workers, supervisors and apprentices in all industries, both public and private. It would

---

[142] Sandrine Kott, 'Constructing a European social model: the fight for social insurance in the interwar period', in Jasmien van Daele et al., eds., *ILO histories: essays on the International Labour Organization and its impact on the world during the twentieth century* (Berne, 2010), pp. 173–96, at pp. 176–7.

[143] Treaty of Versailles (1919), Section I, Part XIII.

[144] Workmen's Compensation (Agriculture) Convention (ILO No. 12), 12 November 1921: ratified by the UK on 6 August 1923; Germany on 6 June 1926; and Italy on 1 September 1930, after first modifying its law on compensation for agricultural workers.

[145] Equality of Treatment (Accident Compensation) Convention (ILO No. 19), 1925: ratified by the UK on 6 October 1926; Germany on 18 September 1928; Italy on 15 March 1928. Workmen's Compensation (Occupational Diseases) Convention (ILO No. 18), 1925: ratified by the UK in 1926, but withdrew in 1936; Germany on 18 September 1928; and Italy on 22 January 1934, after first enacting a health insurance law.

[146] Workmen's Compensation (Accidents) Convention (ILO No. 17), 1925. After two decades and the introduction of compulsory accident insurance following the Second World War, Britain ratified the agreement on 28 June 1949. Germany followed suit on 14 June 1955. Italy has not ratified the convention.

[147] *International labour conference: seventh session: Geneva, June 1925: workmen's compensation* (Geneva, 1924).

also apply to the dependants of these workers. The convention also required medical treatment and therapeutic assistance for injured workers, including rehabilitation and prosthetic limbs. Each country that ratified the agreement would be required to extend these measures to its colonies and protectorates. Employers, commercial insurance companies or sickness or disability insurance funds would be required to pay for both compensation and medical assistance. The agreement would require aligning each country's accident system with a new international standard, resulting in the fundamental rethinking of what the social state meant and did.

Various concerns shaped how the ILO conventions were received in each country. Rather than agreeing to new international norms in social legislation, for example, the government in Britain sought finally to settle the question about whether employers should be required to insure workers against accidents. The proposal would effectively overturn a central tenet of the workmen's compensation laws.[148] In Germany, officials instead debated whether to shift authority over workplace accidents from the Imperial Insurance Office, and to a certain extent from the employers' liability funds, to the new Imperial Labour Office in an act of bureaucratic centralisation.[149] And in Italy, the debate about creating a 'global' form of insurance that would address all major ills came to a head after the war, provoking new fears about the 'statalisation' of social problems.[150] On a more essential level, the ideological precepts that underpinned each country's compensation system tempered responses to the movement for binding international norms in the treatment of social risks. In the postwar era of social insurance, as in politics, much remained the same as it had been before war and, in the case of Germany and Italy, revolution and uprisings.

---

[148] The debate was ultimately settled by the 1923 Workmen's Compensation Act and 1925 consolidating Act, which left the policy in place with a few minor adjustments. See TNA: PIN 12/15: unnumbered: Home Office memorandum 'Legislation to Amend the Law as to Workmen's Compensation', 5 August 1920. More information on these debates can be found here: Bartrip, *Workmen's compensation*, pp. 88–119.

[149] A proposal that was, after much interdepartmental wrangling, ultimately rejected. See BArch: R3901: 4527: Unnumbered report of the Imperial Labour Office: n.d. [25 October 1920] 'Umbau der Sozial-Versicherung'; BArch: R3901. 4592: 106–12: *Verband der Beamten und Angestellten der Reichsversicherung*, to the Imperial Labour Minister, 24 January 1924; Kaufmann, *Zur Umgestaltung der deutschen Sozialversicherung*, pp. 6–7.

[150] The result of these discussions was a minor revision to accident insurance in 1922. See ACS: PCM (1916). Bta. 514. Fasc. 12. No. 2: 840: National Accident Insurance Fund, central office in Rome, to the Prime Minister, 30 December 1916; ACS: PCM (1916). Bta. 514. Fasc. 12. No. 2: 136: National Accident Insurance Fund to the Minister of the Interior, 9 October 1916; INAIL: *Atti della Cassa nazionale d'assicurazione per gl'infortuni sul lavoro, sede centrale in Roma: verbale* (n.s.) 26 (31 May–1 June 1920), pp. 91–2; Commissione Reale per il Dopoguerra, *Studi e proposte della prima Sottocommissione presieduta dal Sen. Vittorio Scialoja. Questioni giuridiche, amministrative e sociali: giugno 1918–giugno 1919. Sezione X Legislazione sociale e previdenza (presidente On. Prof. Luigi Rava)* (Rome, 1920), pp. 458–70.

Nonetheless, the conflict had marked a sea change at least in one regard: understandings of individual responsibility for workplace accidents. By the early 1920s, the governments in Italy and Germany began to embrace a form of 'scientific management' which reflected the trend that had begun in Britain under the Health of Munitions Workers Committee during the war.[151] Workplace regulation became more overtly important than it had been before the war, and its newfound centrality was manifested in the health and safety campaigns that were supported directly or indirectly by each government. Significantly, these campaigns emphasised the actions of workers rather than the negligence of employers in securing workplaces. It seemed that wartime research into 'accident proneness' filtered into postwar thinking. For the first time since they introduced laws on accident insurance, the governments in Germany and Italy began comprehensive campaigns to warn workers about the potential risks they could encounter – *and prevent* – at work. Moreover, both governments employed the same method to achieve their goal: cartoon images of workers confronting specific risks (Figure 11 and Figure 12). In Britain, 'safety first' campaigns had advocated the use of similar images even before the conflict. By the early 1920s, in the form of the Royal Society for the Prevention of Accidents and the Safety First Association, they worked together with government to encourage workplaces to adopt related practices. The campaigns in each country appear to have adapted the practice from the United States. Towards the end of the war, American companies, in conjunction with the National Safety Council, had begun relying on visual techniques used by advertising agencies in order to alert workers to possible dangers, but also to encourage them to take action to prevent accidents.[152] Britain, like its continental counterparts, would increasingly shift towards this idiom of individual worker responsibility in securing the workplace.

What seems so novel about this postwar movement for safety regulation is that it focused on *individual* workers. Yet, the ideas behind the movement were not entirely new. On the one hand, the practice was a

---

[151] Mary Nolan, *Visions of modernity: American business and the modernization of Germany* (Oxford, 1994), pp. 30–57.

[152] For example: 'Manifesti murali e prevenzione della cecità in dipendenza d'infortuni sul lavoro', *Rassegna della previdenza sociale* 9/9 (September 1922), pp. 115–18; Georg Müller, 'Unfallverhütung und Gewerbehygiene', *Reichs-Arbeitsblatt* (n.s.) nichtamtl. Teil 5/31 (16 August 1925), pp. 505–8, 508–14; 'Safety first', *British Medical Journal* (19 June 1920), p. 848. On the British movement: Mike Esbester, 'Organizing work: company magazines and the discipline of safety', *Management and Organizational History* 3/3–4 (2008), pp. 217–37; Roger Cooter, 'The moment of the accident: culture, militarism and modernity in late-Victorian Britain', in Roger Cooter and Bill Luckin, eds., *Accidents in history: injuries, fatalities and social relations* (Amsterdam, 1997), pp. 107–57, at pp. 127–8. On the American movement: Mark Aldrich, *Safety first: technology, labor and business in the building of American work safety, 1870–1939* (Baltimore, 1997), pp. 137–41.

FIGURE 11. Italian safety image (1922): 'Don't trust your eyes to your workmate'. *Source*: 'Manifesti murali', p. 115.

continuation of the wartime emphasis on workplace safety in each country. On the other, appealing directly to workers' sensibilities with these warning messages implicated workers in the consequences of their actions. In some ways, the posters and safety campaigns denoted a return to widespread ideas about fault and responsibility of the mid nineteenth century, before the invention of 'occupational risk' and the introduction of compensation laws, when workers alone were held financially (and morally) responsible for the majority of workplace accidents. To be sure, the First World War and its immediate aftermath furthered the movement from treating accidents as the consequences of specific occupational risks and towards seeing them as social risks that affected all workers – and not just those in dangerous industries – and that should be shared by national communities and governed by the state. Military and economic mobilisation meant that new categories of workers were exposed to dangers, but it also meant that the divide between the spheres of war, work and daily life dissolved.

FIGURE 12. German safety image (1925): 'Watch out or you'll get lead poisoning'.
Source: Müller, 'Unfallverhütung und Gewerbehygiene', p. 520.

As a means to address these new risks, all three governments took similar action during and after the war, from introducing new safety provisions to adjusting compensation amounts to account for inflation. The emphasis on workplace regulation during and after the war suggests, however, that the meaning and nature of occupational risk remained contested, and discourses about blame and accountability had never disappeared entirely. They had instead been reconstituted and stretched in various ways, from individual court cases to regulations on health and safety. Moreover, just as the idea of occupational risk emerged across Europe almost simultaneously in the last third of the nineteenth century, its rearticulation during and after the war appears to have been a common European, and possibly international, experience. Nonetheless, as the cases of Britain, Germany and Italy demonstrate, the ways in which each country identified and reformulated occupational risk, and concomitant responsibilities for both individuals and the state, differed – and sometimes markedly.

Conclusion

In the autumn of 1898, the Oxford law professor Albert Venn Dicey delivered a series of lectures at Harvard University on what seems, at first glance, a rather uninspiring theme: 'The Development of English Law during the Nineteenth Century in Connection with the Course of Public Opinion in England'. Despite the drab title, what Dicey proposed was a passionate polemic. The constitutional lawyer saw Britain moving away from an era of individualism, marked by a traditional form of liberalism that prioritised negative freedoms, towards a new age characterised by collectivism. The timing of the lecture series, a year after Britain had enacted its first workmen's compensation policy, was significant. For Dicey, 1897 was the moment when 'legislation took a completely new turn'. This new legal era inverted the model of societal progress that had been outlined several decades earlier by the British comparative jurist Henry Maine. According to Maine, modern societies were based on the rights of individuals to agree contracts, and not on arbitrary distinctions of social status that were customarily tied to kinship – that is, to community. For Dicey, the 1897 law had put Britain on an altogether new path because it meant that 'the rights of workmen in regard to compensation for accidents have become a matter *not* of contract, but of status'.[1] The collectivist age had begun, and the risk of workplace accidents was shared across society.

Dicey's conception of the transition from individualism towards collectivism echoes the story of the socialisation of risks put forward in numerous accounts of modernisation theory. It also maps onto the account of neo-Foucauldian scholars of the increasing legislative intervention into the 'social' which would

---

[1] Author's italics. A. V. Dicey, *Lectures on the relation between law and public opinion in England* (2nd edn, London, 1914), pp. 282–4; Henry Sumner Maine, *Ancient law: its connection with the early history of society and its relation to modern ideas* (1861; London, 1908), pp. 149–51.

mark modernity. This coincidence is, of course, not accidental; a century after Dicey, others were similarly anxious about what they saw as the anti-liberal tendencies of the welfare states that had crystallised across the globe after the Second World War. The question remains, however, whether risk was indeed 'socialised' or, in Dicey's phrase, 'collectivised'. Moreover, was this process universal, with the result that all modern societies became 'risk societies'? As we have seen, the last third of the nineteenth century saw a radical reformulation of ideas about individual responsibility and social risk. It implied a new role for the state, and a novel understanding about the function of the law, in governing what were perceived as social problems. The state became what I call a 'social state', with a primary role as a mediator of social risks: through everyday interactions, government and members of society carved out a new role for the state as risk manager, alongside new roles for individuals as both objects at and subjects of risk. As a consequence, the risk of occupational accidents was shared on a new, industrial basis and was gradually extended to a wide variety of social groups. After the First World War, the majority of the workforce in Britain, Germany and Italy, as in many other countries across Europe, could claim compensation for occupational accidents, regardless of the cause. Fault was no longer an issue, as compensation became a social right.

If, however, we look closely at the processes involved in making accident compensation a social right, the various iterations of the 'collectivist' story become less persuasive. On the one hand, as the cases of Britain, Germany and Italy show, governments managed risk differently for a variety of reasons. Moreover, the governments in each country gradually and self-consciously developed their own mode for addressing questions about the role of the state in regulating social problems: each government came to develop its own culture of risk. There was, therefore, no single story of a path towards collectivism. Common to all three governments, however, was the legal gaze with which risk was handled, from initial discussions about the 'accident problem' to later debates about the application of the compensation policies. From this legal perspective, questions about risk were always tied to considerations of responsibility. Risk and responsibility were two sides of the same coin: every accident, and every claim for redress, would need to take into account what was at the same time a philosophical and a technical conundrum that encapsulated questions about morality and agency as well as dilemmas about cause and effect. On the other hand, and precisely due to its legal nature, the governance of risk transformed and reformed over time depending on specific historical contexts, interpretations and circumstances. As a consequence, interpretations of social problems were always subject to modification. For this reason, it was possible for each government to move from viewing accidents as the natural outcome of occupational risk to seeing them as one of many social risks that would need to be borne collectively. And it was possible to retreat from expansive understandings of social risk and return to ideas about individual responsibility.

The treatment of workplace risk, therefore, points to broader issues of governance and concomitant statehood. It illuminates the ways in which modern governments attempt to manage what they identify as 'risks' by learning about social problems and acting on them, taking into consideration both tangible constraints, as well as cultural and political values. From this perspective, the story of workplace accidents confirms a more general paradigm of state building through making 'social problems' into social policy.[2] However, the British, German and Italian experiences with workplace accidents also expose the contingencies within that process: learning about the accident problem did not mean that these governments would act at all, let alone in a particular way. Officials were constantly confronted with questions about whether and how to address workplace risk. And they responded with particular assumptions and values – even if they argued, as in Britain, that they were not involved in administering the details of the policies. The case of workplace accidents reveals the essential role which governmental bureaucracies play in creating social states, as well as the contingency and emotionality involved in the process – even though administrations may feign 'indifference' to particular political and social agendas or claim to be 'objective' about the matter at hand.[3] That apparent rationality, which was carefully embedded in legal reasoning and administrative arguments in the framing and perpetual reformulation of the accident problem, often masked the shadow side of social risk: questions about blame.

Sociologists and, to a certain extent, historians have aimed to chart a genealogy of risk by tracing it back to a primordial distinction between risk and security.[4] According to this thinking, although the word 'risk' had much older roots, the modern concept emerged in Europe around the sixteenth century. Before this time, understandings of possible misfortune abounded but were predicated on divine action (or inaction). Amidst growing faith in human rationality, ideas about risk came to be positive. By taking a 'gamble', for example in purchasing life insurance or stock shares, there was a chance of hitting the jackpot, even if that chance was predicated on the possibility of losing money (or even a life!).[5] In this light, by the twentieth century, societies could come to agree on 'acceptable risks', such as cancers linked to the use of potentially beneficial technologies like pesticides and nuclear energy.[6] Taking a risk was a

---

[2] Oliver MacDonagh, 'The nineteenth century revolution in government: a reappraisal', *Historical Journal* 1 (1958), pp. 52–67; Niklas Luhmann, *Political theory in the welfare state* (Berlin, 1990), pp. 47–50.

[3] Michael Herzfeld: *The social production of indifference: exploring the symbolic roots of Western bureaucracy* (Chicago, 1992), pp. 81–2.

[4] For example: Wolfgang Bonß, *Unsicherheit und Gewissheit in der Moderne* (Hamburg, 1995); Niklas Luhmann, *Risk: a sociological theory*, trans. Rhodes Barrett (New York, 1993), pp. 19–20.

[5] Gerd Gigerenzer et al., *The empire of chance: how probability changed science and everyday life* (Cambridge, 1989), pp. 19–26. Luhmann, *Risk*, pp. 8–11, 30, 46, 81, 166–72, 191–2.

[6] William Boyd, 'Genealogies of risk: searching for safety, 1930s–1970s', *Ecology Law Quarterly*, 39 (2012), pp. 895–987, at pp. 964–77; Tom Barker and Jonathan Simon, eds., *Embracing risk: the changing culture of insurance and responsibility* (Chicago, 2002).

means to secure an unknown, yet predictable, future, even if that future could not, in reality, ever be managed. It could, however, be insured.[7]

This connection between risk and security is inherently epistemological: it is a problem about knowledge and how to act on it. In this light, social *security*, that neologism of the twentieth century, and compensation are legal and administrative forms of redress for foreseeable, but unavoidable, harms. Owing to this epistemological nature of risk, some have even argued that efforts to secure the future (that is, to make it 'carefree', or *sē* [without] *curitās* [care]) only lead to further insecurity and, as a result, further efforts to engender security.[8] Alongside this binary of risk and security, however, lingers another logic, a rationality based on ethics. Beneath a rhetoric of social risk or social solidarism lay the reappropriation of what could also be cast as individual responsibilities. One could even contend that languages of risk embody new moral norms of acceptable behaviour, for example, by distinguishing good citizens from their irresponsible counterparts who make poor 'lifestyle choices' or negligent errors at work. According to this thinking, deeply rooted social inequalities based on class, race and gender disappear from view, as new norms of correct behaviour take centre stage.[9] By exploring the processes through which risk was managed over time and in different contexts, this book has suggested another reading which complements the genealogical tale of security and nuances these moral narratives of inclusion and exclusion. In the case of workplace accidents, risk and responsibility formed two poles on a common spectrum along which social questions could be rendered and recast in an unending range of iterations.[10] The paradox of social risk was its enduring connection between the individual and the community, for example, between individual obligations to the local community of the workplace, and communal obligations to share social harms such as occupational accidents. Across Europe in the late nineteenth century, this connection came to be seen as both defined and governed by the state. Nonetheless, along this spectrum, responses to misfortune took form in different ways in different circumstances. The meaning of risk was always specific to individual historical, cultural and institutional contexts that embodied a range of assumptions about personal agency, social responsibility and government as the manager of collective security. The law played a key role in mediating these

---

[7] François Ewald, 'Insurance and risk', in Graham Burchell et al., eds., *The Foucault effect: studies in governmentality* (Chicago, 1991), pp. 197–210.

[8] John T. Hamilton, *Security: politics, humanity and the philology of care* (Princeton, NJ, 2013), pp. 3–5, 25–6. See also Robert Castel, *L'insécurité sociale: qu'est-ce qu'être protégé?* (Paris, 2003); Julia Moses and Eve Rosenhaft, 'Moving targets: risk, security and the social in twentieth-century Europe', *Social Science History* 9/1 (2015), pp. 25–37.

[9] Deborah Lupton, *Medicine as culture: illness, death and the body* (1994; 3rd edn, London, 2012), pp. 92–4; François Ewald, *L'État providence* (Paris, 1986). See also: Nikolas Rose, *Powers of freedom: reframing political thought* (Cambridge, 1999), pp. 259–63.

[10] See also: Ian Hacking, 'Risk and dirt', in Richard V. Ericson and Aaron Doyle, eds., *Risk and morality* (Toronto, 2003), pp. 22–37, at pp. 22–3.

assumptions about ethics and formed the basis for how risk was managed in each country.

The case of accident compensation in Britain, Germany and Italy therefore suggests that we need to move beyond methods founded on modernisation theory, as well as narratives of collectivisation or the socialisation of risk, and towards an approach that takes fuller account of the diverse and complexly interdependent factors that shape social welfare. This book has shown that various aspects informed how workplace accidents became an object of social policy. Conceptions within each government about the role of the state and the function of the law in mediating social problems proved decisive. Nonetheless, many other factors shaped both the introduction of the accident laws and, significantly, their everyday implementation, which in turn informed how social legislation came to be regarded as a matter for the state. These included the nature of each country's legal system, the configuration of political institutions and economic structures, such as levels of industrialisation, and the availability and nature of market-based and alternative private options for compensation. Yet, less concrete factors played a role as well, including the availability of specialist expertise, social structures, such as the relationship between workers and employers, as well as the relative strength of workers' and employers' organisations, and the availability of information on workplace accidents from both domestic and transnational sources. The influence of these features varied from country to country and over time. Nonetheless, broad similarities governed how workplace accidents became a matter for social legislation because of the juridical nature of the problem at hand. Each government found that it needed to approach questions about occupational risk from a legal and administrative gaze. As a result, Britain, Germany and Italy encountered the same three phases when developing and refining their early laws for the compensation of workplace accidents. Through the process, the government in each country helped to create the idea that its state was not only real, but that it was a kind of social state to which citizens could turn in times of hardship.

Each country first experienced a planning phase that involved two activities: recognising a problem with occupational accidents and looking for a solution to that problem. Following the introduction of new technologies, and mechanisation in particular, contemporaries began, from the beginning of the nineteenth century, to reflect on workplace accidents as negative aspects of modernity rather than the consequences of fate or an individual's actions. The fact that accident numbers were increasing along with new technologies and that accidents, such as railway derailments, were often more spectacular and disastrous than before, meant that administrators in each country felt compelled to act. Nonetheless, the configuration or inadequacy of administrative structures limited the available options. In Germany and Italy, moreover, governments initially exhibited a strong preference for minimal intervention in social affairs. Italy and Germany only unified in 1861 and 1871, respectively, and the Italian and German states approached workplace accidents from the perspective of economic management. As a result, they enacted few laws that addressed accidents directly, choosing instead to devolve to employers substantial authority over accident prevention and the provision of care for injured workers. The British government also avoided approaching the issue of workplace accidents with comprehensive and interventionist policies and instead pursued a programme of investigation, supplemented by minimal regulations that primarily targeted young and female workers. All three governments in the early and mid nineteenth century proceeded from the firmly rooted assumption that workplace accidents were a matter of personal responsibility that was defined and addressed – however implicitly – in the labour contract, which workers, as free and rational agents, could choose to accept. They therefore saw a problem with occupational accidents only in special cases – those involving large numbers of workers or the 'vulnerable', that is, women and children – that spoke to popular humanitarian sensibilities about communal responsibilities.

By the mid nineteenth century, however, the British, German and Italian governments began to conceptualise workplace accidents in general, and not merely those involving seemingly dependent members of society, as political problems. Accidents were increasingly seen as matters that should be studied with the expert knowledge of legal scholars, scientists and statisticians, and with the aid of national factory inspectors in Britain and local and regional government in Germany and Italy. New 'tools' of governmental knowledge, such as statistics,[11] and growing specialisation within the civil service in each country became important means to learn about the accident problem. The information gathered from these sources further facilitated thinking about accidents in terms of risks that were inherent to work and therefore part and parcel of 'modern industry' – rather than as dangers that individual workers could avoid by acting responsibly. Moreover, a corollary of the process of professionalisation, in which governments increasingly drew on expertise based in civil society, was the acceleration of transfers of ideas about accidents through transnational networks. Transnational organisations that specialised in statistics, the study of industrial hygiene and the prevention of and insurance for accidents played crucial roles in transmitting information about occupational risk and forging common understandings of the concept across borders. Intergovernmental exchanges of information about policies on workplace accidents bolstered these understandings.

By the end of the century, each government began contemplating compulsory, no-fault compensation as a possible solution to workplace accidents. At this point, all three governments possessed institutional capacities that facilitated acting on workplace risk. And British, German and Italian administrators had come to share similar conceptions of occupational risk as a result

[11] Peter Becker and William Clark, eds., *Little tools of knowledge: historical essays on academic and bureaucratic practices* (Ann Arbor, MI, 2001).

of their common experiences in recognising accidents as political problems and also due to transnational and international connections. However, each government spearheaded a unique compensation policy that reflected a deeply entrenched national culture for governing risk. Officials' values about the role of the state in regulating social problems played the most important role here. Yet, their concerns about a variety of more specific factors, such as the nature of existing schemes for compensation, the aspirations of particular groups within civil society and the nature of the national economy, also proved significant.

When devising the compensation laws, all three governments self-consciously reflected on their actions against the backdrop of international developments in social policy and adopted a rhetoric of national difference. This rhetoric revealed governmental aspirations to create compensation policies that addressed nationally specific objectives and issues. In Germany, officials were especially anxious to address the accident problem while simultaneously securing economic stability and governmental authority in the newly unified country. The government's concerns about economic and social stability, as well as the deeply rooted links between government and the mining sector, meant that administrators were particularly open to adopting a corporatist system of accident insurance which derived from practices in that industry. In Italy, by contrast, officials were primarily concerned with addressing what they perceived to be problems with national economic and political backwardness in the newly unified country, and they recognised that adopting a policy of accident insurance could foster credibility not only for the central government but also for the country as a whole in the eyes of foreign and domestic observers. At the same time, administrators were anxious not to depart too dramatically from liberal economic and political traditions within Italy, and they reflected on both the British and German compensation systems when deciding to steer a middle course between the two. The fact that Italy had adopted a voluntary accident insurance fund years before these debates also contributed to administrators' decision to adopt a system of compulsory accident insurance.

Officials in Britain also observed developments in Germany, and, like those in Italy, they were concerned about falling behind international economic and political developments. Administrators in Britain were also concerned about the arguments of a variety of groups, such as friendly societies, trade unionists and small employers, who believed that compulsory insurance would run against their interests. The fact that the British government lacked strong links with the mining sector and had not established a national accident insurance fund also contributed to the decision to adopt a policy of workmen's compensation rather than accident insurance. Above all, however, the British government was anxious about departing from the common-law and liberal political traditions that had governed the country for centuries, which prioritised individual responsibility rather than state action in resolving problems in civil society. In this light, Britain's workmen's compensation policy reflected a peculiarly British mode of risk management.

The second phase in this process of making social states through managing workplace accidents was characterised by administration. It was in this period that the British government's methods for regulating risk diverged more clearly from those in Germany and Italy. After enacting policies on accident compensation, all three governments were confronted with questions about interpreting the law. Greater involvement in the administration of risk brought each government to recognise more sources of uncertainty, which included questions about the meaning of accidents and danger and about the social and geographical boundaries of risk. As a result, compensation was granted more leniently and to a wider segment of the population in each country. Although all three countries shared this process of reinterpreting and extending the policies through a legal gaze, each government differed in its approach to these matters. In fact, it was during this phase in the development of the compensation policies that each administration relied more and more on its own experts and less on the shared assumptions and findings of transnational networks.

Britain, Germany and Italy shared this process of interpretation and administration, but, for the most part, acted in parallel rather than in unison. The British government, unlike its German and Italian counterparts, consistently declined requests to make decisions about the interpretation of the law and insisted that judges and physicians deal with this aspect of policy administration. Due to the structure of the German system of accident insurance, in which the Imperial Insurance Office acted as the final court of appeal, civil servants in Berlin consistently interpreted the law. With the assistance of legal and scientific experts, such as the physicist Hermann von Helmholtz, they answered the question 'what is an accident?' in terms of the law. By contrast, the Italian government relied on courts of cassation and tribunals for decisions about accident insurance. However, it closely monitored judicial arguments, and it consulted legal experts when revising the policy. Unlike the British government, the German and Italian governments frequently articulated their interpretations of the law in the public sphere, such as in domestic, transnational and international congresses and through governmental publications, and they closely followed the discussions of transnational communities of legal and scientific experts. In this respect, both governments acted on their anxieties about garnering legitimacy at home – and prestige abroad – through their treatment of the accident problem. In addition, both the German and Italian governments closely monitored incidents involving fraud and malingering. The British government, by contrast, registered early concerns voiced by county court judges about unscrupulous or fraudulent insurance companies, but it did not act on these.

These differences in each country's approach to administration reflected underlying concerns about the purpose of the state in managing 'social problems'. In Germany, officials continued to worry about maintaining social

stability through social insurance while, at the same time, effectively managing
the economy. It was therefore imperative in administrators' eyes to ensure that
all participants in the system of accident insurance understood how it operated and acted fairly within that system. It seemed that the effective operation
of accident insurance would determine whether government appeared com-
petent and legitimate to citizens and whether Germany seemed economically
and politically advanced in the eyes of foreign observers. In Italy, officials were
similarly anxious about the smooth operation of accident insurance, as its failings could point directly to the incompetence of the government in Rome in
overseeing the new country. This line of thinking amongst the German and
Italian governments held significant implications for resolving questions about
social security, individual responsibility and the attribution of blame, as evidenced by the heated debates in both countries about fraud and malingering.
Yet, the government in Italy, unlike that in Germany, sought to stand above
the fray in these discussions. It had never attempted to oversee the details of
the accident insurance system. As some claimed when first debating whether
to enact social insurance, Italy should attempt to find a compromise between
'state socialism' and 'liberalism'. As a consequence, Rome relied largely on the
existing legal system and attempted to maintain aspects of the young country's
liberal political heritage. The government in Britain resembled Italy in these
respects, and it maintained a policy of noncommitment when specific questions
about the administration of workmen's compensation arose.

Despite these dissimilarities in administrative practices, the policies in each
country were predicated on the same concept: occupational risk. Officials in
each country thus came to similar conclusions when confronted with questions about to whom the law on accident compensation should be extended
and whether compensation should be seen as a *social* right that served to
address workplace risks in general rather than the risks associated with 'dangerous industries' in particular. As in earlier governmental discussions about
the meaning of occupational risk, these later decisions were greatly influenced
by international and transnational exchanges, in particular, about the extension of accident compensation policies to migrant workers. It was during
these negotiations about interpreting the compensation laws that each government's conception of risk began to shift from emphasising dangers at work
towards focusing on the needs and wishes of society as a whole. Workplace risk
appeared to be a common phenomenon, affecting not only railway shunters
but also shop workers, and the findings of doctors, lawyers and other experts
only served to confirm this impression.

Nonetheless, officials decided against the mass extension of accident compensation to all workers. In all three countries, they continued to prioritise
workers in traditional industries rather than those in white-collar professions.
In addition, each government prioritised migrant workers in cases that were
most important for their national economy. Moreover, in Italy, administrators
were reluctant to extend accident insurance to workers in agriculture, as they

constituted the majority of the economy. Despite broad similarities in responses to occupational risk, therefore, different cultures of risk management determined how each government acted. These cultures reflected officials' views about their own state as a social state and implied specific assumptions about the role of individuals in taking responsibility for their lives as well as the lives of those around them. As a result, the majority of the British and German workforces were entitled to accident benefit by 1914, while a fraction of those in Italy could claim the same. Moreover, all recipients of accident pensions were subject to the same systems that had been in place since the 1880s and 1890s. As before, the British government allowed civil society to provide insurance or payments out of pocket by choice, while Germany required all new categories of workers to join a regimented system of state-regulated employers' liability funds. Italian employers continued to choose from a variety of state-sanctioned commercial insurance and mutual funds when insuring their workers.

The final phase in this early episode of governing risk through social policy was characterised by consolidation, and it began during the First World War and stabilised in the mid 1920s. The experience of war had a profound impact on perceptions of occupational accidents and the role of different population groups within the workforce. The war meant that greater numbers of women, the elderly and youths worked in factory settings, which influenced both the perception of workplace accidents and their numbers. The war also meant that each country was confronted with new types of work-related accidents, such as those related to military aviation. The new structural situation that war brought with it, in the form of corporatist arrangements for military and economic mobilisation, meant that all three governments were more invested than previously in managing the risks of workplace accidents. Moreover, the experience of war meant that officials saw that they needed to address risks related to work because, more than ever before, work was a matter for the national community rather than individual workers and their families. As such, the state came to be seen in explicitly national terms, and seemed obliged to care for its injured workers on the home front, just as it did for those on the battlefield.

The violence of war meant, however, that normal workplace accidents lost political salience. Each government focused on addressing the exceptional risks of wartime and their impact on workers that previously lay beyond the remit of the compensation laws. In all three countries, but especially in Italy and Germany, this wartime focus on special cases involving workplace accidents contributed to an exclusionary discourse that focused on specific groups of workers as especially accident-prone or likely to defraud pension funds and therefore dangerous for the body politic. At the same time, the war led each government to focus on the disabilities of soldiers and veterans – as workers on the battlefront – and revealed how the ideas behind accident compensation had begun to filter into domains beyond the workplace. Long-standing questions about occupational risk and personal responsibility transformed with the outbreak of military conflict, and all three governments came to focus on the growing expectations of recipients of accident pensions and workers who supported the war effort on the home front. Each government's culture of risk management, alongside the social, economic and political circumstances within each country, shaped how officials responded to the vast challenges of this period. The German administration had long seen its function in addressing workplace accidents as part of a more general role in governing the economy. When Germany introduced subsidies for severely disabled accident pensioners during inflation, it continued this tradition. By contrast, by introducing pension subsidies, thereby intervening directly in labour relations, the British government seemed to break with its earlier stance on managing risk. The exigencies of the wartime and postwar economy brought this momentary lapse in earlier practices. It was also, therefore, possible during the war for the Italian government finally to extend accident insurance to agricultural workers. As a result, it assuaged longer-term dissatisfaction about their exclusion from the law. Nonetheless, agricultural workers were subjected to the same system of accident benefit that had been in place for decades.

The war and its aftermath had contradictory effects on the governance of workplace risk. After the war, workers returned to the factories and took up their former jobs, meaning that the employment of inexperienced women, youths and the elderly was no longer an issue for the three governments. Moreover, the British and German pension subsidies stopped once the economic crisis had stabilised in each country. Debates about the abuse of accident insurance, which focused on so-called 'accident neurotics' and 'pension vampires' in Germany and Italy, also subsided after the war, in part in response to amendments to each country's policy on accident compensation. The experiences of this period of wartime and postwar instability did, however, alter the governance of workplace risk in one regard. The economic mobilisation on the home front, along with the demobilisation of millions of injured veterans, led each government to emphasise workplace regulation, including the related issues of industrial efficiency and safety at work, as well as retraining, which changed the general tone of discussions about occupational accidents. In this respect, the war was a crucial turning point, as it brought all three governments to begin prioritising health and safety over accident compensation. Along with this changed emphasis came new considerations about personal agency in preventing accidents, revealing that the binary partner to occupational (and social) risk – individual responsibility – had been recast once again.

It was the nationally specific instantiation of this core binary that lent stability to each country's social state. What officials in the nineteenth century had regarded as their unique national models of social statehood, adopted in the 1880s and 1890s and based on social insurance or workmen's compensation, remained in place over subsequent decades. Over the entirety of this period, none of the three governments opted to depart from these initial policies. It is telling, therefore, that transnational observation proved less important for decision making after officials had selected a policy to address the 'accident problem'. The spectrum that bound questions of risk and individual responsibility united Britain, Germany and Italy in a common experience when engaging with the social problems surrounding accidents at work. Nonetheless, each government approached this spectrum with its own style of governance, and addressed every question about risk and responsibility from the specific legal and administrative gaze that derived from that style. For the British, German and Italian governments, therefore, the basic decision in favour of social insurance or workmen's compensation reflected profound differences of opinion about the role of government in managing workplace risk and, on a more fundamental level, regulating the social sphere. As the case of workplace accidents reveals, the origin of the social state in Germany was always about social insurance, based on forward planning and governmental intervention, in contradistinction to the mixed system in Britain that is based on taxation, direct contributions and interpersonal compensation.[12] Social provision in Italy, based on a combination of public and private insurance and limited governmental involvement, was situated between these two poles – precisely because Italian officials sought to carve out their own path that emulated aspects of governance in both Britain and Germany.

These early policy choices – and the ideals about statehood upon which they were based – shaped how each government dealt with the accident problem and related questions of risk in subsequent years. How officials responded to these questions remained open to historical circumstance, and new queries were cast along the broad spectrum of social risk and individual responsibility. Yet, each country retained the same basic approach to spreading and managing occupational risk. As the interwar period progressed, therefore, the British government continued to debate whether social insurance should replace workmen's compensation in order to spread social risk, once and for all, on a broader basis. Yet, it remained unable to resolve the issue. The 1934 Nicholson Act required coal mines to insure their workers against accidents, and, in 1938, a Royal Commission was set up to investigate extending insurance to all sectors of the economy. However, the Commission was postponed in 1940 due to the outbreak of the Second World War, and it would never reconvene. During this period, therefore, Britain saw more change in its treatment of occupational illness. Like its counterparts in Germany and Italy, the British government continued to extend coverage to more diseases, for example, by setting up a scheme in 1931 to compensate sufferers of asbestosis.[13] Pressure from international organisations continued to play a role in these considerations

[12] E. P. Hennock, *The origin of the welfare state in England and Germany, 1850–1914: social policies compared* (Cambridge, 2007).

[13] P. W. J. Bartrip, *Workmen's compensation in twentieth-century Britain: law, history and social policy* (Aldershot, 1987), pp. 160–1, 168–71; P. W. J. Bartrip, *The way from dusty death: Turner & Newall and the regulation of occupational health in the British asbestos industry, 1890s–1970* (London, 2001), pp. 1–30, 84–8.

about the nature of occupational risk. The International Labour Organization, in particular, pushed throughout the 1920s for the extension of accident benefit to various groups, such as migrant and rural workers, and it would continue into the 1930s and beyond to press for compensation for occupational illnesses such as silicosis.[14]

In Germany, despite the swift and dramatic transition in 1933 to a new style of government under National Socialism, accident insurance remained more or less intact and continued the framework put in place under the Weimar Republic, including the 1925 codification of accident insurance and extension of compensation to occupational illnesses. The language around social welfare had, of course, changed, as it had in Fascist Italy, as the notion of a 'people's community' took rhetorical pride of place. In this context, the state seemed the apotheosis of that community, and individuals were made, more than ever before, responsible for fulfilling their obligations to the state as well as to each other. Nonetheless, the essential structure of accident insurance stayed in place, with the employers' funds continuing as they had since the 1880s. Nominally, they had lost their right to self-administration after being subjected to the rule of the *Führer*. The most significant repercussions of this transition stemmed from the exigencies of economic and military mobilisation for the Second World War. On the one hand, Germany saw a growing disregard for workplace safety in certain sectors, such as mining, in an effort to increase productivity.[15] On the other hand, as in the First World War, Germany saw a wide range of citizens, both young and old, male and female, join the workforce, sparking anxieties about protecting these members of the 'people's community'. In 1942, therefore, the government completed the gradual extension that had been ongoing since the 1880s: all workers would now be covered by accident insurance. The policy would no longer cover *Betriebsunfälle*, accidents associated with particular businesses, but it would apply to *Arbeitsunfälle*, workplace accidents. The link between dangerous trades and social insurance had finally been broken.[16]

As in Germany, in Italy, the move to extend accident insurance that had begun during the First World War, with the inclusion of rural labour, would continue under the Fascist government. In 1928, a national health insurance policy was finally adopted, with the result that occupational illnesses received coverage the following year – after decades of debate. Similarly, the long-standing moves to centralise and simplify accident insurance were finally achieved in

[14] Paul-André Rosental, 'La silicose comme maladie professionnelle transnationale', *Revue Française des Affaires Sociales* 2–3 (2008), pp. 255–77.
[15] Josef Boyer, *Unfallversicherung und Unternehmer im Bergbau: die Knappschafts-Berufsgenossenschaft, 1885–1945* (Munich, 1995), pp. 240–8.
[16] Michael Stolleis, 'Historische Grundlagen: Sozialpolitik in Deutschland bis 1945', in Hans Günter Hockerts et al., eds., *Geschichte der Sozialpolitik in Deutschland seit 1945*, vol. I: *Grundlagen der Sozialpolitik* (Baden-Baden, 2001), pp. 199–332, at pp. 320–4.

1926, when the number of registered accident funds was reduced, and again in 1933, when they were organised centrally in the new National Fascist Institute against Workplace Accidents (INFAIL). In part, these initiatives were connected to novel ideas about state corporatism and economic modernisation that were intrinsic to the 1927 Fascist Labour Charter, and they were embodied in the creation of similar social policies and agencies, such as the National Maternity and Child Welfare Institute (1925) and the National Institute for Health Insurance (1943). Nonetheless, the reforms of this era, like those in National Socialist Germany, were largely consistent with previous strategies for managing social risks.[17]

After the Second World War, the Italian and German governments continued to manage risk in much the same way as before. First, however, the German liability funds shed the *Führer* principle, regaining their rights to self-administration in 1951, while the INFAIL lost a letter, becoming the National Institute for Insurance against Workplace Accidents (INAIL). In subsequent years, Germany continued to build its social state on the basis of social insurance, despite discussions under the Christian Democratic Chancellor Konrad Adenauer to reform the system fundamentally and despite moves to recast welfare as part of the country's shift towards a 'social market economy'. Laws on health insurance (1955) and pensions (1957) were enacted and ran alongside other forms of social policy such as child allowances (1954) and social assistance (1961). Like other forms of social insurance, accident benefit would continue as before in West Germany, although several codifications and minor adjustments to the policy were carried out in 1949, 1963 and again in 1996 and 2008. Throughout this period, accident prevention and rehabilitation were increasingly emphasised, and the net of insurance was also cast further. In 1971, even school children were covered by special public accident funds in order to compensate injuries from physical education lessons or accidents on the way to school. As part of the planned economy in East Germany, accident insurance would see a more radical transformation, as the liability funds were dissolved with the creation of a single, national fund. Upon reunification in 1989, however, employers' liability funds, alongside the new public accident funds, would again come to govern insurance throughout the country. And the accident funds would continue to operate as they had for decades, even if they began to merge and reorganise in order to spread risk – and prevent accidents – more efficiently.[18]

---

[17] A point emphasised by Franco Bonelli: 'Appunti sul "welfare state" in Italia', *Studi Storici* 33 (1992), pp. 669–80. On the reforms: Maria Sophia Quine, *Italy's social revolution: charity and welfare from liberalism to fascism* (Basingstoke, 2002), chs. 4–5.

[18] Hans F. Zacher, 'Grundlagen der Sozialpolitik in der Bundesrepublik Deutschland', in Hockerts et al., eds., *Geschichte der Sozialpolitik*, vol. I, pp. 333–684, at pp. 465, 513, 551; *Sicher arbeiten – 125 Jahre gesetzliche Unfallversicherung in Deutschland, 1885–2010* (Berlin, 2010), pp. 14–21.

In postwar Italy, as in Germany, welfare programmes continued to expand on the basis of social insurance as new social risks were identified and reformulated, and as the central state gained greater prominence and legitimacy in the postwar order. The end of the Second World War saw a radical reconsideration of social policy in Italy, as a parliamentary commission headed by the Socialist Senator Ludovico D'Aragona attempted to simplify and centralise the complex system of social provision that had been erected over the preceding five decades. The plan was expansive and would finally extend accident insurance to all employees, including self-employed workers, across the peninsula.[19] In the end, it was dropped by the postwar Christian Democratic government, although the period from the 1950s to the 1970s did witness a major transformation in social provision, including pension reforms in 1952 and again in 1969 and the establishment of the National Health Service in 1978. Accident insurance was also revised repeatedly, for example, in 1963, with the extension to artisans, and again in 1965, with the coordination of a scheme on occupational illnesses and injuries. The reconfiguration of social and occupational risk throughout this period was, however, varied. The 1990s saw a 'season of reform' for Italian social policy amidst pressure from the European Union to lower public spending.[20] Yet, by 1999, accident insurance saw its most radical extension: to housewives (and husbands), or 'domestic workers', who were now obliged to insure against accidents at home.[21] Throughout this long era of transition, much, however, remained the same, and the INAIL continued to govern occupational risk, even for 'domestic workers'.

In contrast to Germany and Italy, postwar Britain appeared to embark on a dramatic new course in its approach to managing social risks. In the form of the Disabled Persons (Employment) Act of 1944, the government began advocating the rehabilitation of injured workers as part of a general programme that targeted disabled servicemen as well. Although it had encouraged workers after the First World War to take responsibility for safety, the government had not taken a strong stance at the time on returning to work. The 1944 policy was, therefore, a significant change.[22] More noteworthy was the dissolution of the workmen's compensation system in 1946 with the creation of the National Insurance (Industrial Injuries) Act. The Act was the outgrowth of long-standing

[19] An excellent reconstruction of the debates from this period: Ilaria Pavan, '"These new rights": social security in the postwar Italian debate', *Journal of Modern Italian Studies* 22 (2017), pp. 175–93.

[20] Maurizio Ferrera and Elisabetta Gualmini, 'Reforms guided by consensus: the welfare state and the Italian transition', in Maurizio Ferrera and Martin Rhodes, eds., *Recasting European welfare states* (London, 2000), pp. 187–208, at pp. 188–90; Maurizio Ferrera, 'Italy', in Peter Flora, ed., *Growth to limits: the Western European welfare states since World War II*, vol. II: *Germany, United Kingdom, Ireland, Italy* (Berlin, 1986), pp. 385–500, at pp. 290, 392, 398, 409.

[21] Legge 3 dicembre 1999, n. 493.

[22] A. F. Young, *Industrial injuries insurance: an examination of British policy* (1964; London, 1998), pp. 80–5.

debates, going back to the years immediately preceding the First World War, about the excessive litigation and inefficiency inherent to Britain's system of workmen's compensation. The more immediate impetus for the policy was, alongside trade union pressure,[23] William Beveridge's efforts to streamline the complex system of social provision in Britain. His 1942 *Report on social insurance and allied services* sought to tackle the 'Five Giants' of want, disease, squalor, ignorance and idleness. The policy that resulted set up the country's first National Health Service (1948), as well as a universal, flat-rate National Insurance system (1948) that covered pensions, unemployment and sickness. Other programmes, such as non-means tested family allowances (1945) and free, compulsory education for children up to age 15 (1944), rounded out the reforms. Against this backdrop, a 1944 White Paper on Industrial Injuries outlined the accident scheme.[24]

Like the other measures of this period, however, the National Insurance (Industrial Injuries) Act closely mirrored, and clearly emerged from, earlier trends in British social policy. On the one hand, for the first time, all injured workers were entitled to accident compensation. Moreover, accident benefit would be provided through social insurance. On the other, however, the scheme was run with a combination of tax money and contributions from employers and workers. The policy seemed to echo the tone of the Beveridge Report, in that it provided a sort of national minimum based on contributions by all, rather than a wage-related social insurance system along the lines of those in Germany and Italy.[25] Nonetheless, creating an insurance scheme at all – and departing from the principles of employers' fault that lingered in the workmen's compensation laws – was significant. However, as before, workers in Britain, unlike their continental counterparts, could continue to sue employers in tort cases under liability law. The new system of accident insurance had been kept separate from the rest of National Insurance expressly for this reason. Since some industries were seen to be especially dangerous, and since disabled workers could be more liable to injury while carrying out their jobs, the authors of the White Paper on Industrial Injuries saw that it was necessary to maintain a mechanism for workers to hold their employers accountable.[26] Moreover, after 1948, workers were allowed for the first time to bring cases against their employers even if they received compensation through National Insurance. By 1978, court cases against employers, alongside tort claims against a variety of other harms, had skyrocketed in Britain, amounting to almost 50 per cent of personal injury suits. The growth in tort cases, including those related to workplace accidents, had become so severe that a Royal Commission for Civil

[23] Howard Glennerster, *British social policy: 1945 to the present* (3rd edn, Abingdon, 2007), pp. 25–8.

[24] Bartrip, *Workmen's compensation*, pp. 179–80, 201–2, 206.

[25] Glennerster, *British social policy*, pp. 5, 28–39.

[26] Young, *Industrial injuries*, pp. 90–1.

Liability and Compensation for Personal Injury (the Pearson Commission) was established in 1973 to investigate.[27] Although the Pearson Commission suggested clamping down on litigation by enacting no-fault insurance schemes for workplace accidents and road accidents, no legislative action was taken.

Debates about social rights, individual responsibility and the sharing of risk would, therefore, continue to resound in Britain in subsequent years, provoking outcry against the emergence of a 'compensation culture' that not only encouraged workers to sue their employers but also brought parents to seek damages for accidents at children's birthday parties.[28] It is noteworthy that these discussions about tort reflected broader debates about dismantling the 'welfare state' that had begun in earnest under Margaret Thatcher in the 1980s and would continue to guide the Conservative Party into the twenty-first century.[29] Similar discussions have become increasingly widespread in Germany since the 1980s, amidst anxieties over an ageing population and rising unemployment. To a lesser extent, they have taken place in Italy since the 1990s. Social provision in the peninsula has historically been uneven, however, with the result that debates have focused on redistributing welfare to new and ostensibly more deserving groups rather than cutting it back entirely.[30]

These discussions about recasting the 'welfare state' – or even dismantling it altogether – have neglected an essential point. Moral rhetoric about 'scroungers' – or, as sometimes seen in the case of workplace accidents, 'pension vampires' – rests on an assumption that state provision, whether for accidents, housing or a range of other needs, leads to the erosion of individual responsibility. It regards individual responsibility and statehood as two opposing positions in a zero-sum game. My analysis of the social state reveals, however, that the governance of social risks has always been intimately connected to expectations of individual responsibility. In each country examined in this study, the nineteenth century saw the rise of the social state: the state seemed to provide for the social body because the social body constituted the state. Nonetheless, *individuals* never ceased to be seen as the foundations on which that social body rested. Differences, of course, existed between different social

---

[27] Richard Lewis, 'Employers' liability and workers' compensation: England and Wales', in Ken Oliphant and Gerhard Wagner, eds., *Employers' liability and workmen's compensation* (Berlin, 2012), pp. 137–202, at pp. 140–1.

[28] For example: 'Bouncy castle payout threatens children's parties', *Daily Telegraph*, 8 May 2008; 'David Cameron to crack down on compensation culture', *Daily Telegraph*, 1 December 2009.

[29] Michael Lobban and Julia Moses, 'Introduction', in Michael Lobban and Julia Moses, eds., *The impact of ideas on legal development* (Cambridge, 2012), pp. 1–33, at pp. 30–2.

[30] Jochen Clasen, 'From unemployment programmes to "work first": is German labour market policy becoming British?', in Jochen Clasen, ed., *Converging worlds of welfare? British and German social policy in the 21st century* (Oxford, 2011), pp. 266–81; Valeria Fargion, 'Italy: a territorial and generational divide in social citizenship', in Adalbert Evers and Anne-Marie Guillemard, eds., *Social policy and citizenship: the changing landscape* (Oxford, 2013), pp. 173–97. See also Silja Häusermann, *The politics of welfare state reform in continental Europe: modernization in hard times* (Cambridge, 2010).

states. Within different societies, at different historical junctures, different cultures of risk took form and shaped these connections between individuals, on the one hand, and the state, as the guarantor of the social body, on the other. It was through the law and everyday acts of bureaucracy that this connection was governed, by setting normative principles, loose guidelines based on precedence and common practices, and legislative regulations. Through the law, individual cases of need were assessed, on a case-by-case basis, holding every individual accountable, even if his needs were distributed to a wider social net. Despite liberal political philosophy of the nineteenth century, and neoliberal arguments of the late twentieth century, this essential connection between individual responsibility and the governance of social risks has remained in place. There never was a simple transition from contract to status, from individualism to collectivism. And despite political decisions and arguments to the contrary, there never could be, and never can be, an undoing of that connection without damaging the very foundations of modern statehood.

Appendix

TABLE 1. *Sequencing of accident laws in relation to other social-security policies[a]*

	Sequence rank average	Year of introduction		
		First	Last	Average
Accident insurance	1.8	1884	1971	1914
Health insurance	2.4	1883[b]	1963	1923
Old-age insurance	2.2	1889	1946	1922
Unemployment insurance	3.6	1911	1967	1930

Notes
[a] Across Austria, Belgium, Denmark, Finland, France, Germany, Italy, the Netherlands, Norway, Sweden, Switzerland and the United Kingdom.
[b] Germany's national Sickness Insurance Act was adopted in 1883 as a means to complement the accident insurance legislation, which was predicated on workers first seeking assistance from sickness insurance funds before receiving accident benefit.
(*Source:* adapted from Peter Flora and Jens Alber, 'Modernization, democratization, and the development of welfare states in western Europe', in Peter Flora and Arnold J. Heidenheimer, eds., *The development of welfare states in Europe and America* (New Brunswick, NJ, 1981), pp. 37–80, at pp. 50–1.)

TABLE 2. *Global spread of accident compensation laws, 1884–1918*[a]

Germany	1884	New York (USA)	1913
Austria	1887	Iowa (USA)	1913
Norway	1894	Minnesota (USA)	1913
Finland	1895	Nevada (USA)	1913
United Kingdom	1897	Arizona (USA)	1913
France	1898	Illinois (USA)	1913
Italy	1898	Portugal	1913
Denmark	1898	Connecticut (USA)	1913
Australia	1900	West Virginia (USA)	1913
New Zealand	1900	California (USA)	1913–1917
Spain	1900	Maryland (USA)	1914
Greece	1901	Louisiana (USA)	1914
Sweden	1901	Ontario (Canada)	1914
Netherlands	1901	South Africa	1914
Luxembourg	1902	Hawaii (US territory)	1915
Mississippi (USA)	1902	Maine (USA)	1915
Montana (USA)	1903	Nova Scotia (Canada)	1915
Belgium	1903	Vermont (USA)	1915
Oregon (USA)	1903	Victoria (Australia)	1915
Mexico	1906	Colombia	1915
Hungary	1907	Colorado (USA)	1915
Newfoundland	1908	Alaska (US territory)	1915
Serbia	1910	Indiana (USA)	1915
New South Wales (Austral.)	1910	Oklahoma (USA)	1915
Quebec (Canada)	1910	Argentina	1915
Switzerland	1911	Pennsylvania (USA)	1915
El Salvador	1911	Cuba	1916
Massachusetts (USA)	1911	Kentucky (USA)	1916
Peru	1911	Puerto Rico	1916
Tasmania	1911	Queensland (Australia)	1916
Washington (USA)	1911	British Columbia (Canada)	1916
Ohio (USA)	1911	Manitoba (Canada)	1916
Wisconsin (USA)	1911	Delaware (USA)	1917
South Australia	1911	Nebraska (USA)	1917
New Hampshire (USA)	1911	Idaho (USA)	1917
Kansas (USA)	1911	New Jersey (USA)	1917
Japan	1911	Utah (USA)	1917
West Australia	1912	New Mexico (USA)	1917
Rhode Island (USA)	1912	South Dakota (USA)	1917
Russia	1912	Virginia (USA)	1918
Michigan (USA)	1912	New Brunswick (Canada)	1918
Romania	1912	Alberta (Canada)	1918
Texas (USA)	1913		

Note
[a] In most federal systems, legislation was initially adopted on the state (territory) level.
(*Source*: C. M. Knowles, 'State control of industrial accident insurance', *Journal of Comparative Legislation and International Law* 2 (1920), pp. 29–50.)

TABLE 3. *Proportion of workers within the British, German and Italian compensation systems, 1885–1925[a]*

Year	Britain	Germany	Italy
1885	n/a	18	n/a
1890	n/a	70	n/a
1895	n/a	81	n/a
1900	n/a	75	5
1905	76	72	10
1910	76	87	12
1915	76	78	15
1920	77	75	50
1925	77	72	50

Note
[a] In percentage of the economically active population.
(*Source:* Flora and Alber, 'Modernization', p. 74.)

TABLE 4. *Percentage of economically active population employed in agriculture*

	1881	1891	1901	1911	1921	1931
Britain	12.8	10.4	8.2	8.1	7.4	6.4
Germany	49[a]	36.2	32.7	–	28.6	29
Italy	61.8	–	63.1	59.1	59.1	53.8

Note
[a] German figures calculated for the following years: 1882, 1895, 1907, 1925, 1933.
(*Sources:* Simon Kuznets, 'Quantitative aspects of the economic growth of nations. II: industrial distribution of national products', *Economic Development and Cultural Change* 5 (1957), supplement, here at p. 953; Vera Zamagni, 'A century of change: trends in the composition of the Italian labour force, 1881–1981', *Historical Social Research* 44 (1987), pp. 36–97, here at table A1; Brian R. Mitchell, *British historical statistics* (Cambridge, 1988), pp. 104–5; Wolfgang Fritz, 'Historie der amtlichen Statistiken der Erwerbstätigkeit in Deutschland: ein fragmentarischer Abriß: Darstellung, Quellen, Daten, Definitionen, Chronik', *Historical Social Research* 13 (2001), supplement, pp. 159–62.)

TABLE 5. *Commercial accident insurance premiums*

	Per capita[a]				Per population[b]		
	1890	1909	1912–14		1890	1909	1914
Britain	0.032	–	.363	Britain	1,190,000	–	16,700,000
Germany	0.033	–	.124	Germany	1,629,000	8,195,000	–
Italy	0.001	0.068	–	Italy	42,000	2,336,000	–

Notes
[a] Current values in £.
[b] Net of reinsurances, values in £.
(*Source:* Robin Pearson, 'Towards an historical model of services innovation: the case of the insurance industry, 1700–1914', *Economic History Review* (n.s.) 50 (1997), pp. 235–56, at p. 250.)

Bibliography

ARCHIVES

Britain

Guildhall Archives, London

Accident Offices Association (MS 29198)

Modern Records Centre, Warwick (MRC)

Amalgamated Society of Railway Workers (MRC MSS 127-AS)
Trades Union Congress (MSS 292-143, MSS 292-146)

The National Archives, Kew (TNA)

Board of Trade (BT)
Foreign Office (FO)
Home Office (HO)
Ministry of Labour (LAB)
Ministry of Pensions (PIN)
Ministry of Reconstruction (RECO)
Ministry of Transport (MT)
Pre-nationalisation railway companies, pre-nationalisation canal and related compa-
    nies, the London Passenger Transport Board and successors (RAIL)

Working-Class Movement Library, Salford (WCML)

Amalgamated Association of Card and Blowing Room Operatives (L1/35)
Amalgamated Society of Engineers (S1V/10, S11V/15)
Associate Shipwrights' Society (L26/64)
United Society of Boilermakers and Shipbuilders (L1/79)

Germany

Bundes-Archiv Berlin (BArch)

Imperial Chancellor's Office (R1401)
Imperial Chancellory (R43)
Imperial Insurance Office (R89)
Imperial Labour Office (R3901)
Imperial Office of the Interior (R1501)

Geheimes Staats-Archiv Preußischer Kulturbesitz, Berlin (GStAPK)

Prussian Ministry for *Volkswohlfahrt* (I. HA I. 191)
Prussian Ministry of Finance (I. HA Rep. 151)
Prussian Ministry of Justice (I. HA Rep. 84a)
Prussian Ministry of the Interior (I. HA Rep. 77)
Prussian Ministry of Trade (I. HA Abt. VIII; I. HA Abt. VII; I. HA 120BB;
    I. HA 120A)

Italy

Archivio centrale dello stato, Rome (ACS)

Francesco Saverio Nitti Papers (Arch. Nitti)
Luigi Luzzatti Papers (Arch. Luzzatti)
Ministry of Agriculture, Industry and Commerce: Division of Industry and Commerce
    (MAIC. Div. Ind. & Comm.)
Ministry of Arms and Munitions: Central Committee on Mobilisation (Maem, Ccmi)
Ministry of Labour and Insurance (Min. Lav. Prev. Soc.)
Ministry of the Interior: General Directorate of Public Health (Min. Int.: Dir. Genl.
    San. Pub.)
Prime Minister's Office (PCM)

Camera dei deputati: Archivio storico, Rome (CdAs)

Leg. XV, Sess. 1882–6, Proposte di legge
Leg. XIX, Sess. 1895–7, Proposte di legge
Leg. XX, Sess. 1897–8, Proposte di legge
Leg. XXI, Sess. 1902–4, Incarti delle commissioni incaricato dello studio dei disegni di
    legge e delle proposte d'iniziativa parlamentare
Leg. XXII, Sess. 1904–9, Incarti delle commissioni incaricato dello studio dei disegni di
    legge e delle proposte d'iniziativa parlamentare
Petizione, F.1 (194), 1892

Senato del regno: Archivio storico, Rome

Sess. 1882–3, numero di progetto 73
Sess. 1897, numero del progetto 16

Sess. 1912, numero del progetto 731
Sess. 1917, numero del progetto 360

Historical Archives of the Foreign Office, Rome (MdaeAs)

General Commissariat on Emigration
Political Series A
Political Series P

Istituto nazionale per l'assicurazione contro gli infortuni sul lavoro (INAIL)

Atti della Cassa nazionale di assicurazione per gli infortuni degli operai sul lavoro

Parliamentary Papers and Official Periodicals

Britain

Hansard, House of Commons (HC) (1870–1925)
Hansard, House of Lords (HL) (1870–1925)
Labour Gazette (1893–1922)
Parliamentary Papers (PP) (1833–1925)

Germany

Amtliche Nachrichten des Reichsversicherungsamts (1884–1925)
Die Arbeiter-Versorgung (1884–1925)
Deutscher Reichs-Anzeiger und Preußischer Staatsanzeiger (1871–1925)
Drucksachen des Deutschen Bundesrates (DDB) (1871–1918)
Drucksachen des Deutschen Reichstags (DDR) (1871–1918)
Drucksachen des norddeutschen Bundes (DDNB) (1867–70)
Geschäftsbericht des Reichs-Versicherungsamts (1885–1925)
Monatsblätter der Arbeiterversicherung (1907–22)
Reichsarbeitsblatt (1903–25)
Reichsgesetzblatt (1871–1929)
Statistisches Jahrbuch für das Deutsche Reich (1880–1925)
Stenographische Berichte über die Verhandlungen des Deutschen Reichstags (SBDR)

Italy

Annali del credito e della previdenza (1883–1925)
Atti del consiglio superiore del lavoro (1903–13)
Atti parlamentari del senato del regno (A. P. Sen.)
Atti parlamentari del senato del regno: Documenti (A. P. Sen., Doc.) (1870–1922)
Atti parlamentari della camera dei deputati (A. P. Cam.) (1870–1922)
Atti parlamentari della camera dei deputati: Documenti (A.P. Cam., Doc.)
Bollettino della Cassa nazionale per gl'infortuni degli operai sul lavoro
Bollettino dell'Ispettorato del lavoro

Bollettino di notizie sul credito e sulla previdenza (1883–1918)
Gazzetta ufficiale del Regno d'Italia (1861–1925)

Newspapers and Periodicals

Archiv für Psychiatrie (used selectively)
Archiv für soziale Gesetzgebung und Statistik (1888–1903)
Ärztliche Sachverständigen-Zeitung (1895–1925)
Atti della Cassa nazionale di assicurazione per gli infortuni degli operai sul lavoro: Verbale delle sedute d'insediamento del nuovo Consiglio Superiore (1886–1900)
Atti per l'istituzione della cassa nazionale di assicurazione per gli operai contro gli infortuni sul lavoro (1883)
Avanti (used selectively)
Die Berufsgenossenschaft: Zeitschrift für die Reichs-Unfallversicherung (1885–1925)
Birmingham Daily Gazette (used selectively)
Bollettino dell'agricoltura: Organo della società agraria di Lombardia (used selectively)
British Medical Journal (used selectively)
Bulletin des internationalen Arbeitsamtes (1902–19)
Concordia: Zeitschrift der Zentralstelle für Volkswohlfahrt (1901–20)
Critica sociale: Rivista del socialismo italiano
Daily Chronicle (used selectively)
Daily News (used selectively)
Daily Telegraph (used selectively)
Deutsche Kolonialzeitung: Organ der Deutschen Kolonialgesellschaft (used selectively)
Fraser's Magazine (used selectively)
Giornale degli economisti (used selectively)
Herapeth's Railway Journal (used selectively)
Hannoverscher Courier (used selectively)
Help (used selectively)
Il Secolo (used selectively)
Insurance News (1890–1919)
Jahres- und Kassenbericht der Berliner Gewerkschaftskommission (1901–22/4)
Journal of the Statistical Society of London (1838–86)
The Lancet (used selectively)
Magdeburger Zeitung (used selectively)
Mining Journal (used selectively)
La medicina delle assicurazioni sociali: Infortuni del lavoro: Malattie professionali e comuni maternità, invalidità e vecchiaia, prevenzione delle malattie e degli infortuni del lavoro, assicurazioni sulla vita umana (1912–13)
Monatsschrift für Unfallheilkunde und Invalidenwesen mit besonderer Berücksichtigung der Mechanotherapie under der Begutachtung Unfallverletzter, Invalider und Kranker (1900–21)
Neurologisches Centralblatt (used selectively)
Nuova antologia di lettere, scienze e arti (1866–1925)
Oddfellows Magazine (used selectively)
Railway Service Gazette (used selectively)
Railway Times (used selectively)

Rassegna contemporanea (1908–15)
Rassegna della previdenza sociale (1919–25)
Revue Internationale du Travail (1921–6)
Rheinischer Jacquard: Zeitschrift für Deutschlands Wollen-Industrie und Volkswirth-schaftliche Interessen (used selectively)
Riforma sociale: Rivista critica di economia e finanza (1894–1925)
Rivista di diritto e giurisprudenza. Patologia speciale e medicina forense sugli infortuni del lavoro (1899–1911)
Rivista infortuni (used selectively)
Rivista internazionale di scienze sociali e discipline ausiliarie (used selectively)
Sammlung zwangsloser Abhandlungen aus dem Gebiete der Nerven- und Geistes-krankheiten (used selectively)
Schriften des Vereins für Social-Politik (1873–1925)
Soziale Praxis: Zentralblatt für Sozialpolitik (1894–1925)
The Times (used selectively)
TUC Congress: Proceedings (used selectively)
Vorwärts (used selectively)
Vossische Zeitung (used selectively)
Zeitschrift für Bahn- und Bahnkassenärzte
Zeitschrift für die Gesamte Versicherungs-Wissenschaft
Zeitschrift für Versicherungsmedizin

Miscellaneous Printed Primary Sources

Actes du VIII congrès international des assurances sociales ... Rome 12–16 octobre 1908 (3 vols., Rome, 1909).
Adler, Georg, *Die Frage des internationalen Arbeiterschutzes* (Munich, 1888).
Agnelli, Arnaldo, *Infortuni sul lavoro e assicurazione* (Milan, 1908).
Agnew, T. H., *Relation of general health to length of employment hours and nature of work* (London, 1917).
Aronson, V. R., *The Workmen's Compensation Act, 1906* (London, 1909).
Barnett, H. Norman, *Accidental injuries to workmen with reference to the Workmen's Compensation Act, 1906* (London, 1909).
Bernhard, Ludwig, *Unerwünschte Folgen der deutschen Sozialpolitik* (Berlin, 1912).
Bernhardi, Friedrich von, *Germany and the next war*, trans. Allen H. Powles (New York, 1914).
Berti, Domenico, *Le classi lavoratrici e il parlamento* (Rome, 1885).
Beverly, Frank, ed., *A digest of cases decided under the Workmen's Compensation Acts, 1897–1909 of the House of Lords Court of Appeal in England and Ireland, Division and High Courts in England and Court of Session in Scotland* (1910; 2nd edn, London, 1912).
Bödiker, Tonio, *Die Arbeiterversicherung in den europäischen Staaten* (Leipzig, 1895).
  Die Unfallgesetzgebung der europäischen Staaten (Leipzig, 1884).
Borri, Lorenzo, *Gli infortuni del lavoro sotto il rispetto medico legale* (Milan, 1910).
Brabook, Edward W., *Provident societies and industrial welfare* (London, 1898).
Brentano, Lujo, *Die Arbeiterversicherung gemäss der heutigen Wirthschaftsordnung* (Leipzig, 1879).

Brezina, Ernst, *Internationale Übersicht über Gewerbekrankheiten nach den Berichten der Gewerbeinspektionen der Kulturländer über die Jahre 1914–1918* (Berlin, 1921).

Bury, Giovanni de, *Relazione sul contenzioso della cassa nazionale infortuni, sede compartimentale di Napoli, dal gennaio 1900 al dicembre 1904* (Naples, 1905).

Cabinet Office, 'Central Government's Concept of Operations', 23 April 2013, www.gov.uk/government/publications/the-central-government-s-concept-of-operations, last accessed 10 November 2015.

Cabinet Office, 'National Risk Register', Reports, 27 March 2015, www.gov.uk/government/publications/national-risk-register-for-civil-emergencies-2015-edition, last accessed 5 December 2015.

Caissotti di Chiusano, Luiei, 'Il problema degli alloggi popolari: soluzioni', *Rivista Internazionale di Scienze Sociali e Discipline Ausiliarie* 31/124 (1903), pp. 513–43.

Camera di commercio ed arti di Livorno, *Relazione sulle modificazioni alla legge per gl'infortuni degli operai sul lavoro: Approvata dalla Camera di commercio nell'adunanza del 2 marzo 1908* (Livorno, 1908).

Camera di commercio ed arti in Firenze, *Osservazioni e rilievi al progetto parlamentare degli infortuni sul* lavoro (Florence, 1908).

Camps, William, *Railway accidents or collisions: their effects, immediate and remote, upon the brain and spinal cord* (London, 1866).

Carnelutti, Francesco, *Infortuni sul lavoro* (Rome, 1913).

Cassa nazionale d'assicurazione per gl'infortuni degli operai sul lavoro, sede centrale in Roma, *Assicurazioni e previdenza sociale: per la riforma della legge infortuni* (Rome, 1915).

Cassa nazionale d'assicurazione per gl'infortuni sul lavoro, sede centrale in Roma, *Organizzazione del servizio di assistenza agli infortuni* (Rome, 1922).

Cheysson, E., 'La législation internationale du travail, rapport présenté sur la demande du Comité d'Organisation Exposition universelle de 1889', in *Congrès international du commerce et de l'industrie, tenu à Paris de 22 au 28 septembre* (Paris, 1889).

Chironi, G. P., *La colpa extra contrattuale* (2 vols., Turin, 1887–1903).

Clines, Francis X., 'Clinton signs bill cutting welfare; States in new role', *New York Times* (23 August 1996), http://nyti.ms/194fPhs, last accessed 10 December 2015.

Colajanni, Pompeo,. 'Trois premières années d'application de la loi sur les accidents du travail aux ouvriers des mines de soufre de la Sicilie', in *Congrès international des accidents du travail et des assurances sociales. Sixième session tenue à Düsseldorf* (Berlin, 1902), pp. 731–47.

Collie, John, *Malingering and feigned sickness, with notes on the Workmen's Compensation Act, 1906 and compensation for injury, including the leading cases thereon* (1913; 2nd edn, London, 1917).

Colocci, Adriano, *Gli zingari: storia di un popolo errante* (Turin, 1889).

Commissione per studiare le cause e i provvedimenti preventivi delle malattie professionali degli operai nelle industrie, special issue of *Annali del credito e della previdenza – Anno 1902* (Rome, 1903).

Commissione Reale per il Dopoguerra, *Studi e proposte della prima Sottocommissione presieduta dal Sen. Vittorio Scialoja. Questioni giuridiche, amministrative e sociali: giugno 1918–giugno 1919. Sezione X Legislazione sociale e previdenza (presidente On. Prof. Luigi Rava)* (Rome, 1920), pp. 458–70.

Congrès international des accidents du travail. Deuxième session tenue à Berne ... 1891. Rapports et procès-verbaux (Berne, 1891).

Congrès international des accidents du travail et des assurances sociales. Quatrième session tenue à Bruxelles ... 1897. Rapports, procès-verbaux des séances et communications présentées au Congrès, publiés par les soins du comité belge d'organisation (Brussels, 1897).

Congrès international des accidents du travail et des assurances sociales. Sixième session tenue à Düsseldorf du 17 au 24 juin 1902, publié par les soins du comité allemande d'organisation (Breslau and Berlin, 1902).

Congrès international des accidents du travail et des assurances sociales. Troisième session tenue à Milan ... 1894 ... Rapports, procès-verbaux des séances et communications présentées au Congrès, publiés par les soins du Comité italien d'organisation (Milan, 1894).

Congrès international pour la protection ouvrière à Zurich du 23 au 28 août 1897, circulaire du Comité d'organisation, rapports et proposition, liste provisoire des participants au congrès (Zurich, 1897).

Corsi, Prof. and Invrea, Esq., *Projet de convention internationale pour l'application des lois nationales aux ouvriers étrangers en cas d'accidents sur le travail* (Turin, 1904).

Cotteritz, F. von, *Das Reichs-Unfall-Versicherungs-Projekt: eine sachliche Kritik mit neuen Vorschlägen, dem Reichstag gewidmet* (Berlin, 1881).

Dawson, William Harbutt, *Social insurance in Germany 1883–1911: its history, operation, results and a comparison with the National Insurance Act, 1911* (London, 1912).

The German workman: a study in national efficiency (London, 1906).

Bismarck and state socialism: an exposition of the social and economic legislation of Germany since 1870 (London, 1890).

Dicey, A. V., *Lectures on the relation between law and public opinion in England* (2nd edn, London, 1914).

Direzione generale dell'agricoltura, *Pubblicazioni del Corpo reale delle miniere. Studio sulle condizioni di sicurezza delle miniere e delle cave in Italia* (Rome, 1894).

Discorsi parlamentari di Giovanni Giolitti, 4 vols. (Rome, 1953).

Ellero, Pietro, *La questione sociale* (Bologna, 1874).

Emigrazione e colonie: Rapporti di RR. Agenti diplomatici e consolari publicati dal R. Ministero degli affari esteri (Rome, 1893).

Engels, Friedrich, *Die Lage der arbeitenden Klasse in England* (Leipzig, 1845).

'Review for the *Fortnightly Review*', in *Engels on Capital* (New York, 1937).

Erichsen, John Eric, *On concussion of the spine, nervous shock and other obscure injuries of the nervous system, in their medical and medicolegal aspects* (London, 1875).

Ewald, W., *Die traumatischen Neurosen und die Unfallgesetzgebung* (Berlin, 1908).

Foot, A., *The practice of insurance against accidents and employers' liability* (London, 1909).

Foreign Office, *Report on the present state of the labour question in Germany* (London, 1891).

Report on the question of employers' liability in Germany (London, 1894).

Fusinato, G., *Gli infortuni sul lavoro e il diritto civile* (Rome, 1887).

Generalkommission der Gewerkschaften Deutschlands, *Gewöhnung an Unfallfolgen und anderes zur Rechtsprechung in Unfallrentenstreitsachen* (Berlin, 1914).

Gneist, Rudolf von, *Das englische Verwaltungsrecht* (Berlin, 1883).

Green, T. H., 'Lecture on liberal legislation and freedom of contract (1881)', in R. L. Nettleship, ed., *Works of Thomas Hill Green* (London, 1906), vol. III, pp. 365–86.

Gruner, Édouard, ed., *Exposition universelle internationale de 1889: Congrès international des accidents du travail*, vol. II: *Comptes rendus des séances et visite du congrès* (Paris, 1890).

Grimm, Jacob and Wilhelm, *Deutsches Wörterbuch* (16 vols., 1854–1960; repr. Munich, 1984).

Haerendel, Ulrike, ed., *Quellensammlung zur Geschichte der deutschen Sozialpolitik, 1867–1914*, sect. 2, vol. VI: *Die gesetzliche Invaliditäts- und Altersversicherung und die Alternative auf gewerkschaftlicher und betrieblicher Grundlage* (Darmstadt, 2004).

Harris, Henry J., 'The increase in industrial accidents', *Publications of the American Statistical Association* 13/97 (1912), pp. 1–27.

Hartmann, Konrad, *Das Gefahrtarifwesen und die Beitragsberechnung der Unfallversicherung des Deutschen Reiches* (Berlin, 1913).

'Die Entwicklung der Unfallverhütungstechnik in Deutschland ', in *Congrès international des accidents du travail et des assurances sociales. Sixième session tenue à Düsseldorf* (Berlin, 1902).

Schutz gegen Unfallgefahren in gewerblichen Betrieben (Berlin, 1902).

Hobhouse, L. T., *Liberalism* (1911; London, 1919).

Howe, Frederic C., *Socialized Germany* (New York, 1915).

Iagwitz, F. Von, *Die Vereinheitlichung der Arbeiter-Versicherung und der VII. Internationale Arbeiter-Versicherungs-Kongress* (Berlin, 1906).

IIe Congrès international des maladies professionnelles. Bruxelles, septembre 1910: Analyse sommaire des travaux publiés avant l'ouverture du Congrès et des discussions au cours des séances (Brussels, 1910).

Infortuni sul lavoro: Giurisprudenza giudiziaria (vols. 1–7, Rome, 1905–15).

International labour conference: Seventh session: Geneva, June 1925, workmen's compensation (Geneva, 1924).

Kaiserliches Statistisches Amt, Abteilung für Arbeiterstatistik, ed., *Atlas und Statistik der Arbeiterversicherung des Deutschen Reichs. Beiheft zum Reichs-Arbeitsblatt* (Berlin, 1904).

Kaufmann, Constantin, *Handbuch für Unfallmedizin: mit Berücksichtigung der deutschen, österreichischen, schweizerischen und französischen Arbeiter- und der privaten Unfallversicherung: für den akademischen und praktischen Gebrauch* (3rd edn, Stuttgart, 1907).

Kaufmann, Paul, *Zur Umgestaltung der deutschen Sozialversicherung* (Berlin, 1924).

Neue Ziele der Sozialversicherung (Mönchen-Gladbach, 1921).

Wiederaufbau und Sozialversicherung. Vorschläge zur Änderung der Reichsvericherungsordnung (2nd improved edn, Berlin, 1920).

Was dankt das kämpfende Deutschland seiner sozialen Fürsorge? (Berlin, 1917).

Soziale Fürsorge und deutscher Siegeswille (12th repr., Berlin, 1915).

Kay-Shuttleworth, James P., *The moral and physical condition of the working classes employed in the cotton manufacture in Manchester* (London, 1832).

Klein, Gustav Adolf, *Die Leistungen der Arbeiterversicherung des Deutschen Reichs* (Berlin, 1900).

Kocher, Theodor, *Zur Kenntnis der Phosphornekrose* (Biel, 1893).

Kraepelin, Emil, *Compendium der Psychiatrie* (8th edn, Leipzig, 1909–15).

Laband, Paul, *Das Staatsrecht des Deutschen Reichs*, vol. II of *Handbuch des öffentlichen Rechts der Gegenwart in Monographien* (3rd edn, Tübingen, 1902).

Lass, Ludwig, *Reichsversicherungsordnung*, vol. ii: *Unfallversicherung* (3rd and 4th edns, Berlin, 1914).

Lass, Ludwig and Zahn, Friedrich, *Einrichtung und Wirkung der deutschen Arbeiterversicherung: Denkschrift für die Weltausstellung zu Paris, 1900* (Berlin, 1900).

Leigh, Evan, *The science of modern cotton spinning* (2nd edn, 2 vols., London, 1873).

Leo XIII, *Rerum novarum* (On capital and labour), 15 May 1891, quoted from http://w2.vatican.va/content/leo-xiii/en/encyclicals/documents/hf_l-xiii_enc_15051891_rerum-novarum.html, last accessed 23 October 2014.

Levi, E., *Della assicurazione sulla vita e contro gli infortuni: Nota di legislazione e giurisprudenza comparata* (Florence, 1886).

Lohmann, Theodor, *Die Fabrik-Gesetzgebungen der Staaten des europäischen Kontinents* (Berlin, 1878).

Lohmar, Paul, *Schattenseiten der Reichs-Unfallversicherung. Gesundheitlich, sittlich und volkswirtschaftlich nachteilige Begleiterscheinungen der Reichs-Unfallversicherung und ihre Bekämpfung* (Berlin, 1916).

Love, Thomas B., 'The social significance of war risks insurance', *Annals of the American Academy of Social and Political Science* 79/1 (1918), pp. 46–51.

Lowey-Hattendorf, Erwin, *Krieg, Revolution und Unfallneurosen* (Berlin, 1920).

Luzzatti, Luigi, *Memorie autobiographiche e carteggi*, ed. Elena Carli (3 vols., Bologna, 1931–66).

Magaldi, Vicenzo, 'Les accidents du travail en Italie: progrès legislatif – applications de la loi', in *Congrès international des accidents du travail et des assurances sociales. Sixième session tenue à Düsseldorf* (Berlin, 1902), pp. 681–99.

Maine, Henry Sumner, *Ancient law: its connection with the early history of society and its relation to modern ideas* (1861; London, 1908).

Maxwell, Sir Herbert, ed., *The Creevey-papers* (2 vols., London, 1904).

Maxwell, Peter Benson, *On the interpretation of statutes* (4th edn, London, 1905).

Mazzola, Ugo, *L'assicurazione degli operai nella scienza e nella legislazione germanica: relazione a S. E. il Ministro di agricoltura, industria e commercio*, special issue of *Annali del credito e della previdenza* (Rome, 1885).

Mihr, Volker, Tennstedt, Florian and Winter, Heidi, eds., *Sozialreform als Bürger- und Christenpflicht. Aufzeichnungen, Briefe und Erinnerungen des leitenden Ministerialbeamten Robert Bosse aus der Entstehungszeit der Arbeiterversicherung und des BGB (1878–1892)* (Stuttgart, 2005).

Ministero per il lavoro e la previdenza sociale, direzione generale della previdenza sociale, *L'assicurazione obbligatoria contro gli infortuni sul lavoro in agricoltura: Prima relazione sull'applicazione del decreto-legge 23 agosto 1917, n. 1450* (Rome, 1922).

Ministry of Munitions, Health of Munitions Workers Committee, *Final report* (London, 1918).

Mirto, Domenico, 'La simulazione negli infortuni del lavoro', in *Atti del I Congresso per le malattie del lavoro (malattie professionali), Palermo, 19–21 ottobre 1907* (Palermo, 1908), pp. 23–54.

Navarra, Ugo, *Gl'infortuni del lavoro nell'agricoltura* (Florence, 1908).

Oliver, Thomas, *Dangerous trades* (London, 1902).

Oppenheim, Hermann, *Die traumatische Neurose* (Berlin, 1889).

Pantano, Edoardo, *I problemi economic urgenti: voti e proposte per il passaggio dallo stato di guerra allo stato di pace,* report of the Commissione per il dopoguerra (Rome, 1919).

Pappenheim, Louis, *Handbuch der Sanitäts-Polizei nach eigener Untersuchungen* (2 vols., Berlin, 1859).

Pieraccini, Gaetano, *Patologia del lavoro e terapia sociale* (Milan, 1906).

Pubblicazioni del Corpo reale delle miniere: Studio sulle condizioni di sicurezza delle miniere e delle cave in Italia (Rome, 1894).

Puccinotti, Francesco, *Lezioni medicina legale* (Milan, 1856).

Ramazzini, Bernardino, *Le Malattie dei lavoratori (De morbis artificum diatriba): testi delle edizioni del 1700 e del 1713,* ed. Francesco Carnevale (Florence, 2000).

Reichsversicherungsordnung, *Handbuch der Unfallversicherung* (3rd edn, Leipzig, 1909–10).

Rosenblatt, Alfred, 'The civilizing influences of war', *Current History* 5/1 (1916), pp. 103–5.

Rossi, L. E., *Cenni storici e amminstrativi sulla Cassa nazionale di assicurazione degli infortuni degli operai sul lavoro* (Milan, 1911).

Ruegg, Alfred Henry, *The Employer's Liability Act, 1880 and the Workmen's Compensation Act, 1906* (7th edn, London, 1907).

Savigny, Friedrich Carl von, *System des heutigen Römischen Rechts* (8 vols., Berlin, 1840–9).

Scanlan, J. J., *The mutilated hand and the Workmen's Compensation Act, 1906: having special reference to 'missing' fingers* (London, 1913).

Smiles, Samuel, *Die Selbsthülfe in Lebensbildern und Charakterzügen,* trans. Josef M. Boyes (Hamburg, 1866).

Self-help: with illustrations of character and conduct (1859; London, 1970).

Solari, Gioele, *La legge degli infortuni sul lavoro: introduzione al commento della legge italiana 17 marzo 1898 sugli infortuni* (Civitanova-Marche, 1899).

Sommerfeld, Theodor, *Handbuch der Gewerbekrankheiten* (Koblenz, 1898).

Sommerfeld, Th. and Fischer, R., *Liste der gewerblichen Gifte und anderer gesundheitsschädlicher Stoffe, die in der Industrie Verwendung finden: Nach den Beschlüssen des Komitees der Internationale Vereinigung für gesetzlichen Arbetierschutz* (Jena, 1912).

Starsberg, Hugo, *Unerwünschte Folgen deutscher Sozialpolitik? Eine Entgegnung an Prof. Ludwig Bernhard* (Bonn, 1913).

Stein, Lorenz von, *Handbuch der Verwaltungslehre,* vol. 1: *Der Begriff der Verwaltung und das System der positiven Staatswissenschaften* (3rd edn, Stuttgart, 1888).

Strümpel, Adolf, 'Über die traumatischen Neurosen', vol. III in the series *Berliner Klinik: Sammlung klinischer Vorträge,* ed. E. Hahn and P. Fürbringer (Berlin, 1888), pp. 2–10.

Teleky, Ludwig, 'La guerre et les maladies industrielles', *Revue Internationale du Travail* 3 (July–August 1921), pp. 53–5.

Tennstedt, Florian and Winter, Heidi, eds., *Quellensammlung zur Geschichte der deutschen Sozialpolitik 1867 bis 1914,* sect. 2: *Von der kaiserlichen Sozialbotschaft bis zu den Februarerlassen Wilhelms II (1881–1890),* vol. II.i: *Von der zweiten Unfallversicherungsvorlage bis zum Unfallversicherungsgesetz vom 6. Juli 1884* (Stuttgart, 1995).

Quellensammlung zur Geschichte der deutschen Sozialpolitik 1867 bis 1914, sect.
   1: *Von der Reichsgründungszeit bis zur Kaiserlichen Sozialbotschaft (1867–1881)*,
   vol. II: *Von der Haftpflichtgesetzgebung zur ersten Unfallversicherungsvorlage*
   (Stuttgart, 1993).
Thackrah, Charles, *The effects of the principal arts, trades and professions and of civic
   states and habits of living on health and longevity, with a particular reference to
   the trades and manufactures of Leeds and suggestions for the removal of many of
   the agents which produce disease and shorten the duration of life* (London, 1831).
Thiem, C., *Handbuch der Unfallerkrankungen* (Berlin, 1898).
Thomas, G. N. W., *Leading cases in workmen's compensation* (London, 1913).
Tourneux, Félix, *Encyclopédie des chemins de fer et des machines à vapeur* (Paris, 1844).
Ufficio del lavoro, *L'ispezione del lavoro: Studi sull'organizazione di vigilanza per
   l'applicazione delle leggi operaie* (Rome, 1904).
Unfall-Statistik des Deutschen Reichs, special issue of the *Monatshefte zur Statistik des
   Deutschen Reichs für das Jahr 1882*, 53 (Berlin, 1882).
Ure, Andrew, *Philosophy of manufactures* (London, 1835).
Vecchietti, Ettore, *Rilievi ed appunti sulla esecuzione della legge infortuni* (Naples, 1912).
Vernon, H. M., *The health and efficiency of munitions workers* (Oxford, 1940).
   'The human factor and industrial accidents', *International Labour Review* 13 (1926),
   pp. 673–716.
   Industrial fatigue and efficiency (London, 1921).
Virgilii, Filippo, *L'assicurazione degli infortuni sul lavoro agricolo* (Turin, 1913).
Wagner, Adolph, *Der Staat und das Versicherungswesen: socialökonomische und social-
   rechtliche Studien* (Tübingen, 1881).
Walford, Cornelius, *Cyclopaedia of insurance* (6 vols., London, 1871–80).
Weber, Max, *Wirtschaft und Gesellschaft*, ed. Johannes Winckelmann (5th edn,
   Tübingen, 2002).
Weyer, Otto W., *Die englische Fabrikinspektion. Ein Beitrag zur Geschichte der
   Fabrikgesetzgebung in England* (Tübingen, 1888).
Williams, E. E., *Made in Germany* (London, 1896).
Zacher, Georg, *Guide to the workmen's insurance of the German Empire* (Berlin and
   London, 1900).
   Leitfaden zur Arbeiterversicherung des Deutschen Reiches (Berlin, 1893).
Zacher, Georg, ed., *Die Arbeiter-Versicherung im Auslande* (Berlin, 1898–1908).
*Zusammenstellung der Entschädigungssätze, welche das Reichs-Versicherungsamt bei
   dauernden Unfallschäden gewährt hat* (Groß-Lichterfelde, 1912).

Secondary Sources

Abbott, Andrew and DeViney, Stanley, 'The welfare state as transnational event: evi-
   dence from sequences of policy adoption', *Social Science History* 16/2 (1992),
   pp. 245–74.
Abraham, Kenneth S., *The liability century* (Cambridge, MA, 2009).
Abrams, Philip, 'Notes on the difficulty of studying the state (1977)', *Journal of
   Historical Sociology* 1 (1988), pp. 58–89.
Abse, Tobias, 'Italian workers and Italian fascism', in Richard Bessel, ed., *Fascist Italy
   and Nazi Germany: comparisons and contrasts* (Cambridge, 1996), pp. 40–60.

Adler, Franklin Hugh, *Italian industrialists from liberalism to fascism: the political development of the industrial bourgeoisie, 1906–34* (Cambridge, 1995).

Aimo, Piero, *Il centro e la circonferenza: profili di storia dell'amministrazione locale* (Milan, 2005).

Alborn, Timothy, 'Senses of belonging: the politics of working-class insurance in Britain, 1880–1914', *Journal of Modern History* 73/3 (2001), pp. 561–602.

Aldrich, Mark, *Safety first: technology, labor, and business in the building of American work safety, 1870–1939* (Baltimore, 1997).

Allen, Christopher S., 'Germany', in Mark Kesselman, Joel Krieger and William A. Joseph, eds., *Introduction to comparative politics* (5th edn, Boston, 2010), pp. 157–210.

Amari, Monica, *I musei delle aziende: la cultura della tecnica tra arte e storia* (Milan, 2001).

Andersen, Arne, 'Arbeiterschutz in Deutschland im 19. und frühen 20. Jahrhundert', *Archiv für Sozialgeschichte* 31 (1991), pp. 61–83.

Andersen, Arne and Ott, René, 'Risikoperzeption im Industrialisierungszeitalter am Beispiel des Hüttenwesens', *Archiv für Sozialgeschichte* 28 (1988), pp. 75–109.

Antozzi, Oriella, 'I socialisti e la legislazione sul lavoro delle donne e dei fanciulli', *Movimento Operaio e Socialista* 20 (1974), pp. 285–316.

Armitage, David, '"Greater Britain": a useful category of analysis?', *American Historical Review* 104/2 (1999), pp. 427–45.

Ashbee, Edward, 'Neoliberalism, conservative politics and "social recapitalization"', *Global Discourse* 5/1 (2015), pp. 96–113.

Asher, Robert, 'Experience counts: British workers, accident prevention and compensation, and the origins of the welfare state', *Journal of Policy History* 15 (2003), pp. 359–88.

Ashley, Susan A., *Making liberalism work: the Italian experience, 1860–1914* (Westport, CT, 2003).

Le Assicurazioni Generali: cenni storici (Trieste, 1966).

Atiyah, Patrick S., *The rise and fall of freedom of contract* (Oxford, 1979).

Ayass, Wolfgang, 'Regulierte Selbstregulierung in den Berufsgenossenschaften der gesetzlichen Unfallversicherung', in Peter Collin, Gerd Bender, Stefan Ruppert, Margrit Seckelmann and Michael Stolleis, eds., *Regulierte Selbstregulierung im frühen Interventions- und Sozialstaat* (Frankfurt, 2012), pp. 123–43.

Bade, Klaus J., *Migration in European history*, trans. Allison Brown (Oxford, 2003).

Baker, Tom, 'On the genealogy of moral hazard', *Texas Law Review* 75/2 (1996–7), pp. 237–92.

Baldasseroni, Alberto and Carnevale, Franco, 'L'abbandono dell'uso del fosforo bianco nella produzione dei fiammiferi: un lungo processo per la realizzazione di un precoce esempio di vera prevenzione (1830–1920)', in A. Grieco and P. A. Bertazzi, eds., *Per una storiografia italiana della prevenzione occupazionale ed ambientale* (Milan, 1997), pp. 133–87.

Baldasseroni, Alberto, Carnevale, Franco, Iavicoli, S. and Tomassini, L., eds., *Alle origini della tutela della salute dei lavoratori in Italia: nascita e primi sviluppi dell'Ispettorato del Lavoro (1904–1925)* (Rome, 2009).

Baldasseroni, Alberto, Guastella, V. and Tomassini, L., 'Concerning the first International Congress on Work-Related Illnesses – Milan 9–14 June 1906: success – news – reports – motions', *Medicina del Lavoro* 97 (2006), pp. 100–13.

Baldinetti, Anna, *The origins of the Libyan nation: colonial legacy, exile, and the emergence of a new nation state* (London, 2010).

Baldwin, Peter, 'Beyond weak and strong: rethinking the state in comparative policy history', *Journal of Policy History* 17 (2005), pp. 12–33.

The politics of social solidarity: class bases of the European welfare state, 1875–1975 (Cambridge, 1990).

Barker, Tom and Simon, Jonathan, eds., *Embracing risk: the changing culture of insurance and responsibility* (Chicago, 2002).

Barta, Heinz, *Kausalität im Sozialrecht: Entstehung und Funktion der sog. Theorie der wesentlichen Bedingung. Analyse der grundlegenden Judikatur des Reichsversicherungsamtes in Unfallversicherungssachen (1884–1914)* (Berlin, 1983).

Bartolini, Stefano, *The political mobilization of the European Left, 1860–1980: the class cleavage* (Cambridge, 2000).

Bartrip, P. W. J., *The Home Office and the dangerous trades: regulating occupational disease in Victorian and Edwardian Britain* (Amsterdam, 2002).

The way from dusty death: Turner & Newall and the regulation of occupational health in the British asbestos industry, 1890s–1970 (London, 2001).

Workmen's compensation in twentieth-century Britain: law, history and social policy (Aldershot, 1987).

Bartrip, P. W. J. and Burman, Sandra, *The wounded soldiers of industry: industrial compensation policy, 1833–1897* (Oxford, 1983).

Bartrip, P. W. J. and Fenn, P. T., 'The measurement of safety: factory accident statistics in Victorian and Edwardian Britain', *Historical Research* 63 (1990), pp. 58–72.

'The administration of safety: the enforcement policy of the early factory inspectorate, 1844–1864', *Public Administration* 58 (1980), pp. 87–102.

Bashford, Alison, and MacAdam, Jane, 'The right to asylum: the 1905 Aliens Act and the evolution of refugee law', *Law and History Review* 32/2 (2014), pp. 309–50.

Baums, Theodor, 'Die Einführung der Gefährdungshaftung durch F. C. von Savigny', *Zeitschrift der Savigny Stiftung für Rechtsgeschichte* 104 (1987), pp. 277–82.

Beaud, Jean-Pierre and Prévost, Jean-Guy, 'Statistics as the science of government: the stillborn British Empire Statistical Bureau, 1918–20', *Journal of Imperial and Commonwealth History* 33 (2005), pp. 369–91.

Beck, Ulrich, *Risk society: towards a new modernity*, trans. Mark Ritter (Thousand Oaks, CA, 1992).

Becker, Peter, and Clark, William, eds., *Little tools of knowledge: historical essays on academic and bureaucratic practices* (Ann Arbor, MI, 2001).

Bedford, Thomas, 'Obituary: H. M. Vernon', *Occupational Medicine* 1/1 (1951), pp. 47–8.

Behrent, Michael C., 'Accidents happen: François Ewald, the "antirevolutionary" Foucault, and the intellectual politics of the French welfare state', *Journal of Modern History* 82/3 (2010), pp. 585–624.

Béland, Daniel, 'Ideas and social policy: an institutionalist perspective', *Social Policy and Administration* 39 (2005), pp. 1–18.

Béland, Daniel and Lecours, André, *Nationalism and social policy: the politics of territorial solidarity* (2008; rev. edn, Oxford, 2010).

Bellamy, Richard, *Modern Italian social theory: ideology and politics from Pareto to the present* (Cambridge, 1987).

Benenati, Elisabetta, 'Cento anni di paternalismo aziendale', in Stefano Musso, ed., *Tra fabbrica e societa: mondi operai nell'Italia del novecento* (Milan, 1999), pp. 43–84.

Bennett, Colin J., 'What is policy convergence and what causes it?', *British Journal of Political Science* 21(1991), pp. 215–33.

Benson, John, 'Coalminers, coalowners and collaboration: the miners' permanent relief fund movement in England, 1860–1895', *Labour History Review* 68/2 (2003), pp. 181–94.

Berg, Maxine, *The machinery question and the making of political economy, 1815–1848* (Cambridge, 1980).

Berghahn, Volker R., *Imperial Germany, 1871–1918: economy, society, culture and politics* (rev. edn, Oxford and New York, 2005).

Berlinguer, Giovanni, 'La medicina del lavoro all'inizio del secolo XX. Riflessioni sul I Congresso Internazionale (1906) e sul I Congresso Nazionale (1907) per le malattie del lavoro', in A. Grieco and P. A. Bertazzi, eds., *Per una storiografia italiana della prevenzione occupazionale ed ambientale* (Milan, 1997), pp. 107–24.

Bernstein, Peter L., *Against the gods: the remarkable story of risk* (New York, 1996).

Bessel, Richard, *Germany after the First World War* (Oxford, 1993).

Bettin, Cristina M., *Italian Jews from emancipation to the racial laws* (Basingstoke, 2010).

Bevir, Mark, *The making of British socialism* (Princeton, NJ, 2011).

Bhambra, Gurminder K., 'Comparative sociology and the state: problems of method', *Cultural Sociology* 10 (2016), pp. 1–17.

Bianchi, Bruna, *La follia e la fuga: nevrosi di guerra, diserzioni e disobbedienza nell'esercito italiano (1915–1918)* (Rome, 2001).
    'Salute e rendimento nell'industria bellica (1915–1918)', in Maria Luisa Betri and Ada Gigli Marchetti, eds., *Salute e classi lavoratrici in Italia dall'Unità al fascismo* (Milan, 1982), pp. 101–28.

Biernacki, Richard, *The fabrication of labor: Germany and Britain, 1650–1914* (Berkeley, CA, 1995).

Blanc, Paul D., *How everyday products make people sick: toxins at home and in the workplace* (Berkeley, CA, 2007).

Bogacz, Ted, 'War neurosis and cultural change in England, 1914–22: the work of the War Office committee of enquiry into 'shell-shock', *Journal of Contemporary History* 24 (1989), pp. 227–56.

Bonelli, Franco, 'Appunti sul "welfare state" in Italia', *Studi Storici* 33 (1992), pp. 669–80.

Bonß, Wolfgang, *Unsicherheit und Gewissheit in der Moderne* (Hamburg, 1995).

Borscheid, Peter, 'Europe: an overview', in Peter Borscheid and Niels Viggo Haueter, eds., *World insurance: the evolution of a global risk network* (Oxford, 2012), pp. 37–66.

Bosworth, Richard J. B., *Italy, the least of the Great Powers: Italian foreign policy before the First World War* (Cambridge, 1979).

Bouk, Dan, *How our days became numbered: risk and the rise of the statistical individual* (Chicago, 2015).

Bourdieu, Pierre, *Sur l'État: cours au Collège de France, 1989–1992* (Paris, 2012).

Boyd, William, 'Genealogies of risk: searching for safety, 1930s-1970s', *Ecology Law Quarterly* 39 (2012), pp. 895–987.

Boyer, Josef, *Unfallversicherung und Unternehmer im Bergbau: die Knappschafts-Berufsgenossenschaft 1885–1945* (Munich, 1995).

Bradley, Simon, *The railways: nation, network and people* (London, 2015).

Bridge, John C., 'A pioneer of industrial medicine', *Archiv für Gewerbepathologie und Gewerbehygiene* 7 (1936), pp. 431–6.

Briggs, Asa, 'The welfare state in historical perspective', *European Journal of Sociology* 2/2 (1961), pp. 221–58.

Bronstein, Jamie L., *Caught in the machinery: workplace accidents and injured workers in nineteenth-century Britain* (Stanford, CA, 2008).

Brückweh, Kerstin, Wetzell, Richard, Schumann, D. and Ziemann, B., eds., *Engineering society: the role of the human and social sciences in modern societies, 1880–1980* (Basingstoke, 2012).

Bruner, Stephen C., 'Leopoldo Franchetti and Italian settlement in Eritrea', *European History Quarterly* 39 (2009), pp. 71–94.

Bueck, G. A., *Der Centralverband deutscher Industrieller, 1876–1901* (2 vols., Berlin, 1905).

Bufton, Mark W. and Melling, Joseph, 'Coming up for air: experts, employers, and workers in campaigns to compensate silicosis sufferers in Britain, 1918–1939', *Social History of Medicine* 18/1 (2005), pp. 63–86.

Bulhof, I. N., *Wilhelm Dilthey: a hermeneutic approach to history and culture* (The Hague, 1980), pp. 55–79.

Burnham, John C., *Accident prone: a history of technology, psychology and misfits of the machine age* (Chicago, 2009).

'Accident proneness (*Unfallneigung*): a classic case of simultaneous discovery/construction in psychology', *Science in Context* 21 (2008), pp. 99–118.

Campbell, Joan, *Joy in work, German work: the national debate, 1800–1945* (Princeton, NJ, 1989).

Candeloro, Giorgio, *Storia dell'Italia moderna*, vol. VI: *Lo sviluppo del capitalismo e del movimento operaio* (8th edn, Turin, 1981).

Caracciolo, Alberto, 'La crescita e le trasformazione della grande industria durante la prima guerra mondiale', in Giorgio Fuà, ed., *Lo sviluppo economico in Italia*, vol. III (Milan, 1969), pp. 195–248.

Carnevale, Francesco and Baldasseroni, Alberto, 'Gaetano Pieraccini e la medicina del lavoro in Italia nella prima metà del Novecento', *Medicina e Storia* 2 (December 2011), pp. 29–43.

Mal da lavoro: storia della salute dei lavoratori (Rome, 1999).

Carnevale, Francesco and Ravenni, Gian Bruno, *Gaetano Pieraccini medico del lavoro. La salute dei lavoratori in Toscana all'inizio del XX secolo* (Florence, 1993).

Castel, Robert, *L'insécurité sociale: qu'est-ce qu'être protégé?* (Paris, 2003).

Cazamian, Louis, *The social novel in England, 1830–1850: Dickens, Disraeli, Mrs. Gaskell, Kingsley*, trans. Martin Fido (London, 1973).

Cazzetta, Giovanni, *Scienza giuridica e trasformazioni sociali: diritto e lavoro in Italia tra otto e novecento* (Milan, 2007).

Cerasi, Laura, 'Anglophilia in crisis: Italian liberals, the English model and democracy in the Giolittian era', *Modern Italy* 7 (2002), pp. 5–22.

Charlesworth, Lorie, *Welfare's forgotten past: a socio-legal history of the poor law* (London, 2011).

Chatterjee, Partha, *The nation and its fragments: colonial and postcolonial histories* (Princeton, NJ, 1993).

Cherubini, Arndalo, *Beneficenza e solidarietà: assistenza pubblica e mutualismo operaio (1860–1900)* (Milan, 1991).

Medicina e lotte sociali 1900–1920 (Rome, 1980).

Storia della previdenza sociale in italia, 1860–1960 (Rome, 1977).

Cherubini, Arnaldo and Piva, Italo, *Dalla libertà all'obbligo: la previdenza sociale fra Giolitti e Mussolini* (Milan, 1998).

Chickering, Roger, *Imperial Germany and the Great War, 1914–1918* (3rd edn, Cambridge, 2014).

'World War and the theory of total war: reflections on the British and German cases, 1914–1915', in Roger Chickering and Stig Förster, eds., *Great War, total war: combat and mobilization on the Western Front, 1914–1918* (Cambridge, 2000), pp. 35–56.

Choate, Mark I., *Emigrant nation: the making of Italy abroad* (Cambridge, MA, 2008).

Clark, Geoffrey W., *Betting on lives: the culture of life insurance in England, 1695–1775* (Manchester, 1999).

Clark, Martin, *Modern Italy: 1871 to the present* (3rd edn, London, 2008).

Clasen, Jochen, 'From unemployment programmes to "work first": is German labour market policy becoming British?', in Jochen Clasen, ed., *Converging worlds of welfare? British and German social policy in the 21st century* (Oxford, 2011), pp. 266–81.

Cohen, Deborah, 'The war's returns: disabled veterans in Britain and Germany, 1914–1939', in Roger Chickering and Stig Förster, eds., *The shadows of total war: Europe, East Asia and the United States, 1919–1939* (Cambridge, 2003), pp. 113–29.

The war come home: disabled veterans in Britain and Germany, 1914–1939 (Berkeley, CA, 2001).

'Will to work: disabled veterans in Britain and Germany', in David A. Gerber, ed., *Disabled veterans in history* (2000; revised edn, Ann Arbor, MI, 2012), pp. 295–322.

Collini, Stefan, 'Hobhouse, Bosanquet and the state: philosophical idealism and political argument in England, 1880–1918', *Past and Present* (1976), pp. 86–111.

Connolly, Angela, 'Psychoanalytic theory in times of terror', *Journal of Analytical Psychology* 48 (August 2003), pp. 407–41.

Conze, Werner, 'Vom "Pöbel" zum "Proletariat": sozialgeschichtliche Voraussetzungen für den Sozialismus in Deutschland', *Vierteljahrsschrift für Sozial- und Wirtschaftsgeschichte* 41 (1954), pp. 333–64.

Cooke, Chris and Stevenson, John, *A history of British elections since 1689* (London, 2014).

Cooter, Roger, 'The moment of the accident: culture, militarism and modernity in late-Victorian Britain', in Roger Cooter and Bill Luckin, eds., *Accidents in history: injuries, fatalities and social relations* (Amsterdam, 1997), pp. 107–57.

Corner, Paul, 'The road to fascism: an Italian *Sonderweg*?', *Contemporary European History* 11 (2002), pp. 273–95.

Corner, Paul and Procacci, Giovanna, 'The Italian experience of "total" mobilization, 1915–1920', in John Horne, ed., *State, society and mobilization in Europe during the First World War* (Cambridge, 1997), pp. 223–40.

Cornish, William R. and Clarke, Geoffrey de N., *Law and society in England, 1750–1950* (London, 1989).

Corrigan, Philip and Sayer, Derek, *The great arch: English state formation as cultural revolution* (Oxford, 1985).

Cronin, James E., *The politics of state expansion: war, state and society in twentieth-century Britain* (London, 1991).

Crook, Tom, *Governing systems: modernity and the making of public health in England, c. 1830–1910* (Berkeley, 2016).

Crook, Tom and Esbester, Mike, eds., *Governing risks in modern Britain: danger, safety and accidents, c. 1800–2000* (Basingstoke, 2016).

Crosby, Travis L., *Joseph Chamberlain: a most radical imperialist* (London, 2011).

Crowther, M. A. and White, Brenda M., 'Property and the law in Britain, 1800–1914', *Historical Journal* 31 (1988), pp. 853–70.

Cullen, M. J., *The statistical movement in early Victorian Britain: the foundations of empirical social research* (Hassocks, 1975).

Daniel, Ute, *Arbeiterfrauen in der Kriegsgesellschaft: Beruf, Familie und Politik im Ersten Weltkrieg* (Göttingen, 1989).

Davis, Belinda J., *Home fires burning: food, politics and everyday life in World War I Berlin* (Chapel Hill, NC, 2000).

'Review: experience, identity, and memory: the legacy of World War I', *Journal of Modern History* 75/1 (2003), pp. 111–31.

Davis, John A., *Conflict and control: law and order in nineteenth-century Italy* (Basingstoke, 1988).

'Remapping Italy's path to the twentieth century', *Journal of Modern History* 66/2 (1994), pp. 291–320.

Debè, Anna and Polenghi, Simonetta, 'Assistance and education of mutilated soldiers of World War I: the Italian case', *History of Education and Children's Literature* 11 (2016), pp. 227–46.

de Grand, Alexander, 'Comment on Corner: Giolitti's Italy: Sonderweg or well-travelled road?', *Contemporary European History* 11 (2002), pp. 296–300.

de Grazia, Victoria, *The culture of consent: mass organization of leisure in Fascist Italy* (Cambridge, 1981).

Dentoni, Maria Concetta, '"Questioni alimentare" e "questione sociale" durante la prima guerra mondiale in Italia', *Società e Storia* 37 (1987), pp. 612–46.

de Renzi, Silvia, 'La natura in tribunale: conoscenze a pratiche medico-legale a Roma nel XVII secolo', *Quaderni Storici* 36 (2001), pp. 799–822.

de Roover, Florence Edler, 'Early examples of marine insurance', *Journal of Economic History* 5 (1945), pp. 172–200.

de Vries, Jan, *The industrious revolution: consumer behaviour and the household economy, 1650 to the present* (Cambridge, 2008).

Dinsdale, W. A., *History of accident insurance in Great Britain* (London, 1954).

Dolowitz, David and Marsh, David, 'Learning from abroad: the role of policy transfer in contemporary policy-making', *Governance: An International Journal of Policy and Administration* 13 (2000), pp. 5–24.

Duggan, Christopher, *The force of destiny: a history of Italy since 1796* (London, 2007).

Dupree, Marguerite W., 'Other than healing: medical practitioners and the business of life assurance during the nineteenth and early twentieth century', *Social History of Medicine* 10 (1997), pp. 79–103.

Eghigian, Greg, *Making security social: disability, insurance, and the birth of the social entitlement state in Germany* (Ann Arbor, MI, 2000).

Eisner, Marc Allen, *From warfare state to welfare state: World War I, compensatory state building and the limits of the modern order* (University Park, PA, 2000).

Eley, Geoff, *Forging democracy: the history of the left in Europe, 1850–2000* (Oxford, 2002).

Eley, Geoff and Blackbourn, David, *The peculiarities of German history: bourgeois society and politics in nineteenth-century Germany* (Oxford, 1984).

Emy, H. V., *Liberals, radicals and social politics, 1892–1914* (Cambridge, 1973).

Ernst, Wolfgang, 'Negligence in 19th-century Germany', in Eltjo J. H. Schrage, ed., *Negligence: the comparative legal history of the law of torts* (Berlin, 2001), pp. 341–59.

Esbester, Mike, *The birth of modern safety: preventing accidents on Britain's railways, 1871–1948* (London, 2017).

'Organizing work: company magazines and the discipline of safety', *Management and Organizational History* 3/3–4 (2008), pp. 217–37.

Esping-Andersen, Gøsta, *Politics against markets: the social democratic road to power* (Princeton, NJ, 1985).

The three worlds of welfare capitalism (Oxford, 1990).

Euchner, Walter, Grebing, Helga, Stegmann, F.-J. et al., *Geschichte der sozialen Ideen in Deutschland: Sozialismus, Katholische Soziallehre, Protestantische Sozialethik: ein Handbuch* (2nd edn, Wiesbaden, 2005).

Evans, Peter, Rueschemeyer, Dietrich and Skocpol, Theda, eds., *Bringing the state back in* (Cambridge, 1985).

Ewald, François, *L'état providence* (Paris, 1986).

'Insurance and risk', in Graham Burchell, Colin Gordon and Alfred Foot, eds., *The Foucault effect: studies in governmentality, with two lectures by and an interview with Michel Foucault*(Chicago, 1991), pp. 197–210.

Faini, Riccardo and Venturini, Alessandra, 'Italian emigration in the pre-war period', in Timothy J. Hatton and Jeffrey G. Williamson, eds., *Migration and the international labour market* (London, 1994), pp. 72–90.

Fargion, Valeria, 'Italy: a territorial and generational divide in social citizenship', in Adalbert Evers and Anne-Marie Guillemard, eds., *Social policy and citizenship: the changing landscape* (Oxford, 2013), pp. 173–97.

Farrell-Vinay, Giovanna, 'The old charities and the new state: structures and problems of welfare in Italy (1860–1890)' (PhD thesis, University of Edinburgh, 1989).

Feld, Ina vom, *Staatsentlastung im Technikrecht: Dampfkesselgesetzgebung und -überwachung in Preußen, 1831–1914* (Frankfurt a.M., 2007).

Feldman, Gerald D., *Army, industry, and labor in Germany, 1914–1918* (Princeton, NJ, 1966).

The great disorder: politics, economics, and society in the German inflation, 1914–1924 (New York, 1996).

Ferrera, Maurizio, 'Italy', in Peter Flora, ed., *Growth to limits: the Western European welfare states since World War II*, vol. II: *Germany, United Kingdom, Ireland, Italy* (Berlin, 1986), pp. 385–500.

'The "southern model" of welfare in social Europe', *Journal of European Social Policy* 6 (1996), pp. 17–37.

Ferrera, Maurizio and Gualmini, Elisabetta, 'Reforms guided by consensus: the welfare state and the Italian transition', in Maurizio Ferrera and Martin Rhodes, eds., *Recasting European welfare states* (London, 2000), pp. 187–208.

Feuchtwanger, Edgar, *Bismarck* (London, 2002).

Figlio, Karl, 'What is an accident?', in Paul Weindling, ed., *The social history of occupational health* (London, 1985), pp. 180–206.

Finnis, John, *Natural law and natural rights* (1980; 2nd edn, Oxford, 2011).

Fischer-Homberger, Esther, *Die traumatische Neurosen: vom somatischen zum sozialen Leiden* (Berne, 1975).

Fishback, Price V. and Kantor, Shawn E., *A prelude to the welfare state: the origins of workers' compensation* (Chicago, 2000).

Flora, Peter and Alber, Jens, 'Modernization, democratization, and the development of welfare states in Western Europe', in Peter Flora and Arnold J. Heidenheimer, eds., *The development of welfare states in Europe and America* (New Brunswick, NJ, 1981), pp. 37–80.

Foucault, Michel, 'Governmentality', in Graham Burchell, Colin Gordon and Alfred Foot, eds., *The Foucault effect: studies in governmentality, with two lectures by and an interview with Michel Foucault*(Chicago, 1991), pp. 87–104.

Frankel, Oz, *States of inquiry: social investigations and print culture in nineteenth-century Britain and the United States* (Baltimore, 2006).

Frascani, Paolo, 'La disciplina delle industrie insalubri nella legislazione sanitaria italiana, 1865–1910', in Maria Luisa Betri, and Ada Gigli Marchetti, eds., *Salute e classi lavoratrici in Italia dall'Unità al fascismo* (Milan, 1982), pp. 713–35.

'Medicina e statistica nella formazione del sistema sanitario italiano: l'inchiesta del 1885', *Quaderni Storici* 15 (1980), pp. 942–66.

Fraunholz, Uwe, *Motorphobia: anti-automobiler Protest in Kaiserreich und Weimarer Republik* (Göttingen, 2002).

Freeden, Michael, 'The stranger at the feast: ideology and public policy in twentieth-century Britain', *Twentieth Century British History* 1 (1990), pp. 9–34.

Freedgood, Elaine, *Victorian writing about risk: imagining a safe England in a dangerous world* (Cambridge, 2000).

Fressoz, Jean-Baptiste, *L'apocalypse joyeuse: une histoire du risque technologique* (Paris, 2012).

Friedman, Lawrence M., 'Civil wrongs: personal injury law in the late 19th century', *American Bar Foundation Research Journal* 12 (1987).

The republic of choice: law, authority and culture (Cambridge, MA, 1990).

Fritz, Wolfgang, 'Historie der amtlichen Statistiken der Erwerbstätigkeit in Deutschland: ein fragmentarischer Abriß: Darstellung, Quellen, Daten, Definitionen, Chronik', *Historical Social Research* 13 (2001), supplement, pp. 159–62.

Frohman, Larry, *Poor relief and welfare in Germany from the Reformation to World War I* (Cambridge, 2008).

Gabaccia, Donna R., *Foreign relations: American immigration in global perspective* (Princeton, NJ, 2012).

Gabaccia, Donna R. and Ottanelli, Fraser M., eds., *Italian workers of the world: labor migration and the formation of multiethnic states* (Urbana and Chicago, 2001).

Geary, Dick, *European labour protest, 1848–1939* (London, 1984).

Gelder, Ken, *Reading the vampire* (London, 1994).

Geyer, Martin H., *Verkehrte Welt: Revolution, Inflation und Moderne: München, 1914–1924* (Göttingen, 1998).

Geyer, Michael, 'Ein Vorbote des Wohlfahrtstaates: die Kriegsopferversorgung in Frankreich, Deutschland und Grossbritannien nach dem Ersten Weltkrieg', *Geschichte und Gesellschaft* 9/2 (1983), pp. 230–77.

Gibelli, Antonio, *La Grande Guerra degli italiani, 1915–1918* (Milan, 1998).

Giddens, Anthony, 'Risk and responsibility', *Modern Law Review* 62 (1999), pp. 1–10.

Gigerenzer, Gerd, Zweijtink, Zeno, Porter, Theodore et al., *The empire of chance: how probability changed science and everyday life* (Cambridge, 1989).

Gilbert, Bentley B., *The evolution of national insurance in Great Britain: the origins of the welfare state* (London, 1966).

Giles, Audrey C., 'Railway accidents and nineteenth-century legislation: "misconduct, want of caution or causes beyond their control"', *Labour History Review* 76/2 (2011), pp. 121–42.

Ginsborg, Paul, *Italy and its discontents: family, civil society, state 1980–2001* (London, 2001).

Girotti, Fiorenzo, *Welfare state: storia, modelli, critica* (Rome, 1998).

Glennerster, Howard, *British social policy: 1945 to the present* (3rd edn, Abingdon, 2007).

Glootz, Tanja Anette, *Geschichte der Angestelltenversicherung des 20. Jahrhunderts* (Berlin, 1999).

Goetz, Christopher G., Bonduelle, Michel and Geljand, Toby, *Charcot: constructing neurology* (Oxford, 1995).

Golder, Ben and Fitzpatrick, Peter, *Foucault's law* (London, 2009).

Goldman, Lawrence, *Science, reform and politics in Victorian Britain: the Social Science Association, 1857–1886* (Cambridge, 2002).

Gozzi, Gustavo, *Modelli politici e questione sociale in Italia e in Germania fra Otto e Novecento* (Bologna, 1988).

Gray, Robert, *The factory question and industrial England, 1830–1860* (Cambridge, 1996).

Green, Abigail, *Fatherlands: state-building and nationhood in nineteenth-century Germany* (Cambridge, 2001).

Green, E. H. H., *The crisis of conservatism: the politics, economics and ideology of the British Conservative Party, 1880–1914* (London, 1995).

Gregory, Adrian, *The last Great War: British society and the First World War* (Cambridge, 2008).

Grieves, Keith, 'Lloyd George and the management of the British war economy', in Roger Chickering and Stig Förster, eds., *Great War, total war: combat and mobilization on the Western Front, 1914–1918* (Cambridge, 2000), pp. 369–88.

Grimmer-Solem, Erik, *The rise of historical economics and social reform in Germany, 1864–1894* (Oxford, 2003).

Gusejnova, Dina, *European elites and ideas of empire, 1917–1957* (Cambridge, 2016).

Gustapane, Enrico, 'L'influenza tedesca sull'istituzione in Italia della Cassa di previdenza per l'invalidità e per la vecchiaia degli operai', *Jahrbuch für europäische Verwaltungsgeschichte* 5 (1993), pp. 179–214.

Habermas, Jürgen, *Theorie des kommunikativen Handelns*, vol. II: *Zur Kritik der funktionalistischen Vernunft* (1981; repr., Frankfurt, 1995), pp. 530–47.

Hacker, Jacob S., *The great risk shift: the new economic insecurity and the decline of the American dream* (Oxford, 2008).

  The divided welfare state: the battle over public and private social benefits in the United States (Cambridge, 2002).

Hacking, Ian, 'Risk and dirt', in Richard V. Ericson and Aaron Doyle, eds., *Risk and morality* (Toronto, 2003), pp. 22–37.

  The taming of chance (Cambridge, 1990).

  'Was there a probabilistic revolution, 1800–1930?', in Lorenz Krüger, Lorraine Daston and Michael Heidelberger, eds., *The probabilistic revolution*, vol. I: *Ideas in history* (Cambridge, MA, 1987), pp. 45–55.

  'Making up people', in Thomas C. Heller, Morton Sosna and David E. Wellbery, eds., *Reconstructing individualism: autonomy, individuality, and the self in Western thought* (Stanford, CA, 1986), pp. 222–36.

Haferkamp, Hans-Peter, 'The science of private law and the state in nineteenth-century Germany', *American Journal of Comparative Law* 56 (2008), pp. 667–89.

Halford, Peter, 'Lord Campbell and the Fatal Accidents Act', *Law Quarterly Review* 129 (2013), pp. 420–49.

Hall, Peter A. and Taylor, Rosemary C. R., 'Political science and the three new institutionalisms', *Political Studies* 45 (1996), pp. 936–57.

Halttunen, Karen, 'Humanitarianism and the pornography of pain in Anglo-American culture', *American Historical Review* 100/2 (1995), pp. 303–34.

Hamilton, John T. *Security: politics, humanity and the philology of care* (Princeton, NJ, 2013).

Hamilton, Ross, *Accident: a philosophical and literary history* (Chicago, 2008).

Hamlin, Christopher, *Public health and social justice in the age of Chadwick: Britain 1800–1854* (Cambridge, 1998).

Hanagan, Michael, 'Citizenship, claim-making, and the right to work: Britain, 1884–1911', *Theory and Society* 26 (1997), pp. 449–74.

Hanes, David G., *The first British Workmen's Compensation Act, 1897* (New Haven, 1968).

Harrington, Ralph, 'On the tracks of trauma: railway spine reconsidered', *Social History of Medicine* 16 (2003), pp. 209–23.

Harris, Jose, *Private lives, public spirit: Britain, 1870–1914* (London, 1993).

  'Political thought and the welfare state, 1870–1930: an intellectual framework for British social policy', *Past and Present* (1992), pp. 116–41.

  'Victorian values and the founders of the welfare state', *Proceedings of the British Academy* 78 (1992), pp. 165–82.

  'Enterprise and welfare states: a comparative perspective', *Transactions of the Royal Historical Society* (5th Series) 40 (1990), pp. 175–95.

  'Society and the state in twentieth-century Britain', in F. M. L. Thompson, ed., *The Cambridge social history of Britain, 1750–1950* (3 vols., Cambridge, 1990), vol. III, pp. 63–119.

  'The transition to high politics in English social policy, 1880–1914', in Michael Bentley and John Stevenson, eds., *High and low politics in modern Britain* (Oxford, 1983), pp. 59–79.

  'Did British workers want the welfare state? G. D. H. Cole's survey of 1942', in J. Winter, ed., *The working class in modern British history* (Cambridge, 1983), pp. 200–14.

Unemployment and politics: a study in English social policy, 1886–1914 (Oxford, 1972).

Harrison, Barbara, 'Are accidents gender neutral? The case of women's industrial work in Britain, 1880–1914', *Women's History Review* 2 (1993), pp. 253–75.

Not only the 'dangerous trades': women's work and health in Britain, 1880–1914 (London, 1996).

Hart, Jennifer, 'The genesis of the Northcote–Trevelyan report', in Gillian Sutherland, ed., *Studies in the growth of nineteenth-century government* (Cambridge, 1973), pp. 63–81.

Haskell, Thomas L., 'Capitalism and the origins of the humanitarian sensibility, part 1', *American Historical Review* 90/2 (1985), pp. 339–61.

Häusermann, Silja, *The politics of welfare state reform in continental Europe: modernization in hard times* (Cambridge, 2010).

Hay, Douglas, 'England, 1562–1975: the law and its uses', in D. Hay and P. Craven, eds., *Masters, servants and magistrates in Britain and the Empire, 1562–1955* (Chapel Hill, NC, 2004), pp. 59–116.

Hay, Douglas and Craven, Paul, 'Introduction', in D. Hay and P. Craven, eds., *Masters, servants and magistrates in Britain and the Empire, 1562–1955* (Chapel Hill, NC, 2004), pp. 1–58.

Healy, Jonathan, *The first century of welfare: poverty and poor relief in Lancashire, 1620–1730* (Woodbridge, 2014).

Hecht, Gabrielle, *Being nuclear: Africans and the global uranium trade* (Cambridge, MA, 2012).

Heclo, Hugh, *Modern social politics in Britain and Sweden: from relief to income maintenance* (New Haven, 1974).

Henderson, William O., *The rise of German industrial power, 1834–1914* (Berkeley, CA, 1975).

Hennock, E. P., *British social reform and German precedents: the case of social insurance 1880–1914* (Oxford, 1987).

The origin of the welfare state in England and Germany, 1850–1914: social policies compared (Cambridge, 2007).

Herren, Madeleine, *Internationale Sozialpolitik vor dem Ersten Weltkrieg: die Anfänge europäischer Kooperation aus der Sicht Frankreichs* (Berlin, 1993).

Herzfeld, Michael, *The social production of indifference: exploring the symbolic roots of Western bureaucracy* (Chicago, 1992).

Hilton, Boyd. *The age of atonement: the influence of Evangelicalism on social and economic thought, 1785–1865* (Oxford, 1991).

Holzinger, Katharina and Knill, Christoph, 'Causes and conditions of cross-national policy convergence', *Journal of European Public Policy* 12 (2005), 775–96.

Horne, Janet, *A social laboratory for modern France: the Musée social and the rise of the welfare state* (Durham, NC, 2002).

Horne, John, ed., *State, society and mobilization in Europe during the First World War* (Cambridge, 1997).

Horowitz, Daniel L., *The Italian labor movement* (Cambridge, MA, 1963).

Hyde, John Kenneth, *Society and politics in medieval Italy: the evolution of the civil life, 1000–1350* (London, 1973).

Ibbetson, David J., 'The tort of negligence in the common law in the nineteenth and twentieth centuries', in Eltjo J. H. Schrage, ed., *Negligence: the comparative legal history of the law of torts* (Berlin, 2001), pp. 229–71.

Innocenti, Maurizio Degl', *La società volontaria e solidale: il cantiere del welfare pubblico e privato* (Rome, 2012).

Itzen, Peter, 'Who is responsible in winter? Traffic accidents, the fight against hazardous weather and the role of law in a history of risks', *Historical Social Research* 41 (2016), pp. 154–75.

Jackson, Christopher R., 'Infirmative action: the Law of the Severely Disabled in Germany', *Central European History* 26/4 (1993), pp. 417–55.

Jeserich, Kurt G. A., Pohl, Hans and von Unruh, Georg-Christoph, eds., *Deutsche Verwaltungsgeschichte* (4 vols., Stuttgart, 1984).

John, Michael, *Politics and the law in late nineteenth-century Germany: the origins of the civil code* (Oxford, 1989).

Johnson, Paul, 'Class law in Victorian England', *Past and Present* 141 (1993), pp. 147–69.

Joyce, Patrick, *The state of freedom: a social history of the British state since 1800* (Cambridge, 2013).

    Visions of the people: industrial England and the question of class, 1848–1914 (Cambridge, 1994).

    Work, society and politics: the culture of the factory in later Victorian England (Brighton, 1980).

Kaelble, Hartmut, *A social history of Western Europe: 1880–1980* (Dublin, 1987).

Karl, Michael, *Fabrikinspektoren in Preußen: das Personal der Gewerbeaufsicht 1854–1945* (Opladen, 1993).

Kasza, Gregory James, *One world of welfare: Japan in comparative perspective* (Ithaca, NY, 2006).

Kennedy, Paul M., *The rise of the Anglo-German antagonism 1860–1914* (London, 1982).

Kersbergen, Kees van and Manow, Philip, eds., *Religion, class coalitions and welfare states* (Cambridge, 2009).

Kidd, Alan J., *State, society and the poor in nineteenth-century England* (Basingstoke, 1999).

Killen, Andreas, *Berlin electropolis: shock, nerves and German modernity* (Berkeley, CA, 2006).

    'From shock to *Schreck*: psychiatrists, telephone operators and traumatic neurosis in Germany, 1900–26', *Journal of Contemporary History* 38/2 (2003), pp. 201–20.

Kleeberg, John M., 'From strict liability to workers' compensation: the Prussian Railroad Law, the German Liability Act, and the introduction of Bismarck's accident insurance in Germany, 1838–1884', *NYU Journal of International Law and Politics* 36 (2003), pp. 53–132.

Kocka, Jürgen, *Facing total war: German society, 1914–1918* (Cambridge, MA, 1984).

    'The First World War and the "Mittelstand": German artisans and white-collar workers', *Journal of Contemporary History* 8/1 (1973), pp. 101–23.

Korpi, Walter, *The democratic class struggle* (London, 1983).

Koselleck, Reinhart, *Preußen zwischen Reform und Revolution: allgemeines Landrecht, Verwaltung und soziale Bewegung von 1791 bis 1848* (Stuttgart, 1967).

Koskenniemi, Martti, *The gentle civilizer of nations: the rise and fall of international law, 1870–1960* (Cambridge, 2001).

Kostal, R. W., *Law and English railway capitalism, 1825–1875* (Oxford, 1994).

Kott, Sandrine, *Sozialstaat und Gesellschaft: das deutsche Kaiserreich in Europa* (Göttingen, 2014).

'Constructing a European social model: the fight for social insurance in the interwar period', in Jasmien van Daele, Magaly Rodriguez García, Geert Van Goethem and Marcel van der Linden, eds., *ILO histories: essays on the International Labour Organization and its impact on the world during the twentieth century* (Berne, 2010), pp. 173–96.

'Der Sozialstaat', in Etienne François, and Hagen Schulze, eds., *Deutsche Erinnerungsorte*, 3 vols. (Munich, 2001), vol. II, pp. 485–501.

'Éléments pour une histoire sociale et culturelle de la religion en Allemagne au XIX siècle', *Revue d'Histoire Moderne et Contemporaine* 5 (2001), pp. 92–111.

'Gemeinschaft oder Solidarität: unterschiedliche Modelle der französischen und deutschen Sozialpolitik am Ende des 19. Jahrhunderts', *Geschichte und Gesellschaft* 3/3 (1996), pp. 311–30.

Kott, Sandrine and Droux, Joëlle, eds., *Globalizing social rights: the International Labor Organization and beyond* (Basingstoke, 2013).

Knowles, C. M., 'State control of industrial accident insurance', *Journal of Comparative Legislation and International Law* 2 (1920), pp. 29–50.

Kolsky, Elizabeth, *Colonial justice in British India: white violence and the rule of law* (Cambridge, 2009).

Kreis, Steven, 'Early experiments in British scientific management: the Health of Munitions Workers Committee, 1915–20', *Journal of Management History* 1 (1995), pp. 65–78.

Krieger, Joel, 'Britain', in Mark Kesselman, Joel Krieger and William A. Joseph, eds., *Introduction to comparative politics* (5th edn, Boston, 2010), pp. 47–98.

Kurer, Oskar, 'John Stuart Mill and the welfare state', *History of Political Economy* 23 (1991), pp. 713–30.

Kuznets, Simon, 'Quantitative aspects of the economic growth of nations. II: Industrial distribution of national product and labour force', *Economic Development and Cultural Change* 5 (1957), Supplement.

Lacey, Michael J. and Furner, Mary O., eds., *The state and social investigation in Britain and the United States* (Cambridge, 1993).

Langewiesche, Dieter, 'Staat und Commune: zum Wandel der Staatsaufgaben in Deutschland in 19. Jahrhundert', *Historische Zeitschrift* 248 (1989), pp. 621–35.

Laqueur, Thomas W., 'Bodies, details, and the humanitarian narrative', in Lynn Hunt, ed., *The new cultural history* (Berkeley, CA, 1989), pp. 176–204.

Lees, Lynn Hollen, *The solidarities of strangers: the English Poor Laws and the people, 1700–1948* (Cambridge, 1998).

Leese, Peter, *Shell shock: traumatic neurosis and the British soldiers of the First World War* (Basingstoke, 2002).

Legendre, Pierre, *Leçons VI: Les enfants du texte. Étude sur la fonction parentale des états* (Paris, 1992).

Lengwiler, Martin, *Risikopolitik im Sozialstaat: die Schweizerische Unfallversicherung, 1870–1970* (Cologne, 2006).

Lerner, Paul, *Hysterical men: war, psychiatry, and the politics of trauma in Germany, 1890–1930* (Ithaca, NY, 2003).

Le Roux, Thomas, *Le laboratoire des pollutions industrielles: Paris, 1770–1830* (Paris, 2011).

ed., *Risques industriels: savoirs, régulations, politiques d'assistance, fin XVIIe–début XXe siècle* (Rennes, 2016).

Lester, V. Markham, 'The employers' liability/workmen's compensation debate of the 1890s revisited', *Historical Journal* 44 (2001), pp. 471–95.

Levin, Michael, *The condition of England question: Carlyle, Mill, Engels* (New York, 1998).

Levy, Jonathan, *Freaks of fortune: the emerging world of capitalism and risk* (Cambridge, MA, 2012).

Lewis, Jane, 'Gender and welfare in modern Europe', *Past and Present*, Supplement (2006), pp. 39–54.

Lewis, Richard, 'Employers' liability and workers' compensation: England and Wales', in Ken Oliphant and Gerhard Wagner, eds., *Employers' liability and workmen's compensation* (Berlin, 2012), pp. 137–202.

Lindenfeld, David F., *The practical imagination: the German sciences of state in the nineteenth century* (Chicago, 1997).

Linker, Beth, *War's waste: rehabilitation in World War I America* (Chicago, 2011).

Lobban, Michael and Moses, Julia, 'Introduction', in Michael Lobban and Julia Moses, eds., *The impact of ideas on legal development* (Cambridge, 2012), pp. 1–33.

Long, Vicky, *The rise and fall of the healthy factory: the politics of industrial health in Britain, 1914–60* (Basingstoke, 2010).

Lonni, Ada, 'Fatalità o responsabilità? "Le jatture" degli infortuni sul lavoro: la legge del 1898', in Maria Luisa Betri and Ada Gigli Marchetti, eds., *Salute e classi lavoratrici in Italia dall'Unità al fascismo* (Milan, 1982), pp. 737–62.

Lowe, Boutelle Ellsworth, *The international protection of labor* (New York, 1921).

Luhmann, Niklas, *Political theory in the welfare state* (Berlin, 1990).

    Risk: a sociological theory, trans. Rhodes Barrett (New York, 1993).

    Soziologische Aufklärung (6 vols., 2nd edn, Opladen, 1993).

Lupton, Deborah, *Medicine as culture: illness, death and the body* (1994; 3rd edn, London, 2012).

Lyons, Amelia H., *The civilizing mission in the metropole: Algerian families and the French welfare state during decolonization* (Stanford, CA, 2013).

MacDonagh, Oliver, 'The nineteenth century revolution in government: a reappraisal', *Historical Journal* 1 (1958), pp. 52–67.

    The pattern of government growth: the Passenger Acts 1800–1860 (London, 1961).

Machtan, Lothar, 'Risikoversicherung statt Gesundheitsschutz für Arbeiter: zur Entstehung der Unfallversicherungsgesetzgebung im Bismarck-Reich', *Leviathan* 13 (1985), pp. 420–41.

McIvor, Arthur J., *Organised capital: employers' associations and industrial relations in northern England, 1880–1939* (Cambridge, 1996).

    'Employers, the government, and industrial fatigue in Britain, 1890–1918', *British Journal of Industrial Medicine* 44 (1987), pp. 724–32.

McIvor, Arthur and Johnston, Ronnie, *Miners' lung: a history of dust disease in British coal mining* (London, 2007).

McKibbin, Ross, 'Why was there no Marxism in Great Britain?', *English Historical Review* 99 (1984), pp. 297–331.

Maddison, Angus, *Monitoring the world economy, 1820–1992* (Paris, 1995).

Maier, Charles S., *Recasting bourgeois Europe: stabilization in France, Germany and Italy in the decade after World War I* (Princeton, NJ, 1975).

Maifreda, Germano, *La disciplina del lavoro* (Milan, 2007).

Mallalieu, W. C., 'Joseph Chamberlain and workmen's compensation', *Journal of Economic History* 10 (1950), pp. 45–57.

Malinowski, Stephan, *Vom König zum Führer: der deutscher Adel und Nationalsozialismus* (Frankfurt, 2004).

Malone, Carolyn, *Women's bodies and dangerous trades in England, 1880–1914* (Woodbridge, 2003).

Mandler, Peter, 'After the welfare state', *Journal of British Studies* 39 (2000), pp. 382–8.
'Cain and Abel: two aristocrats and the early Victorian factory acts', *Historical Journal* 27 (1984).

Mares, Isabela, *The politics of social risk: business and welfare state development* (Cambridge, 2003).

Marucco, Dora, *Lavoro e previdenza dall'Unità al fascismo: il Consiglio della previdenza dal 1869 al 1923* (Milan, 1984).

Maul, Daniel, *Human rights, development and decolonization: the International Labour Organization, 1940–70* (Basingstoke, 2012).

Mayer, Arno J., 'The lower middle class as historical problem', *Journal of Modern History* 47/3 (1975), pp. 409–36.

Melis, Guido, *La burocrazia: da Monsù Travet alle riforme Bassanini: vizi e virtù della burocrazia italiana* (Bologna, 1998).

Menz, Georg, '*Auf Wiedersehen*, Rhineland model: embedding neoliberalism in Germany', in Susanne Soederberg, Georg Menz and Philip Cerny, eds., *Internalizing globalization: the rise of neoliberalism and the decline of national varieties of capitalism* (Basingstoke, 2005), pp. 33–49.

Micale, Mark S., *Hysterical men: the hidden history of male nervous illness* (Cambridge, MA, 2008).

Micale, Mark S. and Lerner, Paul, eds., *Traumatic pasts: history, psychiatry and trauma in the modern age, 1870–1930* (Cambridge, 2001).

Middlemas, Keith, *Politics in industrial society: the experience of the British system since 1911* (London, 1979).

Milles, Dietrich, 'Produktivität schützen, Wachstum sichern: die Schweiz und der deutsche Arbeiterschutz im 19. Jahrhundert', in Historischer Verein des Kantons Glarus, ed., *Das Glarner Fabrikgesetz und der Arbeiterschutz im 19. Jahrhundert* (Näfels, 2015), pp. 79–116.
'Industrial hygiene: a state obligation? Industrial pathology as a problem in German social policy', in W. R. Lee and Eve Rosenhaft, eds., *State, social policy and social change in Germany, 1880–1994* (1990; Oxford, 1997), pp. 164–202.
Gesundheitsrisiken, Industriegesellschaft und Soziale Sicherungen in der Geschichte (Bremerhaven, 1993).
'Medical opinion and sociopolitical control in the case of occupational diseases in the late nineteenth century', *Dyanmis* 13 (1993), pp. 139–53.

Mitchell, Allan, *The divided path: the German influence on social reform in France after 1871* (Chapel Hill, NC, 1991).

Mitchell, Brian R., *Abstract of British historical statistics* (Cambridge, 1971).
British historical statistics (Cambridge, 1988).
European historical statistics, 1750–1970 (London, 1975).

Mitchell, Timothy, 'The limits of the state: beyond statist approaches and their critics', *American Political Science Review* 85/1 (1991), pp. 77–96.

Mohun, Arwen, *Risk: negotiating safety in American society* (Baltimore, 2013).

Mola, Aldo A., *Giovanni Gioliti: lo statista della nuova Italia* (Milan, 2006).

Monteleone, Giulio, 'La legislazione sociale al parlamento italiano: gli infortuni sul lavoro e la responsabilità civile dei padroni, 1879–1886', *Movimento Operaio e Socialista* 22 (1976), pp. 177–214.

'La legislazione sociale al parlamento italiano: la legge del 1886 sul lavoro dei fanciulli', *Movimento Operaio e Socialista* 20 (1974), pp. 229–84.

Morsey, Rudolf, 'Die öffentlichen Aufgaben und die Gliederung der Kompetenzen zwischen Norddeutschen Bund, Reich und Bundesstaaten, 1867–1914', in Kurt G. A. Jeserich, Hans Pohl and Georg-Christoph von Unruh, eds., *Deutsche Verwaltungsgeschichte*, vol. III: *Das Deutsche Reich bis zum Ende der Monarchie* (Stuttgart, 1985), pp. 128–37.

Die oberste Reichsverwaltung unter Bismarck 1867–1890 (Münster, 1957).

Moses, Julia, 'Policy communities and exchanges across borders: the case of workplace accidents at the turn of the twentieth century', in Davide Rodogno, Bernhard Struck and Jakob Vogel, eds., *Shaping the transnational sphere, 1830–1950* (New York, 2014), pp. 60–81.

'La (re)découverte du risque professionnel: l'indemnisation des ouvriers britanniques dans la perspective d'une histoire croisée', *Le Mouvement Social* 249 (2014), pp. 187–204.

Moses, Julia and Eve Rosenhaft, 'Moving targets: risk, security and the social in twentieth-century Europe', *Social Science History* 39/1 (2015), pp. 25–37.

Mosse, George L., 'Shell-shock as a social disease', *Journal of Contemporary History* 35/1 (2000), pp. 101–8.

Mounk, Yascha, *The age of responsibility: luck, choice, and the welfare state* (Cambridge, MA, 2017).

Muehlebach, Andrea, *The moral neoliberal: welfare and citizenship in Italy* (Chicago, 2012).

Murphy, John, *A decent provision: Australian welfare policy, 1870 to 1949* (Farnham, 2011).

Nacol, Emily C., *An age of risk: politics and economy in early modern Britain* (Princeton, NJ, 2016).

Nelson, Barbara, 'The origins of the two-channel welfare state: workmen's compensation and mothers' aid', in Linda Gordon, ed., *Women, the state and welfare* (Madison, WI, 1990), pp. 123–52.

Nettl, Peter, 'The state as a conceptual variable', *World Politics* 20 (1968), pp. 559–92.

Neuner, Stephanie, *Politik und Psychiatrie: die staatliche Versorgung psychisch Kriegsbeschädigter in Deutschland, 1920–1933* (Göttingen, 2011).

Nolan, Mary, *Visions of modernity: American business and the modernization of Germany* (Oxford, 1994).

Nugent, Walter, *Crossings: the great transatlantic migrations, 1870–1914* (Bloomington, 1995).

Nullmeier, Frank and Kauffmann, Franz-Xaver, 'Postwar welfare development', in Francis G. Castles, Stephan Leibfried, Jane Lewis, Herbert Obinger and Christopher Pierson, eds., *The Oxford handbook of the welfare state* (Oxford, 2010), pp. 81–104.

O'Brien, Patrick, 'Path dependency, or why Britain became an industrialized and urbanized economy long before France', *Economic History Review* 49 (1996), pp. 213–49.

Ogorek, Regina, *Untersuchungen zur Gefährdungshaftung im 19. Jahrhundert* (Cologne, 1975).

Osborne, Thomas, 'Bureaucracy as a vocation: governmentality and administration in nineteenth-century Britain', *Journal of Historical Sociology* 7 (2006), pp. 289–313.

Osborne, Thomas and Rose, Nikolas, 'Do the social sciences create phenomena? The example of public opinion research', *British Journal of Sociology* 50 (1999), pp. 367–96.

Otter, Sandra den, 'Thinking in communities: late nineteenth-century liberals, idealists and the retrieval of community', *Parliamentary History* 16/1 (1997), pp. 67–84.

Pagano, Antonio and Fara, Gaetano, 'Dalla soluzione imposta al consenso acquisito: la storia della prevenzione dalla polizia sanitaria alla promozione della salute', in A. Grieco and P. A. Bertazzi, eds., *Per una storiografia italiana della prevenzione occupazionale ed ambientale* (Milan, 1997), pp. 289–308.

Pagano, Emanuele, *Il comune di Milano nell'età napoleonica (1800–1814)* (1994; Milan, 2002).

Pagden, Anthony, 'The empire's new clothes: from empire to federation, yesterday and today', *Common Knowledge* 12/1 (2006), pp. 36–46.

Palier, Bruno, ed., *A long goodbye to Bismarck? The politics of welfare reform in continental Europe* (Amsterdam, 2010).

Pankoke, Eckart, *Sociale Bewegung – sociale Frage – sociale Politik* (Stuttgart, 1970).

Parisi, Francesco, 'The genesis of liability in ancient law', *American Law and Economics Review* 3 (2001), pp. 82–124.

Paster, Thomas, *The role of business in the development of the welfare state and labor markets in Germany: containing social reforms* (London, 2011).

Pastore, Alessandro, *Il medico in tribunale: la perizia medica nella procedura penale d'antico regime (secoli XVI–XVIII)* (Casagrande Bellinzona, 1998).

Patriarca, Silvana, *Italian vices: nation and character from the Risorgimento to the Republic* (Cambridge, 2010).

    'Indolence and regeneration: tropes and tensions of Risorgimento patriotism', *American Historical Review* 110/2 (2005), pp. 380–408.

    Numbers and nationhood: writing statistics in nineteenth-century Italy (Cambridge, 1996).

Pavan, Ilaria, '"These new rights": social security in the postwar Italian debate', *Journal of Modern Italian Studies* 22 (2017), pp. 175–93.

Pearson, Robin, 'Towards an historical model of services innovation: the case of the insurance industry, 1700–1914', *Economic History Review* (n.s.) 50 (1997), pp. 235–56.

Pedersen, Susan, *Family, dependence, and the origins of the welfare state: Britain and France, 1914–1945* (Cambridge, 1993).

Pellew, Jill, *The Home Office, 1848–1914: from clerks to bureaucrats* (London, 1982).

Perigord, Paul, *The International Labor Organization* (New York, 1926).

Perry, Heather, *Recycling the disabled: army, medicine and modernity in WWI Germany* (Manchester, 2014).

'Re-arming the disabled veteran: artifi cially rebuilding state and society in WWI Germany', in Katherine Ott , David Serlin and Stephen Mihm, eds., *Artifi cial parts, practical lives: modern histories of prosthetics* (New York , 2002), pp. 75–101.

Peruta, Franco della, 'Le opere pie dall'Unità alla legge Crispi', *Il Risorgimento* (1991), pp. 173–213.

Pflanze, Otto, *Bismarck: der Reichskanzler* (1998; Munich, 2008).

Phillips, David, *The German example: English interest in educational provision in Germany since 1800* (New York, 2011).

Pick, Daniel, *Faces of degeneration: a European disorder, c. 1848–1918* (Cambridge, 1993).

Pierenkemper, Toni and Tilly, Richard, *The German economy in the nineteenth century* (Oxford and New York, 2004).

Pierson, Paul, *Dismantling the welfare state? Reagan, Thatcher and the politics of retrenchment* (Cambridge, 1995).

Piva, Italo, 'Problemi giuridici e politici della "responsabilità" alle origini dell'assicurazione infortuni sul lavoro in Italia', *Rivista degli Infortuni e delle Malattie Professionali* 5–6 (1980), pp. 649–66.

Porter, Roy, 'Accidents in the eighteenth century', in Roger Cooter and Bill Luckin, eds., *Accidents in history: injuries, fatalities and social relations* (Amsterdam, 1997), pp. 90–106.

Porter, Theodore M., *The rise of statistical thinking, 1820–1900* (Princeton, NJ, 1986).

Poser, Stefan, *Museum der Gefahren: die Gesellschaftliche Bedeutungen der Sicherheitstechnik: das Beispiel der Hygiene Austellugen und Museen für Arbeiterschutz in Wien, Berlin und Dresden um die Jahrhundertwende* (Münster, 1998).

Probert, Rebecca, 'English exports: invoking the common law of marriage across the empire in the nineteenth century', in Julia Moses, ed., *Marriage, law and modernity: global histories* (London, 2017), pp. 168–83.

Procacci, Giovanna, 'La protesta delle donne nelle campagne in tempo di guerra', Istituto Alcide Cervi, *Annali* 13 (1991), pp. 57–86.

'Popular protest and labour confl ict in Italy, 1915– 1918', *Social History* 14 (1989), pp. 31–58.

'Repressione e dissenso nella prima guerra mondiale', *Studi Storici* 22 (1981), pp. 119–50.

Proctor, Tammy M., *Civilians in a world at war, 1914–1918* (New York, 2010).

Putnam, Robert D., with Leonardi, Robert and Nonetti, Raffaella Y., *Making democracy work: civic traditions in modern Italy* (Princeton, NJ, 1993).

Quine, Maria Sophia, *Italy's social revolution: charity and welfare from liberalism to fascism* (Basingstoke, 2002).

Rabinbach, Anson, 'Social knowledge, social risk, and the politics of industrial accidents in Germany and France', in Dietrich Rueschemeyer and Theda Skocpol, eds., *States, social knowledge, and the origins of modern social policies* (Princeton, NJ, 1996), pp. 48–89.

The human motor: energy, fatigue, and the origins of modernity (Berkeley, CA, 1990).

Rainhorn, Judith, 'Les maux de la mine: Revisiter l'histoire minière au prisme des enjeux de santé au travail', in Judith Rainhorn, ed., *Santé et travail à la mine: XIXe–XXIe siècle* (Villeneuve d'Ascq, 2014), pp. 19–30.

'Randeraad, Nico, 'The international statistical congress (1853–76): knowledge transfers and their limits', *European History Quarterly* 41 (2011), pp. 50–65.

Autorità in cerca di autonomia: I prefetti nell'Italia liberale, trans. David Scaffei (Rome, 1997).

Raphael, Lutz, *Recht und Ordnung: Herrschaft durch Verwaltung im. 19. Jahrhundert* (Frankfurt a.M., 2000).

Rass, Christoph, *Institutionalisierungsprozesse auf einem internationalen Arbeitsmarkt: bilaterale Wanderungsvorträge in Europa zwischen 1919 und 1974* (Paderborn, 2010).

Raw, Louise, *Striking a light: the Bryant and May match women and their place in history* (London, 2009).

Read, Donald, *England, 1868–1914* (London, 1979).

Reid, Elspeth, 'The impact of institutions and professions in Scotland', in Paul Mitchell, ed., *The impact of institutions and professions on legal development* (Cambridge, 2012), pp. 59–88.

Reid, Kenneth and Zimmermann, Reinhard, eds., *A history of private law in Scotland,* vol. II: *Obligations* (Oxford, 2000).

Renwick, Chris, *Bread for all: the origins of the welfare state* (London, 2017).

Retterath, Jörn, *Was ist das Volk? Volks- und Gemeinschaftskonzepte der politischen Mitte in Deutschland, 1917–1924* (Oldenbourg, 2016).

Reulecke, Jürgen, 'Die Anfänge der organisierten Sozialreform in Deutschland', in Rüdiger vom Bruch, ed., *Weder Kommunismus noch Kapitalismus: bürgerliche Sozialreform in Deutschland vom Vormärz bis zur Ära Adenauer* (Munich, 1985), pp. 21–59.

'Pauperismus, "social learning" und die Anfänge der Sozialstatistik in Deutschland', in Wolfgang J. Mommsen and Winfried Schulze, eds., *Vom Elend der Handarbeit* (Stuttgart, 1981), pp. 358–72.

Reynolds, David, *The long shadow: the legacies of the Great War in the twentieth century* (New York, 2014).

Rhodes, Martin, ed., *Southern European welfare states: between crisis and reform* (London, 1997).

Riall, Lucy, 'Elites in search of authority: political power and social order in nineteenth-century Sicily', *History Workshop Journal* 55 (2003), pp. 25–46.

'Progress and compromise in liberal Italy', *Historical Journal* 38 (1995), pp. 205–13.

Rieger, Bernhard, *Technology and the culture of modernity in Britain and Germany, 1890–1945* (Cambridge, 2005).

Rimlinger, Gaston V., *Welfare policy and industrialization in Europe, America and Russia* (1973; Aldershot, 1993).

Ritter, Gerhard A., *Soziale Frage und Sozialpolitik in Deutschland seit Beginn des 19. Jahrhunderts* (Opladen, 1998).

Social welfare in Germany and Britain: origins and development (Leamington Spa, 1986).

Ritter, Gerhard A. and Tenfelde, Klaus, *Arbeiter im Deutschen Kaiserreich, 1871–1914* (Bonn, 1992).

Rodgers, Daniel T., *Atlantic crossings: social politics in a progressive age* (Cambridge, MA, 1998).

Rodotà, Stefano, 'La libertà e i diritti', in Raffaele Romanelli, ed., *Storia dello stato italiano dall'Unità a oggi* (Rome, 1995), pp. 301–63.

Rogers, Edmund, '"A most imperial contribution": New Zealand and the old age pensions debate in Britain, 1882–1912', *Journal of Global History* 9/2 (2014), pp. 189–207.

Romanelli, Raffaele, 'Centro e periferia: L'Italia unita', in *Il rapporto centro periferia negli stati preunitari e nell'Italia unifi cata: atti del LIX congresso di storia del Risorgimento italiano* (Rome, 2000), pp. 215–48.

Il comando impossibile: stato e società nell'Italia liberale (1988; Bologna, 1995).

Sulle carte interminate: un ceto di impiegati tra privato e pubblico: i segretari comunali in Italia, 1860–1915 (Bologna, 1989).

'La nuova Italia e la misurazione dei fatti sociali: una premessa', *Quaderni Storici* 15 (1980, pp. 765–78.

L'Italia liberale (1861–1900) (Bologna, 1979).

Romani, Gabriella, ed., *Postal culture: reading and writing letters in post-unification Italy* (Toronto, 2013).

Romano, Roberto, *Fabbriche, operai, ingegneri: studi di storia del lavoro in Italia tra '800 e'900* (Milan, 2000).

Rose, Nikolas, *Powers of freedom: reframing political thought* (Cambridge, 1999), pp. 259–63.

Rosenhaft, Eve, 'How to tame chance: evolving languages of risk, trust and expertise in eighteenth-century German proto-insurances', in Geoffrey Clark, Greg Anderson, Christian Thomann and J. Matthias-Graf von der Schulenburg, eds., *The appeal of insurance* (Toronto, 2010), pp. 16–42.

Rosental, Paul-André, 'La silicose comme maladie professionnelle transnationale', *Revue Française des Affaires Sociales* 2–3 (2008), pp. 255–77.

ed., *Silicosis: a world history* (Baltimore, 2017).

Rosner, David and Markowitz, Gerald E., *Deadly dust: silicosis and the politics of occupational disease in twentieth-century America* (Princeton, NJ, 1991).

Salvante, Martina, '"Thanks to the Great War, the blind gets recognition of his ability to act": the rehabilitation of blinded servicemen in Florence', *First World War Studies* 6/1 (2015), pp. 21–35.

Scaldaferre, Romilda, 'L'origine dello "Stato sociale" in Italia (1876–1900)', *Pensiero Politico* 19 (1986), pp. 223–40.

Scherpe, Jens, 'Technological change and the development of liability for fault in Germany', in Martín Miguel-Casals, ed., *The development of liability in relation to technological change* (Cambridge, 2010), pp. 134–84.

Schivelbusch, Wolfgang, *Geschichte der Eisenbahnreise: zur Industrialisierung von Raum und Zeit im 19. Jahrhundert* (1977; Frankfurt a. M., 2004).

Schmid, Felix, *Sozialrecht und Recht der sozialen Sicherheit: die Begriffsbildung in Deutschland, Frankreich und der Schweiz* (Berlin, 1981).

Schram, Albert, *Railways and the formation of the Italian state* (Cambridge, 1997).

Scott, James C., *Seeing like a state: how certain schemes to improve the human condition have failed* (New Haven, 1998).

Searle, Geoffrey R., *Morality and the market in Victorian Britain* (Oxford, 1998).

The quest for national efficiency: a study in British politics and political thought, 1899–1914 (Oxford, 1971).

Sellers, Christopher C. and Melling, Joseph, eds., *Dangerous trade: histories of industrial hazard across a globalizing world* (Philadelphia, 2012).

Sellin, Volker, *Die Anfänge staatlicher Sozialreform im liberalen Italien* (Stuttgart, 1971).

Semmel, Bernard, *Imperialism and social reform* (London, 1960).

Sheehan, James, *German liberalism in the nineteenth century* (Chicago, 1978).

Showalter, Elaine, *The female malady: women, madness and English culture, 1830–1980* (New York, 1987).

Sicher arbeiten – 125 Jahre gesetzliche Unfallversicherung in Deutschland, 1885–2010 (Berlin, 2010).

Silei, Gianni, *Lo stato sociale in Italia: storia e document* (Manduria, 2003).

Simitis, Spiros, 'The case of the employment relationship: elements of a comparison', in Willibald Steinmetz, ed., *Private law and social inequality in the industrial age: comparing legal cultures in Britain, France, German, and the United States* (Oxford, 2000), pp. 181–202.

Simons, Rolf, *Staatliche Gewerbeaufsicht und gewerbliche Berufsgenossenschaften: Entstehung und Entwicklung des dualen Aufsichtssystems im Arbeitsschutz in Deutschland von den Anfängen bis zum Ende der Weimarer Republik* (Frankfurt a. M., 1984).

Skocpol, Theda, *Protecting soldiers and mothers: the political origins of social policy in the United States* (Cambridge, MA, 1992).

Smith, Helmut Walser, 'When the Sonderweg debate left us', *German Studies Review* 31 (2008), pp. 225–40.

Snyder, Richard, 'Scaling down: the subnational comparative method', *Studies in Comparative International Development* 36/1 (2001), pp. 93–110.

Sperber, Jonathan, *The Kaiser's voters: electors and elections in Imperial Germany* (Cambridge, 1997).

Stanley, Matthew, 'The pointsman: Maxwell's demon, Victorian free will and the boundaries of science', *Journal of the History of Ideas* 69 (2008), pp. 467–91.

Stark, James F., *The making of modern anthrax, 1875–1920* (London, 2013).

Steber, Martina and Gotto, Bernhard, eds., *Visions of community in Nazi Germany: social engineering and private lives* (Oxford, 2014).

Stedman Jones, Gareth, *Languages of class: studies in English working class history, 1832–1982* (Cambridge, 1983).

Stein, Michael Ashley, 'Victorian tort liability for workplace injuries', *University of Illinois Law Review* 3 (2008), pp. 933–84.

Steinberg, Jonathan, *Bismarck: a life* (Oxford, 2011).

Steinmetz, George, *The devil's handwriting: precoloniality and the German colonial state in Qingdao, Samoa and Southwest Africa* (Chicago, 2008).

'Introduction', in George Steinmetz, ed., *State/culture: state-formation after the cultural turn* (Ithaca, NY, 1999), pp. 1–50.

'The myth of an autonomous state', in Geoff Eley, ed., *Society, culture, and the state in Germany 1870–1930* (Ann Arbor, MI, 1996), pp. 257–318.

Regulating the social: the welfare state and local politics in imperial Germany (Princeton, NJ, 1993).

Steinmetz, Willibald, *Begegnungen vor Gericht: eine Sozial- und Kulturgeschichte des englischen Arbeitsrechts (1850–1925)* (Munich, 2002).

Stevenson, David, *1914–1918: the history of the First World War* (London, 2004).

Stolleis, Michael, *Geschichte des Sozialrechts in Deutschland: ein Grundriß* (Stuttgart, 2003).

'Historische Grundlagen: Sozialpolitik in Deutschland bis 1945', in Hans Günter Hockerts, Franz-Xaver Kaufmann, Gerhard A. Ritter et al., eds., *Geschichte der*

Sozialpolitik in Deutschland seit 1945, vol. I: *Grundlagen der Sozialpolitik* (Baden-Baden, 2001), pp. 199–332.

Strang, David and Meyer, John W., 'Institutional conditions for diffusion', *Theory and Society* 22 (1993), pp. 487–511.

Sweeney, Dennis, *Work, race and the emergence of radical right corporatism in Imperial Germany* (Ann Arbor, MI, 2009).

Swenson, Peter, *Capitalists against markets: the making of labor markets and welfare states in the United States and Sweden* (Oxford, 2002).

Supiot, Alain, 'Grandeur and misery of the social state', *New Left Review* 82 (July–August 2013), pp. 99–113.

Tarrow, Sidney and McAdam, Doug, 'Scale shift in transnational contention', in Donatella della Porta and Sidney Tarrow, eds., *Transnational protest and global activism* (Oxford, 2005), pp. 121–50.

Taruffo, Michele, *La giustizia civile in Italia dal '700 a oggi* (Bologna, 1980).

Tennstedt , Florian, ' Glaubensgewissheit und Revolutionsfurcht: zum sozialpolitischem Wirken Robert Bosses', *Zeitschrift für Sozialreform* 49 (2003), pp. 831–46.

'"Bismarcks Arbeiterversicherung" zwischen Absicherung der Arbeiterexistenz und Abwehr der Arbeiterbewegung', in Hans Matthöfer, Walter Mühlhausen and Florian Tennstedt, eds., *Bismarck und die Soziale Frage im 19. Jahrhundert* (Friedrichsruh, 2001), pp. 51–87.

'Sozialreform als Mission: Anmerkungen zum politischen Handeln Theodor Lohmanns', in Jürgen Kocka, Hans- Jürgen Puhle and Klaus Tenfelde, eds., *Von der Arbeiterbewegung zum modernen Sozialstaat: Festschrift für Gerhard A. Ritter zum 65. Geburtstag* (Munich, 1994), pp. 538–59.

'Sozialgeschichte der Sozialpolitik in Deutschland: vom 18. Jahrhundert bis zum Ersten Weltkrieg (Göttingen, 1981).

Tennstedt, Florian and Winter, Heidi, '"Jeder Tag hat seine eigenen Sorgen, und es ist nicht weise, die Sorgen der Zukunft freiwillig auf die Gegenwart zu Übernehmen": die Anfänge des Sozialstaats im Deutschen Reich von 1871', *Zeitschrift für Soziale Reform* 41 (1995), pp. 671–706.

'"Der Staat hat wenig Liebe – active wie passiv": die Anfänge des Sozialstaats im Deutschen Reich von 1871', *Zeitschrift für Sozialreform* 39 (1993), pp. 362–92.

Thane, Pat, *Old age in English history: past experiences, present issues* (New York, 2002).

'Government and society in England and Wales, 1750–1914', in F. M. L. Thompson, ed., *The Cambridge social history of Britain, 1750–1950* (3 vols., Cambridge, 1990), vol. III, pp. 1–61.

'The working class and state "welfare" in Britain, 1880–1914', *Historical Journal* 27/4 (1984), pp. 877–900.

Thom, Deborah, *Nice girls and rude girls: women workers in World War I* (London, 1998).

Thompson, E. P., 'Time, work-discipline and industrial capitalism', in E. P. Thompson, *Customs in common: studies in traditional popular culture* (New York, 1993), pp. 352–403.

' The peculiarities of the English', in E. P. Thompson, *The poverty of theory and other essays* (New York , 1978), pp. 35–91.

The making of the English working class (New York, 1964).

Thorpe, Andrew, *A history of the British Labour Party* (1997; 3rd edn, Basingstoke, 2008).

Tilly, Stephanie, *Arbeit – Macht – Markt: Industrieller Arbeitsmarkt, 1900–1929: Deutschland und Italien im Vergleich* (Berlin, 2006).

Topalov, Christian, *Laboratoires du nouveau siècle: la nébuleuse réformatrice et ses réseaux en France, 1880–1914* (Paris, 1999).

Tooze, Adam, *The deluge: the Great War and the remaking of global order, 1916–1931* (London, 2014).

Statistics and the German state, 1900–1945: the making of modern economic knowledge (Cambridge, 2001).

Tore, Gianfranco, 'Miniere, lavoro e malattie nell'Italia postunitaria (1860–1915)', in Maria Luisa Betri and Ada Gigli Marchetti, eds., *Salute e classi lavoratrici in Italia dall'Unità al fascismo* (Milan, 1982), pp. 75–99.

Torp, Cornelius, *Gerechtigkeit im Wohlfahrtsstaat: Alter und Alterssicherung in Deutschland und Grossbritannien von 1945 bis heute* (Göttingen, 2015).

Tribe, Keith, *Governing economy: the reformation of German economic discourse, 1750–1840* (Cambridge, 1988).

Uekötter, Frank, *Von der Rauchplage zur ökologischen Revolution: eine Geschichte der Luftverschmutzung in Deutschland und den USA, 1880–1970* (Essen, 2003).

Ullmann, Hans-Peter, 'Industrielle Interessen und die Entstehung der deutschen Sozialversicherung', *Historische Zeitschrift* 229 (1979), pp. 574–610.

van Daele, Jasmien, Rodriguez García, Magaly, Van Goethem, Geert and van der Linden, Marcel, eds., *ILO histories: essays on the International Labour Organization and its impact on the world during the twentieth century* (Bern, 2010).

Vecoli, Rudolph J., 'The Italian diaspora, 1876–1976', in Robin Cohen, ed., *The Cambridge survey of world migration* (Cambridge, 1995), pp. 114–22.

Vernon, James, *Hunger: a modern history* (Cambridge, MA, 2008).

Wall, Rosemary, *Bacteria in Britain: 1880–1939* (London, 2013).

Waltermann, Raimund, *Sozialrecht* (8th edn, Heidelberg, 2009).

Wasserstein, Bernard, *Herbert Samuel: a political life* (Oxford, 1992).

Watson, Alexander and Porter, Patrick, 'Bereaved and aggrieved: combat motivation and the ideology of sacrifice in the First World War', *Historical Research* 83 (2010), pp. 146–64.

Wehler, Hans-Ulrich, *Deutsche Gesellschaftsgeschichte*, vol. III: *Von der deutschen Doppelrevolution bis zum Beginn des Ersten Weltkrieges, 1849–1914* (Munich, 1995).

The German empire, 1871–1918 (Leamington Spa, 1985).

Weindling, Paul, 'The medical profession, social hygiene and the birth rate in Germany, 1914–18', in Richard Wall and Jay Winter, eds., *The upheaval of war: family, work and welfare in Europe, 1914–18* (Cambridge, 1988), pp. 417–38.

Wickenhagen, Ernst, *Geschichte der gewerblichen Unfallversicherung: Wesen und Wirken der gewerblichen Berufsgenossenschaften* (2 vols., Munich, 1980).

'Gedanken zum Territorialprinzip in der Sozialversicherung', in Arbeitsgemeinschaft der Knappschaften der Bundesrepublik Deutschland and Bundesverband der Betriebskrankenkassen, ed., *Beiträge zur Sozialversicherung: Festschrift für den Herrn Präsidenten des Bundesversicherungsamts Kurt Hofmann aus Anlaß seines 60. Geburtstages* (Berlin, 1964), pp. 83–97.

Zwischenstaatliches Sozialversicherungsrecht (Bonn-Bad Godesberg, 1957).

'Das Territorialitätsprinzip und seine Ausnahmen in der gesetzlichen Unfallversicherung', *Die Berufsgenossenschaft* 2 (February 1954), pp. 66–70 and 3 (March 1954), pp. 106–9.

Zwischenstaatliches Sozialversicherungsrecht (Bonn-Bad Godesberg, 1957).

Wieacker, Franz, *A history of private law in Europe: with particular reference to Germany* (Oxford, 1995).

Wildt, Michael, *Hitler's* Volksgemeinschaft *and the dynamics of racial exclusion: violence against Jews in provincial Germany*, trans. Bernard Heise (New York and Oxford, 2012).

Wilensky, Harold L. and Lebeaux, Charles N., *Industrial society and social welfare* (New York, 1958).

Wilson, Arnold and Levy, Hermann, *Workmen's compensation* (2 vols., London, 1939–41).

Winkler, Heinrich August, ed., *Organisierter Kapitalismus: Voraussetzungen und Anfänge* (Göttingen, 1974).

Winter, Jay, 'Demography', in John Horne, ed., *A companion to World War I* (Chichester, 2012), pp. 248–62.

Wisselgren, Per, *The social scientific gaze: the social question and the rise of academic social science in Sweden* (London, 2015).

Witt, John Fabian, *The accidental republic: crippled workmen, destitute widows and the remaking of American law* (Cambridge, MA, 2004).

'The transformation of work and the law of workplace accidents, 1842–1910', *Yale Law Journal* 107 (1998), pp. 1467–502.

Wohl, Anthony S., *Endangered lives: public health in Victorian Britain* (London, 1983).

Wong, Aliza, *Race and the nation in Liberal Italy, 1861–1911* (Basingstoke, 2006).

Woolf, Stuart, 'Statistics and the modern state', *Comparative Studies in Society and History* 31 (1989), pp. 588–604.

Woollacott, Angela, *On her their lives depend: munitions workers in the Great War* (Berkeley, CA, 1994).

Young, A. F., *Industrial injuries insurance: an examination of British policy* (New York, 1964).

Zacher, Hans F., 'Grundlagen der Sozialpolitik in der Bundesrepublik Deutschland', in Günter Hockerts, Franz-Xaver Kaufmann, Gerhard A. Ritter et al., eds., *Geschichte der Sozialpolitik in Deutschland seit 1945*, vol. 1: *Grundlagen der Sozialpolitik* (Baden-Baden, 2001), pp. 333–684.

Zamagni, Vera, *The economic history of Italy, 1860–1990* (Oxford, 1993).

'A century of change: trends in the composition of the Italian labour force, 1881–1981', *Historical Social Research* 44 (1987), pp. 36–97.

Zimmermann, Reinhard, *The law of obligations: Roman foundations of the civilian tradition* (Oxford, 1996).

Zitt, Renate, *Zwischen Innerer Mission und staatlicher Sozialpolitik: der protestantische Sozialreformer Theodor Lohmann (1831–1905)* (Heidelberg, 1997).

Zweierlein, Cornel, *Der gezähmte Prometheus: Feuer Sicherheit zwischen Früher Neuzeit und Moderne* (Göttingen, 2011).

Index